FOUNDATIONS: THEIR POWER AND INFLUENCE

FOUNDATIONS: THEIR POWER AND INFLUENCE

BY

RENÉ A. WORMSER

FIRST PUBLISHED IN 1958 BY —

THE DEVIN-ADAIR COMPANY, NEW YORK

Covenant House Books
P. O. Box 4690
Sevierville, TN 37864

615-428-5176

ISBN 0-925591-28-9

PREFACE

THE MOST DIFFICULT assignment of my thirty years in the Congress of the United States was the chairmanship of the Special Committee to Investigate Tax Exempt Foundations, informally referred to as the "Reece Committee." This investigation required embarrassingly close scrutiny of the intellectual activities supported by the great and highly respected American names of Carnegie, Rockefeller, and Ford. As a minority member of the Cox Committee, which in the previous Congress had attempted but virtually abandoned this project, I had sensed the power that would spring up in opposition to a complete investigation.

The obstacles were obvious from the first. We knew that the influential "liberal" press, characterized by *The New York Times,* the *New York Herald Tribune,* and the *Washington Post-Times Herald,* would throw its editorial power against the Committee. We knew that even the bulk of the conservative press could not be unmindful of the enormous power of these foundations. We knew that many prominent educators, regardless of what they felt, could not be unmindful of the dependency of their institutions upon continued largess from the foundations involved. We knew that the group of prominent men whose decisions would have to be judged extended even to intimates of the White House.

But I felt that the work of the Cox Committee left several important unanswered questions, of which the gravest was: *to what extent, if any, are the funds of the large foundations aiding and*

v

*abetting Marxist tendencies in the United States and weakening
the love which every American should have for his way of life?*

So we set out to find the answers. We wanted to explore the
problems of foundations by examining their actions, not their
statements for the public. We felt that there are involved in the
concepts under which foundations operate and grow in the
United States certain dangers for the public welfare. We were not
blind to the undoubted merits of the contributions of numerous
tax-exempt foundations to worth-while causes. It was our intention to find the factual basis for preserving their constructive
functions and at the same time for supplying guidance for future
legislation and administrative action against the use of foundation
power for political ends. The story of that adventure, of what we
found, and of the harassments to which we were subjected, is
included in this book by René A. Wormser, who was general
counsel to the committee of which I was chairman and is widely
recognized in America and Europe as outstanding in the field of
estate planning and taxation. The book contributes essentially,
however, the philosophical and juridical reflections of this distinguished lawyer, based upon the material our committee disclosed and upon other data which have appeared since the
closing of our inquiry. He discusses problems of foundation administration and control which are grave indeed and has rendered a great service in preparing this sober and thoughtful work.

BRAZILLA CARROLL REECE

INTRODUCTION

IN HIS COLUMN in the New York *Daily News* of December 21, 1954, John O'Donnell said that the Reece Committee had the "almost impossible task" of telling "the taxpayers that the incredible was, in fact, the truth." "The incredible fact," he continued "was that the huge fortunes piled up by such industrial giants as John D. Rockefeller, Andrew Carnegie, and Henry Ford were today being used to destroy or discredit the free-enterprise system which gave them birth."

It is not easy to investigate foundations, not even for Congress to attempt it: the giant foundations are powerful and have powerful friends. A special committee was created by the House of Representatives of the 83rd Congress to investigate tax-exempt organizations. It is generally referred to as the "Reece Committee" after its chairman, Congressman B. Carroll Reece of Tennessee. It was successor, in a way, to the "Cox Committee," created by the previous Congress. The Reece Committee had perhaps the most hazardous career of any committee in the history of Congress.* It survived its many perils, however, to bring to the attention of Congress and the people grave dangers to our society.

These dangers relate chiefly to the use of foundation funds for political ends; they arise out of the accumulation of substantial economic power and of cultural influence in the hands of a

---

* See Appendix B for the Story of the Reece Committee. The Committee's findings are quoted in Appendix A.

vii

class of administrators of tax-exempt funds established in perpetuity. An "élite" has thus emerged, in control of gigantic financial resources operating outside of our democratic processes, which is willing and able to shape the future of this nation and of mankind in the image of its own value concepts. An unparalleled amount of power is concentrated increasingly in the hands of an interlocking and self-perpetuating group. Unlike the power of corporate management, it is unchecked by stockholders; unlike the power of government, it is unchecked by the people; unlike the power of churches, it is unchecked by any firmly established canons of value.

This book grew out of my conviction that some of the materials examined by the Reece Committee, for which I acted as general counsel, deserve broader circulation. My own reflections, based upon the committee's work and upon additional material and continued studies, might also contribute to a sharpening of the issues, which deserve wide public consideration.

The "foundations" which the Committee investigated did not all carry that label. In addition to primary sources of foundation grants, such as The Ford Foundation, The Rockefeller Foundation, and The Carnegie Corporation of New York, the Committee examined secondary distributors of grant moneys, especially organizations such as The Social Science Research Council, The Institute of Pacific Relations, and The American Council on Education, which are supported by the major foundations and used in selecting ultimate recipients. A dictionary definition of the term "foundation" might run: "an endowed institution, corporation or charity." This would include colleges, hospitals, churches, and other institutions of a character far different from that of the foundations with which we are dealing. These are essentially recipients of money for their own use and not in the business of handing out grants to others. They are, in relation to the foundations, mentioned above what the consumer is in relation to his supplier.

Limited to the types of organization we have in mind, the total number now existing in the United States can be estimated at over 7,000. Most were created under state corporation laws; some as trusts; a very small number by Federal charter. Accurate statistics are impossible to obtain, but the aggregate capital of these foundations seems to be about nine billion dollars, their income running into hundreds of millions per year. Total foundation wealth is generally underestimated. Some foundations (among them The Duke Foundation, The Ford Foundation, The Ford Motor Company Fund, the Guggenheim foundation and The Rockefeller Brothers Fund) report their assets on a book-value basis—market value usually being much higher. In the case of The Ford Foundation, the actual value of its assets turned out to have been six times their book value. Moreover, many foundations are vehicles for continued donations, whether by gift or legacy—they are in a state of growth. Indeed, some have only nominal capital today but will contain vast sums on the deaths of those who created them.

While there is much overlapping, foundations might be divided into three classes: those which are purely granting foundations; those which use their money for their own research and operations (operating foundations); and those which might be called "intermediaries," "clearing houses," or "retailers" for other foundations. Some of the intermediaries have no endowment and thus, strictly speaking, may not be "foundations"; however, they came within the committee's scope as "tax-exempt organizations," because of the practice of major foundations of delegating to them the selection of beneficiaries.

Other classifications are possible, such as those foundations which have special purposes and those which are concerned with general research. In his recent book, *Philanthropic Foundations,** Mr. F. Emerson Andrews, an executive of The Russell Sage Foundation, says: "Although the foundations that can now be classified as 'general research' probably do not exceed 150 in number, they control more than half the assets of all foundations and are the ones most in the public eye. To a large degree they are the leaders and standard setters for the foundation movement."

* Russell Sage Foundation, 1956.

The birth rate of foundations is rapidly accelerating. The Commissioner of Internal Revenue so testified, as would any expert in estate and business planning. The chief motivation in the creation of foundations has long ceased to be pure philanthropy—it is now predominantly tax avoidance or minimization.* The charitable tax exemptions were intended to advance the public welfare by offering exemption for philanthropic purposes. The increasing tax burden on income and estates has greatly accelerated a trend toward creation of foundations as instruments for the retention of control over capital assets that would otherwise be lost. The Internal Revenue Service, according to a press report,† says it sometimes receives up to 10,000 applications a month for tax-free status!

The creation of a new foundation very often serves the purpose of contributing to a favorable public opinion for the person or corporation that endows it. Among public-relations consultants the practice of publicly establishing the virtue of a previously despised person or institution by forming a tax-exempt foundation and beating the drum for it is quite common. Some of our largest foundations, established before the introduction of Federal income and estate taxes, were created largely to glamorize a name not previously identified as conspicuously charitable.

Mr. Andrews, in his *Philanthropic Foundations,* speaks of the mushroom growth of foundations in the past decade (1945-1956). He attributes truly charitable motivation to many donors, and mixed motives to others, but admits that many foundations are created for primarily selfish reasons and sometimes for fraudulent purposes. He sees it as obvious enough that tax reasons should stimulate the creation of foundations, pointing out that, to the very rich, whose income is taxed at the highest brackets, a donation to a charitable purpose would cost in some instances only nine cents per dollar. If gifts are made in the form of appreciated assets instead of money (stocks, land, or other property that has gained in

---

* See *The Charitable Trust (The Foundation) As an Instrument of Estate Planning.* René A. Wormser, 18 *Ohio St. L. J.* 219 (1957).
† Scripps-Howard, March 13, 1957, from Washington.

value since its acquisition), the donor in the highest tax brackets will have more money left after the donation than if he himself had liquidated the asset, paid a 25% capital-gains tax, and given nothing away!

Perhaps the best example of the use of foundations in estate and business planning is offered by the largest, The Ford Foundation. This foundation received about 90 percent of the stock of the Ford Motor Company, all nonvoting stock. Had not the Ford family created this foundation, it would have had to dispose of a large part of its ownership in the Ford Company to the public, for it is hardly possible that the family had enough liquid capital to pay the hundreds of millions of estate taxes which would have been due upon the deaths of two proprietors, Henry Ford and his son Edsel. It might have been difficult to make such a public sale without endangering their control of the company.

The foundation, however, offered a way out. The family, by transferring about 90 per cent of its Ford holdings to a foundation, escaped estate taxes on approximately 90 percent of its fortune. At the same time, it retained voting control of the company and had the satisfaction of knowing that even the nonvoting stock was in friendly hands. When part of the foundation's holdings of Ford stock was sold in 1956, after being converted into voting stock, the distribution was carefully controlled to make sure that no large blocks would be held by any one investor. One reason behind this might have been the conviction that the more Ford stockholders there were, the more Ford customers and enthusiasts there would be. Another motivation might have been the simple one of not wishing any minority stockholder to acquire enough stock to make him too interested in challenging the management.

In this manner, and by other uses of foundations, control of an enterprise is often retained by a family, while a huge part of a decedent's fortune is removed from death taxes. A direct donation to an existing philanthropic institution, like a college or a church, would save the same tax, but the creation of a foundation enables the family itself to have the pleasure, power, and satisfaction of managing the wealth donated to "charity."

There have been "business" abuses of the tax law, of course. The Reece Committee report gave one rather shocking example of a type of tax avoidance. This was the case of The Reid Foundation, which holds millions of dollars in notes of the publishing company which owns and publishes the New York *Herald Tribune*. These notes were transferred to the Reid Foundation partly by direct donation of the late Ogden M. Reid and partly by his will, the estate thus saving a large sum in death taxes. As the committee report said:

> It is the conclusion of this Committee that what was intended was a business arrangement. We conclude that the Foundation was not to be engaged solely in charitable work. . . . It was to exercise charity in behalf of the New York *Herald Tribune*. It was to subordinate whatever philanthropic work had been planned to the welfare of that newspaper and the interest of the Reid family in it. It was a business deal. There was no free gift of the notes. They were transferred pursuant to a contract under which the Foundation agreed to assist the publishing company in its financial problem and, by inference, but clear inference, to make this objective superior to its presumed charitable function.*

It was the committee's opinion that no charitable exemption should have been allowed The Reid Foundation.

The extent to which foundations are today being used—in a manner generally similar to that of The Ford Foundation—to solve the problem of paying death taxes when a major part of the assets of the estate consist of stock in a closely held corporation, largely prompted me to include this comment in an address at the University of Chicago in 1952:

> It seems to me that the ingenious legal creatures developed by tax experts to solve the unusual social, economic, and legal problems of the past several generations will become

---

* *Report* of the Special Committee to Investigate Tax-Exempt Foundations (Reece Committee), p. 9. Reference to *Report* throughout this book will concern the report of this committee.

Frankensteins, though perhaps benevolent ones. It is possible that, in fifty or a hundred years, a great part of American industry will be controlled by pension and profit-sharing trusts and *foundations* and a large part of the balance by insurance companies and labor unions. What eventual repercussions may come from such a development, one can only guess. It may be that we will in this manner reach some form of society similar to socialism, without consciously intending it. Or it may be, to protect ourselves against the strictures which such concentrations of power can effect, that we might have to enact legislation analogous to the Statutes of Mortmain which, centuries ago, were deemed necessary in order to prevent all England's wealth from passing into the hands of the church.

The overwhelming majority of foundations have had careers quite beyond any criticism, and some of those which have been most criticized have notable accomplishments to their credit. The work of both the Rockefeller and Carnegie foundations in some fields of medicine, public health, and science, for example, deserves the thanks of the American people. Many unquestionably commendable accomplishments should not, however, immunize a foundation from criticism for mistakes involving what may be termed a breach of trust.

It is in the fields of education, international affairs and what are called the "social sciences" that the greatest damage can be done to our society. For this reason the Reece Committee confined its inquiry almost entirely to these areas.

Foundations achieve their tax-exempt status, even their initial license to exist, because they are dedicated, in one way or another, to the public welfare. They must be so dedicated. The state laws which govern the creation of foundations give considerable latitude. The donor is permitted to satisfy his idiosyncrasies, if he cares to, by designating purposes limited to certain classes of beneficiaries and certain classes of benefactions, as long as the whole operation is truly philanthropic. The Federal tax law, in turn, is equally generous in permitting even idiosyncratic philanthropies to qualify for tax exemption. Underlying both the State and Federal laws applying to foundations, however, is the concept of public dedication—a fund administered by fiduciaries (whether called "trustees" or directors") for public benefit.

The tax relief which foundations and their donors enjoy causes the public to pay more taxes than would be the case if the exemptions were not granted. Consequently, and because foundations are public trusts,* the public has the right to expect those who operate them to exercise the highest degree of fiduciary responsibility.

A study of the place of foundations in our society calls for an initial clarification of the method applied in such an inquiry. Obviously the great variety of foundation goals and activities makes it impossible to apply the sampling procedures so fashionable among contemporary social scientists. One cannot arrive at a quantitatively correct description of all foundations from examination of a selected number. Consequently, the investigator must be satisfied with an opportunity to arrive at conclusions regarding possible merits and demerits of foundation practices by examination of a reasonably large number of cases. The result will be a better understanding of the principles of human behavior involved in operating tax-exempt activities and a more practical approach to the formulation and application of the law protecting the public interest.

Limited as it was by time and money, the Reece Committee could attempt only a partial investigation of some of the less desirable features of foundation management in the United States. Its main contribution was to expose instances in which the promotion of political ends, favored perhaps by foundation managers, had been disguised as charitable or educational activity. Political activity of this kind endangers the future of the foundation as an institution.

---

* Objection is sometimes made to calling a foundation a 'public trust.' However, while it is privately administered, it is public in the sense that it must be dedicated to the public—the public is its beneficiary.

The often stormy hearings of the Reece Committee stimulated a widespread reexamination of the goals and methods of the major foundations. In the resulting public discussion, even some of the most stalwart supporters of the criticized foundations were obliged to admit to certain deficiencies; indeed, some major changes in personnel and in operating policies ensued.

The following pages are offered as a contribution towards a better understanding of the public issues arising out of the existence of powerful tax-exempt institutions. They point to some of the abuses of the past to illustrate the dangers inherent in the absence of effective measures for preventing political activity by foundations.

Greenwich, Conn.   RENÉ A. WORMSER

CONTENTS

FOUNDATIONS: THEIR POWER AND INFLUENCE

1   THE STUDY OF FOUNDATIONS

CONGRESSIONAL INVESTIGATION IS NOT ENOUGH

WHEN the 82nd Congress appointed a select committee to investigate foundations, this committee was directed to conduct a full and complete investigation and study of educational and philanthropic foundations and other comparable organizations which are exempt from Federal income taxation. The committee, later known as the "Cox Committee," was instructed "to determine which such foundations and organizations are using their resources for purposes other than the purposes for which they were established and especially to determine which such foundations and organizations are using their resources for un-American and subversive activities or for purposes not in the interest or tradition of the United States."

Similarly, the Special Committee to Investigate Tax-Exempt Foundations and Comparable Organizations appointed by the 83rd Congress, "the Reece Committee," was instructed to make a study of the use of such resources for "un-American and subversive activities; for political purposes; propaganda, or attempts to influence legislation." Consequently, both House committees in their observations concentrated largely on alleged subversive aspects of foundation activities.

Like all studies by Congressional committees, the investigations took place in an atmosphere of some political passion. The clash of personalities, outside efforts to prevent a full airing of the problems of foundations, the short time available for research and hearings, and the absence of sufficient funds substantially impaired committee work. Yet these Congressional committees have accomplished much. They have pointed up the importance of tax-exempt organizations in our social structure. They have disclosed serious weaknesses and dangers. They have exposed a great number of unexplored problems arising out of foundation activity. But they have not finished the study which the social importance of foundations requires.

The American foundation is a social invention, created to contribute to the improvement of the public welfare. Like any invention, it creates new situations, changing with the tides of our social life. The impact of foundation programs and operations in many of the focal areas of our civilization requires constant reevaluation. Congressional committees can contribute very substantially to such appraisal.

The significance of tax-exempt private organizations transcends the importance of occasional or frequent errors of judgment committed by foundation trustees or their managers. These institutions may exert political influence, support subversion, or exhibit tendencies conflicting with our national traditions. The emergence of richly endowed juridical persons with self-perpetuating boards of directors, free from any formal responsibility for their policies and actions and growing in number and wealth, deserves the fullest attention of all who are concerned for the future of our Republic.

There are substantial dissimilarities between the purposes, characteristics, and operators of the various organizations. A stereotype picture of what "the foundations" have contributed or are guilty of, will always do injustice to some. Congressional reports, by necessity, highlight certain features of a limited number of tax-exempt foundations and are likely to invite generalizations from a few explored data. But a "typical foundation" is as nonexistent as an "average man" or an "average corporation" in real life. Furthermore, as it is with human beings and their societies, the individual foundation itself undergoes change; what may be

true of specific intentions and performance today may not be true
any longer tomorrow.

The emphasis of the Reece Committee on the need for further
study came from the recognition of the existence of many more
problems than the ones it touched upon. But the far-from-com-
pleted investigation did disclose sufficient instances of questionable practices to permit an understanding of some of the general
precautions that ought to be applied to foundation management.
The Committee sought out guiding principles for future foundation behavior rather than grounds for punishing past errors. If,
therefore, this study will use some of the less flattering data on
tax-exempt operations uncovered by the Congressional investigation, the purpose is not to create a stereotyped prejudice against
foundations in general. It is rather to record the possible dangers
to the public welfare and so, in the end, to serve the interest of
foundations in their continued service to the public better than
complacent silence would do.

THE "WALSH COMMISSION"

The problems of foundations are not new. They have been aired
by Congressional inquiry before. The manner of their exploration
has always reflected the concern of the day with specific dangers
to the public welfare. The Commission on Industrial Relations examined foundations more than forty years ago under a Congressional Act of August 23, 1912. Its main purpose was to study
labor conditions and the treatment of workers by major industrial
firms. Starting with a study of labor exploitation, it went on to investigate concentrations of economic power, interlocking directorates, and the role of the then relatively new large charitable foundations (especially of Carnegie and Rockefeller) as instruments
of power concentration. The fears of foundation power prevalent
in that generation are best expressed by the statement to the Commission made by a prominent lawyer and student of social problems who later became a justice of the Supreme Court.

Louis D. Brandeis testified on January 23, 1915, as to why he
was gravely concerned with the growth of concentrated economic

power. He spoke of corporate power first; then, of what appeared to him a similar problem in relation to the large foundations. He said:

> But when a great financial power has developed, when there exist these powerful organizations, which can successfully summon forces from all parts of the country, which can afford to use tremendous amounts of money in any conflict to carry out what they deem to be their business principle, and can also afford to suffer losses—you have necessarily a condition of inequality between the two contending forces.*** The result in the cases of these large corporations, may be to develop a benevolent absolutism, but it is an absolutism all the same; and it is that which makes the great corporation so dangerous. There develops within the State a state so powerful that the ordinary social and industrial forces existing are insufficient to cope with it.*

Brandeis said that foundations express a desire, a zealous purpose, to aid humanity. But he also stated that he felt a "grave apprehension at times as to what might ultimately be the effect of these foundations when the control shall have passed out of the hands of those who at present are administering them to those who may not be governed by the excellent intent of the creators." He reiterated his fear of abuse of power and termed the whole system "inconsistent with our democratic aspirations."

At these hearings, under the chairmanship of Senator Frank P. Walsh,† a great number of other prominent witnesses appeared and testified on their ideas and observations regarding foundations.

Samuel Untermyer, counsel to the U. S. Steel Corporation and himself a prominent philanthropist, stated his belief in the capitalist system. He attributed the propaganda success of socialism, communism, and syndicalism to the blunders of capitalism. He saw a remedy in the enlightened self-interest of capitalists that

* *Walsh Commission Hearings,* p. 7659.
† 64th Congress, 1st Session, Senate Document 415, vol. VII.

would lead to social reforms. Criticizing the Rockefeller, Sage, and Carnegie foundations, he said:

> The Rockefeller Foundation sought a Federal charter, but was not satisfied with the terms it was offered by Congress. It wanted our fundamental laws against perpetuities ignored and repealed so far as concerned its powers and limitations. It promptly secured from the New York State legislature what Congress refused to grant; the Sage and Carnegie foundations did the same. If New York had not given them what they wanted they would have passed along from State to State until they found a corporate habitation on their own terms, without in the least interfering with their operating wherever they chose. This ought not to be possible.

Mr. Untermyer did not share the fear and distrust of foundations expressed by others. He believed in the unselfish public spirit of their founders and saw them doing "incalculable public good and no harm." He advocated, however, that they should:

(1) be organized under a uniform Federal law instead of under special State charters;

(2) not be given perpetual charters, because of the possibility that entirely different social structures and conceptions of education in 50 years might make these institutions appear most repugnant;

(3) be limited in their size;

(4) not be permitted to accumulate income.

He also advocated (5) that the government should be represented when the time comes for replacing the present trustees.

Dr. John Haynes Holmes, an eminent Protestant minister, testified to his concern with the power of the self-perpetuating foundation boards:

> We have here in the midst of a society supposed to be democratic that which is essentially an autocratic system of administration, of an institution which represents power, which is, of course, simply stupendous, and that relationship

therefor, of the most serious character to mankind, the autocratic administration on one hand and the democratic administration [of government] upon the other.*

He contended that a democratic society did not need the services of outside agencies "to study a community from its own standpoint and to apply remedies from funds at its disposal." He feared greatly the "paralysis of the possibilities of democracy" when powerful foundations take over. Dr. Holmes, as it appears, was an ardent advocate of cooperative socialism, and represented what today would be called "liberalism." He recommended appointment of foundation trustees by the government. He was so much opposed to the large foundations that he would "rather see democracy die of its own corruption than be favored by the autocratic benefaction or service of any one particular individual."

John D. Rockefeller, Jr., testified that as a corporate director he had represented foundation investments as well as his family interests on the boards of directors of several corporations. He had given considerable study to the question of the relation of private benevolence to social and economic conditions.† Testifying for several days, beginning on June 25, 1915, he answered the question whether large foundations constituted a possible menace either to the general cause of education or to the industrial welfare of the people. He said: "These foundations, as is true of all modern corporations, are subject to the reserved power of legislative bodies which created them—to modify or repeal their charters whenever the public interests require." ‡

Asked whether he saw any dangers in interlocking directorates of foundations, he replied, "I should think on the other hand there might be a great strength in that," and generally spoke in favor of multiple services of the same persons as directors of several foundations.§ In essence, he recognized the public's right to know and through legislation to control foundation activities.

* P. 7917.
† P. 7849.
‡ P. 7854.
§ P. 7859.

He advocated voluntary public reports of federally chartered foundations "on fiscal matters" but not introduction of a law requiring such reports; he wanted to leave the contents of such reports to the judgment of the directors and to their understanding of the public interest. He did not think that any method of public inspection was desirable or necessary.*

Asked about the power of foundations to influence independent thought and action in the investigation of social conditions, Mr. Rockefeller said there should be no public restrictions. He contended that proper selection of directors would sufficiently protect the public interest and that the financial power of large foundations would be felt only in the realm of investment. He advocated academic freedom and complete independence in the use of grants by recipient educational institutions of higher learning. Chairman Walsh was concerned lest the granting of funds for schools might result in "persons being educated taking the viewpoint, consciously or unconsciously, of the man that gave the money or the foundation that gave the money." †

Mr. Rockefeller, with regard to higher education, answered: "There is a possible danger, if the giver retains any kind of control; I think it unwise." Regarding other forms of education, however, he considered continued help in developing the middle school system as desirable and as involving much more remote danger.

In 1915, when these opinions were expressed, obviously nobody expected the emergence of intermediary organizations serving foundations in the distribution of grants and their resulting power in the academic world. "Progressive education," soon to be favored by substantial support, was in its infancy; what has been called the patronage network of Teachers College of Columbia University had not yet conquered the organizations of the teachers with the aid of tax-exempt donations.

Approving the principle of public control and, implicitly, future

* P. 7860.
† P. 7866.

Congressional study of foundations, Mr. Rockefeller said that it was never contemplated that his father or his associates

> could continue to have their influence felt; but at any time in any generation, when the board having the charge of such a foundation is not, in the judgment of the public, a proper board, the legislation can introduce an amendment, limiting, qualifying or modifying the method of electing directors and adding at that time any restriction which it may think desirable.

It was Mr. Rockefeller's thought to "leave each generation to put up such barriers and safeguards as it may think necessary at that time." *

In its final report, Mr. Basil M. Manly, the director of research of the Commission on Industrial Relations, dealt at length with foundation problems. Commissioners Weinstock, Ballard, and Ashton, while dissenting and calling the report partisan and unfair regarding certain labor issues, concurred in its conclusions regarding the foundations.

Concerned with the "concentration of wealth and influence," the report concluded from the evidence examined: that a small number of wealthy and powerful financiers held in their hands the final control of American industry; that control through actual stock ownership, in spite of the large number of stockholders, rested with a very small number of persons; and that in each great basic industry a single large corporation dominated the market.

In these respects the Commission set the pattern for future investigations of Big Business, among them the studies of the Temporary National Economic Committee (TNEC) and many successors. Its observations have been adopted and repeated by many succeeding reformers, including the theorists of the New Deal, though the changes of our economic power structure and legisla-

* P. 7876.

tive reforms have substantially altered the conditions of business since 1915.

Many of the conclusions of the foundation critics of 1915 have lost their cogency because of evolutions in the social structure. Foundations, too, have changed. We may no longer fear them as instruments of capitalism. Today many fear them as promoters of big government. Yet, under totally different economic and social conditions, the findings of 1915 are still significant. They point to essential peculiarities of private endowments manifest in any social climate, irrespective of the current fashions of contemporary social criticism or of current political trends.

The report of Mr. Manly, for the majority of the Commission, saw "the domination by the men in whose hands the final control of a large part of American industry rests *** rapidly extended to control the education and 'social service' of the Nation." Referring especially to Rockefeller's and Carnegie's foundations, it said:

> The control is being extended largely through the creation of enormous privately managed funds for indefinite purposes, hereinafter designated "foundations," by the endowment of colleges and universities, by the creation of funds for pensioning teachers, by contributions to private charities, as well as through controlling or influencing the public press.*** The funds of these foundations are exempt from taxation, yet during the life of their founders are subject to their dictation for any purpose other than commercial profit. In the case of the Rockefeller group of foundations, the absolute control of the funds and of the activities of the institutions now and in perpetuity rests with Mr. Rockefeller, his son, and whomsoever they may appoint as their successors. The control of these funds has been widely published as being in the hands of eminent educators and publicly spirited citizens. In the case of the Rockefeller foundations, however,*** the majority of the trustees of the funds are salaried employees of Mr. Rockefeller or the

foundations, who are subject to personal dictation and may be removed at any moment.

The report expresses concern that the policies of these foundations "must be inevitably colored, if not controlled, to conform to the policies" of the corporations in whose securities their endowment was invested. On the reasoning that these funds were the result of wealth created by exploiting either American workers or American consumers, it was concluded that "the funds, therefore, by every right, belong to the American people." Concern was expressed about the "practically unlimited powers of these foundations."

In discussing The Rockefeller Foundation, President Schurman of Cornell, himself a trustee of The Carnegie Foundation, said that one of these tax-exempt organizations was free to participate in practically any activity concerning the life and work of the nation, with the exception of activities for profit. Among the permitted foundation activities he listed: defense of the Republic in time of war; economic and political reforms which the trustees deem essential to the vitality and efficiency of the Republic in time of peace; championship for free trade or protectionism; advocacy of socialism or individualism; underwriting the respective programs of the Republican or the Democratic parties; introduction of Buddhism in the United States.

The absence of legally enforceable public control was seen in the report as an important deficiency because "past experience indicates *** that the public can be aroused only when the abuses have become so great as to constitute a scandal."

After listing examples of the alleged use of the Rockefeller foundations as instruments for advancement of the Rockefeller business interests, the report reviews the extent of the possible influence of these foundations and private endowments on institutions for education and public service. Evidence in the possession of the Commission supported the following complaints:

1. That the Bureau of Municipal Research of New York adopted

a definite line of policy to meet the conditions imposed by Mr. Rockefeller in connection with proposed contributions;

2. That several colleges and universities abandoned their sectarian affiliations and charter clauses relating to religion in order to secure endowments from the Carnegie Corporation.

This led the report to comment: *"It would seem conclusive that if an institution will willingly abandon its religious affiliations through influence of these foundations, it will even more easily conform to their will any other part of its organization or teaching."* *

The report concluded:

> As regards the "foundations" created for unlimited general purposes and endowed with enormous resources, their ultimate possibilities are so grave a menace, not only as regards their own activities and influence but also the benumbing effect which they have on private citizens and public bodies, that if they could be clearly differentiated from other forms of voluntary altruistic effort, it would be *desirable to recommend their abolition.*

It was therefore recommended that Congress enact legislation limiting the amount of funds and the exercise of power by fund managers. Provisions against accumulation of unexpended income and against expenditure in any year of more than 10 percent of capital were demanded, together with rigid inspection of finances (investment and expenditure) and complete publicity through open reports to the Government. In addition, the report proposed the creation of an investigatory body for the continued study of activities of foundations and of their affiliates. Finally, the recommendations called for increased Government activity in education and the social services to balance the power of foundations.

Commissioners John R. Commons and Florence J. Harriman, in their separate report, requested a further investigation of foundations before new legislation was adopted. They recommended

* P. 123. Emphasis supplied.

a study of endowed charities, religious organizations, universities, and colleges, and concluded: "It would be a misfortune if private endowments, unless plainly shown to have committed abuses, should be prohibited." There should be, however, "no alliance between these private foundations or endowments and the Government. The State or Government should neither subsidize them nor be subsidized by them, nor cooperate with them. Such cooperation has often led to public scandal. Instead of calling upon private foundations for help, the Government should treat them as competitors. No effort on the part of Government officials to secure financial assistance from them should be allowed." *

THE TEXTRON INVESTIGATION AND BUSINESS ABUSES

Congressional investigations have, on occasion, given sharp attention to improper business uses of foundations. In 1948, for example, a subcommittee of the Senate Committee on Interstate and Foreign Commerce (80th Congress, 2nd Session) investigated the operations of the Textron Corporation, which had used several tax-exempt foundations in complex business manipulations. Essentially, the Textron idea was to provide tax-free shelter for business interests, but in organizations which could remain under control. The investigation opened the eyes of many to the extent to which foundations could be and had been used in tax evasion and tax avoidance.

It disturbed this Congressional Committee that no agency of government had any information of consequence on the subject, nor any data regarding the resultant unfair competitive advantages enjoyed by foundations operating in business fields. The Committee expressed concern over the number of "family" foundations, and quoted *Fortune* magazine, which had described the practices of these organizations as "excessively secretive." These organizations were apparently considered by the families which controlled them to be their own private affair. The Committee castigated this secretiveness as unjustified and indefensible, as such foundations received their preferred tax treatment from so-

* P. 387.

ciety and hence owed a definite obligation to satisfy their public sanction.

The Senate Committee endorsed two recommendations which had been offered by The Russell Sage Foundation: that compulsory reporting of financial and other operational activities of foundations be required; and that tax exemption be restricted to organizations with an active program of public welfare.

The Textron disclosures, and studies of other abuses of the tax laws through the use of charitable foundations, led to a strengthening of the Internal Revenue Code. It is no longer as easy as it was to use foundations for business manipulations intended to evade or avoid the imposition of taxes. It is not the purpose of this study, however, to discuss the business or tax-avoidance use of foundations in detail. The Internal Revenue Service seems alert to the problem involved and is likely to propose successive, corrective legislative measures whenever new business abuses of the tax-exemption privilege appear. My concern is with the cultural and intellectual aspects of foundation activity. It is in the field of ideas that foundations exert the greatest influence on our lives and on the future of our country.

This is a field in which private inquiry should be encouraged. Congress is limited in its authority and in its approach. Almost all foundations are created under state law, and their rights and privileges are, for the most part, determined by state law. The leverage of the Congress, in attempting to hold them to proper activity, rests almost solely in the tax laws. The Federal Government has no power to regulate foundations in a direct way. It can only withhold the privilege of exemption from Federal taxes if they do not meet certain criteria of conduct delineated by the tax statutes.

Under these and associated handicaps, a Congressional inquiry cannot hope to do the thorough study which the subject requires. The Cox and Reece Committees did touch on some of the major cultural and intellectual aspects of foundation operation, but in this area private inquiry could promise wider and even more penetrating study.

Congressional investigation of foundation activity should continue; the subject is too grave to suffer Congressional neglect. On the other hand, the searching minds of students who are unconcerned with political consequences could contribute much to an understanding of the impact of foundations on public affairs and the consequent hazards.

THE SOCIAL SIGNIFICANCE OF TAX-EXEMPT INSTITUTIONS

Many authors have found a challenging object of study in the social implications of charitable activity by juridical persons. Charity is a virtue attributed to physical persons. The great religions since time immemorial have identified it with personal salvation. As a concern of lay institutions organized to dispense benefaction to the poor and deserving, it is of a more recent nature. Originating with religious bodies, organized charity has been used as an instrument of power from time to time over the centuries by its administrators. Is the potential of power of a great and wealthy charitable organization any the less a danger because it has no religious affiliation? Humanity has found that even a religious identity has not always kept powerful charitable organizations from conflicting with the public interest.

This conflict frequently required action by the sovereign against a power position established under the guise of religious charity. Usually, the curbing of privileged and tax-exempt charitable organizations took place because of their economic power. But there are also instances of intercession by the government for the declared reason that such bodies, established for charity, frequently exercised thought control. Indeed, there have been few instances in which both these motives have not been present simultaneously in varying proportions.

In 767, the Byzantine Emperor Constantine Kopronymos, after first attempting to tax the holdings of the numerous monasteries which had become too powerful, confiscated their properties, which had been donated by generations of Christians for charitable purposes and pious causes. He started a pattern of secularization which was often repeated by popes, kings, and revolutionary governments.

On May 6, 1312, Pope Clement V dissolved the very powerful order of the Knights Templar. The Templars had become a symbol of charity and culture; they had also grown enormously wealthy and had become a very strong influence in the western world. By the 12th century they had come to own 9,000 manors and had become rich to obvious excess. Their contributions to the security and civilization of Europe, their performance during the Crusades were soon forgotten. Acting in concert with the princes, the Pope suppressed the order; it had antagonized the secular states by its enormous aggregation of tax-exempt wealth, and the Church by some of its heretical beliefs and practices. Like some of our modern foundations, it had gone into politics. A later Pope, referring to this precedent in dissolving the Jesuit order, described the consequences of excessive wealth and influence as general disrepute (*ob universalem diffamationem suppressit et totaliter extinxit*).

The Roots of the Reformation were not in dogma alone. It gave the princes an opportunity to secularize the property of the Church. At the time of the reign of Henry VIII in England, the Church held two thirds of the votes in the House of Lords; owned one third of the land, and the best of it; and possessed an income two and one half times that of the Crown. The Spanish Crown, facing an increasing shrinkage of taxable land in the American colonies, forbade transfers of real property to religious institutions. Such institutions already owned about half the real estate in Mexico. Several Catholic powers, sometimes with the very approval of the Church, confiscated property accumulated from charitable donations and legacies in the hands of religious orders and societies.

It was in 1773 that Pope Clement XIV dissolved the Jesuit order, which had already been expelled from Spain (in 1767), France (1764), and Portugal (1759). This order had contributed very substantially to the preservation of the Roman Catholic

Church during the Reformation. Its charitable activities were immeasurable. In education, it had created methods of teaching and institutions of learning unexcelled at the time and exemplary even today. But its wealth and influence had aroused bitter and powerful resentment. This resentment lay partly in the political activity of some of the guiding managers of the Order. As a friendly historian put it: "Their disobedience to the rule—to abstain from politics—besmirched the name of the society and destroyed the good work of the other Jesuits, who were faithfully carrying out their own proper duties." A less friendly historian commented: "Their perpetual meddling in politics and even in speculation and finance, stank in the nostrils of every government in Europe; while their high-handedness and corrupt greed in the matters of ecclesiastical privileges and patronage alienated the clergy."

Islamic nations had their share of the problem of vast accumulations of wealth in religious organizations. Such accumulations, against a background of increasing population and decreasing free arable lands, made eventual confiscation inevitable; the increasing loss of revenue through the growth of the tax-exempt rolls made the problem more acute. The pious sultans of the Ottoman Empire contributed to the problem by donating land consistently to religious foundations. Upon each conquest, they regularly separated one fifth of their new territories for the use of charitable foundations (vakuf). When the Ottoman Empire fell, two thirds of all real property in its domains was owned by religious foundations. The withdrawal of such property from circulation and from taxation was one of the causes of the Empire's downfall.

Critical students of foundations have always been concerned with their potential of power. In modern times, however, changing political concepts have sometimes produced special criticism related to the trends of the moment. In 1950 Prime Minister Attlee of England appointed a committee to investigate charitable trusts. It questioned the merits and the place of voluntary charitable endowments in a welfare state. It concluded, however, that they must be given room and opportunity to contribute to the search for social advances. At the time, there were some 110,000 charitable trusts in England, 30,000 of them in the field of education.

In 1930 appeared a book written by Frederick P. Keppel, *The Foundation, Its Place in American Life.** Dr. Keppel, a former Dean of Columbia College and a leading exponent and manager of foundations, reviewed the relative responsibilities of private endowments and government. He conceived of foundations as clearing houses for ideas (p. 98), holding that they must be willing to take the initiative and must show courage as well as prudence (p. 94). They must, he said, be ever on guard against indulging in propaganda, even virtuous propaganda; he obviously saw the danger of political identification in charitable work, mindful of the suspicions disclosed by the Walsh Commission's hearings on Industrial Relations. There may have been some inconsistency in that he implored foundations not to wait for applications but to initiate their own programs, while at the same time he cautioned them against propaganda.

Dr. Keppel agreed with Beardsley Ruml, another eminent foundation manager: "In general, private funds are most appropriately used for work of a more experimental character, or for activities *** not a public responsibility." (P. 43.) He supported the proposition that foundation money should be used as "venture capital" in matters concerning welfare and culture. He advocated reliance on expert advisory boards, acting as intermediaries for foundations, presumably competent to counsel on the relative merits of applications and the proper priority of causes. In taking this position, Dr. Keppel may have been partly responsible for many of the foundation practices relating to patronage and the selection of projects which have come under recent severe criticism. Yet he, himself, said, "The administrative camel has crowded the intellectual pilgrim out of his tent" at the same time that he referred to criticism of bureaucratic practices as "often unreasonable criticism."

Dr. Keppel encouraged a pattern of operation which tends to make foundations the ultimate guides and judges of merits in the

* Macmillan, 1930.

intellectual world. He did this by implying that foundation trustees and managers should and could assume leadership in the realm of ideas with the help of intermediary expert organizations supported, in turn, by foundation funds.

Edward C. Lindeman, another leader in the world of tax-exempt organizations, reviewed foundation significance in his book *Wealth and Culture*.* Whereas, the report of the Walsh Committee had expressed mainly the fear of capitalist political machinations by the large foundations, Lindeman, then a socialist, seems to have believed in and approved of their power to contribute toward social change. He said:

> The New State of the future will need social technicians who will be asked to engage in cultural planning just as technological experts and economists will be called upon to plan for orderly material production and distribution. Those who have exercised a similar function during the individualist-competitive phase of modern economy have been, to a very large extent, associated with foundations and trusts. Consequently it becomes pertinent to discover how these culture-determiners have operated in the past.

Lindeman presented the true facts of life in the relation between foundations and the recipients of support. His observations are in conflict with the apologetic contentions of those managers of endowments who testified in later Congressional hearings that they did not interfere with the intellectual pursuits of grantees. "Foundations," he says (p. 19),

> do not merely exercise powers over those who accept their money. Such influence is obvious even when the foundation making grants insists on the contrary. A more subtle and much more widespread control comes about by reason of the multitude of indirect relationships in which foundations play a part. Those who accept foundation grants often turn

* Harcourt, Brace & Company, 1936.

out to be radical critics, in private, of the control which has been exercised over them and their programs. Those who live in anticipation of receiving foundation grants are more servile. Another device for projecting foundation control has become popular in recent years: foundations frequently supply the initial funds for a new project, these funds to be used for exploratory and conferencing purposes. In many cases the foundation acts as host for such preparatory groups. By the time the final project is formulated, it becomes clear that nothing will be proposed or performed which may be interpreted as a challenge to the orthodox conception of value which characterizes foundations as a whole. Very few important cultural projects of any size are consummated in this country without having experienced either the direct or indirect impact of foundation philosophy and influence.

Here we have an expression of concern not any longer with economic power or political intention to protect capitalism but generally with the control of thought practiced by the dispensers of financial support.

Lindeman, too, was suspicious of the secrecy under which so many endowments operate. He expressed surprise to discover that those who managed foundations and trusts did not wish to have these instruments investigated "by his privately conducted survey." He felt that as semi-public institutions they owed the public information about their activities. Looking at them as symbols of surplus wealth, he considered them "a consistently conservative element in our civilization." (P. 12.) Speaking of trustees (p. 59), he condemned the

repugnant arrogance of those who presume to impose cultural norms upon a society on no basis of warrant other than their pecuniary success under the dispensation of a competitive economy.*** In a decent society creative persons should not be expected to debase themselves as persons in order to gain the economic security which permits them to work. When they do so their true creativeness evaporates with tragic suddenness.

The change in prevalent fashions of thinking and in the social climate arising during and after the Depression altered the style of foundation performance so much that later analysts of their impact on our culture have more and more expressed their concern at a record of anticonservative performance. A generation of critics that feared the adverse effect of "capitalistic" bias of trustees was succeeded by observers who, from their study of the support of ideas and organizations by tax-exempt foundations, concluded that foundations had become the breeding ground for socialist and related political movements and action. This more recent generation of students, while equally impressed with the potentials of control of education and of public affairs in general by self-perpetuating, wealthy organizations beyond public control, has become concerned over the danger of foundation support of various undesirable concepts and movements having political implications. Among these are the ideas of the welfare state; the principles of economic determinism; excesses in the promotion of progressive education; the impairment of our national sovereignty; and even subversion. Hence the support by a majority in Congress of both the Cox and Reece Committee inquiries.

Frank Hughes, in his book *Prejudice and the Press** in connection with an analysis of the Report of the Hutchins-Luce Commission on Freedom of the Press, points to the emergence of professional foundation executives as the group actually in control of the billions of dollars of foundation resources. (P. 292.) He suggests that the business men holding positions as trustees had abandoned their responsibility to a professional class of administrators. As authority for this contention he quotes a book by Harrison and Andrews, both of The Russell Sage Foundation†: "The primary function of the board of trustees is the broad de-

---

* Devin-Adair, 1950.
† *American Foundations for Social Welfare*, 1946, p. 44.

termination of policies in harmony with the foundation's charter. However completely authority has been vested in the board, it has neither the time nor usually the special knowledge required for detailed administration of the work of the larger foundations***." Because administrators come from teaching and administrative jobs in colleges and universities (he says virtually all are educators or former educators), Hughes argues that they exhibit the progovernment bias prevalent in university circles. He attributes this to the "big business" nature of higher learning and its dependence on government favor and government support.

In the influence of the administrators on the choice of causes and recipients supported by grants, Hughes sees a real danger to the Republic. He accuses foundations of commonly practicing interlocking management together with some of the large universities (pp. 284-297); of giving money, with exceptions only, to supervised projects; of acting as, and supporting, propaganda agencies; of making little money available to foster individual and independent thought and research. "A more tight and monopolistic control of great wealth would be hard to find in any other segment of American economy." Their interlocking with the boards of large universities is documented by numerous names of multiple trusteeship holders. He points to the invasion of foundation boards of trustees by the trustees of universities, in addition to the emergence of university teachers as the professional managers of foundations. He quotes a study that found fifty-four trusteeships in twenty-nine foundations held by men who were also trustees of universities.

Frank Hughes fears for the freedoms of America. He is a conservative, but his criticism, like that of the generation of Senator Walsh or Edward C. Lindeman, is essentially based on the abstract fear of bigness and concentration of power as a political factor. Like earlier students of foundations, he is concerned with foundation support of selected political ideas and favored institutions. Like his predecessors from the opposing political camp, he gives insufficient attention to the impact of foundation giving on cultural patterns and on the motivations for creativity. Whether one agrees with the political bias of today's or yesterday's analysts of the impact of tax-exempt organizations on public affairs, the problem of the relationship between money and creative genius demands major examination.

Such examination has been undertaken recently, among others, by William H. Whyte, Jr., an editor of *Fortune* magazine, in his book *The Organization Man.** Whyte, who had previously covered the story of The Ford Foundation in magazine articles, is well informed about current foundation practices. In his book he deals with the disastrous impact of organization techniques on the life of America. He attributes to them a growing force for conformism, threatening in the end to destroy all vestiges of genius, individual responsibility and initiative, and with them the concepts of individual independence and liberty so dear to earlier generations. In the corporate mechanics of the foundations he sees one of the most menacing trends resulting from the social patterns of an age controlled by organization bureaucrats. He contends that the flow of really good ideas and scientific achievement is hindered rather than advanced by the habitual bigness of corporation- or foundation-supported research projects.

America, he says, has been borrowing ideas from Europe, especially in basic research, from nations favored neither by large industrial-research operations nor by the bounty of giant tax-exempt foundations. Organization support favors team research. Our learned journals are increasingly publishing papers by two or more authors, indicating a preference for group performance over individual problem study. Planning of scientific work by committee has become the accepted pattern. Consequently scientists do not merely submit their findings to the judgment of others—as has been the case through the ages of learned discourse. They now depend on others also in the early stage, when they decide what specific problems to investigate. Even if committees of organization functionaries do not form an interlocking directorate, according to Whyte, they are "a reflection of the concentrations of influences normal in the academic world. But for that very reason,

* Simon & Schuster, 1956.

the ambitious younger man—and scientists are just as ambitious as anybody else—takes his cues from these guides, and those who prefer to look into questions unasked by others need a good bit of intellectual fortitude to do so." (P. 222.)

Whyte believes that the distraction offered by the lure of funds for organization-favored projects seriously impairs the creative potential of our scientists. He quotes an example of a meeting of twenty top scientists in a particular field for the purpose of listening to the plans of a chairman of a great foundation. About eight of these men were on the verge of some really important work, he reports. But as no indication of interest in the preferences of the scientists was given by the foundation chairman, the meeting dealt only with his plans and projects calling for fresh starts. The feeling prevailed that the work to be financed by the foundation would "be in the long run a net subtraction" of the scientific assets previously accumulated by the participating scholars. Whyte fears the consequences of such usurpation of the basic role of the scientist by a scientific and fund bureaucracy. "The most fertile new ideas," he says, quoting L. L. Whyte, "are those which transcend established, specialized methods and treat some new problem as a single task*** cooperative groups, from great industrial concerns to small research teams, inevitably tend to rely on what is already acceptable as common ground***."

The increasing dependence of research on support by grants forces scientists into a vicious circle, described by Curt Richter of Johns Hopkins in the following words quoted from W. H. Whyte, Jr. (p. 225):

> In making application for a grant before World War II, a few lines or at most a paragraph or two sufficed for the experimental design; now it may extend over six to eight single-spaced typewritten pages. And even then committee members may come back for more details. Under these circumstances, passing the buck has come to be practiced very widely. Projects are passed from Committee to Committee —to my knowledge, in one instance six Committees—largely

because at no place along the line did any one believe that he had adequate information to come to a firm decision.

The control imposed on a scientist by the requirement that his research designs be approved by the members of numerous giant committees will bring his ideas down to the lowest intellectual common denominator. It will impose on him the most powerful pressure to conform to a pattern of mediocrity. Whyte ridicules the argument presented for scientific teamwork: that the group, even in the realm of thought, is superior to the individual. The foundations have not responded to the challenge to invigorate individual research. "Instead of countering the bureaucratization of research they are intensifying it." (P. 230.)

It is no wonder that so many creative individuals have been conditioned to abandon individual projects. The climate produced in the world of ideas by the large foundations, upon whose support so many scholars must rely for research, is not favorable to individual projects. Such scholars are often seduced into group research because of the difficulty of getting individual grants and because of the financial lure of generous foundation subsidy for large projects. This lure draws many away from potentially creative work and the pursuit of new discovery, and leads them into sterile fields tended by conformists. Whyte states that, with few exceptions (the Guggenheim foundations being an outstanding one), the great foundations concentrate their giving on institutions and on big team projects. Where individual grants are eventually contemplated, these foundations generally rely on other organizations and institutions to select from among applications. Whyte gives this shocking example of "projectitis" and the neglect of the individual researcher. He says that he approached thirteen top sociologists "not working on currently fashionable problems but who were thought first rate." (P. 238.) He found that seven had applied to one of the big three foundations (Ford, Rockefeller, and Carnegie) for grants and all but one had been turned down. He said that, with one exception, they all felt they would not get sympathetic consideration by these foundations.

In pointing out their achievements, foundations offer a long list of contributions made by their grantees in the sciences, and a shorter list of outstanding foundation-supported accomplishments in the arts. Yet, again and again, they have been severely criticized for the general sterility of their products and for the tendency to elaborate old ideas instead of venturing into the daring unorthodoxies.* Whyte points out what has become a bureaucratic feature of this big-project process fostered by most of the large foundations—the tendency toward project self-perpetuation. He says: "Many a project gets to a point where its main reason for being is to produce more research to justify a grant for more research***." (P. 236.)

He quotes J. A. Gengerelli, head of the Psychology Department of the University of California, Los Angeles:

> We have a social force that selectively encourages and rewards the scientific hack. There is a great hustle and bustle, a rushing back and forth to scientific conferences, a great plethora of $50,000 grants for $100 ideas. I am suggesting that scientific, technical, and financial facilities are such in this country as to encourage a great number of mediocrities to go into science, and to seduce even those with creative talent and imagination to a mistaken view of the nature of the scientific enterprise. (P. 239.)

The unquestionable merits of a substantial part of what foundations have done and continue to do for the public welfare should not absolve them from criticism whenever their chosen preferences, or the unintended by-products of their manner of operation, develop into dangers to the Republic. Such dangers have been demonstrated by public investigators and by private observers in the potential and real influence of foundation power in the field of politics. To this observation has now been added a fear of the far-reaching influence of foundation-controlled money

---

* My use of the term "unorthodoxies" requires explanation. What is orthodox today may be daring tomorrow; and what was daring twenty or thirty years ago may be orthodox today. A certain form of "liberalism" is currently orthodox in intellectual circles.

in the realm of ideas and on patterns of creative behavior of scientists and artists.

Whether foundation managers like to admit their influence or not, foundation giving most obviously has an enormous impact on education, on social thinking, and ultimately on political action. This influence reaches the public through the schools and acaddemies, through publicity, and through educational and other associations dedicated to public and international affairs. Foundations *per se* are neither good nor bad. It is the people who run them who must account, morally, to the public. It is these managers who are responsible for foundation performance. The laws under which foundations operate are, to say the least, imperfect. But a reform of the law can impose only negative checks and balances on foundation spending and can never convert juridical persons to a truly creative pattern of action. Short of hampering foundations to a point of ineffectiveness, all the legislator can do is to protect the public against certain abuses of power. Only the trustees and managers of foundations themselves can direct the application of tax-exempt funds more intelligently to the public welfare.

FOUNDATION RESPONSIBILITY

In his statement to the Reece Committee in 1954, Mr. H. Rowan Gaither, then President of The Ford Foundation, estimated the annual contributions to philanthropy in the United States at $5,600,000,000. Of this sum, he said, less than 3 percent came from foundations. There can be no doubt that foundations represent, financially, but a small part of the philanthropic world. According to figures published by The American Association of Fund-Raising Counsel, Inc., annual charitable donations in 1956 had reached the astounding figure of $6,100,000,000. Endowments and properties of privately supported religious, educational, health, and welfare institutions had increased in 1956 by an estimated $1,400,000,000 and now exceeded $42,000,000,000. Of this total, religious institutions owned about $12,200,000,000; and about 53 percent of all donations were for religious purposes.

Education consumed 9 percent of the total; contributions to philanthropic and charitable foundations, something like 3 percent. The Association of Fund-Raising Counsel, Inc., estimates that, out of about 40,000 organizations listed by the Internal Revenue Service as tax exempt, the number of those engaged in giving is about 6,000. It estimates, further, that such foundations own assets running between $7,000,000,000 and $9,500,000,000.

Mr. Gaither was on weak ground, however, if he sought to prove the relative unimportance of foundations through financial comparison with other philanthropic media. Foundations occupy a unique place in our society for many reasons, of which two are peculiarly important for distinguishing them from other philanthropic bodies. One is that foundations are not subject to the normal forms of control by which other institutions are checked, such as responsibility to a constituency or membership, or to an academic body. The second is that, under the influence of the "venture capital" theory, so much foundation money has been channeled in favor of social change.

Only a minority of foundations has fallen victim to the obsession for social change. But among this minority are to be found some of the wealthiest and some of the oldest endowments. They have adopted the concept that foundations should be clearing-houses for ideas, and they must accept responsibility for the results of their selected patronage. Such responsibility, as John D. Rockefeller, Jr., put it at the hearings of the Walsh Commission, may result in legislative steps to protect the interests of the public.

Foundations cannot deny their public responsibility. The Russell Sage Foundation, a leader in the foundation world, specializing in philanthropic research, has repeatedly insisted upon public accounting of foundation finances and activities. Mr. Dean Rusk, President of The Rockefeller Foundation and of the General Education Board, said, in his statement to the Reece Committee: "We are convinced that tax-exempt organizations should make regular public reports about their funds and activities." Many, though not all, of the large foundations have, for years, issued public reports, thus implicitly recognizing their responsibility to the public.

Large foundations can do more harm, as well as more good, than smaller foundations. But even comparatively small foundations can have an impact on society disproportionate to their monetary size, particularly when promoting a seductive idea promising better things for society. When they are ready to tamper with the public welfare by pursuing particular brands of social philosophy advocated by their managers, the dynamics of their use can give these smaller foundations an importance far beyond their arithmetical magnitude.

Mr. F. Emerson Andrews, in his *Philanthropic Foundations,* writing of the venture capital concept, has this to say:

> Because of their relative freedom from governmental and other controls, it has been suggested that foundations may have a special mandate to enter fields of controversy, where the explosive nature of the issues would make suspect the findings of less independent organizations and where the needed financing from any other source may prove difficult. (P. 19.)

Following this interpretation of the venture-capital concept, the work of even comparatively small foundations can obviously have enormous impact on our society. A few examples will illustrate:

The Carnegie Endowment for International Peace, a substantial foundation, but a dwarf compared with the giants like Ford, Rockefeller, and the Carnegie Corporation, has achieved stupendous importance and power. By 1953, its net assets, despite heavy disbursements, had about doubled to $20,000,000. Spending annually between $500,000 and $600,000, the endowment achieved a key position in the areas of foreign relations and international organizations. Its influence, increasing over the past 47 years, has reached into the Department of State, into the law schools where international law is taught, into the foreign offices of other nations, and into the United Nations and its associated organizations.

Through concentrated efforts in publishing, in the organization and management of conferences, and in cooperation with various other groups, some subsidized, it has reached a position of world-wide influence. It is no longer a mere clearing-house for ideas; it has become a proponent of the particular ideas of its trustees, its staff, and an entourage sympathetic to certain special concepts of international relations promoted by the foundation itself. The strategic use of its relatively small funds has resulted in the mobilization of additional funds behind causes favored by the endowment, in the form of matched grants supplied by other foundations within its sphere of influence. Large funds have also come from membership contributions to organizations supported by the endowment and, in some instances, created or fathered by it.

Some smaller foundations, like The Hillman Foundation, have found their influence greatly amplified through the granting of annual awards. Five were recently announced, of $500 each. These small awards received considerable newspaper publicity. They were granted, the newspapers reported, "for outstanding work in journalism, magazines and books in 1956." The "outstanding" works selected, however, were all political. Consistent with the policy of The Hillman Foundation, they concerned political goals of the Amalgamated Clothing Workers of America, of which the late Mr. Hillman, as a tribute to whom the foundation had been created, had been president. In addition to an award to *The New York Times* for its editorial treatment of the Near East crisis a reporter of the Des Moines Tribune received one for articles on segregation; an editor of Harper's, one for an editorial attacking censorship efforts of private organizations; Robert Penn Warren, one for an article in *Life* on segregation; and Professor Walter Gellhorn of Columbia, one for his book on *Individual Freedom and Government Restraints.*

Other foundations have offered public prizes and, in this way, multiplied their public visibility and increased immeasurably their opportunities for propaganda. The Nobel prize, as well as the Stalin prize, illustrate this method of publicity-producing giving. Though the purpose of the Nobel prize is essentially apolitical, while the Stalin prize (or whatever has taken its place since

Stalin's loss of standing in Russia) is merely a political propaganda gesture, both evidence the publicity impact which a relatively small amount of money can have if used strategically.

An example of the sometimes explosive nature of foundation giving is the support by foundations of the late Dr. Kinsey in what he called sex research.* The Rockefeller Foundation supported the National Research Council's Committee for research in problems of sex, with a total of $1,755,000 from 1931 to 1954. Of this sum, the activities conducted by Dr. Kinsey received some $414,000 from 1941 to 1949, as reported by The Rockefeller Foundation to the Reece Committee. This amount is microscopic compared with the total of $6,000,000,000 annually spent on philanthropy in the United States. But the impact of this comparatively small sum on one subject was quite out of proportion to the relative size of the two figures. One may approve or disapprove of Dr. Kinsey's efforts, and judge variously their impact upon our sex mores. But the Kinsey incident does show that comparatively small donations may have big repercussions in the realm of ideas.

WHAT IS "PROPAGANDA" AND WHAT IS "EDUCATION"?

What control the Federal Government may exercise over foundations is based almost entirely on the tax law. The State under whose laws a foundation is organized might penalize it in various ways or even dissolve it for misconduct. All that the Federal Government can do, however, is to withdraw its tax exemption and the corresponding tax benefits to donors. What, then, are the bases for such punishment?

The tax law is woefully weak. The controlling statute is worded quite generally and loosely; the courts have been inclined to interpret these loose provisions in favor of the foundations; and, in any event, the Internal Revenue Service is not equipped or manned to do the "policing" necessary to determine when the law has been violated.

* The substance of his activity will be discussed in chapter 4 as an important case illustrating the attempt by foundations to evade responsibility for the results of their grants.

The most important limitation in the law is the one which prohibits political activity. This prohibition is now covered principally by Section 501 (c) (3) of the Internal Revenue Code of 1954 (formerly paragraph [6] of Section 101) in this way: a foundation may qualify for tax exemption,

> no substantial part of the activities of which is carrying on propaganda, or otherwise attempting, to influence legislation, and which does not participate in, or intervene in (including the publishing or distribution of statements), any political campaign on behalf of any candidate for public office.

This test, quantitatively, is weak. What is a "substantial" part of its activities? Dollars? Numbers of grants? Impact? It is also weak qualitatively. Is legislation "influenced" only if a foundation directly supports the passage or the defeat of a particular piece of legislation—or does a foundation also "influence" legislation by promoting a political theory which indirectly results in a change of law or is intended to?

The term "propaganda" is not defined in the statute. Certainly there could have been no intention to prohibit all propaganda, as that would have constituted an attack on the churches, which are entitled to engage in religious propaganda. "Political" propaganda was intended, certainly, but the phrase "to influence legislation" can be interpreted to be attributive to "propaganda" and thus to limit it.

The wording of the statute created many ambiguities. It is sometimes extremely difficult to draw the line, for example, between those forms of education which are essential or desirable in our democratic society and those which have as their ends the promotion of political value-concepts in the realm of ideas. Numerous foundations pursue their political ways free of interference by the Internal Revenue Service because of the ambiguity and weakness of the statute referred to.

For example, The Robert Schalkenbach Foundation of New York, a small foundation with an intensive publishing and training program, is dedicated to the promotion of Henry George's single tax idea. This endowment spends its money to persuade the public that real estate taxes can and should replace all other forms of taxation. It probably abstains from lobbying and from any direct interference with the legislative process. But it has probably indoctrinated thousands of more or less intelligent citizens. What it does, must, in the end, amount to propaganda to influence legislation. Yet the foundation would undoubtedly claim its efforts to be "educational."

A foundation has, for years, supported the World Calendar Association and the efforts of Miss Elizabeth Achelis to introduce, world-wide, a new method of computing the calendar year. Her efforts may be meritorious, but this seemingly apolitical activity does have legislative aspects. How can a new calendar be adopted without legislative action?

Supported by a foundation for world government endowed with $1,000,000 by Mrs. Anita McCormick Blaine, a tax-exempt Committee to Frame a World Constitution, under Chancellor Robert Hutchins of the University of Chicago, wrote a program for a World Republic in 1948. The foundation was to finance "a public educational campaign in the principles of world government." The proposed constitution advocated, among other things, a national surrender to a World Government of expropriation rights; control of plans for the improvement of the world's physical facilities; the power of taxation, regulation of transportation, and similar prerogatives of national governments. Dr. Hutchins, now President of The Ford Foundation's off-shoot, The Fund for the Republic, stated in 1948, and may well have believed, that "world government is necessary, therefore it is—or must be made —possible." But the expression of such a belief was hardly apolitical, and the support by a tax-exempt foundation of the program which Dr. Hutchins supported was hardly the support of "education."

The American Labor Education Service, Inc., is a tax-exempt organization. Among its purposes, it lists: "to cooperate with the labor movement in intensifying education in the field of international affairs; and to encourage the study of such issues within the groups and unions." It becomes apparent, however, from an examination of this organization's literature, that the "education" referred to is essentially propaganda for the political labor movement. In announcements of ALES activities are to be found these "educational" topics: "How Can Workers' Education Advance Labor's Economic and Political Objectives"; "Political Action for Labor"; and "Political Action Techniques." In a news letter discussing the Taft-Hartley Bill, the ALES said: "The passage of the Taft-Hartley Bill indicates among other things the need for an intensive 'push' in labor education. The American Labor Education Service is equipped to furnish this 'push'***."

Other examples of the political nature of this foundation's work will be found in Chapter 6 and in the staff report on the ALES to the Reece Committee.* This foundation received financial support from The Rockefeller Foundation. Perhaps the presence of the word "Education" in the name of the American Labor Education Service was sufficient to prove that its work was purely "educational."

Another strange "educational" tax-exempt organization is The League for Industrial Democracy, formerly The Intercollegiate Socialist Society. In a booklet entitled, significantly, "Revolt," it described its work as follows:

> The League for Industrial Democracy is a militant educational movement which challenges those who would think and act for a "new social order based on production for use not for profit." That is a revolutionary slogan. It means that members of the LID think and work for the elimination of capitalism, and the substitution for it of a new order, in whose building the purposeful and passionate thinking of the student and worker today will play an important part.

The LID has only a modest budget of $50,000 a year, some of it supplied by foundations, but its influence has been wide and deep.

* Reece Committee *Hearings,* Part II, p. 1158 *et seq.*

It is understandable that the Bureau of Internal Revenue contested the tax-exempt status of the LID. However, the U. S. Circuit Court of Appeals, in 1931,* upheld its tax exemption by applying the broadest possible interpretation of the term "education," against the contention of the Collector of Internal Revenue that the organization was political. It has enjoyed tax exemption ever since; it goes about its business of promoting socialism, without harassment by the Internal Revenue Service.

In a lengthy letter submitted to the Reece Committee, Dr. Laidler of the LID insisted upon a similarity between the work of the LID and some college courses in the social sciences. He said that books and pamphlets published by the LID were, in fact, used in some college courses. Using this as a major premise, and the fact that colleges are educational as a minor premise, he produces a syllogism with the conclusion that the work of the LID is also educational.

Semantic difficulties in interpreting statutes are not unusual in our system of law, or in any other. Admittedly our courts have a problem in trying to draw the line between education in its acceptable sense and "education" which is political propaganda intended to influence legislation. They are inclined to interpret punitive statutes liberally in favor of the litigant, strictly against the government. This should probably be so. But decisions such as that in the LID case exhibit a generosity of interpretation so extreme as to make the punitive statute virtually worthless in so far as it proscribes propaganda activities by foundations directed toward influencing legislation. If tax exemption is available to the LID, which "educates" to socialist ends, there is no reason why it should not be available to organizations which educate to other partisan and political ends such as segregation, other forms of racial and religious discrimination, polygamy, nudism, and fascism.

If the law is sufficiently ambiguous to permit political propaganda under the guise of education, this ambiguity does not, however, justify foundation managers in supporting such activities.

* *Weyl v. Commissioner*, 48 F. (2d) 811.

An interpretation of the venture capital theory permitting the use of tax-exempt funds for partisan purposes would be a palpable absurdity. It is a different matter with organizations created to pursue partisan ends and using the dues of members for this purpose. The managers of tax-exempt endowments act as trustees not only for the donors to such foundations but also for the public. They have as little right to use their trust funds for partisan ends as they have to put them into their own pockets.

Not all tax-exempt foundations have received as generous treatment from the courts as did the League for Industrial Democracy. The Twentieth Century Fund lost its tax exemption for the years 1935 to 1939 because of its advocacy of enabling laws on credit-union extension. In 1925 the World Peace Foundation lost its tax-exempt status because it acted as a distributor of League of Nations literature, then considered partisan propaganda. It regained its exemption in 1928 because, by that time, its activities were no longer deemed an attempt to influence legislation. Recently the exemption of The Institute of Pacific Relations was revoked for reasons which shall be discussed later. There have been other cases of exemption denial. Looking at them together, one is impressed with their lack of consistency, and this is no wonder. Each case depends upon the semantic interpretation of the controlling statute which appeals to the court before which it is heard.*

WHAT IS "RELIGIOUS"?

The courts are faced with another semantic difficulty when obliged to determine which organizations are entitled to tax exemption because their activities are truly within the scope of the term "religious," and which ones cross the line and serve political ends. In the course of their legitimate religious activities, churches and religious bodies often develop ancillary programs which are not religious in the strict sense of the word. In our complex so-

---

* In his testimony before the Reece Committee, Assistant Commissioner of Internal Revenue Norman Sugarman offered a most interesting discussion of the cases and of the principles applied by the courts and the Revenue Service. See Hearings, p. 429 *et seq.*

ciety, religious groups frequently become involved in legislative problems. They fight for school buses for religious schools, for public support of such schools, for temperance, for Sunday observance. They participate actively in public discussions regarding the divorce laws, birth control, religious instruction in the public schools, etc.

There are in existence many para-religious organizations whose only relationship to religion is that their membership comes from only one confession. Such organizations claim tax exemption, though principally devoted to the advancement of political group interests in legislation. Some of them maintain registered lobbyists in Washington. They are dedicated to such diverse causes as the political and financial support of the State of Israel; the fight against segregation; the liberalization of the immigration laws for the benefit of their co-religionists; and opposition to the political aims of certain other religious groups.

There can be little doubt that some of these militant organizations, spending their tax-exempt funds openly to influence legislation, should be deprived of their tax advantage. But there is little promise of this happening. Both the legislature and the courts are understandably reluctant to take any steps which, rightly or wrongly, might be called an interference with the freedom of religion. In addition, as far as the courts are concerned, the law is regrettably ambiguous as it stands.

FOUNDATION RESPONSIBILITY IN SUPPORTING SOCIAL CHANGE
In statements filed with the Reece Committee, some foundation managers maintained that they were not responsible for the frequency with which grants have been applied to the advancement of social change toward anticapitalism. They attributed the prevalence of New Deal sentiment, in the literature and programs which they have supported, to the political and intellectual climate of the times. If foundations have favored quasi-socialist "liberal" causes and discriminated against "conservative" programs, it may well be due to some extent, to the fact that the preference

had already existed in the academic world. Also, there may have been a penetration of foundation boards and administrative ranks by anticonservative professionals (academicians, scholars, and administrators), with a resulting adoption of their current idiosyncrasies by the endowments.

This tendency was accelerated by the use of intermediary agencies and individual "expert" consultants. The judging of the merits of grant proposals was delegated to these agencies and consultants. Such delegation cannot, however, shift responsibility away from the foundation managers. Advisory experts were chosen for their standing in the academic world. But the structure of academic life does not differ from other structures in this sense —it encompasses a web of political forces. The politically minded manipulator often is rewarded with eminent status, whether he is a true scholar or not. The symbol of academic prestige is not necessarily an evidence of learning or of sound social judgment. Once an academician is selected to act as an "expert," he becomes one in the public eye because he has been so chosen. He may have succeeded in coming into office chiefly because he had developed good "public relations." If that was the case, he is likely to support whatever fads and foibles enabled him to succeed, rather than the thought of truly creative minds.

These "experts" have almost invariably followed the current fashion which grew up among teachers and political scientists under a barrage of communist and socialist propaganda and under the impact made by the depression of 1930. This fashion is one of confidence in the power of man to create heaven on earth by manipulating the structure of government. The belief in radical change is manifested by the statement of William C. Carr, Executive Secretary of the National Education Association of the United States, to the Reece Committee. According to the NEA, it is not the American ideal to be hostile to change. It attributes the greatness of America to the freedom of its citizens "to propose and adopt modifications in the structure of the Government, and of their other institutions." The NEA believes it is the right and duty of good citizens to adapt their political and social institutions, within the broad circumstances of our constitutional freedoms, to meet new circumstances and conditions.

Mr. Carr is quoted not to contest his point but to bring out that the change which he supports is clearly political. It would seem apparent, therefore, that the advocacy of such change, having essential political implications, is not a proper field for a foundation whose tax exemption is granted by the grace of the entire public. Yet some of the large foundations seem to have adopted an almost religious belief in change for change's sake. Even in the absence of a conspiracy among foundations to promote change, the cumulative effect of this almost unison approach, and the absence of any substantial support for contrary movements looking toward social stability, seems to warrant questioning whether these foundations are truly performing their trust duty to the public.

Trends come into being, from time to time, and may persist whether foundation-supported or not. The real responsibility of foundations rests in their ability to provide war chests in the battle of ideas. However much foundation managers may talk about their right and duty to use their trust funds as venture capital, there can be little doubt that in their "ventures" they have given preference to the political ideas held by cliques of academicians and to the proponents of the ideas who are generally identifiable as leftist.

Foundations should be responsible for a balanced application of their support. The normal checks and balances in our public life can be annihilated through one-sided foundation support of the forces calling for change. Obviously, change is often desirable and even necessary, but not *per se*. The uncritical support by foundations of the idea that we must have change for change's sake justified two recent Congresses in suspecting foundations of being agencies frequently favoring undesirable and destructive goals.

2 THE POWER OF THE INDIVIDUAL FOUNDATION

RAMIFICATIONS OF THE POWER

THE GIANT FOUNDATION can exercise enormous power through the direct use of its funds. Moreover, it materially increases this power and its influence by building collateral alliances which serve greatly to insulate it against criticism. It is likely to find friends among the banks which hold its great deposits; the investment and brokerage houses which serve its investment problem; the major law firms which act as its counsel; and the many firms, institutions, and individuals with which it deals and which it benefits. By careful selection of a trustee, here and there, from among proprietors and executives of newspapers, periodicals, and other media of communication, it can assure itself of adulation and support. By engaging "public relations counselors" (ethically, and even legally, a questionable practice), it can further create for itself a favorable press and enthusiastic publicity.

All its connections and associations, plus the often sycophantic adulation of the many institutions and individuals who had received largess from the foundation, give it an enormous aggregate of power and influence. This power extends beyond its immediate circle of associations, to those who hope to benefit from its bounty. Institutions and individuals are powerfully attracted to the policies of the foundation within their circles of interest and, as long as the magnetic force in the form of funds persists, are unlikely to change their orientation.

The foundation's direct power is the power of money. Privately financed educational institutions have had a bad time during the period of rapidly increasing costs. Foundation grants have become so important a source of support that college and university presidents cannot often afford to ignore the opinions and wishes of the executives who distribute foundation largess. Such administrators will freely admit that they do not like to receive restricted or earmarked grants and would far prefer to be unfettered in their disposition of money given to their institutions. But they will also admit that they usually dare not turn down a grant, however inconsistent with their policy, priority of goals, or urgent needs it may be, for fear they might earn the displeasure of the granting foundation.

The situation permits large foundations to exercise a profound influence upon public opinion and upon the course of public affairs. For academic opinion today, as the Reece Committee report put it, "is the opinion of the intellectuals of tomorrow and will very likely be reflected into legislation and in public affairs thereafter***."

Nor is the control exercisable by a great foundation limited to its direct relations with the executives and trustees of educational institutions. Pressure starts at the very bottom of the academic ladder. A foundation grant may enable a beginner to attain the precious doctorate which is the first rung. To secure such assistance, is it not likely that he will conform to what he may believe would please those who give him their financial grace? Then he becomes a teacher, at a salary sometimes below that of an ordinary laborer. Without supplemental help through a foundation grant, he can support his family only in poverty; he cannot set aside the time or the money necessary to enable him to do such study, research, and writing as may advance him in his career. Is he, then, likely to run counter to what may be wanted by a foundation considering him for a grant? This teacher finds, as he progresses in his career, that he has few sources from which to increase his income other than the foundations; without such accessory income, he cannot achieve those extracurricular but academic distinctions which give him prestige and advance him in the education hierarchy. These distinctions come often from research and writing. Great, dispensing intermediary organizations control learned journals and university presses; they hold the key to academic publications and form an effective instrument of patronage.

Foundations rarely impose conformity in any direct manner. But they often do so through the selection of grantees and the rejection or approval of suggested subjects and methods of research. An academician who is "in" with a great foundation can hope for advancement to the top. One who is not can still get there, but it is infinitely more difficult. And, as the Reece Committee said:

> Just as the president of the institution, whose main job today may well be fund raising, cannot afford to ignore the bureaucrats' wishes, so the academician cannot. Scholars and fund raisers both soon learn to study the predilections, preferences and aversions of foundations' executives, and benefit from such knowledge by presenting projects likely to please them.*

Foundation power poses a problem quite aside from the momentary preferences of the managers of these funds. These managers may be no less conscientious than public servants. But, through the fact that they are free from the checks and controls by which public servants are restrained, there is less probability that their errors will ever be discovered; and, if they are discovered, that they will be reversed.

HOW THE POWER IS ADMINISTERED
In small foundations the trustees usually assume the actual work and responsibility for the examination of applications and the dispensing of grants. In the great ones it is almost standard practice for the trustees to act largely as window dressing. They may exercise the full power of management and direction if they wish, but

* *Report*, p. 36.

they do not do so. They go through the motions of control. They often debate issues; they frequently pass on and determine principles of operation; they consider and take action on many specific grants. But the limited time they devote to such work is not enough to enable them to exercise the degree of control and responsibility which their duty requires.

It is not inattention, it is not an unwillingness on the part of the trustees to accept responsibility, which creates this situation. It is the fact that most of the great foundations have chosen to operate in such complex fashion that it is impossible for otherwise busy trustees, working for the foundation only part time, to perform adequately. Innumerable errors of a serious nature have been acquiesced in by eminent and intelligent trustees merely because they have not had the time to study, check, and follow the detailed operation of the foundation sufficiently—nor have they been able to discover and weigh factors of importance which came to the attention only of the foundation's executive employees.

The unmanageable volume of business which confronts the trustees of a great foundation does not, however, excuse that delegation of power so often practiced. Such a delegation may be in order in a business enterprise, where the failure of its directors adequately to shoulder responsibility results merely in an unhappy profit-and-loss statement; all that can be lost is money. Foundation responsibility is not mere financial responsibility but, far more importantly, social responsibility. The power to venture into the realm of thought, to support and promote ideas, should not be delegated except in a minor, administrative sense. If the volume of work becomes excessive, it might be necessary to increase the number of trustees and to expect of them full-time attention to their duties. An alternative would be to let unquestionably responsible institutions, such as universities, take over the function which otherwise would be delegated to foundation employees or subsidized intermediary organizations.

In many cases, as Dr. Charles W. Briggs, Professor Emeritus of Columbia University, testified before the Reece Committee, the true operating heads of these foundations present a program to the trustees which is "so general as to get approval and yet so indefinite as to permit activities which in the judgment of most competent critics are either wasteful or harmful * * *."* Even the formulation of glittering generalities is usually left to administrative officers; the selection and proposal of individual grants and grantees, almost always. Where express approval by the trustees is required, they are, all too often, insufficiently informed—indeed, so often, rubber stamps. Such abandonment of trustee duties has led to the indefensible practice of leaving the selection of grantees to the professional managers of organizations created for the purpose of retailing the distribution of wholesale grants.

An extreme instance of this is The Institute of Pacific Relations, itself a foundation and one of the retailers used by other foundations. To it, The Carnegie Corporation, The Carnegie Endowment for International Peace, and The Rockefeller Foundation contributed millions of dollars. Its record is now well known. The Internal Revenue Service disclosed in 1955 that it had revoked its tax exemption. Some years ago, after a detailed investigation of this foundation, the McCarran Committee came to the conclusion that The Institute of Pacific Relations had been virtually an organ of the Communist Party of the United States. It held that "at least since the mid-1930's,"

> the net effect of IPR activities on United States public opinion has been pro-Communist and pro-Soviet, and has frequently and repeatedly been such as to serve international Communist and Soviet interests, and to subvert the interests of the United States.†

On the board of directors (trustees) of The Institute of Pacific Relations were men of high caliber and excellent reputation. How, then, were officers of the Institute able to turn its activities to pro-Soviet objectives? Professor David N. Rowe explained this to the Reece Committee. Professor Rowe is an academician of the highest standing. Recently on special assignment in Formosa, he had

---

* *Ibid.*, p. 23.
† McCarran Committee *Report,* p. 84.

been a member of the Yale Executive Committee on International Relations since 1950 and was Director of Studies from 1951 to 1953. He is one of our foremost authorities on the Far East.

Professor Rowe had himself been a director of The Institute of Pacific Relations for several years, resigning when he discovered some of its derelictions and found that he had no power as a director. The directors were dummies. The organization was run by an inner group of its executives. This controlling inner group managed to assemble directors who would either do their will or be too lax in diligence to discover the true nature of that to which they gave their assent.

Professor Rowe testified that the executives, on one occasion, had refused to disclose to the board the names of those whom they were considering for the position of executive secretary. Asked what he did about it, Professor Rowe replied:

> What could I do? I was practically a minority of one. The board upheld their decision not to do this. It was not long after that, as I remember it, that I resigned from the board. They had a monopoly and they were bringing people like me in for the purposes of setting up a front and . . . giving a different kind of coloring to the membership of the board.*

Now let us look at the other side of this picture. Why did the trustees of The Rockefeller Foundation, for example, continue to make substantial donations to The Institute of Pacific Relations long after the time when, as the McCarran Committee indicated, there was evidence that the Institute had become an agent of communism?

It is a harrowing story. In 1944, Alfred Kohlberg, a director of the Institute who had become suspicious of its activities, brought facts to the attention of The Rockefeller Foundation that showed beyond any reasonable doubt the real character of the Institute. Even after discussion of the criticized conditions, The Rockefeller

* Reece Committee *Report*, p. 29.

Foundation continued to make substantial donations to it.* Its excuse, that it wanted to help "reform" The Institute of Pacific Relations, is not tenable. One does not go on making contributions to a pro-Communist organization in the hope of converting it away from communism. One cuts off its support.

The answer, in the case of The Rockefeller Foundation, must be that its trustees were not fully aware of what was happening. Like the trustees of so many large foundations, they left most decisions to their employees, the officers of the foundation. The results were disastrous for our country. The IPR probably had more to do than any other single factor with conditioning our people to abandon the mainland of China to the Communists. Its influence even penetrated the State Department. And its support came chiefly from large tax-exempt American foundations.

Kenneth Colegrove, Professor Emeritus of Politics at Northwestern University (at the time of his testimony he was on a temporary teaching assignment at Queens College), had this to say before the Reece Committee about foundation trustees:

> The large number of famous names on the list of trustees is due to an old superstition that our institutions must be headed by a famous group of men. And I will say frankly it is to impress Congress as well as the American people; to impress public opinion as much as possible. It is an old superstition. It is not necessary at all.†

Professor Colegrove, an authority of the first rank, who had for eleven years been secretary-treasurer of The American Political Science Association, elaborated:

> Yes; undoubtedly many of the trustees would not serve if they felt that they would be called upon to do much more than go to the meetings, hear the reports and sometimes say

---

* Mr. Joseph Willits was head of the Social Sciences Division of The Rockefeller Foundation during the period in question. He was recently in charge of a Ford Foundation survey of the University of Pennsylvania. One wonders whether this survey will be as penetrating as the Rockefeller study of The Institute of Pacific Relations.

† *Ibid.*, p. 28.

not a single word. You would not have as brilliant, as lofty, as remarkable, a collection of men as trustees if you required a little more responsibility on their part.*

THE FOUNDATION BUREAUCRATS

In effect, then, most of the very large foundations are operated by professional employees who assume the functions of designing programs and determining and selecting grants and grantees. These functions are the essence of the fiduciary duty of the trustees. It was most distressing to the Reece Committee to find that such professionals, without themselves having fiduciary responsibility, exercise such vast power. As Professor Colegrove testified:

> In the aggregate, the officers of these foundations wield a staggering sum of influence and direction upon research, education and propaganda in the United States and even in foreign countries.

The Committee had before it a mass of evidence of this bureaucratic power. Even its predecessor, the Cox Committee, had such evidence. It had, for example, received a letter from Dr. J. Fred Rippey, Professor of American History at Chicago, to which it apparently had paid little attention. Professor Rippey was incensed at the extent to which decisions of vital importance were left to foundation bureaucrats, and expressed this opinion of them:

> But I have never been impressed by the superior wisdom of the foundation heads and executive committees. The heads tend to become arrogant; the members of the committees are, as a rule, far from the ablest scholars in the country.†

The late Dr. Frederick P. Keppel, president of The Carnegie Corporation, once said that the officers of foundations steadily tend toward "an illusion of omniscience and omnipotence."

* *Ibid.,* p. 27.
† *Ibid.,* p. 37.

Foundation bureaucrats have become a unique class. Professor Colegrove testified that academicians "fawned" over them. The late Professor Merriam, in his day perhaps the most powerful figure in the foundation world, once said: "Money is power, and for the last few years I have been dealing with more power than any professor should ever have in his hands." *

Dwight Macdonald gives a good view of these "philanthropoids," or professional foundation administrators:

A philanthropoid*** is the middleman between the philanthropist and the philanthropee. His profession is the giving away of other people's money, and he is the key figure in most of today's great foundations now that the original donors are safely dead. Some two hundred and thirty people are employed by the Ford Foundation. [Most of these occupy subordinate positions or are delegated to special work, Macdonald continues.]

This leaves the forty-odd philanthropoids, who, for all practical purposes, *are* the Ford Foundation. They screen the thousands of applications for grants that come in every year; they look into new fields for spending; they think up problems worth solving (the first problem a foundation faces is what *is* the problem) and select the institutions or the people to try to solve them; they carry on the negotiations, often protracted, and the inquiries, often delicate, that may or may not lead to a grant, and they follow up the grants that are made; they dictate the systolic flow of memoranda that is the blood stream of a modern foundation. Through all these activities, and always subject to the final vote of the trustees, the philanthropoids determine that this enterprise of benevolence or scholarship shall be nourished with Ford money, while that one shall not.†

* *Ibid.*, p. 57.
† *The Ford Foundation, the Men and the Millions—An Unauthorized Biography* (New York: Reynal & Co., 1956), pp. 95, 96. First published as a series of "Profiles" in *The New Yorker* magazine.

These philanthropoids, then, are the men with the power. Wherever they go in academic circles, they are received with extraordinary respect and listened to with concentrated attention. The president of a great university will hang on their words, hoping to catch some clue to the possibility of a substantial and badly needed grant. A professor, eminent and loaded with deserved honors, will listen deferentially to every word of this young man, whose opinions on academic subjects, relatively untutored though he may be, are of far more practical importance than those of his distinguished listener. A mere suggestion by one of these young men from the foundations can materially influence the direction of a project proposed by an institution or an academician. And to turn down a project suggested by this young man himself—that is far too dangerous for any university or professor to consider lightly. It is, indeed, rarely done. The risk is too great.

I think of several trustees of great foundations, men with whom I happen to be acquainted and for whom I have great personal admiration. They have genuine stature and deserve every bit of the success and acclaim which they have earned by intelligence, energy, and common sense in their own industrial fields. They are active or retired top executives of great corporations which were built partly upon their executive ability. Their extraordinary capacities for direction, and their experience, qualify them for an important voice-in-council in our society. They have, however, only the most peripheral understanding of many of the fields of activity in which their foundations engage.

They understand neither the lingo nor the substance of the materials with which academicians work in these fields after a lifetime of training. If they are convinced, for instance, by a foundation executive that the foundation should enter the field of "behavioral science" or "educational theory," they can do little more than approve of the generality of appropriations for the purpose and leave all else to the hired executives who presume to know how to act as intermediaries between the trustees and the field. The trustees are at sea. They have the intelligence but not the time to absorb the subject. Thus, they cannot exercise judgment but must leave this to the professionals whom they employ. Nor can they even check the work of the professionals. They can only transfer their power to them and hope for the best.

Something is wrong with such a method of operation. Trustees who direct great enterprises would never sanction methods of this kind in their own organizations.

THE PROBLEM OF BIGNESS

In his *Philanthropic Foundations,* F. Emerson Andrews illustrates the financial power of a few big endowments. His figures are based on the number of foundations listed in directories (4,162), which is clearly a low figure; and upon an estimate of aggregate wealth ($7,000,000,000) which is at least 2 billion too low, but the comparisons he makes are, nevertheless, instructive. Of the 4,162 foundations listed, 77, in 1953, held 3 billion of the aggregate of 7 billion in assets. Among the 77, six reported assets of more than $100,000,000 each, their combined value being $1,269,500,000. These giants are listed as Ford ($520,000,000), Rockefeller ($318,000,000), Carnegie Corporation ($196,000,000), W. K. Kellogg ($109,800,000), Duke ($108,000,000), and Pew Memorial ($104,900,000).* Mr. Andrews listed another seven foundations with assets running between fifty and one hundred millions each. Some other foundations are so closely allied in origin with some of the big six as possibly to be bracketed with them. Among these would be The Ford Motor Company Fund ($16,- 500,000); The Rockefeller Brothers Fund ($59,700,000); The Carnegie Foundation for the Advancement of Teaching ($20,- 600,000); The Carnegie Institution of Washington ($65,100,000); The Carnegie Endowment for International Peace ($20,600,000).

Of the big six, only Carnegie, Rockefeller, and Pew reported assets at market value. Consequently, we have good reason to assume that the combined value of the assets of the big six might be well in excess of $4,000,000,000. It is probable that The Ford

---

* These six are listed together because of size, not because of similarity of operation. The investigation by the Reece Committee disclosed no criticism whatsoever of the Kellogg, Duke, or Pew foundations.

Foundation, for example, should have been listed at close to $3,000,000,000, instead of a mere $520,000,000.

There is a powerful school of political scientists which contends that bigness, *per se,* is a danger to society. It maintains that the economic power of great corporations should be suppressed by dissolutions and break-ups. Whole libraries have been written about the alleged threat to the public welfare in the form of the growth of giant enterprises. Congressional hearings on the problems of small business, on mergers and antitrust issues, and on proposals to apply discriminatory legislation against large corporations, have filled tens of thousands of printed pages a year.

Under the influence of the antibigness philosophy, the Supreme Court, in dealing with antitrust cases, has veered toward a position that bigness, in itself, constitutes a restraint on competition. There is thus a tendency to consider that bigness, in itself, when it is capable of corrective restraint, is sufficient justification for remedial legislation, even when there is no actual evidence of unfair competition or of collusion.

A subschool of the "antibigness" political scientist has recently found a new problem-of-bigness to attack. Many corporations which formerly engaged in only one activity have now seen the wisdom of diversification and have entered various, sometimes unassociated, industries. Some opponents of bigness now wish to prevent diversification, even when the collateral activities of a great corporation give it no preponderant or even commanding position in the collateral industries. Their basic objection is no longer "unfair competition" or "restraint of trade" but mere bigness and the fear of the aggregate power which goes with bigness.

There is a clear analogy between bigness in industry and bigness in the world of foundations. Each of the great foundations can exercise influence in the field of ideas so powerful that it justifies a fear of mere bigness. The argument can be made, as it has been made in relation to Big Business, that it is not necessary to prove that the power reposing in bigness has actually been abused. It is enough to show that the power exists.

Professor Harold D. Lasswell of Yale is one of the academicians upon whom foundation patronage has been bestowed lavishly. He is one of the influential "experts" in the social sciences on whom foundation managers have so often relied for the selection of projects and the allocation of funds. In 1956, his prestige, largely on the basis of his position in the foundation world, contributed to his election as president of the American Political Science Association. It seems fair to assume that his inaugural address, delivered in Washington in September 6, 1956, may represent the position of social scientists enjoying foundation support. Speaking of economic control, Professor Lasswell asks:

> Shall we rely upon a 30-40-50 rule to guide public policy in regard to the permissible degree of market control permitted to private interests? (For example: When one interest has 30% control of output, shall it be subject to special regulations designed to nullify the side-effects of power that go along with economic control? When one interest rises to 40% shall we put governmentally appointed trustees on the Board of Directors? At 50% shall government trustees predominate?)

He says, further:

> The same approach—the search for rules of proportion—applies to every institutional and personality pattern in a body politic. What are the optimum proportions of community resources to devote to elementary, intermediary, advanced and ultra-advanced education? To research and development in science and technology?

The validity of the political theory which opposes bigness in business enterprises is, of course, subject to grave question. Such enterprises operate in a competitive economy and under an effective system of counterweighing power. Business is subject to checks and balances by pressures from labor, from competitive or substitute goods and services, from government, and from the political action of many citizen pressure groups. If, however, there is any justice in opposing bigness in business enterprises, there is even more in fearing bigness among foundations. The generally accepted practice of matched grants multiplies the impact of foundation giving. This technique of fund raising results in a far-reaching *Gleichschaltung* of public charity—a general adoption of the policies of the large foundations which offer the matching.

Foundations owe their existence to the public. It makes a sacrifice to give foundations tax exemption, assuming that the public will, in turn, be properly rewarded for its generosity through an application of the tax-exempt funds to the public welfare. For this reason, if no other, foundations must have the approval of the public to carry on; the public, indeed, would be fully justified in applying legislative restrictions on foundation operations where there seemed to be danger to the public welfare. The problem of foundation bigness *per se* may thus arise seriously to concern the general public unless foundation managers become alert to the inherent dangers of bigness by avoiding, in the future, the techniques of joint planning; of joint support of intermediary organizations which thus achieve commanding positions in the world of ideas; and of eliminating or destroying counterweighing competition in the support of ideas. The conformity which these techniques foster is socially unsound and highly undesirable. It stems partly from the use of a common group of "experts" and a common application of funds to the support of the intellectual fashions of the day instead of applying the venture-capital theory equitably by giving proportionately, at least, to the preservation of the values of the past.

THE CORPORATE FOUNDATIONS

Related to the problem of bigness is that of the foundation created and maintained by an individual business enterprise. Such foundations are comparative newcomers on the American scene but are rapidly increasing in numbers. There are now perhaps two thousand of them. Their aggregate capital is very substantial. As a corporation is granted an annual income-tax deduction of up to five percent of its net income, for philanthropic donations, such corporate foundations could grow to immense importance in our society and could, indeed, even overshadow the individual-created foundations in the course of time. Limited by lack of time and funds, the Reece Committee made no attempt to study these corporate foundations. Nor have I collected any material regarding them. But any comprehensive study of foundations in their relation to our society would have to take corporate foundations into account.

The corporate foundations have, so far, escaped the type of criticism leveled at some of the individual-created foundations because they have generally avoided controversy and have confined themselves to direct grants and to objectives (often local) with which the public could not well quarrel. But several interesting criticisms of them have been made, which do merit consideration by thoughtful students of the general foundation problem.

There is the basic concern of some regarding the operations of juridical persons in the field of charity, in this instance juridical persons created by juridical persons. That difficult and obscure problem, I shall leave to the philosophers and jurists.

Two forms of criticism have appeared from within the corporations which have created foundations. Stockholders have objected to the "dissipation" of profits through donations to a foundation which, they say, are really the property of the owners of the business, the stockholders. Labor, on the other hand, has sometimes complained that, if the corporation is so affluent as to be able to create and maintain a foundation of its own, it could afford to pay higher wages.

A third form of complaint comes from competitors, who assert the unfairness of enabling a great corporation, through the tax-deduction vehicle, to advertise itself and promote public relations and, thus, to take unfair advantage of competitors. Complaints of this kind have been registered against the Ford Motor Company. On the other hand, a foundation can operate in reverse, in regard to public relations. There was a time when many people in the United States refused to buy Ford products because of the antics of the Ford Foundation-created Fund for the Republic and even for some of the acts of The Ford Foundation itself.

A graver criticism lies in the fact that, while Federal laws prevent combinations in business in restraint of trade, it is possible for foundations to act in concert to the attainment of common objectives. Such objectives might conceivably be political, in which event, combinations of huge foundations created by huge corporations could constitute a potential highly dangerous to our society. It is to be hoped that those who manage the great corporations will be alert to this danger and carefully avoid it.

3 THE CONCENTRATION OF POWER

INTERLOCKS

ALTHOUGH the Cox Committee recognized that the responsibility of a foundation trustee was "onerous to the point that it would seriously interfere with the work of the average business man," it found it "understandable that the services of an outstanding man should be sought by more than one foundation." Its only serious criticism of a concentration of trustee power was geographic. It expressed the opinion that a "wider geographical distribution would go far towards establishing greater public confidence in foundations and would dispel much of the distrust which shelters under the traditional fear of Wall Street." Thus, the Cox Committee completely missed the point. What mattered was not that foundation trustees were concentrated on the Eastern Seaboard but that a pattern of interlocking operations existed at various levels of management. The geographical location of the majority of foundation trustees was of small consequence.

That interlocks among foundation boards existed was clear enough. F. Emerson Andrews, in his *Philanthropic Foundations*, mentions two complex cases as evidence of the national prominence of many foundation trustees. In one case, the foundation had 20 trustees who held a total of 113 positions as trustees or officers of other philanthropic organizations, or an average of 5.6 each. The range of outside positions ran from 0 to 14. The Board of the other foundation which Mr. Andrews cited was composed of 14 trustees, holding a total of 85 outside philanthropic positions, or an average of 6 per trustee; the range being from 0 to 13. If, as the Cox Committee held, a foundation trustee's job was "onerous" to the point of "seriously interfering" with his business, one wonders how any man could simultaneously fill thirteen or fourteen philanthropic offices effectively and conscientiously.

Overlapping of foundation administrators is an old story. In his foundation, John D. Rockefeller employed some of the same men to whom Andrew Carnegie had entrusted his endowments. Dean Rusk, speaking for the Rockefeller Foundation, explained that consultation among foundations arose "from the desire on the part of each one to use its funds to the best advantage." He defended discussions among foundation officers as a desirable means of exchanging information, to avoid duplication of effort, and to permit funds to be used wisely. However, the intimate associations which Mr. Rusk lauds can be dangerous. They can operate to force our culture into a uniform pattern. It would be far better for society to face the occasional waste which lack of interfoundation planning might cause than to take the risk of losing a truly competitive intellectual climate. Indeed, there is similarity between Mr. Rusk's plea for cooperation among foundations and the arguments given for industrial cartels and for regulated competition—for that matter, with the rationale for a socialist planned economy.

The men who operate foundations do have power often greater than that of elected or appointed government officials. The law applying to public servants is very strict in defining conflicts of interest. They are held strictly to an exact loyalty. There are no similar limitations applying to trustees or officers of foundations. They may support their pet causes. They may cause donations to be made to institutions or funds on whose directive boards they sit. They may be donors and recipients at the same time. They may favor their friends or relatives and pay salaries and fees without limitation. Hundreds of years ago, the Church introduced rules against nepotism. No such rules prevent those in control of foundations from using power to gain more power, through combinations with others, mutual endorsements and support, and the many subtle forms of collusion available to them under our foundation system.

If there is need for clearing houses in educational, scientific, and public pursuits, that does not justify a domination of these institutions by foundations and their staffs. To continue the widespread practice of simultaneous directorships in grant-giving and grant-receiving institutions is against the public interest. Abstention from voting, where there is a conflict of interest, does not adequately protect the public. The very presence of a trustee or officer with dual allegiance can have an improper effect on the foundation's decisions. It seems fair to require individuals to choose whether they wish to operate on one side of the street or the other—as givers or receivers. Moreover, a switching back and forth, frequently observed, seems highly undesirable. In the interest of continuing a free market for ideas, the managements of granting and receiving institutions should be carefully separated and kept clear of any taint of conflict of interest.

The effective interlock which exists in the foundation world finds expression in many ways, among them:

1. Trustees serving on more than one tax-exempt organization, often both granting and receiving organizations;

2. Joint support and/or control by several foundations of fund-receiving institutions, particularly "clearing-house organizations" and scientific, educational, and public affairs councils or associations;

3. Issuance of matched grants, or promises of grants with the proviso that funds are to be supplied only if and when others support the same project or cause;

4. Service of foundation personnel, simultaneously or in short succession, on staffs of foundation-supported institutions; and

5. Service of foundation officials (trustees or managers)

on government advisory boards, in control of government
policy or spending in fields identified with foundation philanthropy.

Their independent, uncontrolled financial power often enables
foundations to exert a decisive influence on public affairs. They
have a power comparable to political patronage. The propagandistic effects of this patronage can often reach far beyond the immediate beneficiaries of foundation support. The emergence of
dominating agencies in various fields of learning and teaching
was a likely development. Foundations were originally created to
support existing institutions and to undertake certain "operating"
functions. Today, and all too frequently, new recipient organizations are created by foundations, or with their subsidy, while
needy and worthy existing institutions are ignored. The Ford
Foundation in its early years created many subfunds for research
and education which duplicated existing, similar organizations. In
the twenties, several influential scientific and educational councils
were set up jointly by cooperating foundations.

De facto, almost all major foundations insist on approving the
selection of personnel in the recipient organizations. They wish to
know who will spend their grants or benefit from them. An apparent donation is often, in reality, a disguised financing of a foundation department. It is attached to an outside institution or organization, but little is left to it to do except bookkeeping and related
administrative functions. Universities, hospitals, institutes and
learned societies sometimes supply nothing but their name labels
affixed to what is actually a pet project of foundation managers. In
effect, everything from the budget to the choice of *ad hoc* appointed professors or researchers is controlled and decided by
foundation officials.

The concentration of power has measurable influence on our
cultural life. The Social Science Research Council once published
a study of its own granting activities. This clearly showed a preference for five of the largest universities in the United States. Similarly, the National Science Foundation, an agency of the U.S.

Government, found that the same foundation-sponsored institutions had received the major share of hundreds of million dollars of government contracts. Such a concentration of private support by foundations and public support through government agencies is distinctly to the detriment of higher education in our country. Favoritism for institutions and for scholars of a few such institutions tends to cause a migration of talent from the neglected to the pampered universities and gives a few schools of higher learning an élite character, at the same time reducing both the comparative prestige and the potential of the others.

INTERMEDIARIES AS JOINT INSTRUMENT OF SEVERAL FOUNDATIONS

Americans have never liked monopoly or a concentration of power in private hands, free of public control. When they have found it in the business world, they have legislated against it. They are not likely to be pleased to find a quasi-monopoly operating in intellectual areas which are not mere "ivory tower" but influence our society very materially.

A system of interlocks among major foundations and associated organizations has long existed in social-science research and education. No group of men sat down deliberately to plan this thing over-all. It just grew into being, but it is none the less dangerous as a concentration of power. It came about largely through the use of intermediary organizations to which foundations could donate wholesale funds for retailing grants. The system was so convenient and intriguing that clearing houses were brought into existence further to amplify this system of delegation.

What seemed to justify the use of these intermediaries was the belief that they would bring about greater efficiency. In a way, they did. Each specialized in some field of research or of social action and often could act with more detailed understanding than could the contributing foundations which scattered their interest over large areas. On the other hand, as Professor David N. Rowe testified before the Reece Committee, efficiency is by no means the most desirable factor in research. Moreover, by using the convenience of intermediaries, to delegate power and thus to escape the arduous duty of detailed programming and selection, the trustees of a contributing foundation removed themselves further from the ultimate results of their expenditures, and were less and less able to follow and check the application of their funds.

In large industrial enterprises and in government, the delegation of authority is an essential management device. The proper use of the same instrument in the area of ideas has distinct and narrow limitations. In industry and government, the delegation is one of operational responsibility within the framework of a given value system, the policy of the organization. That is quite different from the form of delegation all too often employed in foundations. Here, in effect, the delegation is of actual policy decisions. These policy decisions may deeply effect our society.

No better example of this could be found than the case of The Institute of Pacific Relations, to which I have referred, used by The Rockefeller Foundation, The Carnegie Corporation, The Carnegie Endowment for International Peace, and others as a distributing agent. The Institute became *the* specialist in the Far East. The tragedy was that it also became a specialist in promoting the Communist cause in Asia, succeeding so well in this endeavor because of the vast financial support given to it by the major foundations.

The donating foundations sought to absolve themselves of responsibility for what resulted. But, as Professor Rowe stated in his testimony,* the granting foundations cannot escape responsibility for what their agents have done. They granted these agents great power, a power immensely enlarged when foundations, acting in concert, supplied such substantial financing that the intermediary agent became a dominating force in its specialized area.

The potential power of the major intermediaries was illustrated by Professor Rowe in his testimony. I had asked him whether the intermediary system did not operate against the competitive factor which is intrinsic in our American way of life. He testified:†

* *Report*, p. 60.
† *Ibid.*, p. 59.

There is no question but what an organization like *The Social Science Research Council* has a tremendous amount of power. This power which it exerts, it exerts very heavily on educational institutions and their personnel because when you get down to it, who is it that does research in social science? It is educational institutions, because they have the faculties in the various fields, like political science, economics, anthropology, sociology, geography and so on. That is where the people are.***

This, therefore, means that there is a tremendous responsibility here to apportion their awards in a just way—in such a way as takes into account the differences of approach and the differences of opinion in these fields; the theoretical differences from one school to another. *The possibility exists that at all times in any of these organizations that the people in charge thereof become convinced that there is one way to do a job in the social science field, and that only this way will get their support. If and when that time comes— I don't know whether it is here or ever will come—then you will have a combination in restraint of trade within the limits of public acceptability that may have very deleterious effects upon our intellectual community.* [Emphasis supplied.]

WHAT MAKES UP THE INTERLOCK IN THE FINANCING OF SOCIAL-SCIENCE ACTIVITIES

The report of the Reece Committee described the "network or cartel" in the social sciences* as having five components. The *first* is a group of foundations, composed of the various Rockefeller and Carnegie foundations, The Ford Foundation (referred to as "a late comer but already partially integrated"), The Commonwealth Fund, The Maurice and Laura Falk Foundation, The Russell Sage Foundation, and others.

The *second* component consists of the "intermediaries" or "clearing houses," such as:

* *Ibid.,* pp. 45-47.

The American Council of Learned Societies
The American Council on Education
The National Academy of Sciences
The National Education Association
The National Research Council
The National Science Foundation
The Social Science Research Council
The Progressive Education Association
The John Dewey Society
The Institute of Pacific Relations
The League for Industrial Democracy
The American Labor Education Service

The learned societies in the several "social sciences" were listed as the *third* component.

The *fourth* consists of the learned journals in these areas.

The *fifth* was "certain individuals in strategic positions, such as certain professors in the institutions which receive the preference of the combine."

The report proceeded:

> *The patterns of interlocking positions* of power may take various shapes. The following are the most frequent ones:
>
> (1) Trustees or employed executives are successively or simultaneously trustees and executives of several foundations.
>
> (2) Trustees or executives serve successively or simultaneously as officers of other tax exempt organizations receiving grants and/or retailing the wholesale grants from their own foundations.
>
> (3) Trustees or executives accept appointments to positions of power in control of education and/or charity so as to multiply their influence beyond the budgetary powers of their foundation resources.
>
> (4) Foundations jointly underwrite major projects, thus arriving at a condition of coordination restraining competition.

(5) Foundations jointly create and support centralized coordinating agencies that operate as instruments of control by claiming supreme authority in a field of education, science, the arts, etc. without any resemblance of democratic representation of the professionals in the management of these agencies.

(6) Rather than distribute money without strings attached, foundations favor projects of their own and supply the recipient institutions not only with the program, but also with the staff and the detailed operations budget so that the project is actually under control of the foundation, while professionally benefiting from the prestige of the recipient institution. The choice of professors often is one by the foundation and not one by the university. Foundation employees frequently switch from work in the foundation, or in the councils supported by the foundation, to work on sponsored projects and in professional organizations supported by their funds. They become most influential in the professional organizations, are elected to presidencies and generally rule the research industry.

As an example of interlocking directorates, the report cited the case of The Rand Corporation. This is a corporation in the nature of a foundation, which plays a very important part in government research. It would warrant special attention in connection with any study of the extent to which foundation interlocks have influenced government. Among the trustees and officers of The Rand Corporation were found the following who had material connections with other foundations:

Charles Dollard (trustee)	Carnegie Corporation
L. A. Dudbridge (trustee)	Carnegie Endowment
	National Science
	Foundation
H. Rowan Gaither, Jr.	
(trustee)	Ford Foundation

Philip E. Mosely (trustee)	Ford Foundation
	Rockefeller Foundation
Harvey S. Mudd (trustee)	Mudd Foundation
	Santa Anita Foundation
	American Heritage Foundation
Frederick F. Stephan (trustee)	Rockefeller Foundation
Clyde Williams (trustee)	Batelle Memorial Institute
Hans Speier (officer)	(Ford) Behavioral Science Division

This example of interlocking is specially interesting because the Chairman of this semi-governmental organization, The Rand Corporation, was, at the same time, president of The Ford Foundation, which granted it one million dollars in 1952 alone.

The following list of social-science consultants serving the Research and Development Board of the Defense Department at one time (1953) illustrates the frequency with which foundation executives are appointed as "experts" controlling the expenditure of government funds in research:

Leland De Vinney	Rockefeller Foundation
John W. Lardner	Carnegie Corporation
Pendleton Herring	Social Science Research Council (formerly, Carnegie Corporation)
William C. Menninger	Menninger Foundation
J. A. Perkins	Carnegie Corporation
Don K. Price	Ford Foundation

Closely allied to the practice of interlocking directorates (and interlocking advisers and executives) is the practice of the major foundations of favoring a limited number of institutions and individuals. Mr. Andrews, in his *Philanthropic Foundations,* defends this practice by saying that "adequate research facilities and the ablest personnel are largely concentrated in these places." If this were so, then the foundations have contributed to an unbalanced condition, and the country would be better off if they reversed themselves and sought to bring up the standards of neglected institutions by being more generous to them in their research allotments.

Mr. Andrews's explanation does not seem persuasive. The most favored institutions (Harvard, the University of Chicago, Columbia, California, Yale, Wisconsin, North Carolina, and MIT seem usually to head the list) are not in a class by themselves. I am not sure what Mr. Andrews refers to in mentioning "adequate research facilities"; whatever equipment may be needed for social-science research could be rented readily enough. But Mr. Andrews's contention about "the ablest personnel" would be hotly contested by many informed academicians, among them Professor Colegrove who, in his testimony before the Reece Committee, pleaded for a wider, as well as a greater, use of our colleges and universities. He said there is "a wealth of brains, a wealth of competence, in our small colleges and universities, which does not have its share in research grants at the present time."*

The preference extends not only to selected institutions themselves but even to graduate students in them. For example, the Social Science Research Council, in 1952, reported that 856 graduate students working for a degree had received Council grants. A total of 47.6 percent went to students at Columbia, Harvard, and the University of Chicago. Add Yale, the University of California, and Wisconsin, and students at these six received an aggregate of 63.4 percent of the grants. Students at a total of 16 institutions received 89.1 percent of the grants, while 93 others received, among them, only 10.9 percent; and the more than a thousand remaining institutions received none. If any Catholic institutions were represented in the SSRC list, I missed them.

THE SOCIAL SCIENCE RESEARCH COUNCIL

"Foundations," said the Reece Committee report, "becoming more numerous every day, may some day control our whole intellectual

* *Ibid.,* p. 80.

and cultural life—and with it the future of this country. The impact of this interlock, this intellectual cartel, has already been felt deeply in education and in the political scene."

The report then discussed The Social Science Research Council,* taking it as an example of the "association or individual foundations with one of the intermediary or executive foundations"— another form of interlock. Among the foundations which have supported this distributing agent are these:

> The Laura Spelman Rockefeller Memorial
> The Russell Sage Foundation
> The Carnegie Corporation
> The Commonwealth Fund
> The Julius Rosenwald Fund
> The Carnegie Foundation for the Advancement of Teaching
> The Maurice and Laura Falk Foundation
> The General Education Board (Rockefeller)
> The Grant Foundation
> The Scripps Foundation for Research in Population Problems
> The American Philosophical Society
> The John and Mary R. Markle Foundation
> The Ford Foundation
> The Twentieth Century Fund
> The East European Fund
> The Rockefeller Brothers Fund

With support such as this, and even government support, it is no wonder that The Social Science Research Council has become the greatest power in social-science research. Its 1929-1930 annual report disclosed some pride in the fact that it has been closely interlocked in an important network:

> With our sister councils, the National Research Council,† the American Council of Learned Societies, and the

---

* *Ibid.,* p. 47 *et seq.*
† Active in the natural sciences.

American Council on Education, cooperation remains good and becomes increasingly close and significant. *There are interlocking members* and much personal contact of the respective staffs. (Emphasis supplied.)

Despite many such acknowledgments as this, representatives of the foundations and their intermediaries have firmly denied the existence of an interlock. These denials cannot be sincere. There is a mass of evidence to indicate the close working-together to which the SSRC report quoted above alluded. Professor Colgrove testified that there was a tendency by the clearing houses to move to Washington and to cause their "constituent" societies to move there also. This concentration in one city improves efficiency—efficiency in a "cooperation" which goes far beyond the ordinary connotations of that term. Professor Colegrove said:

> * * * There is more day-to-day conversation and consultation between the officers of the professional societies and the officers of the operating societies, like the American Council of Learned Societies, and the officers of the foundations.
>
> I think the officers of the professional societies are extremely good listeners and follow pretty carefully the advice that is given them by the foundation officers.

Professor Colegrove also said that there had been a conscious concentration of research direction through the clearing-house organizations.*

The intermediaries are not merely distributive agencies in the simple sense. They assume a directive function. This is indicated by a statement by Messrs. Donald Young and Paul Webbink in Vol. i, issue No. 3 of *Items,* a publication of The Social Science Research Council, in which these gentlemen present the role of the SSRC in improving research:

> The particular role of the Council, however, is that of a central agency to promote the unity of effort in attacking social problems which is required to assure maximum re-

---

* *Ibid.,* pp. 47-48.

turns from the work of a multitude of individual social scientists and of independent private and public institutions.

They continued that the Council does not "attempt to operate as a coordinating agency in any compulsive sense." However, its very availability and the wide support given to it by major foundations have actually given the SSRC a control over research in the social sciences which is, said the report of the Reece Committee, "in its effective use, undoubtedly compulsive."

Dr. Pendleton Herring, president of The Social Science Research Council, proudly quoted, in the September 1950 issue of *Items*, this statement of The Ford Foundation:

> The Social Science Research Council has been included in this program because it is the instrumentality most used by individual scholars, universities and research organizations for interchange of information, planning and other cooperative functions in the fields described. * * *

The Ford grant was not, therefore, to be used for the support of more independent research projects, but to help pay the SSRC overhead to "enhance the service it performs for other organizations and scholars."

The Reece Committee report described this sociographic pattern of operations in the SSRC:

Constituent societies:
   Represented at various other nationwide "councils."
Financial support:
   By closely cooperating foundations, which themselves interlock through directorates.
Supported scholarly activity:
   Concentration on graduates of a few major institutions, which also supply most of the directors of the Council, who since a change of by-laws are chosen by the Council board, not any longer freely elected by constituent associations.
Influence of government spending for research:

SSRC or similar foundations-supported groups decisively influence *National Science Foundation* policy and Defence Department spending on research via its officers serving as consultants and board members."*

The Committee was impressed with the peculiar form of management within The Social Science Research Council. As is the case in foundations generally, the management is self-perpetuating. The SSRC, however, purports to represent seven of the individual social-science disciplines through their respective professional societies. Its stationery gives this impression, which is misleading. These societies are not actually members of the SSRC. They are permitted to elect directors to the SSRC Board, but only from among panels of candidates nominated by the SSRC itself.

This practice cannot help but produce conformity to the ideas of the clique which rules The Social Science Research Council. It was introduced in substitution for an earlier system of permitting the professional associations to elect representatives of their choosing. They are no longer permitted to select such as they believe competent and wise, but only from among those nominated by the clique.

The Reece Committee held this to be a rather undemocratic procedure, to say the least. It pointed out that the totalitarian character of this organization, so important in social-science research in the United States, is increased by the fact that its "members" are not the societies which it purports to represent but its former directors. One of these directors explained that the change in the election rules arose from the need to exclude "old-fashioned" social scientists who would oppose the preference for statistical and empirical projects.

It is easy to see, in this peculiar organization of the SSRC, an operation of the "élite" concept. If the assumedly "constituent" professional societies were permitted freely to elect the management of this centralizing organization, those who control it might lose their power. But they are the "élite." They want on their board a

* *Ibid.*, p. 48.

clear majority, or even a unanimity, of social scientists who agree with their theses. Do they not know better than others, better even than the membership of the professional societies of social-science professors, what is good for the country! It is not a pleasant concept under American traditions.

The Reece Committee report found that

> the SSRC has in the past gained leadership, among other reasons, because it successfully created the impression of representing the majority of all social scientists in America.

In a democratic sense, at least, the SSRC did not represent American scholarship in the social sciences. It thrived, however, by giving the impression that it did. Its power grew as the impression mounted and as it became a constant beneficiary of major foundations.

"The power of the *SSRC*," said the Reece Committee report, "seems to be used to effect control of the field of social sciences."* This statement was not lightly made. "There is evidence," said the Committee, "that professional appointments all over the United States are influenced by *SSRC* blessing."

One example is sufficiently powerful to justify the statement. The 1933-1934 report of the National Planning Board was actually prepared by a committee of The Social Science Research Council. It stated:

> The *Council* [the *SSRC*] has been concerned chiefly with the determination of the groups and persons with whom special types of research should be placed.

Keeping in mind that this organization, The Social Science Research Council, is supported by a group of major foundations, the hazards involved are significant. If it has the function which was described, of deciding what groups and individuals should be used for various research projects, it has a control power which carries with it enormous danger.

The Committee suggested a special investigation of the extent

* *Ibid.*, p. 50.

to which The Social Science Research Council and organizations associated with it control book reviews and the literary production —journals, textbooks and other publications—of social scientists. It is a characteristic of the American world of scholarship that academicians are rated largely on their publications, and the test is often quantitative rather than qualitative. Whether or not a social scientist can procure publication of a paper has a lot to do with his advancement in his career. Similarly, the nature of the reviews given to his paper may be of vital importance.

Professor Rowe,* testifying regarding the influence of foundations in educational institutions, said:

> * * * you have to realize * * * that advancement and promotion and survival in the academic field depend upon research and the results and the publication thereof. Here you have, you see, outside organizations influencing the course of the careers of personnel in universities through their control of funds which can liberate these people from teaching duties, for example, and making it possible for them to publish more than their competitors.

If, then, control over an academic journal is concentrated in a few hands, it would be easy enough to impose concepts and philosophies on a generation of scholars, and upon school teachers and textbook writers. In more than one instance this has undoubtedly happened. Such control may take the form of denying space to a nonconformist. It may also influence commercial publishers via the expert readers to whom books are submitted before publication. It is very likely that these experts would be selected from those favored by the journal. Publishers may be reluctant to publish a nonconformist's book because the conformists, articulate and welcomed in the pages of a professional journal, may pan it with unfavorable reviews or freeze it out of circulation by withholding reviews in the controlled learned journals and in book-review sections. The controlling group has the power forcefully to recommend books for purchase in public and school libraries and

* *Ibid.,* p. 50.

to advocate the use or rejection of selected textbooks. All this can add up to conformity. Instead of supporting such power, foundations bear the duty to exercise the greatest care, lest their funds be used for such ends of thought control.

There are other groups powerful in the social sciences besides The Social Science Research Council—The (Ford) Behavioral Science Fund, The Twentieth Century Fund, The American Academy of Political and Social Sciences, and others—but, as the Reece Committee pointed out, "with almost all of them there exist personal and organizational ties and cross connections via supporting foundations." There is, in fact, a similarity of approach among these groups. They all favor the "liberal" point of view. It is possible that this could be mere coincidence, but it is extremely unlikely.

President Grayson Kirk of Columbia University, in an address of May 31, 1954, wisely asserted that we "must maintain the greatest possible opportunities for the free clash of opinions on all subjects, trusting to the innate good judgment of men and women to reach decisions that are beneficial to society." Anything in the nature of a concentration of power or an interlocking is pregnant with the possibility of coercive influence.

The Reece Committee was shocked to find that one so important in the foundation world as Charles Dollard, then president of the powerful Carnegie Corporation, had contributed an article to the Social Science Research Council's publication, *Items,* in which, referring to mistakes in poll taking and in the Kinsey research, he made this statement:

> The third strategic move which I would suggest is that *social science initiate a more rigorous system of internal policing.**

That social scientists financed by foundations may have performed sloppy work is apparent enough, but the Reece Committee found the concept of "policing" terrifying. Who would do the po-

* *Ibid.,* p. 51.

licing? The Social Science Research Council? Some board of censorship?

Efficiency might be increased by a system of "policing." But it would be at the cost of freedom, so precious in academic and intellectual fields. Researchers might easily be squeezed into a common mold. "Few," said the Reece Committee report, "could risk criticizing, few academicians at least. There would emerge what has been called a 'Gresham's Law in the field of professorships in the social sciences.' "

Whatever reasons may have been in the minds of those who created them, the "cartel bureaus" have, to all practical purposes, assumed the functions of accrediting agencies. The growing tendency toward *Gleichschaltung* (elimination of nonconformism) in our schools and professional societies is exhibited by the current preference for "projects." Money is more easily obtainable today for "projects" chosen by foundation boards than for general purposes with no strings attached. The school administrator approaching a foundation, hat in hand, and eager to propose a project which conforms to the known leanings of the foundation executives, is a sad product of our age. No longer does the scholar carry the initiative. He is degraded to a recipient of alms handed out by an almoner who is no longer responsible to the prince.

Power is often exerted by foundations to promote projects, rather than to support institutions, because of the desire of managers to do business in public, to publicize themselves and their services.

The Reece Committee report ended its discussion of The Social Science Research Council by admitting that this organization, like others within the "concentration of power" or interlock in the social sciences, can "point to admirable and valuable work which they have done." These organizations have a great deal to their credit. But they have also exercised control and a restrictive influence on scholarship in many ways. Moreover, they have become a power the existence of which, "dealing with public trust funds," seemed to the Committee "to involve at least a potential danger or risk, however benevolently to date its relative despotism may have acted."*

THE AMERICAN COUNCIL ON EDUCATION

The American Council on Education is an intermediary to which the Reece Committee also gave special attention.† It is a council of national education associations, financed by membership dues, by government contracts, by heavy contributions from major foundations, and by donations of associated organizations. Among its supporters have been:

> The General Education Board (Rockefeller)
> The Carnegie Corporation
> The Carnegie Endowment for International Peace
> The Carnegie Foundation for the Advancement of Teaching
> The Rockefeller Foundation
> The Ford Fund for Adult Education
> The Alfred P. Sloan Fund
> The Payne Fund
> B'nai B'rith
> The Edward W. Hazen Foundation
> The Grant Foundation
> The Ellis L. Phillips Foundation

I have used the term "clearing house." The American Council on Education has called itself that in a pamphlet issued in July 1953‡:

> More specifically, the Council has been a clearing house for the exchange of information and opinion; it has conducted many scientific inquiries and investigations into specific educational problems and has sought to enlist appropriate agencies for the solution of such problems; it has stimulated experimental activities by institutions and groups of institutions; it has kept in constant touch with pending legislation

* *Ibid.*, p. 51.
† *Ibid.*, p. 52 *et seq.*
‡ *"A Brief Statement of the History and Activities of the American Council on Education."*

affecting educational matters; it has pioneered in methodology that has become standard practice on a national basis * * *; it has acted as liaison agency between the educational institutions of the country and the federal government and has undertaken many significant projects at the request of the Army, Navy and State Departments and other governmental agencies; and * * * it has made available to educators and the general public widely used handbooks, informational reports, and many volumes of critical analysis of social and educational problems.

The same pamphlet reports on the Council's Research Policy Committee as follows:

Established 1952 to study the interrelationships of sponsored research from the viewpoints of federal agencies, industries, and foundations, sponsoring such research, and the effect on institutions doing the research. This latter angle involves the distribution of grants among institutions and the concentration of research in fields at the expense of other fields and the distortion of the institutional picture as a whole. The magnitude of the problem is shown by the fact that 20 or more federal agencies are currently subsidizing more than $150,000,000 worth of research a year; industrial and business concerns and private foundations also sponsor research.

The numerous "special interests" involved may approach the same problems in different ways and come up with different solutions. *It is the aim of this Council committee—*composed of college presidents, vice-presidents for research, business officers, and faculty members directly engaged in sponsored research projects—*to attempt to formulate a policy for the national level based on cooperative relationships.* (Emphasis supplied.)

Thus, this Council, like The Social Science Research Council, is an interrelating or coordinating agency, which establishes policy and acts as a distributing agent for foundations whose business is grant making, along planned and integrated lines. Again, we have the emphasis on "efficiency," as though this were the most desirable objective in research. The Reece Committee report commented*:

> As Professor Rowe and others have said: it would seem far better to lose efficiency and give individuals of quality the opportunity to go in their own respective directions unhampered by any group control, direction or pressure.
>
> However laudable much or most of its work may have been, the *Council* has certainly been one of the media through which foundation funds have been used to effect considerable control or influence over education in the United States. Some may argue that this control or influence has been wholly good—were this so, we would still believe that the power of great foundations to affect educational policies and practices is one which should concern the public. By the same token, we believe that "clearing house" organizations, while they may serve a purpose in the direction of efficiency, are of questionable desirability when interlocked financially or by personnel with these foundations. *The aggregate power involved in such a concentration gives us concern.*

OTHER ASPECTS OF INTERLOCK

The clearing-house organizations themselves are interconnected, forming veritable associations of associations, and councils of associations and councils. Three times removed from their constituent individuals and institutions, these express the desire so prevalent among foundation executives to avoid duplication and to bring in what they conceive to be order.

There is, for example, a Conference Board of Associated Research Councils, through which The Social Science Research

* P. 52.

Council, The American Council on Education, The National Research Council, and The American Council of Learned Societies get together "to facilitate action on matters of common concern," continuing "earlier informal consultations of the executives of the Councils." To whatever types of action this conference of councils may be limited by its documents of organization, its meetings nevertheless afford an opportunity for coordinated planning through conferences of the respective executives.

A council to finance higher education has been created jointly by the Carnegie, Rockefeller, Ford, and Sloan foundations, each of which contributes $60,000 to it annually for a period of three years. This money does not go to the direct support of higher education. It pays for a staff under Mr. Wilson Compton which spends its time advising industrial corporations and other donors how to give money, and assisting institutions in their fund-raising campaigns. These foundations have thus, in combination, created another power position of influence in education.

Periodical meetings of foundation executives now take place in New York, informal in nature, perhaps, for the purpose of discussing policy problems and determining common action.

De Tocqueville, in one of his famous observations about democracy in America, reported with some amazement the propensity of this nation for the formation of voluntary associations for common ends. But he saw the working of democratic forces in this expression of freedom of assembly. The competing power of groups produced an effective method of checks and balances, preventing a domination of the people by autocratic forces. The more recent urge for nationwide, hierarchic, so-called clearing houses, fostered by foundations, was not foreseen by De Tocqueville. These are in reality instruments for ideological and political *Gleichschaltung*. Is the difference essential, or only a matter of degree, between an organization of scientists or authors subject to the monetary control of power cliques and the so-called associations and academies operating in totalitarian countries? With good luck, an American scientist may find an independent publisher and emancipate himself from the clique's financial control. But such cases are rare and confined to men of great courage and of contempt for economic rewards.

The United States government now spends far more money on social-science research than do all the foundations combined. This might constitute a counterforce to the influence of the foundation complex were it not for the fact that, to a great extent, the same persons who control or expend the funds of the complex in the social-science fields also direct or advise on the expenditures of the Federal government in these areas. It is not surprising, therefore, that government agencies operating in social-science areas have exhibited the same preferences and idiosyncrasies as has the foundation complex. It is a case of Tweedledee and Tweedledum—or, to put it another way, a condition of constant exchange of men and ideas between the complex and government.

THE INFLUENCE OF FOUNDATION MANAGERS IN THE INTERLOCK
Almost all the executives within the foundation complex whom I have met have been exceptionally pleasant and highly intelligent men. My criticism of them is confined to their almost universally common characteristic of permitting their social, intellectual and, principally, their political predilections to affect their work as administrators of public trusts.

When it has been called to their attention that an amazing amount of conformity and uniformity exists in the operations of the major foundation complex, apologists for these organizations have sometimes suggested that this is not because of the preferences of the foundation managers. They say that this phenomenon stems from a prevailing bias in favor of what is called "liberalism." These apologists tell us that the foundation executives follow the fashions of the times; in this manner, they "play safe." That may be so. It is difficult, in a situation such as this, to establish a cause-and-effect relationship with accuracy—to determine the extent to which foundation managers have followed or created trends. We do know, however, that the existing conformism within the social sciences has been nurtured abundantly by foundation support.

Foundation executives often pay lip service to nonconformism, and pride themselves on their contribution to "new" and "unorthodox" ideas. But the cooperation among the managers within the foundation complex does not favor the nonconformist. On the contrary, it has produced an excess of mediocre, routine work. Nor is much of what these managers point to as "new" and "unorthodox" really so. Most of it may have been "new" or "unorthodox" twenty or thirty years ago. These amazingly like-minded men have contributed substantially to converting into current orthodoxy what were revolutionary ideas during the twenties. They have supported for so long what they euphemistically call the "New Deal" (but what is really a modified form of socialism) that they are no longer capable of recognizing that other concepts of value may be held *bona fide* by thinkers and scholars.

What these professionals choose to call themselves is of no consequence. One maintained to me that he was a "conservative." Yet he is one of the most radical-minded of the foundation managers.

A stereotyped bureaucracy has developed among the major foundations and their satellite organizations. It has common ideas both as to concepts of responsibility and business affairs. The ideas and concepts of this bureaucracy are based heavily on the assumption of a cultural lag—the need to adjust law, values, and human affairs in general to a tempo dictated by our rapid technological progress. The adoption of this interpretation of society, somewhat related to Marx's economic determinism, impels its believers to strive for permanent and continual revolution, a position not too easy to differentiate from the materialistic concept of history.

They have become almost a guild, the bureaucrats of the foundation complex. As the Reece Committee report said*:

> The professionals, who exert so important an influence
> upon thought and public opinion in the United States,
> form a sort of professional class, an élite of management of
> the vast public funds available to their will. They can

* P. 37.

scarcely avoid getting an exaggerated idea of their own importance and becoming preoccupied with holding and enlarging their roles.

Clearly enough, foundation executives are entitled to their political opinions as private individuals. If they were not acting in concert, one could even excuse the impact of such political opinions on their work as individuals within foundations. What is wrong is permitting any *Gleichschaltung* or even the appearance of it. Anything in the nature of a cartel-like coordination in education and in such vital fields as foreign relations and the social-science studies tends to reduce competition and, through a form of collusion, to endanger the freedom of our intellectual and public life.

The emergence of this special class in our society, endowed with immense powers of thought control, is a factor which must be taken into account in judging the merits of contemporary foundation operations. The concentration of power, or interlock, which has developed in foundation-supported social-science research and social-science education is largely the result of a capture of the integrated organizations by like-minded men. The plain, simple fact is that the so-called "liberal" movement in the United States has captured most of the major foundations and has done so chiefly through the professional administrator class, which has not hesitated to use these great public trust funds to political ends and with bias.

4   SOCIAL SCIENCE AND
SCIENTISM

POLITICS IN THE SOCIAL SCIENCES

IN CHICAGO in 1949 a group of social scientists adopted the term "behavioral sciences." They gave their reasons for selecting the new term: "first, because its neutral character made it acceptable to both social and biological scientists and, second, because we foresaw a possibility of some day seeking to obtain financial support from persons who might confound social science with socialism." That confusion has existed in some minds is evidenced by one legislator who said that social science was the pursuit of long-haired men and short-haired women.

While such confusion may be amusing, foundation support in the social sciences does take on special and serious importance. Though much of the research and teaching in these disciplines may have no relationship whatsoever to politics, legislation, or even to public affairs, a large and vociferous sector of the social scientists actively seeks to redesign our government and our public life. It is difficult to understand how tax-exempt funds can properly be used to support the idiosyncrasies of these self-appointed reformers. In the face of the weakness of the controlling tax law which I have pointed out, it behooves foundations to exercise care and restraint.

Here is an illustration of aggressive political-mindedness from the words of one of the leaders of the foundation-supported social-science world, Professor Harold D. Lasswell, in his inaugural address as president of the American Political Science Association:

One of our professional responsibilities is to expedite the development of more perfect institutions specialized to continual self-observation on a global scale * * * originating policy alternatives by means of which goal values can be maximized.

Professor Lasswell continues:

Compared with an entire university, which has become a non-communicating aggregate of experts, each department of political science can be a true center of integration where normative and descriptive frames of reference are simultaneously and continuously applied to the consideration of the policy issues confronting the body politic as a whole over the near, middle and distant ranges of time. The profession is advantageously situated therefore to take the lead in a configurative approach to the decision process in society. Where it plays this part, political science is the policy science, *par excellence.* * * * Part of our role, as the venerable metaphor has it, is scanning the horizon of the unfolding future with a view to defining in advance the probable import of what is foreseeable for the navigators of the Ship of State. It is our responsibility to flagellate our minds toward creativity, toward bringing into the stream of emerging events conceptions of future strategy that, if adopted, will increase the probability that ideal aspirations will be more approximately realized.

If these involved phrases leave any doubt about the political intention of social scientists of Professor Lasswell's mind, their actions in association with government do not. Many of these scholars, including Professor Lasswell, serve as "experts" and advisers to numerous governmental agencies. Social scientists may be said to have come to constitute a fourth major branch of government. They are the consultants of government, the planners, and the designers of governmental theory and practice. They are free from the checks and balances to which the other three branches of government (legislative, executive, and judicial) are subject. They have attained their influence and their position in government mainly through foundation support; and this support, in the past, has been chiefly given to persons, institutions, and ideas of a progressive-liberal, if not Socialist, coloring.

In a pamphlet entitled "Science as Morality," published by the Humanist Press in 1953, George Simpson adds his voice to the growing criticism of the peculiar fashions, the current orthodoxies, in the social sciences. He criticizes the retreat from morality and the reliance on subsidy. He says: "It would seem that the retreat from morality by science is now full, for the dominant view in social science today is that social scientists might well learn from natural scientists how to achieve a new social status derivative from what can be subsidized rather than from what requires investigation." (P. 10.) He criticizes social scientists for surrendering their birthright as analysts and critics of social structures and for having become hired men doing little jobs for corporations, fund-raising associations, magazines interested in market research, and oddments of American culture. (P. 37.) More importantly, he says:

> Nor should sociologists continue to be solicitors of funds from agencies who tell them what they want research done on. Sociologists should make it possible to get funds for research without selling their souls. * * * The ideology of our so-called "applied" social research people appears to be the same as that of the foundations or corporations who give them money. Since many jobs are created this way, and jobs (sometimes partly paid for with degrees) attract graduate students and enhance sociology's respectability, any suggestion that this is the road to moral ruin sounds evangelical to those sociologists who have long lingered with Beelzebub. (P. 43.)

Simpson recommends the giving of "unmarked" grants to universities and to professional societies of sociologists, to avoid domination by foundations. The difficulty, he remarks, is that neither universities nor societies have prepared adequately for such responsibility. "They have become so addicted to absentee ownership of social research, that many sociologists would be unable to find any research to do unless somebody told them what he wanted done." (P. 43.) From his "liberal" point of view, he argues that the subsidizers are afraid of "dangerous" topics, but he says that the scholars themselves and not those who supply research money should decide what research needs doing.

Simpson has this to say regarding the current preference for empirical research:

> To be sure, empirical research is absolutely indispensable in reaching sociological conclusions. But empirical research today has become a magical phrase; if you say you are doing it, the gods bless you. Even if you are not doing it, it is still good to say you are. But sociologists must regain their respect for the necessity of sitting in an arm chair long enough to know what they are going to do empirical research on, what their hypothesis is, whether it is worth prosecuting, what contribution to human knowledge they intend to make, and, simply, to make their ideas clear. Indeed, it may even be found profitable to read a book. It is not good to attack a calculating machine or draw up a questionnaire with little in our heads. The pendulum has swung too far in one direction. It is time to resynthesize learning and techniques, theory and research, education and thinking, morality and sociology, and even the Social Sciences. (Pp. 44-45.)

THE EXCLUSION OF THE DISSIDENT

Dr. A. H. Hobbs of the University of Pennsylvania is a living example of the danger of criticizing foundations and foundation practices. He is only an assistant professor. He wryly calls himself "the oldest assistant professor east of the Rockies." To the shame of his university, he has been told in no uncertain terms by his superiors there that he has no hope of rising in the hierarchy. Why? Because he is a dissident.

The treatment of Professor Hobbs at the University of Pennsylvania is a black mark upon the record of that great institution. It is an outstanding example of suppression of academic freedom. Yet, as far as I know, none of the "liberals" who cry out so loudly that freedom is being suppressed whenever a Communist professor is discharged have entered even the mildest protest against the persecution of Professor Hobbs, whose only sin has been to have an independent mind and the strength of character to use it.

Behind the persecution of Professor Hobbs, and accountable for it, lies the fact that the foundation-supported "concentration of power" has been angered by his independence of mind and his frank criticism. He has been a strong critic of many of the methods used in contemporary social-science research, methods which the foundation complex has fostered.

Professor Hobbs, in his book *The Claims of Sociology: a Critique of Textbooks*, published in 1951, analyzed more than 100 leading textbooks on sociology used in high schools and colleges. He discovered that practically *all* of them, in varying degrees, were slanted toward collectivism. In the case of economics, Professor Hobbs wrote:

> Only a few (six) texts attempt to present an objective, integrated view of the principles and processes which characterize the economic institutions of the United States. Characteristically, the major portion of the treatment of economics is devoted to criticism, to emphasis on maldistribution of wealth and income, and to presentation of remedies or alternatives for prevailing economic principles and processes.*

The single point of view taken by virtually all the examined books was characterized by attacks on big business; adulation of big government; emphasis on maldistribution of wealth (even at-

* *The Claims of Sociology,* p. 81.

tributing to it the major cause for divorce); pleas for some sort of modernization of religion to eliminate its "mysticism" and relate it to "modern society"; and the development of a "humanitarian" point of view. This "humanitarianism," says Professor Hobbs, involves:

> lamentation about war, economic maldistribution, and individual unhappiness. It appears, however, to be secular, materialistic, short-term humanitarianism. It is "liberal" if the term applies to doctrinaire criticisms of economic maldistribution, of inequalities between sexes, classes and races, and of social controls which inhibit each person's full expression of his own personality. It is not completely liberal, however, if this term implies a tolerant historical perspective and a balanced and unbiased presentation of controversial issues in society. It is "objective" if this term applies only to critical emphasis against institutions and traditions. It is lacking in objectivity, however, in uncritical acceptance of platitudinous remedies and goals for society. It is "scientific" if this term includes a process of selection of only certain aspects of quantitative data and certain types of studies. It is not scientific if the term excludes the use of unverified hypotheses in proceeding from unwarranted assumptions to untenable conclusions.

Professor Hobbs is not alone in these criticisms. Many eminent professors agree with him. But he has been one of those few who have had the courage to express their opinions. Those who dominate foundation-supported social-science research profess to advocate freedom of opinion, but they do not encourage the expression of opinions contrary to their own. They profess to advocate "controversy" and assert their right to use foundation funds for its promotion. More often than not, however, it is but one side of a controversy that they wish heard, when it has political implications—the side to the left.

Professor Hobbs is a sociologist. He is brilliant and exceptionally well informed. He is given to independent thought, a precious commodity in our society. But he pays the price of independence. He supports his family on the salary of a laborer. He stands as one of the object-lessons to academicians: Conform or Be Damned.*

FOUNDATION-FOSTERED SCIENTISM

Professor Hobbs testified before the Reece Committee that the many millions of dollars poured annually into "social-science" research by some of the large foundations and their satellites or interlocked organizations, such as The Social Science Research Council, are largely wasted and unproductive of anything substantial or useful. But the waste involved was not his most severe criticism. He gave example after example of such research which offered a direct danger to our society. What goes under the name of "social science" today is often quackery. It is what Professor Hobbs called "scientism." †

Underlying the prevailing approach to research and teaching in the "social sciences" is the concept that social problems can be solved in the same manner as some physical problems, by a "scientific" method. Obviously enough, the collection of certain kinds of empirical data can be of enormous value. But overindulgence in the concept that there is a "scientific" solution for social problems, an overindulgence which some of the foundations have closely fostered, produces absurdity and peril. Professor Hobbs pointed out that the solution of social problems invariably involves the integration of intangible factors, such as love, patriotism, sentiment and other elements which cannot be measured with calipers, a slide rule, or an adding machine.

The jury-tapping project financed by The Ford Foundation, conducted in connection with a "sociological" project of the University of Chicago, illustrates the danger of overindulgence in the empirical approach. The problem of the project, I suppose, was to

---

* Professor Hobbs's persecution is described in E. Merrill Root's *Collectivism on the Campus* and also is referred to in an article in the April 18, 1956, issue of the *National Review* by Russell Kirk, in which the latter said, "Sociology is thoroughly dominated by an entrenched orthodoxy," an orthodoxy which will not tolerate an independent mind such as Professor Hobbs's.

† See A. H. Hobbs, *Social Problems and Scientism*, Stackpole, 1953.

determine whether or not the jury system could be improved. To go about this by eavesdropping on juries to find out how they deliberate is fact-finding of a nature which is extremely dangerous. The term "facts," in itself, is misused by the overanxious empirical researcher. Of what value is the well-known "fact" that jurymen spend part of their time discussing the baseball scores, and that much of their argument would hardly do on a debating team. Have these "facts" any scientific fact-value? Are we to conclude, through a collection of such "facts," that jurymen are not competent to fulfill the function which our legal system has assigned to them? Are such "facts" to be the basis of a plea that we should, in some way, control juries to make them more attentive to duty, or screen them to confine jury duty to those with a high I.Q.?

The jury-tapping procedure was an abortive attempt to solve a problem through empirical "science." If juries are to be abolished, or the jury procedure radically amended, it should be only after a most careful reconsideration of the historical origins and the philosophical rationale of the jury as an institution and not upon the basis of statistical "fact" collection by eavesdroppers. It may well be that the jury system as it stands should be most carefully preserved, even though jurymen represent only a cross-section of intelligence and even if jurymen do waste time discussing baseball.

THE "SOCIAL ENGINEERS" AND THE "FACT-FINDING MANIA"

The "social scientists," who have followed the course which has been so widely encouraged with foundation money, have become hypnotized, it seems, by the title of "scientists" which they have misappropriated. They have concluded that only "social *scientists*" can solve our social problems. They have made themselves into an "élite"—they have called themselves "social engineers." They have been touched with the *Führer* complex—they have become convinced that they are qualified to lead us into better pastures. How? Through the "scientific method."

The Reece Committee found many expressions of this "élite"-"social engineering" concept among social-scientist writers and publicists. Dr. Pendleton Herring, president of The Social Science Research Council, expressed it this way in an article in the SSRC *Items* of March 1947:

> One of the greatest needs in the social sciences is for the development of skilled practitioners who can use social data for the cure of social ills as doctors use scientific data to cure bodily ills.*

The "social doctors" have acquired a "fact-finding mania"— they have gone overboard on empiricism. Trying to imitate the use of the empirical method as one of the necessary tools of natural science, they have all too often forgotten that the natural scientist deals with measurable facts while the social scientist can measure comparatively little;† that the natural scientist sets up conditional hypotheses and tests them through experiment, while the social scientist can hardly experiment with human beings outside of a totalitarian concentration camp.

As Professor Hobbs put it in his *Social Problems and Scientism*‡:

> An over-emphasis on facts as facts is one of the characteristics of what is sometimes called the empirical approach. Ideally, empiricism could mean that the investigators relied solely upon controlled observation and experimental evidence. Actually, much of the empiricism in social science involves no rigid experimentation, and the facts are questionable, fragmentary, and slanted. Empiricism in social science seems to owe its extreme popularity more nearly to desperation rather than plan. Philosophic and scientific jus-

---

* Reece Committee *Report*, p. 127.
† Like Professor Hobbs, Professor Sorokin has pointed out sharply that, where there are no units, the quantified qualities cannot be measured with any scientific accuracy—measurements of them are "bound to be fictitious rather than real, arbitrarily superimposed upon the phenomena rather than giving objective measurement of them." Again: "Where there are no units and numbers, all the formulae and equations are either void or represent a subjective ranking, weighing, and scoring by the devotees of a misplaced quantification." *Fads and Foibles in Modern Sociology*, Regnery, 1956, Chapter Seven.
‡ *Ibid.*, p. 63.

tification for the type of empiricism generally employed in social science is extremely tenuous. It seems to spring more from a frantic effort to acquire the external appearance of science and the accolade of "practicality" than to grow out of any carefully thought out system of either philosophy or science. * * * A belief appears to exist that somehow empiricism is more advanced, more modern, than reliance on reason and logic, such as rationalism involves.*

In his *Fads and Foibles in Modern Sociology,* Professor Sorokin† blasts the "illusion of operationalism" and the measuring-phobia in social-science research. Among his most devastating arguments against the excessive use of the empirical approach is the following:

> * * * if the operationalists had really studied how an overwhelming majority of the most important scientific discoveries, technological inventions, the greatest religious, philosophical and technical verities, and the highest artistic achievements really originated and grew, they would have learned, first, that they were born in intuition; second, that the intuitional idea was developed and elaborated by logical and mathematical thought which was used in making all the necessary deductions or consequences from the intuitional (or "postulational") principle; and finally, that in the field of science these deductions were tested by again rationally devised experimental, inductive, or operational method.‡

* Professor Sorokin, in his *Fads and Foibles in Modern Sociology,* puts it this way: "Most of the defects of modern psychosocial science are due to a clumsy imitation of the physical sciences. * * * most of the numerous 'experimental' studies in sociology and psychology are * * * pseudo-experimental, and have a very remote relationship, if any, to real experimental method. * * * we should by all means use a real experimental method in our studies whereever it can be applied, and the more it is used the better. But we should not fool ourselves and others with sham-experimental procedures. They do not and cannot contribute to the real knowledge of psychosocial phenomena. If anything, they corrode the real experimental method and psychosocial science itself."
† Chapter Three.
‡ Pp. 35-36.

And again:

> To abandon intuitional insight and logical thought in favor of operational method would amount to castrating creative thought generally, and in science particularly. Without intuition and logic no real progress in science, religion, philosophy, ethics, and the fine arts has been or will be possible.

Professor Sorokin ridicules the wide use of the poll-taking method of operation, calling it unscientific, vague, indeterminate and, more often than not, "hearsay" in its product.

> Even their "hearsay" material is ordinarily collected not by the investigators themselves, but by their assistants and hired pollsters. Imagine physicists or chemists operating in this fashion and then tabulating the collected opinions and giving the results in the form of various statistical tables and other paraphernalia to point to the "objectivity" of their "scientific" and "operational" techniques.

Moreover, says Professor Sorokin, "what is true or false cannot be decided by majority vote."

"The tidal wave" of the quantitative, empirical method of research is now so high, says Professor Sorokin, "that the contemporary stage of the psychosocial sciences can be properly called *the age of quantophobia and numerology.*"

The "comptometer compulsion," the "fact-finding mania" of these foundation-supported "social scientists" induce them to accept the principle of moral relativity—that moral laws are only relative—"the facts" speak for themselves and must dictate moral law; whatever "the facts" disclose is right.

The accepted moral law must be taken into consideration in any attempt to find socially acceptable solutions to social problems. As Professor Rowe testified: "Ideas and concepts and values are far more important * * * than much of the indisputable, completely noncontroversial factual material that political scientists seem to occupy themselves with so much in the present day."* But the

* Reece Committee *Report,* p. 65.

"social engineers" who are dedicated to "engineering" us into better ways reject this principle. Thus, if Dr. Kinsey concludes that girls would be happier in the long run if their marriages were preceded by considerable, and even unusual, sex experience, then, say these "social engineers," the moral and legal concepts which proscribe it should be abandoned.

Nor, say these "social engineers," are any political principles to be accepted as basic. If, for example, a function can be more efficiently exercised by the Federal government than by the individual states, it should be so exercised, regardless of the principle of limited Federal jurisdiction which is fundamental to our system and is our greatest protection against totalitarianism.

Nor, inasmuch as social "scientists" deem themselves exclusively competent, are political principles to be determined by such incompetents as lawyers, doctors, farmers, and businessmen. As The Social Science Research Council said in its statement filed with the Reece Committee, the social scientists

> command the analytical methods for most effectively getting at such questions in basic and tangible terms.*

And its 1927 report included among its aims:

> to make possible the substituting of more scientific social control for the rule-of-thumb methods which men have happened upon in their effort to live together.†

One more quotation, again from Dr. Herring, the president of The Social Science Research Council, in its first issue of *Items:*

> Here we wish simply to emphasize that in our generation efforts are being made to arrange and control human relationships more consciously, more deliberately, and, it is to be hoped, more responsibly than during the last century. An interdependent world is being forced to an

* *Ibid.,* p. 126.
† *Ibid.,* p. 128.

awareness of the limitations of individual freedom and personal choice.*

With these quotations we can now finally understand the theory of the "social engineers" in The Ford Foundation who approved of eavesdropping on juries. Those in charge of the jury project were dealing with an aged institution, the jury, which had been adopted by our society through "rule-of-thumb" methods and not by the "scientific" method of which the social engineers were allegedly capable. True, the jury is one of our fundamental protections, almost universally approved by our lawyers, jurists, statesmen, legislators, and public. But these are not "scientists." Only the social "scientists" are capable of understanding whether the jury system is sound or not. This they can determine by getting at "the facts." So they were getting at the "facts" by violating the privacy of jurors.

To make this situation doubly clear, I shall quote once more from The Social Science Research Council, because it is, more or less, the guiding spirit in social-science research. Its 1928-1929 report discloses one of its purposes:

> * * * a sounder empirical method of research had to be achieved in political science, if it were to assist in the development of a scientific political control.†

Political control is thus to be left in the hands of the "élite," the "social engineers." What the people want is not necessarily good for them; they are not competent to decide. The *Führers* must decide it for them, so that we can have a scientifically based and intelligent society.

The Reece Committee report quoted a distinguished professor, Dr. Carl O. Sauer of the University of California:

> In American social science it has indeed become a dominant folkway to associate progress with putting the job inquiry into large-scale organizations, under formally pre-

* *Ibid.*, p. 126.
† *Ibid.*, p. 125.

scribed methods, and with limited objectives. Having adopted the name "science," we are impressed by the "Method of science" as inductive, quantitative, experimental. We are even told that such is the only proper method.*

This eminent academician minced no words in discussing the part played by the complex composed of certain of the foundations and intermediary organizations concerned with direct research, such as The Social Science Research Council. He said:

A serious and delicate problem is posed by the growing role of the national research council and foundation, the last years having seen a continually increasing concentration of influence.

And, he said, social scientists have developed

hierarchies of conference members who speak a common language, obscured from us by its own ceremonial terms. They become an élite, fashioning increasingly the directions and limits of our work, as they become more and more removed from the producers.

The foundation-supported concept of "social engineering," with its political implications, was castigated by Professor Sauer in these words:

Research programs are set up in terms of social goals, and it is assumed that professional training provides the deep insight needed. Having set up schools for the training of prophets, it gratifies us to hear that the great task of social science is to remake the world.†

Among the material used by the Committee were letters received from three of the leading sociologists of today, Professor Pitirim A. Sorokin of Harvard, Professor Carle C. Zimmerman of Harvard, and Professor James H. S. Bossard of Pennsylvania. Professor Zimmerman went so far as to say:

* *Ibid.*, p. 83.
† *Ibid.*, p. 84.

The tax-exempt foundations in the United States have unfairly and undesirably emphasized empirical research to such an extent that the whole meaning of social-science research has come to be ridden with sham and dubious practices.*

Professor Sorokin said†:

The futility of excessively favoring this sort of research [the empirical] particularly is well demonstrated by its sterility—in spite of the many millions of dollars, enormous amount of time and energy expended by research staffs. Almost all of the enormous mass of research along this line in the United States of America for the last 25 or 30 years has not produced either any new significant social theory or any new method, or any new technique, or any scientifically valid test, or even any limited causal uniformity.

Professor Sorokin's judgment of the sterility of most foundation-supported social-science research is supported by an address, "New Concepts in Education," by Dr. Stuart A. Courtis, made to the American Association for the Advancement of Science in 1950, part of which is quoted in the Reece Committee report‡:

As a result we are today in possession of mountains of quantitative data whose interpretation is not furthered by our experiments, and we have discovered no laws as the exact sciences know law. We possess only large masses of quantitative conclusions nearly worthless for purposes of prediction.

Referring to the mass production of research, Professor Sorokin has said:

The research factories manufacturing such products have become the dominant industry of sociological and psycho-

* *Ibid.,* p. 64.
† Report, p. 78.
‡ P. 63.

logical research. Their products are manufactured on a mass scale, moving along the assembly line almost as mechanically as automobiles. As a result, scientific journals, texts and monographs are filled mainly with this sort of research. Its total volume has already become so large that nobody, except "the All-Remembering, All-Indexing, and All-Tabulating Electronic Robot," can know, remember, and use this cosmic mass of research. Human scholars and scientists can hardly master it; after all, human memory is limited, and human life is too short. Moreover, it is not certain whether these products are worth remembering. Many real scholars refuse to waste their time and energy in plodding through miles and miles of this monotonous research. * * * Preoccupation with this time-and-fund-consuming research leaves little time for the researchers to study more important sociocultural phenomena, or to acquaint themselves with the vast fund of real knowledge accumulated by hundreds of eminent social thinkers. In this research industry the researchers have hardly any time even for seriously thinking about the problems studied and still less time for cultivating intuition or incisive rational thought, or for developing their minds generally. As a result of this mechanized research industry, we have a vast army of "research-factory hands" who, in the terms of Lao-Tze, "are never wise men, while wise men are never researchers." No wonder, therefore, that this vast army has not enriched our knowledge by many new discoveries or verities.*

Professor Bossard expressed his concern over the effect that the recent emphasis (by foundations) on the "comptometer approach" would have upon research. He wrote:

The monies and influence of the large foundations naturally do a great deal to set the norms of professional acceptance in a given field, and it is in this respect, difficult to measure

* *Fads and Foibles in Modern Sociology*, pp. 299-300.

statistically but possibly of very great importance, that a distinct disservice may be done to sociological research by an undue emphasis upon any particular emphasis or methodology.*

To quote Professor Sorokin again:

> In the raging epidemic of quantophrenia everyone can be "researchers" and "scientific investigators," because everyone can take a few sheets of paper, fill them with all sorts of questions, mail the questionnaires to all possible respondents, receive the answered copies, classify them in this or that way, process them through a tabulating machine, arrange the results into several tables (with all the mechanically computed percentages, coefficients or correlation, Chi-Square indices, standard deviations and probable errors), and then write a paper or a book filled with the most impressive array of tables, formulae, indices, and other evidence of "objective, thorough, precise, quantitative" research. These are typical "rites" in "contemporary quantitative research" in sociology, psychology, and other psychosocial sciences. * * * Hence the rising tide of quantophrenic studies in these disciplines. * * * The Nemesis of such simulacra is sterility and error—and this Nemesis is already walking abroad among the contemporary psychosocial sciences.†

Similar statements were made by various academicians who were reluctant to have their names disclosed for fear of reprisal from the foundation world. One renowned professor of economics, whose teachings conflict with the ruling interventionist school, a man of worldwide prestige and of independent thought, stated to me that no student of his could get a grant from any of the foundations which form part of the complex (which the Reece Committee referred to as a "concentration of power") because he does

---

* Reece Committee *Report,* p. 64.
† *Fads and Foibles in Modern Sociology,* pp. 172-173.

not follow the comptometer school of research which the major foundations promote.

The nonconformists and their students stand little chance of receiving support for research from those foundations which have delegated the selection of grant recipients to professional councils which are strictly controlled by majorities adhering to the current orthodoxies. It is no wonder that so much sterility has resulted in social-science research fields. There is little controversy in such kept "science." Researchers work in a foundation-created climate which offers rewards for conformity and the penalty of abandonment for dissent. The degrading effect of this upon the academic world accounts for the general sterility of social-science research in the United States.

ROCKEFELLER FINANCES DR. KINSEY'S SCIENTISM

Professor Hobbs rightly asserted that social scientists should exercise the greatest care in informing the public when their work is not truly "scientific." The very term "social science" implies that their conclusions are unassailable because they are "scientifically" arrived at. There is the constant danger, then, that laymen will take these conclusions as axiomatic bases for social action. Perhaps the best illustration of this is the remarkable number of writings which appeared after the publication of the reports on the Rockefeller Foundation-supported Kinsey studies.* With the assumedly "scientific" character of Dr.

---

* The Rockefeller Foundation's statement filed with the Committee explained its connection with the Kinsey studies in this way. In 1931 it "became interested in systematic support for studies in sexual physiology and behavior." It had become increasingly interested in the "life sciences" and less in the "physical sciences." And, it continued, "support for studies in reproductive physiology and behavior constituted an obviously necessary part of this program since the ability to reproduce is one of the elementary characteristics of living organisms." Its work in these areas was chiefly in connection with the "committee for research in problems of sex of The National Research Council," to which, by 1954, the Foundation had granted $1,755,000, in annual grants running from $75,000 to $240,000. Beginning about 1941, a considerable portion of these funds was supplied to Dr. Kinsey's studies, and one grant was made direct to Dr. Kinsey. The NRC grants to these studies were with the knowledge and approval of the Foundation.

The work of the NRC produced some results of truly noteworthy impor-

Kinsey's work behind us, we had such things offered to the public as this by one Anne G. Freegood, in the September 1953 issue of *Harper's:*

> The desert in this case is our current code of laws governing sexual activities and the background of Puritan tradition regarding sex under which this country still to some extent operates.

Later on she wrote that the first Kinsey report "has already been cited in court decisions and quoted in textbooks as well as blazoned from one end of the country to the other."

Professor Hobbs, in *Social Problems and Scientism*, p. 93, described the aftermath of Dr. Kinsey's Rockefeller Foundation-supported first report as follows:

> Despite the patent limitations of the study and its persistent bias, its conclusions regarding sexual behavior were widely believed. They were presented to college classes; medical doctors cited them in lectures; psychiatrists applauded them; a radio program indicated that the findings were serving as a basis for revision of moral codes relating to sex; and an editorial in a college student newspaper admonished the college administration to make provision for sexual outlets for the students in accordance with the "scientific realities" as established by the book.

Some of these Kinseyites have said that our laws are wrong because they do not follow the biological "facts." Published reports such as those of Kinsey can do immeasurable harm when they falsely pretend to disclose biological "facts." A great part of the Kinsey product is without basis in true "fact" and is mere propaganda for some personally intriguing concepts.

---

tance and great value to society in the field of physiology. I intend no criticism of the Foundation's grants in so far as they were used for physiological studies. But the much-publicized "best-seller" Kinsey studies base an advocacy of criminal and social reform on the very *unscientific* material which Dr. Kinsey had collected and permitted to be widely disseminated.

Professor Hobbs pointed out that Dr. Kinsey ridiculed "socially approved patterns of sexual behavior," calling them "rationalizations," while usually referring to socially condemned forms of sexual behavior as "normal" or "normal in the human animal." This presentation, said Professor Hobbs, "could give the impression, and it gave the impression to a number of reviewers, that things which conform to the socially approved codes of sexual conduct are rationalizations, not quite right, while things which deviate from it, such as homosexuality, are normal, in a sense right."*

Professor Hobbs stressed the fact that such pseudoscientific presentations could seriously affect public morality. Here is part of his testimony:

> For an illustration, in connection with the question of heterosexuality compared with homosexuality, Kinsey in the first volume has this statement:
> "It is only because society demands that there be a particular choice in the matter (of heterosexuality or homosexuality) and does not so often dictate one's choice of food or clothing."
> He puts it in [these] terms . . . it is just a custom which society demands.
> In the second volume it is stressed, for example, that we object to adult molesters of children primarily because we have become conditioned against such adult molesters of children, and that the children who are molested become emotionally upset, primarily because of the old-fashioned attitudes of their parents about such practices, and the parents (the implication is) are the ones who do the real damage by making a fuss about it if a child is molested. Because the molester, and here I quote from Kinsey, "may have contributed favorably to their later sociosexual development." That is, a molester of children may have actually, Kinsey contends, not only not harmed them, but may have

* Reece Committee *Report,* pp. 69-70.

contributed favorably to their later sociosexual development. Especially emphasized in the second volume, the volume on females, is the supposed beneficial effects of premarital sexual experiences. Such experiences, Kinsey states: "provide an opportunity for the females to learn to adjust emotionally to various types of males."
That is on page 266 of the volume on females.
In addition, on page 327 he contends that premarital sexual experience may well contribute to the effectiveness of one's other nonsexual social relationships, and that many females—this is on page 115—will thus learn how to respond to sociosexual contacts.
On page 328, that it should contribute to the development of emotional capacities in a more effective way than if sexual experiences are acquired after marriage.
The avoidance of premarital sexual experience by females, according to Professor Kinsey, may lead to inhibitions which damage the capacity to respond, so much that these inhibitions may persist after years of marriage, "if, indeed, they are ever dissipated." That is from page 330.
So you get a continued emphasis on the desirability of females engaging in premarital sexual behavior. In both these volumes there is a persistent emphasis, a persistent questioning of the traditional codes, and the laws relating to sexual behavior. Professor Kinsey may be correct or he may be incorrect, but when he gives the impression that the findings are scientific in the same sense as the findings in physical science, then the issue becomes not a matter of whether he as a person is correct or incorrect, but of the impression which is given to the public, which can be quite unfortunate.* (Hearings, pp. 129, 130.)

The special responsibility of The Rockefeller Foundation for having financed the Kinsey "best sellers" comes sharply to roost in this quotation from an article by Albert Deutsch in *Harper's*:

* *Ibid.,* p. 70.

So startling are its revelations, so contrary to what civilized man has been taught for generations, that *they would be unbelievable but for the impressive weight of the scientific agencies backing the survey.**

Note how impressive is the word "scientific." And how false. How dangerous to society if foundations support the theory that social problems can be scientifically solved by mere interviewing techniques. Apart from the doubtful veracity of the samples of men and women questioned by Kinsey, his statistical methods have been seriously criticized by organs of the American Statistical Association and several scholarly reviewers. But even if the sampling had been representative of American attitudes on sex, and even if all the persons interviewed had been willing to give truthful answers and were psychologically capable of doing so, it seems preposterous to propose that social change should be justified upon empirical inquiry alone.

Should concepts of value (legal, religious, ethical ideas) be abandoned merely because any number of men find them oppressive and neglect to live up to them? Are we justified in advocating a change in the criminal law because certain types of crimes are practiced widely? Shall we abrogate punishment for speeding, for theft, for adultery, for fraudulent voting, for income-tax evasion, if we find that such illegalities are practiced by a majority? By twenty percent of our people? By eighty percent? What percentage of our population must express itself, either by response to interviews or by action, in favor of an illegality to convince a social scientist that the law proscribing it should be abrogated? Similar questions might be asked in relation to the weighing of existing ethical concepts such as patriotism, respect for parents and elders, and tolerance of dissidence.

The basic fallacy of the Kinsey approach and that of the ruling research clique in the social sciences stems from a confusion between what is a fact, what is an expression of opinion, and what is an *a priori* concept of value. The puerile doctrine that change

* *Ibid.,* p. 71.

is always necessary has led many of these "scientists" to believe that there are no longer any "inalienable rights," no longer any unchanging duties. They deem themselves justified, with the support of foundation grants, to label their prejudices as truth and to experiment with society. The Reece Committee report puts it thus:

> *It seems to this Committee that there is a strong tendency on the part of many of the social scientists whose research is favored by the major foundations toward the concept that there are no absolutes, that everything is indeterminate, that no standards of conduct, morals, ethics and government are to be deemed inviolate, that everything, including basic moral law, is subject to change, and that it is the part of the social scientists to take no principle for granted as a premise in social or juridical reasoning, however fundamental it may heretofore have been deemed to be under our Judeo-Christian moral system.**

THE AMERICAN SOLDIER, PRODUCED BY THE SSRC

Poll taking has become one aspect of the fact-finding mania. Professor Hobbs testified regarding *The American Soldier*, a book prepared and edited under the auspices of The Social Science Research Council. He described the process by which social scientists, against the repeated objections of the military authorities, managed to "incorporate their own ideas in a matter of highest military significance." This was the method of discharge to be used by the military forces at the end of hostilities in World War II. Most of these "scientists" were foundation connected. Their work was praised by Frederick Osborn, a trustee of The Carnegie Corporation, as a "typical example of social-science prediction." What was this "example"? These "scientists" decided that men should be discharged individually from the army according to a table of weighted factors, and that these factors should be determined by taking a poll of the men themselves. In

* *Ibid.,* p. 72.

other words, regardless of military necessities, the men were to determine what weight should be given to length of service, front-line duty, and other factors in determining the order of release.

The traditional method of demobilization called for the successive release of whole units from the armed forces, leaving unimpaired the strength of the remaining units. The method recommended by the social scientists, based upon alleged "scientific" findings, shattered the effectiveness of individual units.

These "scientists" prevailed. As a result, there can be little doubt that, if we had been forced into a resumption of hostilities, our army would have been reduced to a nadir of inefficiency. As the Committee report put it:

> The military policymakers were defeated by the social scientists. This was another victory in the struggle of the "social engineers" to gain control of all the throttles of control. * * * A few more such victories for "social engineering" might indeed be fatal.*

In his statement filed with the Reece Committee, Mr. Charles Dollard, President of the Carnegie Corporation, defended the authors of *The American Soldier,* holding that our military forces themselves initiated the study and, inferentially, were responsible for the outcome. Obviously enough, the study could not have been made without express military authorization. But it is inconceivable that any truly military minds could have initiated the study. Nor does that seem to have happened. The introduction to *The American Soldier* states that the officers responsible for advancing the project were General George C. Marshall and Brehon Somervell. But the actual officer in charge was General Frederick Osborn. General Osborn was no professional soldier. He had been a civilian, an official of a factoring company, and it is of no little consequence that he was a trustee of the Carnegie Corporation. He had achieved some attention in social-science circles through various writings. His service in

* *Ibid.*, p. 75.

the army, where he rose to the rank of major general, seems to have been confined to the nonmilitary work of acting as director of the Information and Education Division, the unit through which the studies of demobilization methods were made.

Among General Osborn's staff were Dr. Samuel A. Stouffer, director of the professional staff, Dr. Carl I. Hovland, and Dr. Leonard S. Cottrell, Jr., all identifiable as closely associated with The Social Science Research Council. In all probability it was some of these men, or some of the employed consultants, who generated the idea of the study. A two-page list of such consultants appears in the beginning of volume II of *The American Soldier;* many of these, in later reviews of the book, expressed enthusiastic praise for the work to which they had contributed.

The introduction boasts: "Never before had modern methods of social science been employed on so large a scale by such competent technicians." It also said: "The conservatism natural to professional men everywhere, and often particularly ascribed to the professional soldier, was broken down by the imaginative grasp of the abler leaders." It would be interesting to know the full story of how these "leaders"—if military men were meant—were sold this "grasp." At any rate, while the book cites that even the President approved of the project, it states: "The idea of a point system for demobilization had been conceived in the Research Branch * * *." This branch of the armed forces was operated not by military men but by social scientists. It is equally clear that there was powerful and consistent opposition to the point system from truly military men who realized how disastrous to our security the suggested discharge system could become. This point system contributed substantially to that grave weakness in our forces which left us unprepared for the Korean War, coming so soon after the close of World War II.

Looking back, it is incredible that a group of so-called "scientists" could have been so blind to reality as to propose that military decisions be made through the process of finding out what the soldier in the ranks wanted. Moreover, the scientific value of this effort to justify a military decision by the poll-taking method has been questioned by many critics. Arthur M. Schlesinger, Jr., a historian who is certainly not suspect of being a conservative, lashed out at the study in a review, "The Statistical Soldier." He said:

> Too many obvious frauds were at last committed in the name of sociology * * * So the old and toothless beast was put out to pasture. In its place has come its more carnivorous son, known in his more modest mood under some such name as "social relations," or, more often, in a tone of majestic simplicity, as "social science" * * *
>
> Well, the "social science" machinery has been grinding away for some years now. Occasionally skeptics approach the devout and say with proper humility: You have basked in the smile of the deans and in the favor of foundations. You are discovering the secret of the ages. We wish to share in the new enlightenment you are bringing us. But what, oh wise one, should we read? Can you name a single book that would give some idea of the great revelations that lie in wait? The oracle at that point used to become muffled. Then one began to hear of *The American Soldier*. This work one was told was the real stuff; this would settle the doubts.*

Schlesinger continues:

> Indeed, the more basic questions are raised, not by relatively innocuous practice of "social science" but by its mystique—its pretensions to Know Knowledge and new certitude—Most of *The American Soldier* is a ponderous demonstration in NEWSPEAK of such facts as [one can] find described more vividly and with far greater psychological insight in a small book entitled *Up Front* by Bill Mauldin. What Mauldin may have missed will turn up in the pages of Ernie Pyle. * * * Bursting onto university campuses after the war, overflowing with portentous if vague

* *Partisan Review*, August 1949.

hints of mighty wartime achievements (not, alas, to be disclosed because of security), fanatical in their zeal and shameless in their claims, they [the social scientists] persuaded or panicked many university administrators into giving their studies priority. Needless to say, they scored an even more brilliant success with foundations. Certain foundation directors even decided that virtually all their funds for research in the social sciences should be expended on projects of the "social science" variety; the individual scholar, so far as they were concerned, was through. * * * The whole [is] happily subsidized by the foundations, carrying to triumphant completion their ancient hope of achieving the bureaucratization of American intellectual life.

Apart from his criticism of the underlying scientific fadism, Schlesinger considers *The American Soldier* a "harmless book." But most of the social scientists (and perhaps General Marshall also) considered *The American Soldier* a monumental contribution to military policy and to the social sciences. In the words of Paul Lazarsfeld, one of the project's consultants: "The results of both volumes are without parallel in the history of the social sciences."

The American Soldier comprised two out of four volumes of a series. The flyleaf says:

The four volumes in this series were prepared and edited under the auspices of a Special Committee of the Social Science Research Council comprising
Frederick Osborn, Chairman
Leonard S. Cottrell, Jr.
Leland C. De Vinney
Carl I. Hovland
John M. Russell
Samuel A. Stouffer
Donald Young, ex officio.
The data on which these volumes are based were collected by the Research Branch, Information and Education Di-

vision, War Department, during World War II. In making the data available the War Department assumes no responsibility for the analyses and interpretations contained in these volumes, which are the sole responsibility of the authors.

These volumes were prepared under a grant from the Carnegie Corporation of New York. That corporation is not however the author, owner, publisher or proprietor of the publication, and is not to be understood as approving by virtue of its grant any of the statements made or views expressed therein.

(This last reservation is typical of the method by which some foundations seek to use the "risk capital" theory and yet escape all responsibility for unhappy risk.)

In *Items,* the official publication of The Social Science Research Council, issue of March 1949, an anonymous author boasts: "The point system was actually invented by the Research Branch and 'sold' to the Army on the basis of attitude studies made in all parts of the world." According to the SSRC, more than a half million soldiers were studied. These American soldiers were guinea pigs for social scientists, to satisfy their curiosity and their penchant for statistical analyses. Their persuasive promises of military benefits had sold the program to the authorities. This gave the associated professors jobs in Washington during the war time and an opportunity to gain prestige for a mysterious contribution to the war effort. It also almost wrecked our military strength.

FOUNDATIONS GENERATE *THE PROPER STUDY OF MANKIND*

In the face of the evidence produced by the Reece Committee, to deny that the major foundation complex slanted its research and its work to the left is futile. An example is the production of *The Proper Study of Mankind,* written by Stuart Chase, at the instance of Donald Young, then of The Social Science Research Council, and Charles Dollard, then of The Carnegie Corporation, to portray the condition and functioning of the social sciences.

This book had enormous impact. Approximately 50,000 copies had been sold, which, for a book of this kind, is truly monumental.

Mr. Chase was described by Professor Hobbs as a man who "has in his work definitely indicated his leanings towards collectivism and social planning * * *." *

Mr. Chase had had a long history as a pamphleteer. In 1922 he wrote for the League for Industrial Democracy, the declared object of which was "Education for a New Social Order Based on Production for Use and Not for Profit." His book *A New Deal,* published in 1932,† recommended (1) a managed currency; (2) a drastic redistribution of the national income through income and inheritance taxes; and (3) a huge program of public works. He advocated nationwide economic controls "from the top," proposed a National Planning Board, and claimed that his plan attempted "to dissolve capitalism with a minimum of government interference" (p. 24). His blueprint for a new America ends with this question: "Why should Russians have all the fun of remaking a world?"

In 1935 his book *Government in Business*‡ reprinted several of his magazine articles extolling the New Deal. Not satisfied with the degree of control already exercised by the Federal government, he advocated clearing the road through a straightforward revision of the Constitution§ and presented a long list of activities to be assumed by the Federal government. In his later books, he consistently pleaded for government control of and interference with private investment. He did not depart from the cooperative-Socialist line until he began to write for Standard Oil of New Jersey after World War II.

Mr. Chase was retained by The Twentieth Century Fund to write, among other books, *Goals for America,* which appeared in 1942. This work advocated a "mixed economy." In 1946 ap-

* Report, p. 85.
† Macmillan.
‡ Macmillan.
§ *Supra,* p. 287.

peared his *For This We Fought.** He had the advantage of advice and criticism from the Twentieth Century Fund staff, but the Fund took the precaution to say that "the opinions and conclusions expressed by these books are those of Mr. Chase." Among his conclusions were these: He recommended a government-manipulated economy; as a new twist he asked for an "intensive stimulation of the social sciences, to help them to begin to catch up with the runaway physical sciences."

The first edition of his *The Proper Study of Mankind, an Inquiry into the Study of Human Relations*† includes an introduction, "How This Book Came to Be Written." It is quite clear, from this introduction, that Mr. Chase was chosen by two eminent foundation executives, Donald Young (then president of The Social Science Research Council and now president of The Russell Sage Foundation) and Charles Dollard (then president of The Carnegie Corporation of New York), to write a book for them. The book was intended as a popular publicity piece, to interpret the meaning and goals of the social sciences to the general public. Both these gentlemen must have been familiar with Mr. Chase's previous work and with his well-publicized political convictions. The conclusion is inescapable that they selected Mr. Chase because they approved his bias, unless, indeed, one grants them complete indifference to his convictions.

Mr. Chase had conferences with Messrs. Dollard and Young in the course of his work, and they participated in the sending out of a questionnaire to social scientists and exchanged ideas with Mr. Chase. Their tax-exempt organizations assumed the financial risk involved in the project. The book, in fact, may rightly be held to have been a semi-official publication of The Social Science Research Council.

The book registers many examples of economic *achievement* in the social sciences. Several are of extreme interest. Mr. Chase said:

---

* These assignments came from Evans Clark, a former director of the Department of Information, Bureau of the Representative in the United States of the Russian Socialist Federal Soviet Republic (1920), later for many years executive director of The Twentieth Century Fund.
† Harper, 1948.

"There is Harry White of the Treasury arguing with Lord Keynes as to the best form of the World Bank and the International Currency Fund—then known as the Bretton Woods Plan." * And he lauded Lauchlin Currie as an able economist, a contributor to the federal agencies of the New Deal, and mentions his function on the board of economic warfare. The involvement of both Harry Dexter White and Lauchlin Currie in Communist networks is well known.

The second edition of Mr. Chase's book tones down the role of Messrs. Young and Dollard in the creation of the book, and omits the references to Messrs. White and Currie. Mr. Chase, in expounding the concepts of foundation-supported and -directed social-science research, lays it on the line. We are to be managed by these experts, these social divines, with the new "scientific method" which he says can be "applied to the behavior of men as well as to the behavior of electrons." "Prepare now for a surprising universal," says Mr. Chase:

> Individual talent is too sporadic and unpredictable to be allowed any important part in the organization of society. Social systems which endure are built on the average person who can be trained to occupy any position adequately if not brilliantly.†

And how is this "scientific" management to take place? One gathers from Mr. Chase's book, which seems to represent the official line of the foundation complex, that it is to be through "cultural determinism," via a molding of our minds by propaganda. Mr. Chase wrote:

> Theoretically, a society could be completely made over in something like 15 years, the time it takes to inculcate a new culture into a rising group of youngsters.

Professor Hobbs in commenting on the book, saw "cultural determinism" as a weapon both of fascism and communism, a va-

---

* P. 211.
† Reece Committee *Report*, p. 87.

riety of "brainwashing" reminiscent of the Russian Pavlov's experiments on the conditioning of dogs.*

To quote Professor Hobbs again, he has said that the "zealots" of the new research in the social sciences

> lead people to believe that techniques exist in social science which provide accurate description and enable prediction of social behavior. We are told to pattern our behavior and to change our society on the basis of such conclusions regarding criminality, race relations, marriage, mental health, war, divorce, sex, and other personal and social affairs. Yet in these areas of behavior the pertinent knowledge is extremely limited and unreliable, the rules of behavior are vague and changeable, the techniques are crude and untested, and even the basic units required for measurement are non-existent. [Again:] Character and integrity are dissolved in the acid ridicule of cultural determinism.†

CARNEGIE PRODUCES *AN AMERICAN DILEMMA*

To the tune of $250,000, The Carnegie Corporation of New York financed a study of the race problems in the South. Dr. Gunnar Myrdal of Sweden was selected to run this study. He reported his findings in a book which became very influential, entitled *An American Dilemma*. Dr. Myrdal was assertedly selected because he was a foreigner and thus could be an unprejudiced observer. Now, if the foundation moguls who thought a study of the southern race situation was desirable (and I have no doubt that it was) concluded that a foreigner should be chosen to make it, why did they select a socialist for the job? This was no accidental selection. Dr. Myrdal's politics were well known. Professor Kenneth Colegrove had been Secretary-Treasurer of The American Political Science Association for eleven years and knew a Socialist when he saw one. He testified that Dr. Myrdal was a "very left-wing socialist." ‡ It would be incredible to suppose that

---

* *Ibid.*, pp. 86-87.
† *Ibid.*, p. 72.
‡ *Ibid.*, p. 91.

those who chose Dr. Myrdal did not realize the danger in giving him heavy foundation subsidy to study a problem of highly delicate political character.

In *An American Dilemma*, Dr. Myrdal libeled and insulted the American people unmercifully. Our Constitution, he said, turned its back on the Declaration of Independence and was "dominated by property consciousness and designed as a defense against the democratic spirit let loose during the Revolution." He referred to our "nearly fetishistic cult of the Constitution," continuing: "This is unfortunate since the 150-year-old Constitution is in many respects impractical and ill-suited for modern conditions * * *." "Modern historical studies," said the good Dr. Myrdal, "reveal that the Constitutional Convention was nearly a plot against the common people."

Dr. Myrdal accused Americans of "a relatively low degree of respect for law and order." He referred to an "anarchistic tendency in America's legal culture," complicated by "a desire to regulate human behavior tyrannically by means of formal laws." We are a desperately low order of humanity: "We have to conceive of all the numerous breaches of law, which an American citizen commits or learns about in the course of ordinary living, as psychologically a series of shocks which condition him and the entire society to a low degree of law observance." He talks about the possibility that, "in the course of time, Americans" might conceivably be "brought to be a law-abiding people." *

Professor Colegrove had this to say about *An American Dilemma*†:

> Dr. Myrdal was a Socialist, pretty far left, indeed extremely left. He was not unprejudiced. He came over here with all the prejudices of European Socialists. And the criticism that he makes of the American Constitution, the criticism that he makes of the conservatives of the United States, are bitter criticisms. He didn't have any praise at

* *Ibid.*, p. 89 *et seq.*
† Report, p. 91.

all for the conservatives. He did praise what he called the liberals. And he implied that it was the conservatives in the United States who created the problem and who continued the difficulties of any solution. I felt the foundations did a great disservice to American scholarship in announcing his study as an objective nonpartisan study whose conclusions were wholly unbiased. It was almost intellectual dishonesty.*

There is this strange aftermath to *An American Dilemma,* which illustrates the dangers when foundations finance studies in the social sciences without making certain that the product is to be objective. In a recent instance, the Supreme Court of the United States based one of its most important decisions in part upon the authority of this book. This was in the segregation cases (*Brown v. Board of Education,* 347 U.S. 483 and 349 U.S. 293). This feature of its decisions was aptly ridiculed in an article which appeared in the *American Bar Association Journal* of April 1956, written by Eugene Cook, the Attorney General of Georgia, and William I. Potter, of the Kansas City Bar. These writers expressed astonishment that the Court had "cited as authority college professors, psychologists, and sociologists," rightly asking:

> Should our fundamental rights rise, fall or change along with the latest fashions of psychological literature?

They continued:

> The book, *An American Dilemma,* written by Swedish socialist Gunnar Myrdal on a grant from the Carnegie Foundation, was cited in its entirety by the Supreme Court as an authority for its ruling.

> It was *in this book* that Myrdal declared the United States Constitution to be "impractical and unsuited to modern conditions" and its adoption to be "nearly a plot against the common people." Furthermore, he openly avowed that

* *Ibid.,* p. 91.

liberty must be foresaken for the benefit of what he called "social equality."

Has the present Supreme Court now adopted Myrdal's view of the Constitution?

In an article, "The Supreme Court Must Be Curbed," appearing in the May 18, 1956, issue of *U. S. News & World Report,* the former Justice of the Supreme Court, James F. Byrnes, cried out against the Court having supported its decision "not by legal precedents but by the writings of sociologists." He noted its citation of the Myrdal book and said that "the files of the House Committee on Un-American Activities show that many of Myrdal's associates are members of organizations cited as subversive by the Department of Justice under Democratic and Republican Administrations."

It is not my purpose here to discuss whether the Supreme Court's decision in the *Brown* case was right or wrong, but merely to point out that *scientism,* financed by great foundations, can find unexpected and startling places to roost.

Charles Dollard of The Carnegie Foundation, in his statement filed with the Reece Committee, defended the selection of Dr. Myrdal for the race study, partly by attempting to show that the Swedish scholar was not a Socialist in the sense we use the term. He said it was "common knowledge, that the program inaugurated in Sweden by the Social Democrats is vastly different from what we in this country normally think of as socialism." This comment begged the question. Whatever program may have been "inaugurated" in Sweden by her Socialists, their objectives were those we rightly attribute to socialism. It is the objectives which count; these alone should count in appraising the bias of an author who is being considered for research in a delicate and political field of social science.

There can be no doubt that the program of the Swedish *Social Demokratiska Partie* is anticapitalist. It preaches class struggle, expropriation of the means of production, a new regulation of income and property distribution. The by-laws of this party declare as its purpose: "in cooperation with the socialist parties of other countries to recreate the economic order of bourgeois society and to achieve liberation of the exploited classes." Raymond Fusilier, in his *Le Parti Socialiste Suèdois* (1954), reports that the party advocates nationalization of oil, banking, and insurance.

Messrs. Young and Dollard are highly intelligent, exceptionally well-informed men. There were plenty of unbiased and objective European scholars to choose from. Both Young and Dollard knew that the race problem was, indeed, one of great political delicacy. That they would not have cared what the political bias of a scholar selected for such an investigation might be, would attribute to them negligence foreign to their characters. The conclusion seems fair that Dr. Myrdal was chosen not in spite of his collectivist bias but because of it.

In one of his books, *Warning Against Peace Optimism* (1944), Dr. Myrdal admits to an initial excitement and enthusiasm over the Russian Revolution, stating, however, that he was later repelled by the general absence of individual liberties in Russia. But he has never given up hope apparently, that Russia would come through to lead the world. After a three-week trip through Russia in 1941, he announced that he had become excited over the warm, human attitudes in the Soviet Union. He said that Russia is still a puzzle to him, but that he wants to believe in Russia, not only in her future might but in the force of her "internationalist, democratic ideals."

On another occasion (in *Kontakt mit Amerika,* 1942), this "scientific" observer, selected by leaders in the social-science section of the foundation world to study our race problem, offered this opinion: "The ideals of Soviet socialism, even if up to now not its practice, are democratic. Russia even has the most democratic constitution in the world." He demonstrates his deep understanding of the international situation by adding: "America must free the Russians from fear and permit Russia to develop her democratic ideals."

Far from contributing to a solution of the American race problem, *An American Dilemma*, sponsored by tax-exempt foundations, supplied ammunition for use by Communist, neutralist, and other agitators to undermine America's position in a world populated by colored majorities. Myrdal said: "The treatment of the Negro is America's greatest scandal." This is not the language of science, but clearly the formulation of a political agitator. He said that the Negro's situation in the U. S. A. is "salt in the wounds of colored people all over the world, whose rising influence is axiomatic."

No sensible person doubts that the race problem in the United States is a difficult and vital one, crying for sound and fair solution. But it is clear that the assignment given to Dr. Myrdal by Carnegie Foundation and Social Science Research Council executives involved incendiary matter which, it might readily be expected, a leader of international socialism would delight in exploiting. This must have been foreseen by Dr. Myrdal's sponsors.

One more note on Dr. Myrdal. According to Fusilier, Myrdal's radicalism in domestic affairs antagonized a great part of the social democratic constituency in Sweden. This resentment against him may have led to his change of environment. He has become an important official of the United Nations, as Secretary of the U. N. Council for Europe. Here he works for economic integration between East and West, opposes American influence in Europe, accuses American industry of exploiting European customers, and generally plays an active anti-American political role.

THE ENCYCLOPEDIA OF THE SOCIAL SCIENCES

The examples of scientism which I have given so far, slanting sharply to the left, are not isolated cases—"sports" of major foundation investment. One or two, or three or four, or even more, could be excused as accidents. But I am reminded of what Dr. Frederick P. Keppel once said to a student at Columbia when he was Dean of the College. He had informed the student that he was expelling him for excessive cuts.

The young man replied: "But, Dean, I have had an excuse, every time."

"Yes," answered the Dean, "but you have had too many excuses."

Dean Keppel himself later became president of The Carnegie Corporation.

The Encyclopedia of the Social Sciences is the basic reference book in the "social sciences." Though it was even then somewhat out of date, it was estimated that, in 1952, it was consulted about half a million times. It is a book of tremendous importance and influence. The creation of the *Encyclopedia* was financed or materially supported by The Rockefeller Foundation, The Carnegie Corporation, and The Russell Sage Foundation. It was a highly desirable venture. Objectively prepared, it could have taken a proud and meritorious place in our library of basic reference books. The objectivity which was essential to its propriety as a foundation-supported project, however, was markedly missing in the product which was turned out.

I do not suggest that the foundations which financed the project should have censored it or in any way controlled its production. I do suggest that they should have made sure that those who would edit and create it would have the necessary objectivity. This they failed to do.

The key man in editing the *Encyclopedia,* apparently, was Dr. Alvin Johnson, an associate editor. Dr. Johnson was a teacher of economics, who had been the editor of the *New Republic,* a co-founder of the New School for Social Research, and an experienced rewrite man and editor of several other encyclopedic publications. He had been employed by The Carnegie Corporation in its public-library program and by The Carnegie Endowment to write a piece, before World War I, on the interest of the labor organizations in peace. He had a flair for catering to the guilt feelings of the rich and to the reform ideas of the foundation bureaucracy.

His patron at Columbia University, Professor Seeligman, a wealthy supporter of the social sciences, became the nominal head of *The Encyclopedia of the Social Sciences*. He lined up a glittering advisory board and the support of foundations and of a number of professional societies which were then not yet tainted by the ascendancy of a ruling, socialist clique. The *Encyclopedia* enterprise served to create a spirit of common work and common goals among these professional societies. Alvin Johnson, a man of wit and shrewd tenacity, became the guiding spirit of the venture. There is little doubt that his association with the enterprise contributed to enabling the propagandists of the left to influence the minds of successive generations of opinion molders in public affairs.

In his autobiography, Dr. Johnson boasts:

> In enlisting assistant editors I forebore all inquiry about infection with Marx. Like the common cold, Marx was in the air, sometimes cutting editorial efficiency but not irremediably. Although I have always regarded myself as a self-effacing scholar, I meant to keep the encyclopedia under my hand. * * * I had two assistant editors who asserted that they were Socialists. That was nothing to me; they were good and faithful workers. And one was so considerate of my reactionary bent as to inform me that a new editor I had taken on was a Communist. I sent for him. "Yes" he said "I was once a Communist. The name by which I go is not my real name." He gave me his real name, which had figured in press accounts of rows in the Communist party. "And so" he said "you are going to fire me." "Certainly not. You are here to do a specific editorial job. Your private political views are your own business. You can't import them into any work you do for me. But you exhibit the frankness of a gentleman and a scholar. All I ask of you is that if ever you feel it your moral duty to slap a little Communist color on your work, you will resign." That he promised, and he kept his promise.*

* *Pioneers Program*, Viking Press, 1952, p. 311.

Dr. Johnson did not make similar reservations regarding Socialist bias. I quote at length from his book because the attitude of this recipient-dispenser of foundation money is so characteristic of the past attitudes of foundation executives. It has been as if, come the revolution, they wished to be sure of a certificate of good conduct from Communist scholars. They treated them with kid gloves, overlooking the primacy of their party allegiance. Dr. Johnson may not today be a Socialist himself, but while he was working on the *Encyclopedia,* his attitude toward ex-Communist and Socialist gentlemen did much to influence American teachers (and opinion leaders influenced by social-science teachers) with socialist ideas.

Dr. Johnson's incomprehensible attitude, that the political bias of an editor of an encyclopedia of the social sciences was of no moment, played its part in the unfortunate result. The *Encyclopedia* contains a large number of articles written by Communists, fellow travelers and Socialist partisans generally. The Reece Committee report gave a partial list of such articles, as follows*:

> The article on *The Rise of Liberalism* was written by Harold J. Laski, a British socialist. He also did the articles on *Bureaucracy, Democracy, Judiciary: Liberty: Social Contract:* and *Ulyanov, Vladimir Ilich* [Lenin].
>
> *Atheism, Modern Atheism* was written by Oscar Jassi, a socialist of Hungarian origin. *Bolshevism* was written by Maurice Dobb, an English radical. *Capitalism,* by Werner Sombart, a socialist who became affiliated with the Nazis.
>
> *Communism* was written by Max Beer, a Marxian of the University of Frankfurt, Germany. *Communist Parties* was written by Lewis L. Lorwin, whose views may be gleaned from this statement in the article: "The view common in the United States that the Communists are either cranks or criminals is largely a reflection of a conservative outlook." He also wrote the article on *Exploitation.*
>
> *Corporation,* written by two New Dealers, Adolph A.

* Pp. 92-93.

Berle, Jr., and Gardiner C. Means, clearly reveals their bias at that time. (Mr. Berle has since written *The 20th Century Capitalist Revolution* and repudiated some of his former views regarding corporations.) They say that the corporation may well equal or exceed the state in power: "The law of corporations, accordingly, might well be considered as a potential constitutional law for the new economic state: while business practice assumes many of the aspects of administrative government."

Criticism, Social, was produced by Robert Morss Lovett, of wide Communist front associations. *Education, History,* was produced by George S. Counts, a radical educator * * * *Fabianism* was written by G. D. H. Cole, a British socialist. He also wrote the article on *Industrialism. Fortunes, Private, Modern Period,* prepared by Lewis Corey, is easily recognizable as a Marxist analysis.

Freedom of Speech and of the Press was written by Robert Eisler of Paris, who destroys the Christian ethic with this authoritative pronouncement: "No one today will consider the particular ethical doctrine of modern, or for that matter of ancient, Christianity as self-evident or natural or as the morality common to all men. The modern relativist theory of values has definitely shattered the basis on which such artificial churches as the various ethical societies orders rested."

Government, Soviet Russia was prepared by Otta Hoetzsch of the University of Berlin who gives us kind thoughts about the Soviets—for example: "Although the elections are subject to pressure of Communist dictatorship, *this workers' democracy* is not entirely a fiction." [Emphasis ours.]

The article on *Labor-Capital Co-Operation* is credited to J. B. S. Hardman, whose Communist front affiliations are recorded in Appendix, Part IX of the Dies Committee Reports, 78th Congress (1944). He also wrote *Labor Parties, General, United States, Masses* and *Terrorism. Laissez-Faire* is the product of the socialist, G. D. H. Cole; his job was done with a hatchet. *Large Scale Production,* by Myron W. Watkins, is an attack on the production methods of Big Business.

Morals is the product of Horace M. Kallen, whose extensive Communist-front associations are a matter of record. *Philosophy* was produced by Horace B. Davis, with ex-Communist-front associations (See Appendix IX). *Political Offenders*, by Max Lerner, a radical, contains a diatribe against the treatment of political offenders. *Political Police* is by Roger N. Baldwin, recorded by Appendix IX as having Communist-front associations. *Power, Industrial*, by Hugh Quigley, seems to be a plea for more control of business. *Proletariat* is by Alfred Meusel of Germany and seems to admire the Soviet system in Russia.

Social Work, General Discussion, Social Case Work, is the work of a Communist-fronter, Philip Klein. *Socialism* was written by a socialist, Oscar Janski.* It is not unsympathetic to Communism.

Stabilization, Economic, was written by George Soule, of extensive Communist-front affiliations. It expresses doubt that "stabilization" can be accomplished under our present order. *Strikes and Lockouts* is by John A. Fitch, of wide Communist-front affiliations. *Vested Interests* is the work of Max Lerner.

One of the theses in *Woman, Position in Society*, by the Communist-fronter, Bernhard J. Stern, is that we are not doing right by our women, while the Soviets are.

This list is not inclusive. Many more instances of radical selection could be given, plus the multitude of articles by moderately slanted writers.

The Committee report commented further†:

What is amazingly characteristic of the *Encyclopedia* is the extent to which articles on "left" subjects have been

* This name was misspelled in the Committee Report. It should be **Oskar Jaszy**. (See also page 122).
† P. 93.

assigned to leftists; in the case of the subjects to the "right," leftists again have been selected to describe and expound them. This is reminiscent of the reviews in the *New York Times* of books on China, in which both pro-and-con-Communist volumes were assigned to pro-Communists for review.

Dr. Johnson has been very adroit in giving the appearance of objectivity at the same time that he has promoted his own brand of social criticism and reform. While Dr. Johnson was associated with the New School for Social Research in New York City, the well-known Mexican Communist painter Orozco was selected to paint murals on the walls of a large hall in the school building. The final paintings, sketches of which must have been submitted in advance, prominently present Lenin, Stalin, and marching Soviet soldiers. Dr. Johnson defended these murals on the theory that they were not intended as propaganda but were symbols of the time. He did not explain why pictures of equally detestable characters, also characteristic of the time, such as Hitler and Mussolini, were not depicted. Surely, if the idea was to present Lenin and Stalin as examples of the horrors of the time, Hitler and Mussolini would have been at least as eminent examples. If the idea was merely to depict the revolutionary movements of the era, then, after all, the movements of Hitler and Mussolini were revolutionary also. It is difficult to escape the conclusion that Hitler and Mussolini were omitted because they were examples of horror and Lenin and Stalin were depicted because they were deemed not to be.

THE SWING TO THE LEFT

The foundation-fostered approach to research in the social sciences, with its "social goals" to which Dr. Carl O. Sauer (professor of geography at the University of California,) referred, in addressing The Social Science Research Council, tends strongly to the left politically. Professor Hobbs so testified and gave many examples. The Committee accumulated a mass of supporting material. Even the Cox Committee had before it indications that this contention of leftward direction is correct. A long and brilliant statement was attached to the Hearings of the Cox Committee* but was apparently ignored in its conclusions. It was prepared by Mark M. Jones, a consulting economist who had been an adviser to private philanthropy for over thirty years. Mr. Jones wrote:

> From the standpoint of the objects supported by foundations, it seems clear that projects classified in the field of the social sciences have been most subject to doubt with respect to the public interest. This is largely because most of such projects have been executed by educational and charitable agencies. Many educational agencies appear to have been so intolerant even of the idea of profits that they naturally inclined toward means and measures not for profit. This inclination, of course, led many into collectivist channels of thought and action, probably without realization of what was happening. When the sophistries of John Maynard Keynes came along, they fell on receptive ground and were quickly made fashionable largely because of this attitude. *We now have so-called social sciences under the aegis of education which are collectivist in character more than anything else. They represent too much socialism and not enough science.* [Emphasis supplied.]

Mr. Jones also said:

> From the standpoint of the place of the foundation, the most important question falls in the category of omissions. I have not heard of grants from foundations or of activities carried on directly by them which have been particularly noteworthy from the standpoint of the improvement of the capitalistic system. * * * Foundations owe their existence to the capitalistic system.

* Cox Committee *Hearings,* p. 767 *et seq.*

Professor Rowe, in his Reece Committee testimony, contributed these comments concerning the leftward slant of so much foundation-supported social-science research:

> I think that the development of the social sciences in this country in the last 40 or 50 years has been very heavily influenced, in my opinion, by ideas imported from abroad, which have been connected with, if not originated in, socialistic mentality, and to say this is to simply say that it is normal in social science to accept today a great deal of economic determinism, to accept a great deal of emphasis upon empirical research over and against basic thinking and the advancement of theory, and to accept a lot of ideas about the position of the social scientist in the society that seem to me rather alien to the American tradition.
>
> *I think it must be kept in mind that the theory of social engineering is closely related to the notion of the elite which we find dominant in Marxism, the notion that a few people are those who hold the tradition and who have the expertness and that these people can engineer the people as a whole into a better way of living, whether they like it or want it or not. It is their duty to lead them forcibly so to speak in this direction.*
>
> That is all tied up with the conviction of the Marxists that they seem to have, rather that they do have, a perfect social science. This is one of the main tenets of Marxism, that they have a social science which is perfect; it not only explains all the past history, but it will lead to the complete victory of the socialist state on a worldwide basis.
>
> I am not maintaining that my colleagues are all dyed in the wool along this line, but there is such a thing as infection. I think some of these ideas have infected us, and have gotten over into a much more influential place in our thinking than many of us understand or realize. The complete respectability of some of the basic ideas I have been talking

about in the framework of American intellectual life can be seen when you ask yourself the question, "When I was in college, what was I taught about the economic interpretation of history, the frontier interpretation of American history, the economic basis of the American Constitution, and things of this kind?"

This is the entering wedge for the economic analysis of social problems which is related to economic determinism, which is the very heart and soul of the Marxist ideology. When we reflect on the extent to which these ideas have become accepted in the American intellectual community, I think we ought to be a bit alarmed, and be a bit hesitant about the direction in which we are going.

For my own purposes, I would much rather complicate the analysis of social phenomena by insisting that at all times there are at least three different kinds of components that have to be taken into account. There is not only the basic economic thing. We all recognize its importance. But there are what I call political factors. These have to do with the fundamental presuppositions people have about the values that they consider important and desirable. These can be just as well related to abstract and to absolute truth, which we are all trying to search for in our own way, as they can be to economic formation and predetermination, if I make myself clear. Along with this you have to take into account the power element in the military field. If you throw all these things in together, I think it rather tends to scramble the analysis and reduce it from its stark simplicity, as it is embodied in the doctrines of communism, into something which is much harder to handle and much more difficult and complicated, but is a good deal closer to the truth. I make this rather long statement only because the subject is extremely complicated. I know I can't discuss it adequately here, and I don't pretend to try, but I am trying to introduce a few of the things which give me the feeling that in our academic community as a whole we have gone down the road in the direction of the dominance of an intellectual élite. We have gone down the road in the direction of economic determination of everything, throwing abstract values out of the window.*

THE MUCKRAKING INFLUENCE OF SOME FOUNDATIONS

Professor Kenneth Colegrove joined those scholars who asserted that foundation-supported social-science research had overemphasized the empirical method and that this resulted in leftist materialism, a decline of morality, and a declining respect for American traditions. He attributed this in part to an overinterest in things "pathological":

> * * * I think there has been unfortunately a tendency on the part of the foundations to promote research that is pathological in that respect, that is pointing out the bad aspects of American government, American politics, American society, and so on, instead of emphasizing the good aspects.†

And he said that such research had been used as a "cloak for reform":

> If you are going to study the pathological aspects, the natural tendency of human nature * * * is to find out how to cure it, how to alleviate it, and so on. And if the foundations contribute overmuch to pathological studies, and not sufficiently to the studies with reference to the soundness of our institutions, there would be more conclusions on the pathological side than there would be conclusions on the sounder traditional side of American government, American history, and so on. That would inevitably follow." ‡

This insistence, fostered by the foundations, on finding things at fault with America, has run through the entire foundation com-

* Reece Committee *Report,* pp. 123-124.
† *Ibid.,* p. 116.
‡ *Ibid.,* p. 117.

plex or concentration of power and has been greatly responsible, in Professor Colegrove's judgment, for the distinct turn "to the left." He attributed to this the growing tendency in the American classroom to think "that intellectualism and liberalism or radicalism were synonymous" and that a conservative "was not an intellectual."

Out of this "overemphasis on the constant need for reform" grew the concept of "social engineering," according to Professor Colegrove. And he offered these astute comments:

> DR. COLEGROVE. That, of course, grows out of the overemphasis on the constant need for reform. The assumption is that everything needs reform, that unless you are reforming you are not progressing. I think it is in large part due to the failure of the foundations, the failure of many of the scholars they choose, to fully understand what the principles of the American Constitution are, what the principles of American tradition are. Some of them, I know, do not accept those principles as sound. They even attack the principles. Of course, we all know that the principles should be examined and re-examined. But there is a tendency on the part of those who get grants from the foundations to think that they must turn out something in the way of reform; not a study which does not suggest a definite reform but a study more like Myrdal's study, *The American Dilemma*, which poses a condition in which there must be reform.
>
> MR. WORMSER. Does that tendency to insist on reform in turn tend to attract the more radical type of scholar, with the result that grants are made more generally to those considerably to the left?
>
> DR. COLEGROVE. I think undoubtedly it does, especially in the cooperative research, where a large number of people cooperate or operate together on one research project.

* * *

Mr. Wormser. Professor, back to this term, "social engineering," again, is there not a certain presumption or presumptuousness, on the part of social scientists, to consider themselves a group of the élite who are solely capable and should be given the sole opportunity to guide us in our social development? They exclude by inference, I suppose, religious leaders and what you might call humanistic leaders. They combine the tendency toward the self-generated social engineering concept with a high concentration of power in that interlocking arrangement of foundations and agencies, and it seems to me you might have something rather dangerous.

Dr. Colegrove. I think so. Very decisively. There is a sort of arrogance in a large number of people, and the arrogance of scholarship is in many cases a very irritating affair. But there is a tendency of scholars to become arrogant, to be contemptuous of other people's opinions.*

MASS RESEARCH—INTEGRATION AND CONFORMITY

Two long articles on foundations by William H. Whyte, Jr., appeared in *Fortune* (October and November 1955) before the publication of his book, *The Organization Man*. One has only to read the first of these articles to understand that he is no friend of the Reece Committee and that he is a strong admirer of the major foundations. Yet his second article, entitled "Where the Foundations Fall Down," is devoted almost entirely to a criticism of the tendency of the great foundations to indulge in mass research. The following quotations are from this latter article:

> In making grants, they channel the bulk of their money to large-scale team projects and programs, only a small part to the individual. This trend, furthermore, is self-perpetuating. Academics joke privately (and bitterly) that it's easier to get $500,000 from a foundation than $5,000; un-

* *Ibid.*, p. 125.

derstandably, many react by inflating their projects, and the more they do so, the more satisfied the foundations are that their way of giving is the proper way.

* * *

Here is the way they apportion the funds * * * 76 per cent of the total—goes to big team projects or institutions.

* * *

The majority of social scientists believe that the foundations wish to support (a) large projects, (b) mapped in great detail, (c) tailored to foundation interests.

* * *

Overblown projects usually turn out badly, but failure doesn't get advertised. Researchers are reluctant to tell the foundation they have been wasting its money; and even if nothing comes out of the project there is always the consolation that the younger people got some good training. Occasionally researchers do confess failure but this is likely to be a disingenuous preface to asking for more money to reach the summit now in sight.

While foundation officials may know that nothing very important came of an overblown project, they demonstrate no sense of a far more negative effect, i.e., the waste of the scholar's time and energies in what ought to be his most productive years. This is the true blight and it affects the big men in the research field quite as much as the newcomer.

* * *

Even when they want to do some small, independent research of their own, top men often have great trouble getting money for it.

* * *

There is, too, the "lone wolf," the man who insists on pursuing his own, independent course. By and large, foundations dismiss him as no problem.

These are serious indictments of the "projectitis" which has beset the great foundations, wasteful of precious talent, tending to create conformity and uniformity, repressing individual initiative, destructive of that intellectual independence which is the most valuable possession of the academician.

Mr. Dwight Macdonald, in his book *The Ford Foundation* was perhaps even stronger in his condemnation of the foundations for their emphasis on mass research. He said:

> An inevitable, and depressing, question is: What is the practical effect of the towering mass of research that Ford and the other foundations have erected with their millions? Does anybody read their findings—*can* anybody read them?
>
> * * *
>
> But while the work of a single scholar may sometimes achieve the intellectual, and even aesthetic, interest that a literary or philosophical production has, and so have a legitimate claim to be judged as an end in itself, rather than as merely a means toward some other end, this almost never happens with the products of modern collective research.*

Mr. Macdonald quoted Abraham Flexner as saying in his *Funds and Foundations:* "Who reads these books?"; Einstein as saying: "I am a horse for a single harness, not cut out for tandem or team-work; for well I know that in order to attain any definite goal, it is imperative that *one* person should do the thinking and commanding."; and Elbridge Sibley, studying the lone-wolf researcher's needs for The Social Science Research Foundation, as saying: "No effective substitute has been or is likely to be found for the individual human mind as an instrument for making fundamental new discoveries."

Professor Rowe, in testifying previously before the McCarran Committee, was asked whether he knew of any efforts by founda-

* P. 106.

tions to "integrate studies and to bring about unanimity of agreement on any particular subject." This led to the following testimony:

> *From my point of view, the foundations and these research organizations like the Institute of Pacific Relations have gone hog wild on the coordination of research. They have committed themselves so thoroughly to coordination of research that in fact instead of supporting a great variety of research projects, which would enrich the American intellectual scene through variegation, which is a value I very basically believe in, you have a narrowing of emphasis, a concentration of power, a concentration of authority, and an impoverishment of the American intellectual scene.*

* * *

> Now, as I said, I am off on a hobbyhorse at this point. But it is of particular interest, because *by exercising power over research in this way, you see, by insisting on the integration of research activity, anybody who wants to, can control the results of research in American universities. And I think this is a very questionable business that the public ought to look at very, very closely, and see whether they want a few monopolies of the money, like, for instance, the Rockefeller Foundation, the Carnegie Corp., who have done immense amounts of good, to emphasize narrow concentration to the extent that they have.*

* * *

I often say that if we try to become as efficient as the really efficient, supposedly, people, the dictators, then we destroy American scholarship and everything that it stands for. And I often wonder whether my colleagues realize who won the last war. *Intellectually speaking, this country has a great danger of intellectually trying to imitate the totalitar-*

ian approach, in allowing people at centers of financial power—they aren't political powers in this sense—to tell the public what to study and what to work on, and to set up a framework.

Now, of course, as you know, scholars like freedom. Maybe they come up with a lot of useless information. But in my value standard, as soon as we diminish the free exercise of unhampered curiosity, free curiosity, by channeling our efforts along this line, we then destroy the American mentality. Because the great feature of the American mentality is the belief in allowing people to rush off in all kinds of different directions at once. Because we don't know what is absolutely right. You can't tell that far in advance.

* * *

If I may just continue one moment more, Senator, I would like to point out to you that Adolf Hitler very effectively crippled atomic research in Germany by telling the physicists what he wanted them to come up with. Now, this is true. And if you can do that in atomic physics, you can do it 10 times as fast in the so-called social sciences which really aren't sciences at all, where really opinion, differentiation of opinion, is the thing that matters and what we stand for in this country.

That is why I become very much inflamed when I even smell the first hint of a combination in restraint of trade in the intellectual sphere.

Now, you see what I am talking about with this interlocking directorate? That is what bothers me about it. I don't mind if the boys go off and have a club of their own. That is their own business. But when you get a tie-in of money, a tie-in of the promotion of monographs, a tie-in of research, and a tie-in of publication, then I say that the intellectuals are having the reins put on them and blinders.

SENATOR WATKINS. Otherwise, they do not get on the team.

Mr. Rowe. That is right. They don't get on the team, and they don't get a chance to carry the ball.

Now to the faculty member, this means money, income, what he lives on. It is vital. It is not just some recreational thing, you see.

* * *

And, of course, remember this. The foundation people have to have jobs. They have to have something to administer. They don't want to give away the money to the universities and say "Go ahead and spend it any way you want." They want to see that the activity pays. That is, we have got to have a regular flow of the so-called materials of research coming out. We want to see this flow in certain quantity. It has to have a certain weight in the hand. And to see that this happens, we do not just give it to a university where they are going to allow any Tom, Dick and Harry of a professor to do his own thinking. "No, we want an integration."

* * *

Senator Watkins. I take it that is a pretty good plea for the university as against the foundation.

Mr. Rowe. Absolutely. And, as a matter of fact, *I couldn't find a better illustration of the dangers of consistently over the years donating very large sums of money to organizations, you see, for research purposes, than is involved in the very Institute of Pacific Relations itself. It is a fine illustration of the fact that power corrupts, and the more power you get the more corrupt you get.**

In testifying before the Reece Committee, Professor Rowe repeated his deep concern over the tendency of the great foundations to create guided research projects instead of supporting the individual researcher in whatever direction he wished to go. His best illustration was that of the study, financed by The Rocke-

---

* Reece Committee *Report,* p. 41 *et seq.* Emphasis supplied.

feller Foundation, to the extent of some $200,000, of the Taiping Rebellion, which occurred in China in the 19th century. This project concentrated the efforts of a considerable group of competent researchers on a subject which had very limited value. Professor Rowe testified:

> I thought that in view of the scarcity of human resources and the need for general training on Far Eastern matters, that this was focusing it down pretty fine. It is a wonderful project from the point of view of research. If you believe in gadgetry, this had all the gadgets you will ever want to find. If you believe that the best way to promote research is to pick out highly trained and able people and set them free in a general field, like Chinese studies, to follow their own interests wherever they may lead them, then you see this is the very opposite of that kind of thing. It does achieve a certain kind of mechanical efficiency, it seems to me, at the expense of inhibiting the kind of thing that Mr. Hays was talking about, namely, the freedom of the individual to go down any number of blind alleys he wants to go down in the free pursuit of his curiosity, in the interests of honestly trying to come up with important things.*

Professor Rowe illustrated another aspect of the tendency by foundations to organize research according to predetermined plans. He cited the attempt by The Carnegie Corporation to induce Yale University "to eliminate the work we were doing in the far-eastern field and to concentrate our work on the southeast Asian field." His testimony proceeded:

> The only reason for my giving you this incident in somewhat detail is to indicate what I consider to be a real tendency in foundations today—in some foundations, not all

---

* *Ibid.,* p. 80. In his testimony before the McCarran Committee, Professor Rowe, referring to the Taiping project, had said: "This kind of thing is supported by foundation money. And, of course, the temptation is to bring everybody in and integrate, through a genteel process of bribery. That is to say, you support the student, you give him a fellowship, if he will buy your subject matter area."

—to adopt a function of trying to rationalize higher education and research in this country along the lines of the greatest so-called efficiency. I used the word "so-called" there designedly, because in my view, the notion that educational and research and scholarly efficiency can be produced this way in a democratic society is unacceptable. It seems to me that in a democratic society we have to strive for the greatest possible variegation and differentiation as between universities along these lines, and the suggestion that any one university should more or less monopolize one field or any few universities monopolize one field, and give the other fields to others to do likewise with, it is personally repugnant to me. It does not jibe with my notion of academic freedom in the kind of democratic society that I believe in.*

As Professor Rowe put it: "What * * * is a professor to think when people with money come along and tell his university that what he is doing there is useless and ought to be liquidated, because it is being done much better some place else?"

* *Ibid.,* p. 35.

5   FOUNDATIONS AND RADICALISM IN EDUCATION

THE CONTROL OF EDUCATION BY FOUNDATIONS

A VERY POWERFUL COMPLEX of foundations and allied organizations has developed over the years to exercise a high degree of control over education. Part of this complex, and ultimately responsible for it, are the Rockefeller and Carnegie groups of foundations. The largest of the foundation giants, The Ford Foundation, is a late comer. It has now joined in the complex and its impact is tremendous; but the operations of the Carnegie and Rockefeller groups start way back.

There is little question that the initial efforts of the Carnegie and Rockefeller foundations in the field of education produced substantial and salutary results. Certainly the standards of our institutions of higher learning were materially improved as a result of the early work of these foundations. Yet the Reece Committee questioned whether their actions were wholly commendable. The reason for this doubt was that coercive methods were used.

Dr. Ernest Victor Hollis, now Chief of College Administration in the United States Office of Education, once explained the background of this coercive approach as follows:

> * * * Unfavorable public estimate of the elder Rockefeller and Andrew Carnegie, made it inexpedient in 1905

for their newly created philanthropic foundations to attempt any direct reforms in higher education.*

The method used, therefore, he said, was one of indirection—"indirectly through general and non-controversial purposes." "For instance," said Dr. Hollis, "there is little connection between giving a pension to a college professor or giving a sum to the general endowment of his college, and reforming entrance requirements, the financial practices, and the scholastic standards of his institution." Yet one was tied to the other. It was a case of conform, or no grant! When to conform meant bathing in a stream of millions, college and university administrators and their faculties were inclined to conform.

About this type of coercion the Committee report said:

> We question, however, whether foundations should have the power even to do good in the coercive manner which was employed. We cannot repeat too often that power in itself is dangerous. What may have been used for a benign purpose could in the future be used for the promotion of purposes against the interests of the people. It does not write off this danger to say that good men ran the foundations. It is power which is dangerous—power uncontrolled by public responsibility.†

Merely to recognize the satisfactory results of benign coercion, to point to the highly desirable academic reforms for which this coercion was responsible, is not enough. Such a mistake was made by those who lauded the internal reforms of fascism in Italy and ignored the cost in freedom and liberty. Power is in itself dangerous. When we make it possible for financial power to exercise substantial control over education, we endanger our welfare. Perhaps the risk is worth taking in order to preserve freedom of action to foundations. But we should be conscious of the risk,

* Reece Committee *Report*, p. 134.
† *Ibid.*, p. 135.

and alert to what transpires. The Walsh Committee had heard witnesses testify to the fact that colleges had abandoned their religious affiliations in or before 1915 to conform to requirements established by foundations! Today, school policymakers anticipate the idiosyncrasies and preferences of foundation officials in a manner similarly producing conformity.

Consider what The Ford Foundation could do with its billions of capital. It could use this monumental fund to promote whatever educational theories a Dr. Hutchins of the moment were to persuade the trustees to support.* Nor need it be difficult for such promotion to succeed. The country is full of colleges and universities starving for endowment. The number of miserably paid academicians is legion. Professors have to eat; and universities have to pay their janitors. While it is possible that the majority of academicians and administrators would resist, their aggregate voices would not be as powerful as those of a minority of academicians subsidized in the publication of their writings, and a minority of administrators whose institutions flowered financially. How difficult to resist if pressure for change in educational concepts were accompanied by a persuasive flow of hundreds of millions, or even billions! †

* I happen to support some of Dr. Hutchins's educational theories. The fact is, however, that he was a power in The Ford Foundation and did promote his own theories with its tax-exempt money. Whether his theories are right or wrong is beside the point. That the power which he exercised in educational circles could exist through the tax-exempt foundation vehicle is a serious matter.

† It is encouraging that some educators, even at schools which have enjoyed special foundation patronage, are beginning to complain against foundations directing education and educational research. Just before this book was sent to the press, there appeared in the New York World Telegram a report of a lecture delivered by Dean Stephen M. Corey of Teachers College, at Columbia University, in which he is reported to have complained that "Philanthropic foundations are beginning to shackle educational institutions in their research projects by depriving them of a free hand in deciding the areas to be looked into." "Decision-making," said the Dean, is being taken out of the hands of the educators.

The report quotes Dean Corey as follows:

It is probably worth noting that within the past few years there seems to have been a decrease in the disposition of foundations to make grants to institutions that had independently arrived at judgments regarding the research they wanted to do. Foundations as donors are

There is much evidence that, to a substantial degree, foundations have become the directors of education in the United States. To what extent this has been brought about by conditions attached to financial support since the early activities of the Carnegie and Rockefeller foundations, it is difficult to assess. We do know that their first efforts to reform the colleges were only a beginning.

Accrediting organizations and other instruments in the form of civic, professional, and school associations were created or supported to implement the reform plans of these two foundation groups. The American Council on Education became their major executive agency. Other clearing-house organizations, operating variously in higher, secondary, and primary education, and later in the field of "adult education," received heavy support. Among them were The National Education Association and associated groups, The Progressive Education Association, The John Dewey Society, The National Council on Parent Education, and The American Youth Commission.

While the results of the first phase of foundation operations in education were entirely beneficial, that cannot be said of later stages. Together with an enormous amount of benefit, the foundations were responsible, as well, for much that has had a decidedly deleterious effect upon our society.

Research and experimental stations were established at selected universities, notably Columbia, Stanford, and Chicago. Here some of the worst mischief in recent education was born. In these Rockefeller-and-Carnegie-established vineyards worked many of

---

coming more and more frequently to designate the problems that they want studied as a result of their gifts.

The Dean was reported as saying that the trend of the foundations to set the pitch "was most clearly illustrated by operations of the Ford Foundation and its subsidiaries. He said they sought out research institutions to go into 'problems or practices that the officials thought critical'."—"A 'pathetic' consequence, in the dean's opinion, has been the great amount of time spent by university personnel developing data that conforms to the 'real or fancied interests of the foundation or government agency.' This, he observed, 'tends to remove the decision-making on research, that should be done, from the persons who are most intimately involved in the research, the investigators themselves.' "

the principal characters in the story of the suborning of American education. Here foundations nurtured some of the most ardent academic advocates of upsetting the American system and supplanting it with a Socialist state.

THE BIRTH OF EDUCATIONAL RADICALISM

Whatever its earlier origins or manifestations, there is little doubt that the radical movement in education was accelerated by an organized Socialist movement in the United States. In 1905 The Intercollegiate Socialist Society was created under the direction of Jack London, Upton Sinclair, and others for the active promotion of socialism. It established branches in many major colleges and universities, where leaders were developed who were to have considerable future influence; among them were Bruce Bliven, Freda Kirchwey, (Senator) Paul Douglas, Kenneth Macgowan, Isador Lubin, Evans Clark, and John Temple Graves, Jr. Robert Morss Lovett, a man with a total of 56 Communist-front affiliations,* became the first president of the Society. Stuart Chase, selected by The Social Science Research Council to write the showpiece on the achievements of social scientists, was an early writer for this organization. This Society was no transient organization. It still exists and operates today as a tax-exempt foundation, having changed its name some years ago to The League for Industrial Democracy.†

The movement generated or accelerated by the League was likened to the Fabian Socialist movement in England by Mr. Aaron Sargent, one of the witnesses before the Reece Committee. Mr. Sargent is a lawyer who has had considerable experience in special investigations and research in education and subversion. He had been a consultant to the Senate Internal Security Committee in 1952 and represented patriotic organizations in numerous public hearings concerned with educational and other tax-exempt activities. At the Reece hearings, Mr. Sargent cited *Fabianism in Great Britain*, a book by Sister Margaret Patricia

---

* Reece Committee *Hearings*, pp. 221-224.
† It will be discussed in some detail in the following chapter.

McCarran, daughter of the later Senator McCarran, in which she described the gradual extension of influence of the Fabian idea. Mr. Sargent called the Socialist movement in America, that propelled by The Intercollegiate Socialist Society, an offspring of the Fabian movement.

The American movement seized upon some of the teachings of John Dewey, who, as Mr. Sargent put it,

> expounded a principle which has become destructive of traditions and has created the difficulties and the confusion, much of it, that we find today. Professor Dewey denied that there was any such thing as absolute truth, that everything was relative, everything was doubtful, that there were no basic values and nothing which was specifically true.

Mr. Sargent added that, with this philosophy,

> * * * you automatically wipe the slate clean, you throw historical experience and background to the wind and you begin all over again, which is just exactly what the Marxians want someone to do.

This rejection of tradition carried with it an undermining of the doctrine of inalienable rights and the theory of natural law which underlie our system of government. It has become intrinsic in the "liberal" philosophy which assumed the Dewey point of view that, while there may be fundamental rights which are sacred, they are subject to constant review. In any event, proceeds this approach, some are not as sacred as others, whether or not they may be listed together in the Declaration of Independence and the original Constitution or its amendments. Certainly these "liberals" believe that the right to private property is only a second-class right, or maybe third-class.

Mr. Sargent very persuasively told the story of the growth of the radical movement in education. The Dewey philosophy took hold just about the time John D. Rockefeller established his first foundation, The General Education Board, in 1902. The era was one of reform agitation, and there is no doubt that much reform was needed in various directions. But the moderate and sensible reformers of the era were very often overwhelmed, and to some extent seduced, by a small army of Socialists, crypto-Socialists, and collectivists who took advantage of the necessary reform movement to propel their own radical philosophies and theories of government. These found grist for their mills in the teachings of John Dewey. As Mr. Sargent said, they took advantage "of the existing discontent to make considerable inroads in academic fields."

The National Education Association became enamored early of the Dewey philosophy. It was at Columbia University, however, the institution in which Professor Dewey taught so long, that perhaps the greatest strides were made in applying this philosophy to teaching. In 1916 the Department of Educational Research was established in Teachers College (part of Columbia University). This department was responsible for the creation of The Lincoln School in 1917, which, to use the words of a Teachers College pamphlet, "kindled the fire which helped to spread progressive education."

The same pamphlet* noted that John D. Rockefeller, through The International Education Board, donated $100,000 to establish an International Institute at Teachers College. It noted as well that a Dr. George S. Counts had been made associate Director of the Institute, and Dr. Counts became one of the leading radicals in education.

The growing radicalism which was beginning rapidly to permeate academic circles was no grass-roots movement. Mr. Sargent cited a statement by Professor Ludwig Von Mises that socialism does not spring from the masses but is instigated by intellectuals "that form themselves into a clique and bore from within and operate that way. * * * It is not a people's movement at all. It is a capitalization on the people's emotions and sympathies toward a point these people wish to reach."

* Reece Committee *Report,* pp. 147-149.

CARNEGIE FINANCES A SOCIALIST CHARTER FOR EDUCATION

Mr. Sargent gave convincing evidence that efforts to use the schools to bring us to a new order, collectivist in nature, followed a plan and that this plan was supported by foundation money. He cited the *Conclusions and Recommendations* of the Commission on Social Studies of The American Historical Association.* The American Historical Association is the professional association of historians and as such one of the organizations participating in The Social Science Research Council. The work of its Commission was financed by The Carnegie Corporation to the extent of $340,000. The *Conclusions* was the last section of the Commission's final report, produced in 1934. It had an enormous and lasting impact upon education in our country.

The *Conclusions* heralds the decline of capitalism in the United States. It does not oppose the movement for radical change. It accepts it as inevitable:

> Cumulative evidence supports the conclusion, that, in the United States as in other countries, the age of individualism and laissez faire in economy and government is closing and that a *new age of collectivism* is emerging. [Emphasis supplied.]

* *Ibid.,* p. 137 *et seq.* In one of his speeches in Congress, Mr. Reece referred to a "conspiracy," and his use of this term brought down on his head the anger and ridicule of the "liberal" press. While the term was a strong one, Mr. Reece had some justification for using it. Since the preparation of my manuscript, a book has appeared, a reading of which leads one to the conclusion that there was, indeed, something in the nature of an actual conspiracy among certain leading educators in the United States to bring about socialism through the use of our school systems. (The book is *Bending The Twig,* by Augustin C. Rudd, published in 1957 by The Heritage Foundation, Inc., a most admirable and illuminating work.) To the extent that the movement to suborn our schools was heavily financed by leading foundations, through the Lincoln School, the Progressive Education Association, the John Dewey Society, units of the National Education Association, and other organizations, these foundations must be held largely accountable for the success of the movement. It is impossible to believe that the countless public utterances of some of these organizations and their leaders which made their program utterly clear, did not penetrate into the administrative consciousness of the managers of the foundations which subsidized them.

But that is not all. It continues:

> As to the specific form which this "collectivism," this integration and interdependence, is taking and will take in the future, the evidence at hand is by no means clear or unequivocal. It may involve the limiting or supplanting of private property by public property or it may entail the preservation of private property, extended and distributed among the masses. Most likely, it will issue from a process of experimentation and will represent a composite of historic doctrines and social conceptions yet to appear. Almost certainly it will involve a larger measure of compulsory as well as voluntary cooperation of citizens in the conduct of the complex national economy, a corresponding enlargement of the functions of government, and an increasing state intervention in fundamental branches of economy previously left to the individual discretion and initiative—a state intervention that in some instances may be direct and mandatory and in others indirect and facilitative. In any event the Commission is convinced *by its interpretation of available empirical data* that the actually integrating economy of the present day is the forerunner of a consciously integrated society in which individual economic actions and individual property rights will be altered and abridged. [Emphasis supplied.]

* * *

> The emerging age is particularly an age of transition. It is marked by numerous and severe tensions arising out of the conflict between the actual trend toward integrated economy and society, on the one side, and the traditional practices, dispositions, ideas and institutional arrangements inherited from the *passing age of individualism,* on the other. In all the recommendations that follow, the transitional character of the present epoch is recognized. [Emphasis supplied.]

* * *

Underlying and illustrative of these tensions are privation in the midst of plenty, violations of fiduciary trust, gross inequalities in income and wealth, widespread racketeering and banditry, wasteful use of natural resources, unbalanced distribution and organization of labor and leisure, the harnessing of science to individualism in business enterprise, the artificiality of political boundaries and divisions, the subjection of public welfare to the egoism of private interests, the maladjustment of production and consumption, persistent tendencies toward economic instability, disproportionate growth of debt and property claims in relation to production, deliberate destruction of goods and withdrawal of efficiency from production, accelerating tempo of panics, crises, and depressions attended by ever-wider destruction of capital and demoralization of labor, struggles among nations for markets and raw materials leading to international conflicts and wars.

The report of the Commission proceeds to say that we must make an "adjustment" between "social thought, social practice, and economic realities" or "sink back" into a *primitive* form of life. This adjustment must be made, apparently, in some collectivist manner, for the report, continuing, says that there are many varied theories to use, "involving wide differences in modes of *distributing* wealth, income, and cultural opportunities." I have italicized the verb "distributing," which forcefully disclosed the collectivist, planned economy objectives of the authors of the report.

But no inferences regarding their intention are needed. They were utterly frank in their recommendations. Teachers must "free the school from the domination of special interests and convert it into a truly enlightened force in society." And the "board of education" must have as its objective *"to support a school program conceived in terms of the general welfare and adjusted to the needs of an epoch marked by transition to some form of socialized* *economy."* * The Commission then discusses "the lines along which attacks can and will be made on the problem of applying its conclusions with respect to instruction in the social sciences." And the "pay-off:"

> As often repeated, the first step is to awaken and consolidate leadership around the philosophy and purpose of education herein expounded * * *.†

This was a call to the teachers in America to condition our children to an acceptance of a new order in process of transition. As to the nature of this intended order, there can be no doubt. Professor Harold J. Laski, philosopher of British socialism, said of the Commission's report:

> AT BOTTOM, AND STRIPPED OF ITS CAREFULLY NEUTRAL PHRASES, THE REPORT IS AN EDUCATIONAL PROGRAM FOR A SOCIALIST AMERICA.‡

Mr. Sargent's comment upon the report, produced by Carnegie Corporation money, is highly significant:

> What these gentlemen propose to do is set forth in their chapter at the end talking about next steps. It says that it is first to awaken and consolidate leadership around the philosophy and purpose of education expounded in the report. That *The American Historical Association* in cooperation with the *National Council on the Social Studies* has arranged to take over the magazine, *The Outlook,* as a social science journal for teachers. That writers of textbooks are to be expected to revamp and rewrite their old works in accordance with this frame of reference. That makers of programs in social sciences in cities and towns may be expected to evaluate the findings. That it is not too much to expect in the near future a decided shift in emphasis from mechan-

---

* Emphasis supplied.
† Reece Committee *Report,* p. 139.
‡ *Ibid.,* p. 141.

ics and methodology to the content and function of courses in the social studies. That is the gist of it.

This report became the basis for a definite slanting in the curriculum by selecting certain historical facts and by no longer presenting others, * * *.*

Did The Carnegie Corporation denounce or renounce this call for a socialization of America? Indeed no. Its 1933-1934 Annual Report said this:

> * * * Both the educational world and the public at large owe a debt of gratitude both to the Association for having sponsored this important and timely study in a field of peculiar difficulty, and to the distinguished men and women who served upon the Commission.†

This reaction of The Carnegie Corporation is most astounding. In his statement to the Reece Committee, Mr. Charles Dollard, the president of this foundation, contended that the *Conclusions* and *Recommendations* of the Commission on the Social Sciences do "not advocate socialism." He said that what the authors were accepting was "not socialism. It was the New Deal." He attributes their attitude to widespread disillusionment concerning our economic system, prevalent during the years of depression. He makes the further apology that once the funds had been granted, the Foundation did not have "the power to censor or rewrite the works produced under its grants." He takes the position that "works will be supported by corporation (foundation) grants containing views that differ from those held by trustees and officers."

Mr. Dollard does not explain the commendatory remarks of the Carnegie foundation after the publication of the last volume of the Commission's report. Nor does he convincingly absolve the foundation from responsibility for the Commission's work. The grant was not one for scientific research, but one essentially for the development of new principles in education. As such, it supported

---

* *Ibid.,* p. 153.
† *Ibid.,* p. 141.

the formulation of a philosophical value system, based on *a priori* assumptions of goals of education and desirable forms of government and social organization. Such a system might well be supported by reference to facts in the manner in which Aristotle's *Rhetorik* advises the use of facts for the end of persuasion. But the basing of principles on *a priori* value concepts is meta-scientific. The work of the Commission was not a scientific search but an effort to persuade America in favor of a new ideal in public life and in education. The support of this project was essentially political.

Mr. Dollard's emphatic denial of the partisan-Socialistic character of the *Conclusions* and *Recommendations* of the Commission could mislead only those who had not read the work itself. He may attempt to identify the concepts of society contained in it as "New Deal," and it is true that some of the Socialist convictions disseminated by the document were shared by the fathers of the New Deal. But the overlapping of the Socialist ideas of the Commission with the New Deal did not absolve the financial supporters of responsibility for this political undertaking. It is clearly desirable that foundations abstain from tampering with scientific research once a grant has been made to an unpolitical scientific organization. When, however, foundation money is offered for a program of a politico-social nature, responsibility for its impact on society cannot be dodged by a semantic manipulation of terms such as "socialism" and "New Deal." It is not the proper work of any foundation to promote the "New Deal" or any other political deal.

There was consistency in the position of Mr. Dollard in defending the Commission's work, in supporting the selection of Stuart Chase and of Dr. Myrdal, and in supporting *The Encyclopedia of the Social Sciences* after its bias became well known. It seems fair to conclude that this consistency had at its base a sympathy for the political objectives which these activities furthered.

One may wonder how it came about that foundations such as Carnegie and Rockefeller, controlled by trustees whose membership was overwhelmingly conservative, could lend themselves to the radical movement in education. One answer I have already given: they left decisions far too often to subordinate employees and to intermediary organizations. Another is that they were totally unaware of the pitfalls in the projects which they financed. Foundation apologists explain it differently. They say that these foundations made grants to respectable organizations and for respectable purposes; having done so, they were obliged to keep their hands off; therefore, they cannot be held accountable for what was produced.

This justification of foundation trustees cannot be accepted by reasonable persons. As I have pointed out, there is an obligation to make sure that objectivity would accompany the operation of a proposed grant. What is equally important—*there is an obligation to examine the product and, if it is found to lack objectivity, to take means to protect the public against its effects.*

The trustees of *The Carnegie Corporation* were acting in a field in which they had only limited competence when they authorized the heavy grant which produced the report of the *Commission on Social Studies.* Granting, for the sake of argument, that they had the right, nevertheless, to take what risks to society were involved, their failure to repudiate the result was a dereliction of duty. Upon learning that this product was "an educational program for a Socialist America," they might have offset whatever negligence or incompetence was connected with the creation of the project, by organizing another project, with at least equal financing, to be made by a group of eminent educators who believed that our governmental and economic system was worthy of preservation and that the schools should not be used as political propaganda machines.

THE RADICAL EDUCATORS
The report of the Reece Committee referred to numbers of the educational élite who supported and followed the plan laid down by the Carnegie-financed Commission on Social Studies. They were all, in various ways, connected with the educational complex

supported by the millions of the Rockefeller, Carnegie, and other foundations.

Among the favorites of this foundation-supported radical movement in education was Professor George S. Counts, a leader in the project to use the schools to reform our political and social order. A pamphlet entitled "A Call to the Teachers of the Nation," published by The Progressive Education Association, a tax-exempt organization largely supported by major foundations, was prepared by a committee of which Dr. Counts was Chairman. It included this "call":

> The progressive minded teachers of the country must unite in a powerful organization militantly devoted to the building of a better social order, in the defence of its members against the ignorance of the masses and the malevolence of the privileged. Such an organization would have to be equipped with the material resources, the talent, the legal talent, and the trained intelligence to wage successful war in the press, the courts, and the legislative chambers of the nation. To serve the teaching profession in this way should be one of the major purposes of the Progressive Education Association.*

In one of his many radical books, *Dare the School Build a New Social Order* (John Day Company, 1932), Professor Counts said:

> That the teachers should deliberately reach for power and then make the most of their conquest is my firm conviction. To the extent that they are permitted to fashion the curriculum and the procedures of the school they will definitely and positively influence the social attitudes, ideals and behavior of the coming generation.

He continued, that a "major concern" of teachers should be "opposing and checking the forces of social conservatism and reaction."

* *Ibid.,* p. 151.

Another professor of education named in the Committee's Report is Professor Theodore Brameld of New York University, who minced no words in an article in *Science and Society:*

> The thesis of this article is simply that liberal educators who look toward collectivism as a way out of our economic, political and cultural morass must give more serious consideration than they have thus far to the methodology of Marx * * *.*

Professor Brameld, along with Dr. Gunnar Myrdal, was among those "experts" cited by the Supreme Court in the *Brown v. Board of Education* segregation decision. These are strange authorities for the Supreme Court to rely upon. That many men such as these (politicians in educators' clothing) have achieved such prominence may be laid closely at the door of foundation support.

Another of these "educators" gives us an idea of how close they come to totalitarianism. In an article in *The Progressive Education Magazine,* Professor Norman Woelfel wrote:

> It might be necessary paradoxically for us to control our press as the Russian press is controlled and as the Nazi press is controlled.†

Professor Woelfel felt strongly that the élite in the social sciences should reform the world. His *Moulders of the American Mind* was dedicated to

> the teachers of America, active sharers in the building of attitudes, may they collectively choose a destiny which honors only productive labor and promotes the ascendency of the common man over the forces that make possible an economy of plenty.‡

And, like so many of his kind, he is against tradition and against codes of morality. He wrote:

* *Ibid.,* p. 152.
† *Ibid.,* p. 153.
‡ *Ibid.,* p. 143.

The younger generation is on its own and the last thing that would interest modern youth is the salvaging of the Christian tradition. The environmental controls which technologists have achieved, and the operations by means of which workers earn their livelihood, need no aid or sanction from God nor any blessing from the church.

*　*　*

In the minds of the men who think experimentally, America is conceived as having a destiny which bursts the all too obvious limitations of Christian religious sanctions and of capitalist profit economy.*

Elsewhere he wrote:

The call now is for the utmost capitalization of the discontent manifest among teachers for the benefit of revolutionary social goals. This means that all available energies of radically inclined leaders within the profession should be directed toward the building of a united radical front. Warm collectivistic sentiment and intelligent vision, propagated in clever and undisturbing manner by a few individual leaders no longer suits the occasion.†

The educators of whom we speak were leaders in their field, prominent in the counsels of that most powerful organization of teachers, The National Education Association, which advertised itself as "THE ONLY ORGANIZATION THAT REPRESENTS OR HAS THE POSSIBILITY OF REPRESENTING THE GREAT BODY OF TEACHERS IN THE UNITED STATES." ‡

THE PROGRESSIVE EDUCATION ASSOCIATION

Quotations already given from publications of the Progressive Education Association will indicate its character. Had it been de-

* *Ibid.*, p. 144.
† *Ibid.*, p. 145.
‡ *Ibid.*, p. 146.

voted entirely to improving educational methods, it might have served a worthy purpose in education. Its leaders, however, were devoted not only to new methods of teaching (many of these methods, found to be entirely impractical, have since been abandoned) but also to following the thesis of the Commission on Social Studies that educators must use the schools to indoctrinate youth into an acceptance of collectivism. Its periodical, *The Social Frontier,* of October, 1934, stated in an editorial, that it "accepts the analysis of the current epoch—outlined—in Conclusions and Recommendations, Report on the Social Studies of the Commission of the American Historical Association."

Its sinews of war were supplied by foundations. Up to 1943, says the Reece Committee report, foundations had contributed $4,257,800 to this Association. What the aggregate figure is to date, I do not know. During its long and intense career, the Progressive Education Association, which later changed its name to the American Education Fellowship, created an unenviable record of leftist propaganda. Its publications, called at various times *The Social Frontier, Frontiers of Democracy,* and *Progressive Education,* contain a long record of attempts to suborn our educational system to an acceptance of radicalism.

Typical is the issue of December 15, 1942, in which Professor Harold Rugg, of Teachers College, Columbia University, contributed a "call to arms." He announced the Battle for Consent. The "consent" was the consent of the people to change. His theory was simple. Education must be used to condition the people to accept social change. The social change was to be that, of course, espoused by Professor Rugg, involving a war against some of our most precious institutions.

THE COLLECTIVIST TEXTBOOKS

There were plenty of teachers ready to follow the lead of the American Historical Association's Commission on Social Studies, and their efforts extended into all aspects of education. New textbooks were required to take the place of the standard and objective works used in the schools. These new books could be used to indoctrinate the students, to give them the pathological view of their country upon which sentiment for collectivism could be built. The writer of a conservative or classic textbook has difficulty getting the funds to enable him to produce his work. At best he must rely on an advance from a publisher, and it is rarely that even a slim one might be forthcoming. In contrast, a foundation-supported textbook writer, as a rule, can apply a substantial part of his time, or all of it, to his writing. Moreover, the very fact of foundation support (or the support of an intermediary distributing organization) for his project, and the consequent inference of approval, will create a favorable climate of opinion for the acceptance of his work by schools. At least before the recent Congressional investigations, radical writers found it a simple matter to get foundation bounty. Under the influence of cliques in the world of teaching, the schools in the United States were flooded with books which disparaged the free-enterprise system and American traditions.

The notorious Rugg textbooks were of this class. They were prepared by Professor Harold Rugg, who began, in the Lincoln Experimental School, financed by Rockefeller foundations, to issue pamphlets which grew into this series of textbooks. Five million copies of the books were poured into American schools up to 1940—how many since, I do not know. They were finally banned from the schools in the State of California after a panel of competent men appointed by the San Francisco Board of Education unanimously held them reprehensible. One of the reasons given by this panel was that these books promoted the thesis that "it is one of the functions of the schools, indeed it appears at the time to be the chief function, to plan the future of society. From this view we emphatically dissent." The panel's report continued:

> Moreover, the books contain a constant emphasis on our national defects. Certainly we should think it a great mistake to picture our nation as perfect or flawless either in its past or in its present, but it is our conviction that these

books give a decidedly distorted impression through over-stressing weaknesses and injustices. They therefore tend to weaken the student's love for his country, respect for its past and confidence in its future.

Mr. McKinnon, one of the panel, added that these books denied moral law; that Professor Rugg was trying to achieve "a social reconstruction through education"; and that they promoted change as apparently desirable in itself, and "experiment" in government, education, economics, and family life as of paramount importance. "Throughout the books," he said, "runs an antireligious bias." *

Let us take a closer look at Professor Rugg. In his book *Great Technology*,† Rugg, who had visited China the previous year on a mission to prepare a "social reconstruction and education" project for that country, said:

> Can independent ways of living be carried on any longer on an irresponsible competitive basis? Must not central public control be imposed on the warring, self-aggrandizing captains of industry? Can this control be set up with the *consent of a large minority of the people* quickly enough to forestall the imposition of dictatorship either by business leaders or by an outraged proletarian agriculture bloc, which seems imminent?

He asked these questions not about China but about the United States!

Millions of textbooks written by this man were used, at one time, in our country. In his *Great Technology*, his *Social Chaos and the Public Mind*,‡ and other works, he advocated social change. Following the *Recommendations* of the Carnegie-financed Commission on the Social Studies, he suggested that such change required the indoctrination of our youth through the

* Report, pp. 149-150.
† John Day, 1933.
‡ John Day, 1933.

schools. He recommended that social science be the "core of school curriculum" to bring about a climate of opinion favorable to his philosophy.

Through the efforts of this and other followers of the *Recommendations,* and through the operation of the patronage network of Teachers College of Columbia University, the educational philosophy which Professor Rugg espoused soon pervaded the American school system. This philosophy involves:

> implementing an expectancy of change; picturing the America of today as a failure; disparaging the American Constitution and the motives of the Founders of the Republic; and presenting a "New Social Order."

Professor Rugg characteristically advocated production for use, not for profit (that old Socialist slogan); reconstruction of the national economic system to provide for central controls, to guarantee a stable and a high minimum living for all; division of the social income, so as to guarantee at least a ten times 1929 minimum for all; measuring wages by some yardstick of purchasing power; reeducation of the "parasitic" middleman in our economy and his reassignment to productive work; recognition that educators are a group "vastly superior to that of a priesthood or of any other selected social class." "Our task," he said, was "to create swiftly a compact body of minority opinion for the scientific reconstruction of our social order. This body of opinion must be made articulate and be brought to bear insistently upon the dictators of legislative and executive action. The alternative to this extension of democracy is revolution." *

In 1941 Professor Rugg denied vehemently that he was a Socialist or that he had ever been one. However, in 1936 he had been a member of a committee of 500 supporting the Socialist candidacy of Norman Thomas. He was a director of The League for Industrial Democracy in 1934-1935. But no collateral evidence of his political position is necessary to disclose his Socialistic point

* See *Undermining Our Republic,* Guardians of American Education, 1941.

of view. He has stated it himself in his numerous writings. His employment of the Socialist plank "production for use, not for profit" is quite enough to identify him.

A group of "liberal" educators defended the Rugg textbooks. Prominent among these was Professor Robert S. Lynd, a former permanent secretary of The Social Science Research Council, himself an advocate of change toward socialism. Professor Rugg was also defended by a number of members of the Committee on Textbooks of the American Committee for Democracy and Intellectual Freedom.

The money for Professor Rugg's six textbooks came indirectly from Rockefeller foundation grants to the Lincoln School and Teachers College. While foundations approached in 1922 had refused direct support of the pamphlets, Professor Rugg reports* that preliminary estimates set the amount of money required at a sum far beyond that which the Lincoln School or Teachers College could be asked to supply. They did, however, support the project in other and altogether indispensable ways. In fact, if they had not given it an institutional connection and a home, no such undertaking could have been started. Even their financial contribution, however, was considerable. It consisted of the writer's salary as educational psychologist in the school (1920-1929) and as professor of education in the college, the salary of his secretary (1920-1930), and an allowance for a part-time assistant during several years.

Mr. Aaron Sargent also testified in detail regarding the *Building America* textbook series, which the Reece Committee report characterized as another "attempt by radical educators financed by foundations to suborn the schools." † It was The General Education Board, a Rockefeller foundation, which provided over $50,-000 for the production of these books, taken over and intensively promoted by The National Education Association.

The State of California barred these books also from its schools, after a legislative committee, the Dilworth Committee, investi-

---

* *Building a Science of Society for the Schools,* 1934, p. 10.
† Reece Committee *Report,* p. 154.

gated and concluded in its report that they were subtle attempts to play up Marxism and to destroy our traditions.

Mr. Sargent pointed out that there had been a "blackout" in history teaching in California for about twelve years; during this time no history textbooks were provided by the Department of Education, which was operating under the radical-devised scheme of "social studies." After an investigation, history books were again furnished, as the law required. In the meantime, the *Building America* books largely took their place, giving children distorted facts and consciously directed misinformation regarding our history and our society.

The report of the Dilworth Committee, as a result of which the California Legislature refused any appropriation for the purchase of *Building America* textbooks, concluded that these books do "not present a true historical background of American history and progress, and that the cartoons and pictures appearing in said books belittle American statesmen, who have been upheld as heroes of American tradition and have been idealized by the American people; yet on the other hand the 'Building America' series glamorizes Russian statesmen and [is] replete with pictures which do great credit to these leaders of Russian thought." The report goes on to say that the "books contain purposely distorted references favoring Communism, and life in Soviet Russia, in preference to the life led by Americans."

In this regard, the Committee felt that pictures representing conditions of starvation among American families hardly presented a true picture of family life in America. When children in the 7th and 8th grades, the Committee said, compare such pictures with the illustrations of Russian family life, they will conclude that family life in Russia is equal or even preferable to that in the United States." It was found that the "books paint present economic and social conditions in America in an unfavorable light and have the opportunity to propagandize class warfare and class distinction." It was concluded, further, that the texts present a materialistic picture of government and economy in America and in the world rather than the idealism of the American way of life. Specific criticism was made of the reference books listed in the *Building America* pamphlets as guides to additional information. These recommended books were found to be highly biased and likely to indoctrinate pupils in a manner contrary to the best traditions of America.

The editors and authors of the *Building America* series were careful enough to present both sides of various problems and questions. This was done, however, in most instances, in a manner strongly indicating editorial bias in favor of Socialist measures and ideas, a preference emphasized by the editors who selected the illustrations. The pictures were likely to impress children even more than the text itself and were selected clearly to arouse doubts about American institutions and American historical figures.

The pamphlet about Russia contains numerous propaganda pictures from Soviet information sources. The "objectivity" of the authors may be illustrated by their statement: "The Russians liked our system of government no better than we liked theirs." This implies that there is much to be said on both sides. It also assumes an absurdity—that the suppressed Russians, unable to speak their minds, favor the system which has been imposed on them.

The Bolshevik revolution and regime are presented as a blessing to the Russian people. In the description of the long road which led to communism, there is not one word of fact or criticism regarding the murderous Red terror of 1917 and 1918, or the treachery of communism in destroying the hopes of Russia's democratic revolutionaries. Conditions in Russia are presented wholly in terms of Soviet apology. There is a chapter on making the State safe for socialism, including this: "Probably no other nation ever made such rapid strides in extending educational opportunities for the people." The depicted image of social progress contains no word of reference to the obliteration of freedom, to the concentration camps, to the purges and to the worldwide, Moscow-directed subversive activities.

Pictures of everyday Soviet life present scenes in a church, in art galleries, in concert halls, and at a meeting of a Soviet "trade union"—the whole gamut of Red propaganda of the period. "As more consumer goods were produced and the scheme for buying and selling improved," it said, the wants of consumers were more satisfied. There is no mention, however, of the actual tragic dearth of consumer goods, even before the German attack; there is nowhere a picture of the privation of the Russian people under communism.

Nor is this all. Fearful lest statements by outsiders might disillusion the child readers of these books about Russia, the authors are careful to prepare a defense. "*Some* writers mention *some* use of force by the government to attain its ends." (I have emphasized the double use of "some.") Yes, *some* writers mention a denial of the right to strike or protest; secret police; the absolute power of one man over the lives of the people; and the lack of any civil liberties in the American sense of the word—but the authors imply that there is another sense, a Soviet sense of civil liberties. The Russians, say the authors, have more self-government than they ever had before; *the new Russians* call their dictatorship the "democracy" of the working classes; there is no more discrimination against certain races and creeds; etc. etc. etc. The authors have the effrontery to say that "rights that mean so much to Americans—freedom of assembly and the press—are little missed in Russia * * * to them [the Russians] the new leadership is better than the old." They indicate also that, though it does not appeal to Americans, the Russian system is here to stay.

The Dilworth report said of the book on China: "This book is peculiarly useful to the Communists as a medium to further disseminate the current party line concerning conditions in China." The pamphlet on civil liberties contains pictures of Sacco and Vanzetti, of the Scopes trial, of Browder, of the Scottsboro Negroes, of strike riots being subdued. The whole collection, in spite of its pretended objectivity, is loaded with "liberal" propaganda. It is a reminder of the "Aesopian" language used by Communists in their communication system.

It is difficult to believe that The Rockefeller Foundation and the National Education Association could have supported these textbooks. But the fact is that Rockefeller financed them and the NEA promoted them very widely. They were still in use in some parts of the country at the time of the Reece Committee investigation.

Another foundation-supported piece of "education" literature is a pamphlet entitled "The American Way of Business." It was one of a series prepared by the National Association of Secondary School Principals and the National Council for Social Studies, both branches of the National Education Association, under a grant from the Rockefeller General Education Board, to provide teachers with source material on some social problems. Who wrote it? Oscar Lange and Abba P. Lerner. Mr. Lange will be remembered as the professor at the University of Chicago, when Dr. Hutchins was its president, who later renounced his American citizenship to accept appointment as the ambassador to the United Nations from Communist Poland. Mr. Lerner has been a collectivist for a long time.

This book gives our children such ideas as these:

> Public enterprise must become a major constituent of our economy, if we are really going to have economic prosperity.
>
> * * *
>
> It is necessary to have public ownership of banking and credit (investment banks and insurance companies).
>
> * * *
>
> * * * it is necessary to have public ownership of monopolistic key industries.
>
> * * *
>
> It is necessary to have public ownership of basic natural resources (mines, oil fields, timber, coal, etc.)
>
> * * *
>
> * * * in order to insure that the public corporations act in accordance with the competitive "rules of the game," a

special economic court (enjoying the same independence as the courts of justice) might be established * * * and that the economic court be given the power to repeal any rules of Congress, of legislatures, or of the municipal councils. * * * "*

These texts, financed by The Rockefeller Foundation and distributed by the National Education Association, must have influenced the thinking of hundreds of thousands of defenseless young Americans. They may well have contributed to the recent philosophy of reckless public spending and overgrowth of government.

These books I have mentioned are but a few examples of what has happened to teaching materials in our schools and colleges. Professor E. Merrill Root gives a quick survey of this development in his *Collectivism on the Campus*,† in which he includes a chapter entitled, "The State Liberals: Their Textbooks." The rise of communism, he says, has produced a strange result among the textbook writers. Conservatism is not even given house room. Communism is disliked, but the only alternative offered is "some such appeasement as welfarism or Fabian socialism." He quotes Professor David McCord Wright of McGill University:

> What sometimes happens, for instance, in economics courses, is that the Marxian indictment is presented, followed by some sort of "social-democratic" or heavily interventionist answer, and that the capitalist case never gets heard at all.

The vast majority of textbooks now used in colleges and schools on subjects in which a political slant could be given are heavily slanted to the left. This was demonstrated by Professor A. H. Hobbs of the University of Pennsylvania, whose work in disclosing some of the vices and foibles of modern sociology earned for him martyrdom in his career. In his analysis of a great number of sociology textbooks in his book *The Claims of Sociology: A Critique of Textbooks*, he found (p. 157):

* *Ibid.*, pp. 155-156.
† Devin-Adair, 1955. See also, *Bending the Twig*, by Augustin C. Rudd.

Inclusion of a chapter on social change is an integral part of the system of sociology textbooks. Such chapters * * * are designed to leave students with favorable final impressions about the subject. After depressing the student with portrayals of the amount of unemployment, poverty, crime, vice, and slums; after shocking him with descriptions of the insidious war propaganda and the horrors of war; after creating in him qualms about the amount of social disorganization and raising him to rebellion against the "dead hand of the past" upon society, the author of contemporary texts must assuage him. Mitigation of the depressive effects of horrendous description of social evils is attained in a chapter which is "constructive" "optimistic" "positive" and "looking - beyond - social - defects - of - the - present - toward - a-bright-future-which-we-can-make-for-ourselves" in outlook.

In seventy out of eighty-three texts, Dr. Hobbs found sections devoted to social change. "There is agreement that traditions, conventions, and social inertia are the principal obstacles to social progress. . . . Authors in sociology texts increasingly emphasize economic security as a fundamental social value and the principal goal toward which social change should be focused." Twenty-seven textbook authors call for the use of the social sciences in a program of social planning. As used in these texts, the term "planning" or "social engineering" involves control of social processes by long-range subjection of society to guidance by social scientists.

Dr. Hobbs formulates the attitudes of the majority of the sociology textbooks currently in use with these words:

Educational practices and principles which involve discipline or drill, and the teaching of traditional beliefs about the government, the family, or the economic system are inefficient and harmful. These should be replaced by including educational programs which will train students to think for themselves and to behave only in accordance with self-derived principles of "rationality." Independent think-

ing will emancipate student personalities from the stultify-
ing effects of traditional beliefs and enable them to adjust
to existing social situations and to promote social change.

Democracy is highly desirable but the present form of
government is not democratic, principally because business
interests exert too much control over it. * * * Increased
government control over business and industry is the most
important step toward attainment of the political ends,
but such controls constitute only one phase of broader social
planning.

Maldistribution of wealth and income and unemployment
are the outstanding characteristics of our social system.

It is no wonder that some of our citizens, facing the political
character of so much of what purports to be sociological teaching,
have difficulty distinguishing among the terms "sociology," "the
social sciences," and "socialism."

REFERENCE WORKS

To both teacher and student, reference works are important instruments in the educational process. We have already seen that
the all-important *Encyclopedia of the Social Sciences,* created
under foundation financing, was heavily slanted toward radicalism. Let us look at another reference work, *The Encyclopedia
Americana.*

Financed by The Rockefeller Foundation, both Columbia University and Cornell University established courses described as
an "Intensive Study of Contemporary Russian Civilization." It
was chiefly to the staffs of these projects that the editors of *The
Encyclopedia Americana* turned to write its section on Soviet
Russia. A *dramatis personae* of this venture included such deeply
biased workers as these:

> Sir Bernard Pares (who opposed American help to Greece
> and Turkey and supported the claim of Soviet Russia
> to Constantinople);

Corliss Lamont (whose record of procommunism needs no elaboration);

Harriet L. Moore (named by Louis Budenz as a member of the Communist Party);

Vladimir D. Kazakevich (one of the editors of *Science and Society*, a Marxist quarterly; a frequent contributor to *Soviet Russia*, a pro-Communist publication. Mr. Kazakevich left the United States in 1949 after exposure as a Soviet agent).

and others of very doubtful objectivity.

When the work was completed, Cornell University was so pleased with it that, with the permission of the *Encyclopedia*, it converted the Russian section into a textbook, *USSR*, which was used at Cornell until 1954. In the meantime, many other colleges and universities had adopted it, including Columbia, Rutgers, Swarthmore, Chicago, Pennsylvania, Michigan, Southern California, Washington, and Yale.

At least 15 out of 20 contributors were, according to Professor Warren S. Walsh of Syracuse University, "pro-Soviet in varying degrees." About one third of the material in *USSR* was prepared by Mr. Kazakevich. That he could have been selected for this work was truly amazing. Professor E. Merrill Root, in his *Collectivism on the Campus* quotes these words from Mr. Kazakevich, appearing on February 27, 1940, in *Russky Golos:*

> The crocodiles of imperialism will continue to swallow everything they get. For the neutral countries today the English crocodile is more dangerous than the German one. In order to prevent the lawlessness of this crocodile, you've got to drive a pole into the back of its neck.

Professor Root continues, "Perhaps this chaste language seemed scholarly to the scholars of Cornell, for they invited Kazakevitch to lecture on the campus during the summer. His lectures became a part of *The Encyclopedia Americana* (as he was an 'expert in a special field') and of *USSR*."

Professor Roman Smal-Stocki of Marquette University has said of *USSR* that it is justly called a "fellow-traveling guide to the Soviet Union."

It may, of course, be true that The Rockefeller Foundation bears no direct responsibility for what was produced. Perhaps the projects which it financed were wholly desirable. Perhaps it was entirely the fault of Columbia and Cornell Universities that a strange collection of radicals and pro-Communists were included on the staffs of the Russian projects, and the fault of Cornell that it did not recognize or become concerned over the biased nature of the book which it published. But the fact remains that it all came about through Rockefeller financing. If this is in the nature of that "risk taking" which many foundation executives maintain is the duty of the modern foundation, something is badly wrong, somewhere.

I ask again: is it not the duty of a foundation which takes such risks to examine the results and to repudiate them if they have been unfortunate? As far as I know, The Rockefeller Foundation has done nothing to inform the public that it is not in sympathy with what its financing produced in this instance or in any other. Here, indeed, is a strange situation. Foundations consider themselves entitled to take credit for the outcome of a grant, the results of which are socially approved. On the other hand, when the grant has failed, or if its product meets with disapprobation, or is seriously questionable, then responsibility is shifted to the recipient of the grant. This is an odd interpretation of the "venture capital" concept. "We are entitled to take political 'risks' with the tax-exempt money we administer," say foundation managers. "If the project turns out safely, it is to our credit; if the risk turns out to have been too great, or if the result is an unhappy one, that is not our fault and we have no responsibility either to inform the public of the error or to take any steps to correct the injury done."

THE CITIZENS EDUCATION PROJECT

The Citizens Education Project was created at Teachers College of Columbia University under financing, far exceeding one million dollars, provided by The Carnegie Corporation. "That the *Project* was carried on with considerable bias to the left is unquestionable."* There arises, then, the question of responsibility. The Committee report stated that it was unable, without further inquiry, to determine whether this was the fault or the intention of either the Project managers or of the Carnegie foundation. It continued its comment, however, as follows:

> We do, however, see responsibility lodged with *The Carnegie Corporation*. It may not have had the duty to supervise the project or to direct it in transit—this may even have been unwise. But, as the project represented a substantial investment of public money and its impact on society could be very heavy, it seems clearly to have been the duty of *Carnegie* to examine what had been done and to repudiate it if it was against the public interest. This, as far as we know, *Carnegie* did not do.

What was the objective of this Project? To educate for better citizenship. How was this to be accomplished? One of its chief products was a card-index file. The cards summarized books, articles, films, etc., being arranged topically so that teachers could use the files in teaching citizenship. The files were sold to schools at nominal cost. In essence, this was "canned" material for teachers. The teacher did not have to read a book; he or she could just look in the card file and read a quick digest prepared by the Project. There is some doubt that this method of teaching through canned media is desirable. Granting that it might be, the greatest objectivity would have to be used in preparing the digests and comments on the cards, as well as in the selection of items to be included. As the Committee put it:

> * * * even those who believe in "canned" education cannot defend the slant with which this card system was devised, unless they believe that education should not be

* Reece Committee *Report*, p. 120.

unbiased but should be directed toward selected political ends, and radical ones at that.*

The Committee report gave several, out of many, examples of the radical slant. Books were included which could not be reasonably defended as proper for recommendation to school children—books by Communists and pro-Communists. Radical books were given approbation; conservative books were given the doubtful treatment. Let me give one illustration. *The Road to Serfdom*, by Frederick A. Hayek, a valuable commentary on the fallacies of socialism, is called "strongly opinionated." In contrast, the *Building America* textbooks, to which I have earlier referred, are described as "Factual, Ideals and Concepts of Democracy."

Many conservative books of importance were not even listed. But *A Mask for Privilege* by Carey McWilliams was described as "Historical, Descriptive." (Mr. McWilliams's record of Communist-front associations consume four pages of the Reece Committee report: 337 *et seq.*) *Rich Land, Poor Land* by Stuart Chase (whose collectivist position has been described earlier) was called "Descriptive, Factual, Illustrative." *Building for Peace at Home and Abroad* by Maxwell Stewart (whose Communist-front associations consume about five pages of the Reece Committee report: p. 375 *et seq.*) was labeled "Factual, Dramatic." And Howard Fast's *The American* was called "Historical, Bibliographical." † (Mr. Fast's Communist associations occupy four pages of the Committee report. He has since renounced the Party.)

SEVERAL SLOAN FOUNDATION PROJECTS

The Sloan Foundation, created in 1934, has had its regrettable moments. Its intention seems to have been to specialize in economic education and to seek truth through sound scholarship. But it supported the heavily left-slanted Chicago Round Table Broadcasts to the tune of $35,000 and the Public Affairs Pamphlets with $72,000. It supported a motion-picture-making program at

* *Ibid.*, p. 120.
† *Ibid.*, p. 121.

New York University which concentrated on presenting the darkest image of the backward hinterlands of the South, possibly to arouse compassion but more likely for propaganda purposes. It deserves credit for having supported the sound economic teaching program of Harding College. Whether it merits credit for having contributed $19,000 to the Lincoln School at Columbia University is questionable.

The Public Affairs Committee was directed by Maxwell Stewart, a one-time editor of the Communist English-language newspaper, *Moscow News*. Several witnesses have called Mr. Stewart a Communist,* but we do not know what his party allegiances were during his more than a decade of management of the Public Affairs pamphlets. They had a circulation of millions of copies among high-school and college students, among libraries, adult education groups, and government employees. Among the members of the board of directors of this publishing organization were such well-known "liberals" as Lyman Bryson, Luther Gulick, and Ordway Tead.

We find these names also: Frederick Vanderbilt Field, Mark Starr, and Harry W. Laidler, all of whom may be classed as extreme leftists. The presence of these names on the roster of any organization should have indicated to the Sloan trustees what the publishing venture was all about. Among the authors of the pamphlets we find Louis Adamic, James G. Patton, Maxwell Stewart, and E. C. Lindeman. Stewart wrote by far the largest number of the approximately one hundred pamphlets. The style of these books is reminiscent of the *Building America* textbooks. They show a pretense of objectivity, but in giving both sides of an issue they leave no doubt that they believe the left side is sound.

If my information is correct that The Sloan Foundation reorganized its management and deposed those who were responsible for its leftist orientation, there is ground for rejoicing and for hope that other foundations, whose trustees have lacked alertness in the past, may follow suit.

* See a description of Mr. Stewart's Communist-front associations, *ibid.*, pp. 375-379.

6   REVOLUTION IS NEARLY ACCOMPLISHED

THE THIRD AMERICAN REVOLUTION
"IN THE UNITED STATES we have had two violent revolutions: that which freed us from England and that which sought to divide us. I suggest we are now in the Third American Revolution, none the less serious because it is bloodless. * * * This new revolution is a reform movement gone wrong. It has become an attempt to institute the paternal state in which individual liberty is to be subordinated and forgotten in a misapplication of the theory of the greatest good for the greatest number." I wrote these words in an article published in the *American Bar Association Journal* of May 1953. My statement may not have been entirely accurate. Instead of saying we *are* in the Third Revolution, I might better have said that it is *nearly finished;* that all that can be hoped for is a counterrevolution.

"Liberals" have frequently announced that the revolution is *over.* So said Dr. Mortimer Adler, upon whose judgment The Ford Foundation (through its Fund for the Advancement of Education) relied so heavily as to put him in charge of the philosophical study of freedom, spending $600,000 on support of his philosophical education. Professor Seymour E. Harris of Harvard has put it this way:

> In the 20 years between 1933 and 1953, the politicians, college professors, and lawyers, with little help from business,

173

wrought a revolution in the economic polices of the United States.*

Professor Harris should have added that the revolution was materially aided by foundations.

Over the past few decades the major foundation complex has operated almost as an informal but integral arm of government, acting, to a very considerable extent, as its collateral "brain trust," and determining policy. If a revolution has indeed been accomplished in the United States, we can look here for its motivation, its impetus, and its rationale.

COMMUNIST PENETRATION OF FOUNDATIONS

A good part of the impetus of the "revolution" came from Marxists. To what extent some of it came from actual Communists, we shall probably never be able to piece together adequately—but there can be equally little doubt that much of it was Communist-inspired. The presence of so many disclosed Communists in government during the New Deal and Fair Deal eras makes this conclusion inevitable. There is, moreover, much evidence that Communists made substantial, direct inroads into the foundation world, using its resources to promote their ideology.

The Reece Committee has been castigated for asserting that subversive influences have played a part in the history of foundations in the United States. Yet it was its predecessor, the Cox Committee, which made this utterly plain, in so far as actual Communist penetration of foundations was concerned. That Committee produced evidence which supported its conclusion that there had been a Moscow-directed, specific plot to penetrate the American foundations and to use their funds for Communist propaganda and Communist influence upon our society. There was also evidence that this plot had succeeded in some measure.

We shall never know the full extent of this penetration, but testimony before the Cox Committee disclosed that The Marshall Field Foundation, The Garland Fund, The John Simon Guggen-

* Reece Committee *Hearings*, p. 628.

heim Foundation, The Robert Marshall Foundation, The Rosenwald Fund, and The Phelps Stokes Fund had been successfully
penetrated or used by Communists. The Marshall and Garland
foundations had, in fact, lost their tax exemptions. The Cox investigation also disclosed that almost a hundred discovered grants to
individuals and organizations with extreme leftist records or affiliations had been made by some of the more important foundations, including The Rockefeller Foundation, The Carnegie Corporation, The Carnegie Endowment for International Peace, The
John Simon Guggenheim Foundation, The Russell Sage Foundation, The William C. Whitney Foundation and The Marshall
Field Foundation.

One hundred grants were not many, compared with the total
grants of the foundations. But Professor Rowe made clear, in the
following testimony before the Reece Committee, first, that the
problem is qualitative and not quantitative; and, second, that
the aggregate effect of Communist penetration cannot be measured
by merely considering the number of direct grants to Communist
individuals*:

> *In much of the activity that has to do with identification of
> Communist activity in the United States, it has seemed to
> me that we are going off on the wrong track when we limit
> ourselves to efforts to identify overt Communists, or let us
> say organizational Communists, people who carry a card or
> who can be positively identified as members of an organiza-
> tion subject to organized discipline. For every one of those
> that you fail to identify, and it seems to me we even fail to
> identify most of those, there are a thousand people who
> could not possibly be identified as such, because they have
> never had any kind of organizational affiliation, but among
> those people are many people who advance the interests
> of world communism, in spite of the fact that they are not
> subject to discipline and do not belong to any organization.†*

* Reece Committee *Report*, pp. 199-200.
† Reece Committee *Report*, pp. 199-200.

* * * The people who can be trailed and tagged by the FBI are a very, very small minority. They occupy a very powerful position and a potentially important one, but the people who do the important work are unidentifiable, and if I were planning to infiltrate the United States, I would see to it that they were unidentifiable.

Here it seems to me you have to set up an entirely different category than the two categories of Communists on the one side, and other people on the other side.*

* * *

* * * I would like to add this regarding the IPR and regarding the problem of Far Eastern policy. You remember some of my earlier remarks about the state of Far Eastern studies in the United States 20 or 30 years ago, how I said there was practically none of it; how some of the foundations started to finance the building up and training of personnel. It seems to me this kind of thing has to be taken into account in evaluating foundation grants, namely, that the area of ignorance in the United States about Far Eastern matters was so great that here was the strategic place in which to strike at the security of the United States by people interested in imperiling our security and fostering the aims of world communism. They would naturally not pick the area in which we have the greatest intellectual capacities and in which we have the greatest capacities for defense. They would pick the area of greatest public ignorance, with the greatest difficulty of defending against the tactics of their attack, and so these people naturally poured into Far Eastern studies and exploited this area as the area in which they could promote the interests of world communism most successfully in the general ignorance and blindness of the American people.

So that it is not only quantitative evaluation that counts; it is not only the numbers of grants or the amounts of

* Reece Committee *Hearings*, p. 536. Emphasis supplied.

grants; it is the areas in which the grants are given that are significant. Here, you see, it seems to me, it takes a great deal of subject matter know-how—quite apart from dollars and cents—people and their affiliations or lack thereof, to evaluate the impact on this country of any given foundation grant, I don't care whether it is $50 or $5 million. It is a qualitative matter, not a quantitative matter.*

SOCIALIST PENETRATION

The two recent Congressional investigations were largely concerned with "subversion." The Cox Committee interpreted this term to include only international communism of the Stalinist brand and organized fascism. The Reece Committee, in the course of its work, came to give the term broader or deeper meaning. Neither investigation established sharply, however, the characteristics of Communist activity which would be clearly held to be subversive. In the public mind, the term "subversion" is generally confined to Moscow-directed Communist activity, or that of domestic Communists allied in an international conspiracy.

The emphasis on a search for organized Communist penetration of foundations absorbed much of the energy of the investigators and detracted somewhat from the efficacy of their general inquiry into "subversion." There are varieties of Communist sectarian programs and propaganda of a dissident nature, aside from those directed from Moscow. A follower of Trotsky's brand of communism may be no less a danger to our society because he opposes the current rulers of Russia. It is likely that there are more Trotsky followers in the United States than followers of the Kremlin. Even among the formerly orthodox supporters of the Party line, there has occurred a mass conversion to a domestic form of the Communist theory and method.

Moreover, it is difficult to mark the line beyond which "socialism" becomes "communism." The line may be between methods of assuming power, communism being distinguished from other forms of socialism by its intent upon establishing a dictatorship of the

* *Ibid.,* pp. 541-542.

proletariat. But this line is by no means clear. Socialism has the same ends as communism, though with an allegedly democratic approach. The Communist Manifesto of 1848 is the basis of all socialist parties the world over. Marx himself did not distinguish between socialism and communism. Both advocate centrally planned controls of production and consumption by the State, public ownership of the means of production, and confiscatory measures. They have in common the concept that, through a manipulation of public affairs, man can attain lasting happiness for all, can make want and misery disappear, can eradicate war, and can produce Paradise on earth. The major distinction between the two forms of socialism, as asserted by the Communists, is that they believe in the necessity of a temporary dictatorship of the proletariat before reaching the Golden Age of social justice and universal happiness.

America has had a long tradition of Socialist fads and has listened long to utopian arguments. In the 19th century there were numerous Socialist communities in the United States. Robert Owen, the founder of the cooperative movement and probably the most important of the pre-Marxian Socialists, addressed the Congress of the United States more than 125 years ago. He preached "production for use, instead of production for profits." He advanced the generally discredited theory of surplus value exploited by Marxism in calling the proletariat to arms in a class war held to be unavoidable.

The failure of our numerous experiments in communism has not ended a longing for better forms of social organization. This longing is evidenced in the ease with which preachers of utopian economic systems still gather large followings.

The mandates of both the Cox and Reece Committees went further than a mere exploration of "subversion." The Cox Committee was to inquire into activities which were not in the "interests or tradition of the United States"; the Reece Committee, into the support of "un-American activities." These terms are almost impossible to define with complete certainty. They can only be related to *a priori* standards of value, standards which cannot be arrived at through an empirical approach. There are conflicting ways in which historical facts can be interpreted to prove what the tradition of the United States may be. One can make a case for the claim that various types of sectarian socialism are traditionally characteristic of parts of our farm population. One can submit "proof" in the form of data about continued devotion to ideas originally promoted by early religious community settlements, and their survival in various forms of Federal farm support and soil-banking schemes. However, there was sufficient general clarity in the mandates of the two Committees for inquiry purposes. Socialism is basically antithetical to our system.

All Socialists do not recognize themselves as such. But it is, after all, their private affair. They are entitled to be Socialists if they care to, whether or not they are aware that socialism cannot exist without force and oppression, that it must otherwise fail for economic reasons. In a democracy, the citizen has the right to his reasonable mistakes, disastrous as they may be to the public welfare. The free contest of ideas would usually save us from such evils as doctrinaire socialism. But, in our country, the free market for ideas has rapidly declined. The one-sided support by foundations of the utopian Socialists has created a constricted and limited market place.

So the real problem which faced the two recent investigations was the imbalance in the struggle of ideas, created by the preference of foundation giving in the two decades from 1930 to 1950. The virulent criticism to which Congressional investigation of foundations has been subjected has perverted an investigation of this imbalance into an alleged attack on civil liberties.

The true problem is not whether Socialists or extreme "liberals" are respectable and entitled to their views but rather that their opponents have been discriminated against in the allotment of funds by major foundations. The ascendancy of Socialistic ideas is attributable, partly at least, to this foundation-created imbalance.

The Reece Committee did not disparage liberalism. It said: "We cannot too strongly state that this Committee respects the true liberal and deems him as important to the proper political functioning of our society as is the conservative." It did attack the kind of person who calls himself a "liberal" but is not. Such a "liberal," said the Committee, "travels *IN* if not *UNDER* the same direction" as communism—he may even be "a violent and inveterate opponent of communism," but he gives it support by falling into "the error of wishing to destroy before he knows the significance of that with which he wishes to replace."

And so, continued the Committee, the foundations have frequently been persuaded by these ardent men-in-a-hurry to use trust funds for "risk capital," without fairly measuring the social risk.

This "risk capital" concept, which has found such wide favor among major foundation executives, propels them "into a constant search for something new, a pathological scrutinizing of what we have, on the premise that there must be something better." There is much room for improvement in our society, but much of what we have is considered by the great majority of Americans sound and inviolate. The pathological "liberal" propulsion into taking social risks seems invariably to skip the study of what we have that is good and should be preserved; instead, it supports change for change's sake, or on the general theory that the different thing *must* be better.* Much of this "risk taking" assists communism.

That Socialistic ideas can be legally promoted in the United States, that prominent figures have openly adopted them in the disguise of "reform," does not make them any less "subversive." If one accepts the concepts and principles of the Declaration of Independence and the Constitution as expressions of the existing order, then any attempt to replace them with the concepts and principles of socialism must be considered "subversive" and "un-American." Moreover, there is continued danger that the Communist who has recently been converted over to what might be called simple socialism may switch back again in his allegiance. Many of the intellectuals who departed from communism did so because they disagreed with Stalin; some of these will still support

* **Reece** Committee *Report*, pp. 201-202.

communism of a variety differing only slightly from the old orthodoxy.

If any American should know how the Communists operate, it is J. Edgar Hoover. In an address in October 1955 Mr. Hoover said that the Communists do their most effective work through "fictitious liberals." These he defined as

> individuals who through insidiously slanted and sly propagandist writings and reports oppose urgently needed internal security measures; present the menace of communism as a myth of hysteria; urge that we tolerate the subversive acts of Communists because Communists are only "nonconformists"; pretend that the Communist Party is a political movement and that it is improper to consider it a criminal conspiracy to overthrow our government by force and violence.

Such ideas may be presented even by people of comparatively conservative leanings who fail to recognize the threat of socialism and its incompatibility with our Constitutional rights. The Reece Committee report gives an example of this process out of the mouth of Mr. Pendleton Herring, President of the extremely powerful Social Science Research Council. In an address to The American Political Science Association in 1953, of which he was then President, Mr. Herring touched on a subject which is dear to the hearts of "liberal" extremists and very valuable to Communists—"civil rights." A thesis of extreme "liberals" is that they alone support the fundamental rights granted by the Constitution —that the rest of us are in danger of destroying these precious rights—that a "conservative" is almost *per se* against "civil rights." Mr. Herring contends that he is rather conservative. But he seems to lack understanding of the fact that socialism and communism are eventually destroyers of liberty, however respectable some of their followers may appear.

The Reece Committee report commented on Mr. Herring's typically "liberal" speech as follows:

We regard as unfortunately typical, the address made in 1953 by Mr. Pendleton Herring, now President of *The Social Science Research Council,* to *The American Political Science Association,* of which he was then President. After a discussion of the position and work of the political scientist in America, and after emphasizing the necessity of empirical approaches and of observing the cultural lag theory, he launched into a tirade in the "civil rights" area.

Let us re-quote for guidance, the words of Mr. Hoover— "It is an established fact that whenever one has dared to expose the Communist threat he has invited upon himself the adroit and skilled talents of experts in character assassination." Let us then quote from Mr. Herring's address, made under the cloak of office in *two tax-exempt organizations* supported heavily with the public's money through foundation grace. He speaks of "political quacks" who ask "careers for themselves through exploitation of public concern with the Communist contagion." He does not identify any one man against whom he may have some special animus. His terminology, his selection of phrase, condemns as "quacks" whoever try to expose Communists. He makes no exceptions. He does not exempt from his excoriation any Congressional investigators or investigation. He indicates that investigating Communists may, indeed, be worse than Communism. He repeats the hysterical claim that books have been "burned." How many and how often? Is there truly danger in the United States of "book burning"? He speaks of giving "cool, intelligent treatment" to "the transmission of erroneous information and propaganda"— is it not transmitting "erroneous information and propaganda" to infer that there is widespread "book burning" in this country!

He uses the term "witchdoctors" to characterize the whole breed of exposers of Communism. He speaks of "contrived excursions and alarums"—implying that the Communist menace has been grossly exaggerated for political reasons.

He refers to the whole exposure business as "MALARKY-ISM," putting it in capital letters. He gives us this profound comment upon our concern with the Communist menace:

"We must go from symptoms to the causes. A deep cause, I think, is a failure to understand the forces operating in the world around us. Why do so many Americans feel threatened? It is the stubborn complexity of world problems and the difficulties arising from ideological differences and international rivalries that lead them to seek scapegoats among their fellow countrymen."

That is an astounding statement to come from one of the top rank of those who disburse the public money which foundations control. "You poor dumb Americans," he might well have said, "You are afraid of the Russian Communists only because you do not understand the dears."

Mr. Herring says: "Why assume that the conspiracy of Communism is best exposed where the limelight shines brightest?" He forgets that it has frequently taken a glaring limelight to induce government officials to expose a Communist—witness, among many, the case of Harry Dexter White.

Another example of the "cloak of respectability" (to which Mr. J. Edgar Hoover referred) through eminence in the foundation world, is to be found in public utterances of Mr. Paul Hoffman, formerly Chairman of the Ford Foundation and now Chairman of its offspring, the Fund for the Republic. In an article *To Insure the End of Our Hysteria* in the New York *Times* Magazine Section of November 14, 1954, Mr. Hoffman referred to the California Senate Un-American Activities Committee as a "highly publicized witch hunt."[*]

Messrs. Herring and Hoffman are not ordinary citizens expressing a personal political point of view. They have been two of the

---

[*] *Ibid.*, pp. 115-116.

most important characters among the *dramatis personae* of the foundation complex.

FOUNDATIONS AND "SUBVERSION"

The Reece Committee concluded that because of the essential identity of evolutionary and revolutionary socialism and communism, much of the radicalism which has been supported and financed by foundations was "subversive." It expressed itself as follows:

> Foundation spokesmen have emphatically denied any support of subversion. We question, however, whether in such denials they did not misinterpret the meaning of the term "subversion." Their denials were justified in so far as they are related to the direct support of Communism, but these spokesmen were well aware of the nature of some of the evidence produced before this Committee which showed that foundations had frequently supported those who wish to undermine our society. Their denials of subversion in relation to such activities are without merit.
>
> *What does the term "subversion" mean? In contemporary usage and practice, it does not refer to outright revolution, but to a promotion of tendencies which lead, in their inevitable consequences, to the destruction of principles through perversion or alienation. Subversion, in modern society, is not a sudden, cataclysmic explosion, but a gradual undermining, a persistent chipping away at foundations upon which beliefs rest.*
>
> By its very nature, successful subversion is difficult to detect. It can easily be confused with honest, forthright criticism. In our free society outright and honest criticism is not only permissible but immensely desirable. Individuals who engage openly in such criticism, who criticize political institutions from a political perspective, and economic institutions from an economic perspective, should be given free rein and encouraged. The issues involved in per-

mitting open and honest criticism, however, differ vitally from the issues raised by subversion promoted by foundations. Some of these vital differences (which foundation spokesmen refused to acknowledge, much less discuss, in their conscious misinterpretation of the term "subversive") are these:

Fundamental to the entire concept of tax exemption for foundations is the principle that their grants are to be primarily directed to strengthening the structure of the society which creates them. *Society does not grant tax exemption for the privilege of undermining itself.* Reasonable license is granted to satisfy personal idiosyncrasies, with the result that there is much social waste when grants serve no truly useful purpose to society. But such tolerated waste is something far different from the impact of grants made by foundations which tend to undermine our society. Such grants violate the underlying, essential assumption of the tax-exemption privilege, that the substantial weight of foundation effort must operate to strengthen, improve and promote the economic, political and moral pillars upon which our society rests.

* * *

In the modern usage of the term, "subversion," it is no exaggeration to state that in the field of the social sciences many major projects which have been most prominently sponsored by foundations have been subversive.

Numerous examples of such foundation-sponsored projects, subversive of American moral, political and economic principles, were offered in testimony. Foundation spokesmen failed utterly to provide any evidence that such heavily financed and prominently sponsored projects were in any real sense balanced by projects which promoted or strengthened the principles upon which our society rests. In this sense, the weight of influence of foundation tax-exempt funds applied in the social sciences has been on the side of subversion.

Moreover, the subversive projects have been offered with spurious claims to "science." With this false label they have been awarded a privileged status. They have been offered as "scientific" and, therefore, beyond rebuttal. The impact of these subversive works has been intensified manifold by the sponsorship of foundations."*

HELPLESSNESS OF THE CITIZEN

Unhappily, the average citizen, even the normally well-informed, has no fair chance to combat radical ideas flowing into education and into government through the agency of foundations. The writings of the partisan educators come to the attention of the professional class only. By the time the ordinary citizens know what has happened, they have been "subverted"—a tremendous pressure for the imposition of radical ideas has been built up, and their proponents have become well organized, entrenched, and implemented to impose them.

The report of the American Historical Association's Commission on Social Studies illustrates the inherent danger in foundation meddling in vital areas of public affairs. This report, it will be recalled, was characterized by Professor Laski as "an educational program for a Socialist America." It started a flow of radical ideas into education, ideas for which, it is safe to say, the average American would have scant sympathy. But that average American is not aware, even today, of the responsibility of this Carnegie foundation-supported report for so much of the mischief wrought in our educational system. The damage was done long before there was any possible hope that the people could have been alerted to defend themselves.

It is difficult to trace with any exactness the extent to which foundation-supported ideologies have passed into government, or the exact courses which this flow has taken. But there is evidence enough that the flow has been full and serious. In its report for 1933-1934, the National Planning Board included this statement:

* *Ibid.*, pp. 205-206.

State and interstate planning is a lusty infant but the work is only beginning. Advisory economic councils may be regarded as instrumentalities for stimulating a coordinated view of national life and for developing mental attitudes favorable to the principle of national planning.

The report acknowledged the cooperation, in the scheme for more national planning, of certain "advisory economic councils": The Council of Learned Societies, The American Council on Education; and The Social Science Research Council—a committee of this last having "prepared this memorandum."*

I urge a reading of pages 129-133 of the Committee report, to get a more detailed idea of the concept of national planning which the foundation-supported clearing houses had fostered and brought into government. Consider, for instance, the report of The National Resources Committee, which took the place of The National Planning Board, which went so far as to advise "A New Bill of Rights." Not satisfied apparently with the "Bill of Rights" attached to our Constitution, it contained these new "rights," presumably to be guaranteed by the Federal government.

3. The right to adequate food, clothing, shelter, and medical care.

4. The right to security, with freedom from fear of old age, want, dependency, sickness, unemployment, and accident. (This is the "cradle-to-the-grave" security concept.)

6. The right to come and go, to speak or to be silent, free from the spyings of secret political police.

9. The right to rest, recreation, and adventure, the opportunity to enjoy life and take part in an advancing civilization.

AN EXAMPLE OF FOUNDATION-SUPPORTED ANTICAPITALISM

It would be a vast undertaking, but well worth while, to attempt to ascertain how many anticapitalist books have been foisted on the American public through foundation support. The number is

* *Ibid.*, p. 129.

indeed great. Here is one for which Andrew Carnegie, were he alive, would hardly congratulate his trustees for having financed.

It is *Business as a System of Power,* written by Professor Robert A. Brady, under a grant from The Carnegie Foundation for the Advancement of Teaching. In an introduction, Professor Robert S. Lynd says:

> * * * capitalist economic power constitutes a direct, continuous and fundamental threat to the whole structure of democratic authority everywhere and always.

Dr. Brady repeatedly alleges that BIG BUSINESS is an essential evil. The "great corporations" account for much of the current mischief in our society. "Industrial capitalism," he says, "is an intensely coercive form of organization of society," and great evils flow from it. He is very clearly a collectivist. He just does not like the capitalist system. The business system is "feudal"; it is "completely authoritarian (antidemocratic)"; its leadership is "self-appointed, self-perpetuating, and autocratic." War, he indicates, is essential for capitalist survival—a statement which is reminiscent of Communist propaganda. The National Association of Manufacturers, he likens to the *Reichsverband der deutschen Industrie;* and "Mr. Knudsen, Edward Stettinius and Bernard Baruch are paralleled by Mr. Ogura in Japan, Lord Beaverbrook in England, and Hermann Goering (himself a leading industrialist), Friederick Flick, and their group in Germany." Big business, says this seer, can result in fascism.*

The Carnegie Corporation followed the production of this book very carefully and financed its publication.

THE LEAGUE FOR INDUSTRIAL DEMOCRACY

Some tax-exempt organizations have been bold and forthright in promoting socialism and yet have escaped revocation of tax exemption. One is The League for Industrial Democracy. Its purpose is to educate the American people into an acceptance of socialism. Mr. Ken Earl, a witness before the Reece Committee,

* *Ibid.,* p. 117 *et seq.*

termed it "an adjunct of the Socialist Party," and his conclusion seems amply justified.

After his exposition of the socialist character of the LID, Mr. Earl concluded:

> * * * Mr. Chairman and members of this committee, let me say that in this presentation I do not quarrel with the right of these many people in the LID, and all of those who have been recipients of its awards or have spoken to it, and I don't quarrel with their people, to say and write the things which we have discussed, though I disagree with many of the things which they advocate.
>
> *My thesis is this: If the LID is to continue to fill the air with propaganda concerning socialism; if it is to continue stumping for certain legislative programs; and if it is to continue to malign the free enterprise system under which we operate—then I believe that it should be made to do so with taxed dollars, just as the Democrats and the Republicans are made to campaign with taxed dollars.**

In his statement filed with the Committee, Dr. Harry W. Laidler, executive director of the LID, attempted to show that the organization was no longer "Socialist" and that it was "educational" in its activities. The fact is that comparatively few of its members, associates, and officers are now members of the Socialist Party. But no wonder. That Party, as Norman Thomas, its old leader, has admitted, has shrunk. But socialism is still with us, and far stronger than in the days when there was an active and substantial party. Most Socialists have gone elsewhere. Most now call themselves "liberals." As for the claim that the work of the LID is "educational" under the law, entitling it to receive tax-deductible donations, then if that is so, said the Reece Committee, "something is very wrong with the law."

The League for Industrial Democracy (formerly The Intercollegiate Socialist Society), to which I have earlier referred, started life in 1905. Its name was changed in 1921, but its character re-

---

* *Ibid.,* pp. 105-106.

mained the same. I have pointed out that it called itself a "militant educational movement" to promote a "new social order based on production for use and not for profit," calling this "a revolutionary slogan" and urging "the elimination of capitalism." This organization's publication, *Revolt*, announced proudly the wide dissemination of its inflamatory "educational" literature:

> The LID emergency publications, *The Unemployed* and *Disarm*, have reached a circulation of one-half million. * * * Students organized squads of salesmen to sell these magazines, containing slashing attacks on capitalism and the war system * * *.*

Mr. Earl, in his testimony, piled up quotation after quotation to show the true character of this "educational" organization. They are far too numerous even to digest here. But I shall give a few from the writings and official pronouncements of Dr. Laidler, whose statement to the Committee denied its radical-propagandist nature, and of others of influence or importance in the LID organization (emphasis supplied throughout):

> [The] recourse [of workers and farmers] now is to form a political party which they themselves control, and through which they might conceivably obtain state mastery over the owning class. [Paul R. Porter, in *Revolt*, a publication of the LID.] †
>
> The LID therefore works to bring a new social order; not by thinking alone, though a high order of thought is required; not by outraged indignation, finding an outlet in a futile banging of fists against the citadel of capitalism; but by the combination of thought and action and an understanding of what is the weakness of capitalism in order to bring about socialism in our own lifetime. [*The Inter-Collegiate Student Council of the LID,* an affiliated organization.] ‡

* *Ibid.*, p. 97.
† *Ibid.*, p. 97.
‡ *Ibid.*, p. 96.

Watch now those little flames of mass unrest * * * . Great energy will be generated by those flames of mass revolt. But revolt is not revolution, and even though new blankets of cruel repression fail to smother the fire and in the end only add to its intensity, *that energy may be lost unless it can be translated into purposive action.* Boilers in which steam can be generated—if we may work our metaphor—need be erected over the fire, and that steam forced into engines of reconstruction.

Trotsky, in describing the rule of the Bolsheviks in the Russian Revolution, has hit upon a happy figure of speech which we may borrow in this instance. No man, no group of men, created the revolution; Lenin and his associates were but the pistons driven by the steam power of the masses. *The Marxist Bolshevik party saved that steam from aimless dissipation, directed it into the proper channels. To catch and to be driven by that steam is the function of the radical parties in America today.*

* * *

There are members who would pattern it [the Socialist Party of America] after the German Social Democracy and the British Labor Party, despite the disastrous experiences of two great parties of the Second International. There are members who have lost to age and comfort their one-time fervor, and members who would shrink from struggle in time of crisis.

* * *

They [the Socialists] must overcome the quiescent influence of those whose socialism has been dulled by intimacy with the bourgeois world, and they must speak boldly and convincingly to the American working people in the workers' language.

If their party can rise to these tasks *then perhaps capitalism can be decently buried before it has found temporary rejuvenation in a Fascist dictatorship.* [Paul Porter, in *Re-*

volt. Note: Mr. Porter was an organizer and lecturer for the LID and a missionary to thousands of college students.]*

The crucial issue of industrial civilization today is not between laissez-faire individualism on the one hand and collectivism on the other. History is deciding that question. The question for us is what sort of collectivism we want. *Modern technology makes collectivism inevitable. But whether our collectivism is to be Fascist, feudal, or Socialist will depend * * * upon the effectiveness with which we translate those political ideals into action.*

You cannot fight on the economic front and stay neutral on the legal or political front. Politics and economics are not two different things, and the failures of the labor movement in this country largely arise from the assumption that they are. Capitalism is as much a legal system as it is an economic system, and *the attack on capitalism must be framed in legal or political terms as well as in economic terms. * * * a Socialist attack on the problem of government cannot be restricted to presidential and congressional elections or even to general programs of legislation. We have to widen our battlefront to include all institutions of government, corporations, trade unions, professional bodies, and even religious bodies, as well as legislatures and courts.* We have to frame the issues of socialism and democracy and fight the battles of socialism and democracy in the stockholders' meetings of industrial corporations, in our medical associations, and our bar associations, and our teachers' associations, in labor unions, in student councils, in consumers' and producers' cooperatives—in every social institution in which we can find a foothold * * *.

* * *

But the need of fighting politically within corporations and trade associations and professional bodies, as well as labor

* *Ibid.,* p. 98.

unions, is just as pressing if we think that fundamental social change can be secured in this country only by unconstitutional measures.

In a revolution, when the ordinary political machinery of government breaks down, it is absolutely essential that the revolutionary force control the remaining centers of social power. In Russia the success of the Bolshevik revolution rested with the guilds or soviets, which were not created by the Communist Party and which antedated the revolution. *A socialist revolution in this country will succeed only if our guilds, chief among them our engineering societies, have within them a coherent socialist voice.* [Felix S. Cohen, in *Revolt.*] *

Under a system where the basic industries of the country are privately owned and run primarily for profit, therefore, much of the income of its wealthiest citizens bears little or no relation to their industry, ability or productivity. [Dr. Harry W. Laidler, Executive Secretary of the LID in "Toward Nationalization of Industry," a pamphlet widely distributed by it, which expressly advocates nationalization of forests, coal mines, oil, power, railroads, communications, banking and credit.] †

This Dr. Laidler is the man whose filed statement said the LID was educational and not Socialist!

If The League for Industrial Democracy is entitled to tax exemption, then, like Mr. Earl, I see no reason why an organization which is frankly created for the purpose of promoting the platform of either the Democratic or Republican Party should not be tax exempt. Or is it only Socialist propaganda which deserves tax exemption?

THE AMERICAN LABOR EDUCATION SERVICE

This tax-exempt organization, supported by The Ford Foundation and others, is engaged in the "education" of labor. Its "education"

* *Ibid.*, p. 98.
† *Ibid.*, pp. 102-103.

is of a special kind: political education. Its keynote was sounded in an invitation of October 2, 1946, to attend a conference at Milwaukee:

> At the dinner, we shall consider methods labor must use when collective bargaining does not work, especially methods of dealing with the government.*

The Reece Committee report summarizes the nature of this foundation this way:

> The background of some ALES staff members, together with a list of participants in ALES conferences, suggests an interlock with individuals and groups associated with militant socialism and, in some instances, with Communist fronts.†

The nature of the "educational" program of this Ford-supported organization is indicated by the subjects listed for discussion at various ALES conferences:

> Political Action for Labor;
> Political Action Techniques;
> The Contribution of Labor in Rebuilding Democratic Society;
> The Role of Workers' Education in Political Action.

One conference strongly stressed

> the urgency of participation in political action by labor and the re-evaluation of education in relation to political action.

Nor was foreign policy to be neglected. "International affairs" for labor received wide attention, and labor was urged to take part in *establishing* foreign policy.

Action, action, action—is the constant demand!

The American Labor Education Service distributes two song

---

* *Ibid.*, p. 106.
† *Ibid.*, p. 106.

books, *Songs Useful for Workers' Groups*—some of the music having been contributed by the Communist Hans Eisler—and a *Rebel
Song Book.* It circulates a series of pamphlets "for Workers'
Classes," many of which were published by The League for Industrial Democracy, some of them written by Harry Laidler, the
Socialist executive director of the LID. Plays are provided for the
education of the laboring man, many of them socially incendiary,
written by such eminent educators as Albert Maltz, who served a
jail term for contempt of Congress.

One of the leading lights of the ALES is Mr. Mark Starr, its vice
chairman, who has also been chairman of The League for Industrial Democracy. Mr. Starr has had many opportunities to exercise
his influence for socialism. He has been director of education of
the International Ladies Garment Workers Union, a member of
the United States Advisory Commission on Educational Exchange, labor consultant to Elmer Davis's Office of War Information, a member of the American delegation to establish UNESCO,
a labor-education consultant to the American occupation government in Japan, and a member of President Truman's Commission
on Higher Education. He has also been Chairman of the Public
Affairs Committee.

Mr. Starr has no use for our economic system—he has explained
that carefully. He is a frank collectivist. And, ironic as it may be,
he has been a heavy beneficiary of Ford Foundation (Fund for
Adult Education) largess, though he has expressed himself regarding foundations as follows:

> * * * colleges too often have to go cap-in-hand and ex-
> ploit personal contacts with the uncrowned kings and agents
> of philanthropy * * * . There are, of course, some foun-
> dations which delouse effectively the millions accumulated
> by monopolies and dynastic fortunes; but if one could
> choose a way for the long time support of education, it
> would be done by community intelligence rather than the
> caprice of the big shots of big business who wish to per-
> petuate their names in a spectacular fashion, a process which

196 REVOLUTION IS NEARLY ACCOMPLISHED

may not in all cases coincide with the real educational activity of the college.*

LEFTISTS SUPPLIED TO GOVERNMENT BY FOUNDATIONS

It is an understatement to say that the majority of the Reece Committee was shocked at Professor Kenneth Colegrove's revelations concerning the extent to which foundation-supported organizations had been responsible for the penetration of Communists and Communist sympathizers into the government as advisers.

When advisers were to be selected in social-science areas for our occupation authorities in Germany and Japan, Professor Colegrove submitted, as Secretary of The American Political Science Association, upon request of the government, a list of proposed political advisers. While he himself was appointed and took office as an adviser to General MacArthur (not at his own suggestion), his list was completely ignored. He found, to his dismay, that the advisers had been selected entirely from lists supplied by two other organizations. One was the notorious Institute of Pacific Relations, so generously supported by The Rockefeller Foundation, The Carnegie Corporation, and The Carnegie Endowment for International Peace. The other was The American Council of Learned Societies, another intermediary organization heavily supported by major foundations.

The Communist connections of IPR have been mentioned. In the case of The American Council of Learned Societies, its Executive Secretary was Dr. Mortimer Graves, whose list of Communist-front associations impressed even the Cox Committee. Here we have two of the executive agencies of what the Reece Committee report called the "concentration of power" or the complex supported by some of the major foundations.

Professor Colegrove checked the list of accepted appointees. He testified as follows:

> We checked these names off. Some of them were known to us to be Communists, many of them pro-Communists or fellow travelers. They were extremely leftist.

* *Ibid.*, pp. 108-109.

I went back to the Pentagon to protest against a number of these people, and to my amazement I found that they had all been invited, and they had all accepted, and some of them were already on their way to Japan.*

The Committee report had this to say about Dr. Graves:

We do not accuse Mr. Graves of being a Communist. But it amazes us that one with so evident a lack of political and social discernment, with such apparent lack of objectivity, should be retained as a directing officer in what purports to be the representative organization for all the social sciences and humanities. Mr. Graves still holds his position, though the Cox Committee hearings brought out his extensive record of Communist-front affiliations. This leads us to conclude one of two things; either his personal power is astounding or the extreme political slant of an executive is deemed of no moment by that tax-exempt agency of the foundations.†

In writing the platform for the Communist League, Marx and Engels predicted that the proletariat would "use its political supremacy to wrest, by degrees, all capital from the bourgeoisie, to centralize all instruments of production in the hand of the state, i.e., of the proletariat organized as a ruling class." A considerable number of the planks of the Communist Manifesto have become part of the law of our land; but this has been accomplished not through a seizure of power by a "proletariat" but through the misguided efforts of our intellectuals. Most of these intellectuals lead a life remote from the economic realities of society. Educators, in general, are among the most valuable of our citizens. But they usually do not know the market place; their ideas of how an economy should or can run are often as impractical as they are idealistic. True, they can sometimes support unrealistic theories with a mass of empirical data, but it is usually both incomplete and un-

* *Ibid.*, p. 201.
† *Ibid.*, p. 55.

sound because it excludes vital factors not susceptible to empirical study.

The undeniable fact is that the changes which have taken place in the United States were not the result of the "despotic inroads on the right of property, and on the conditions of bourgeois production." They were the result of continuous propaganda in the form of biased education. This propaganda has nearly convinced the American people that the Marxian formula is good for it.

The fog-bound intellectuals who have advocated change on the theory that things are not as rosy as they should be and, therefore, anything else would be better, have blindly permitted themselves to be led into the path of socialism. Whereas, today they generally despise communism, the intellectual proponents of change in America still consider socialism as eminently respectable. They still do not see the central identity of communism and other forms of socialism; they believe that a gradual transition of our society to one in which "production" is "for use and not for profits" can prevail without any suppression of freedom. The bloody extermination of liberty in Russia is, to these intellectuals, merely an evidence that the Stalinist variety of socialism is reprehensible. They are disappointed lovers, rather than true opponents. They are blind to this fact: whether the approach to socialism is by way of force or soft propaganda, the system will inevitably call for the rape of the masses, for the suppression of liberty and freedom.

The ideas of socialism have too long been supported in our country by fashions of thought which, in turn, have been heavily financed by foundations. Critics of foundation activity have wondered, indeed, why foundations have had so little interest in several obvious fields of "venturing." They might well "venture" heavily into studies of what is worth preserving in our system and in our society; into education that promotes traditions and established values; into public-affairs programs which promote national pride and national ambitions.

There is some hope. The foundations today seem to be slightly more cautious in supporting Socialist politics under the disguise of education and research than before the Congressional investigations took place. But caution is not enough. In addition to taking care to see that their funds are not used for anti-social purposes, it behooves them also to support constructive programs in the social sciences, in education and in public affairs.

A number of foundations have made a substantial effort to this end. The Lilly Endowment made possible, through a relatively modest grant, the publication of the incisive criticism of modern social science to which I have referred, written by Professor Pitirim A. Sorokin, *Fads and Foibles in Modern Sociology and Related Sciences*. The Bollingen Foundation publishes unusually interesting books and supports scholars of merit in fields of culture usually neglected by other foundations. Even The Social Science Research Council must be given a special award of merit for recently supporting the brilliant but unorthodox work of Eric Voegelin, *Order and History*.* The Foundation for Foreign Affairs has supported a number of authors critical of communism, socialism and "liberalism," and authors of conservative books. The Ford Foundation directly and indirectly supports some research in communism and may, in the end, contribute to a better understanding of this scourge of mankind. The work of the Erhart Foundation, the Volker Fund, The Richardson Foundation, the Pew Foundation, the American Economic Foundation, and a few others has been unorthodox enough to support conservative writers and projects.

There is still hope that the trustees of some of those foundations which have acted as the financial underwriters of socialism in the United States may force a change in the ways of the organizations whose cerebral management they have neglected.

* Louisiana State University Press, 1957.

FOUNDATION IMPACT ON
FOREIGN POLICY

THE FOUNDATION COMPLEX IN "INTERNATIONALISM"

FOUNDATION ACTIVITY has nowhere had a greater impact than in the field of foreign affairs. It has conquered public opinion and has largely established the international-political goals of our country. A few major foundations with internationalist tendencies created or fostered a varied group of organizations which now dominate the research, the education, and the supply of experts in the field. Among such instruments are the Council on Foreign Relations, the Foreign Policy Association, the Institute of Pacific Relations, the United Nations Association, and the conferences and seminars held by American universities on international relations and allied subjects.

It would be difficult to find a single foundation-supported organization of any substance which has not favored the United Nations or similar global schemes; fantastically heavy foreign aid at the burdensome expense of the taxpayer; meddling in the colonial affairs of other nations; and American military commitments over the globe. Though the sums of money put up by the internationalist-minded foundations may seem relatively small in comparison with larger grants spent elsewhere, they have enabled their satellite or subsidized organizations to play a conspicuous and dominating role. This was comparatively easy to accomplish because there was no organized or foundation-supported opposition.

The influence of the foundation complex in internationalism has reached far into government, into the policymaking circles of Congress and into the State Department. This has been effected through the pressure of public opinion, mobilized by the instruments of the foundations; through the promotion of foundation-favorites as teachers and experts in foreign affairs; through a domination of the learned journals in international affairs; through the frequent appointment of State Department officials to foundation jobs; and through the frequent appointment of foundation officials to State Department jobs.

At least one foreign foundation has had a strong influence on our foreign policy. The Rhodes Scholarship Fund of Great Britain, created to improve England's international public relations but not registered here as a foreign agent, has gained great influence in the United States for British ideas. It has accomplished this by annually selecting a choice group of promising young men for study in England. The usually Anglophile alumni of this system are to be found in eminent positions in legislation, administration, and education and in the ranks of American foundation officials. They form a patronage network of considerable importance. Dr. Frank Aydelotte in a book, *The Rhodes Trust 1903-1953* published in 1956, reported: "The influence of this group on American educational practice and particularly on the rapidly increasing maturity and breadth of methods of instruction in American institutions of higher learning, has been immense." He continued: "The number of those going into government is constantly increasing."

Of a total of 1,372 American Rhodes scholars up to 1953, 431 held or hold positions in teaching and educational administration (among them, 31 college presidents); 113 held government positions; 70 held positions in press and radio; and 14 were executives in other foundations. Dr. Aydelotte remarks: "One indication of the success of operations of the Rhodes Scholarships in America is the remarkable way in which they have inspired other foundations." He reports that the Guggenheim fellowships and the program of the Commonwealth Fund set up by Mr. Harkness and several similar programs were developed with the aid of officials of the Rhodes fund.

Dean Rusk, president of The Rockefeller Foundation, and several of the staff members of that foundation are Rhodes scholars. Mr. Henry Allen Moe, the director of the Guggenheim foundation, and O. C. Carmichael, former president of the Carnegie foundation, are Rhodes Scholars. Senator J. W. Fulbright, Congressmen C. R. Clason, R. Hale, and C. B. Albert, and 14 American State legislators are also Rhodes alumni. Among the many Rhodes scholars connected with our Department of State are these: Ambassador to the Netherlands S. K. Hornbeck (formerly Chief of Far Eastern Affairs in the Department); B. M. Hulle (former Chief of North European Affairs in the Department); W. Walter Butterworth (former Assistant Secretary of State for Eastern Affairs, U. S. Ambassador to Sweden, Deputy Chief U. S. Mission to London); Walter Gordon (U. S. Embassy in London, in charge of Economic Affairs with the rank of minister); and G. C. McGhee (Ambassador to Turkey). Before becoming president of The Rockefeller Foundation, Dean Rusk served as a deputy Under-secretary of State. Dr. Aydelotte reports that, in addition, 12 Rhodes scholars were attached to various intergovernmental agencies (ILO, UN, etc.).

It may not be merely coincidental to this subject that Cecil Rhodes, who created the Scholarships, and Andrew Carnegie were friends. The latter may have learned from the former the technique of accomplishing great effects with relatively modest means. Carnegie contributed but a small part of his wealth to The Carnegie Endowment for International Peace; yet this comparatively small unit grew to have gigantic influence on American foreign affairs.

Just as there have been interlocks and a "concentration of power" in education and in social-science research in domestic areas, there has been a similar combination in the field of foreign policy. The major components of the concentration in internationalism have been The Carnegie Corporation, The Carnegie Endowment for International Peace, The Rockefeller Foundation, and, recently, The Ford Foundation. I have mentioned some of their more important satellites. Then there are the "conferences."

One of the most important activities of the foundations and associated groups operating in the international field consists of promoting conference after conference and forum after forum for the discussion of international affairs. These would serve a useful purpose were it not for the fact that they are almost invariably made into platforms for the special points of view which these groups favor.

A common character of the meetings frequently held all over the country under the auspices of or in cooperation with the organs of the internationalist foundations is that they regularly present speakers favorable to the sentiments of these supporters. The speakers, almost invariably and *ad nauseam,* advocate aid for underdeveloped countries "with no strings attached"; distribution of American foreign aid through the United Nations rather than through American agencies; recognition of Communist China; membership for Communist China in the United Nations; American abandonment of atomic weapons without guarantees for similar disarmament by our enemy. Through their virtually monopolistic control of the market place for ideas in the area of international relations, these organizations exert an influence far beyond the weight of the general followers of "liberal" politics. Their opponents enjoy little or no financial support. Thus, the intensity of the "internationalist" campaign produces propaganda returns even among businessmen and groups which would ordinarily, without the blasting of such propaganda, be inclined to a more conservative point of view.

For example, the *National Review* of March 7, 1956, called attention to the fact that The U. S. Chamber of Commerce had been among the sponsors of a recent Midwest Residential Seminar on World Affairs, held near St. Louis. It was in strange company. Among the other supporting organizations were The American Labor Education Service, The American Association for the United Nations, The Social Science Foundation, The Institute of

International Relations, The Carnegie Endowment for International Peace, The American Library Association, The Foreign Policy Association, and The American Foundation for Political Education. *The featured speaker at this seminar was John Carter Vincent, discharged from the State Department as a loyalty risk.*

THE PART OF THE CARNEGIE ENDOWMENT

When Andrew Carnegie established The Carnegie Endowment for International Peace, he gave the managers of this fund a difficult task. How were they to go about promoting peace? They seem to have had no very clear idea until Dr. Nicholas Murray Butler, in whose hands Mr. Carnegie put the initial direction of the fund, got excited about the peril of the Allies in World War I and decided that the best way to establish peace was to help get the United States into the War. To this end he began to use the Endowment funds.

When the war was ended, that issue was gone. Support for the League of Nations gave the Endowment one new outlet for its energies and its funds, but more scope than this was needed for the propaganda machine which it had become. A fruitful guide for operations was found in Dr. Butler's personal shibboleth of "the international mind," a phrase to which he was devoted in speeches and writings.

The concept of "the international mind" had considerable value. Americans generally, in Dr. Butler's day, were not as well informed in international affairs as might be desirable; efforts to educate them were commendable enough. But Dr. Butler went further than a mere desire to give us a better international education. He seemed to have had an idea that if only Americans got more "international-minded" the cause of peace would be promoted. Perhaps this is an exaggeration, as I state it, but there is no question that Dr. Butler was somewhat possessed of the concept of "international-mindedness."

At any rate, a powerful propaganda machine came into being. Used objectively, it could have been of enormous service to the country. But, as is likely to be the case, it turned to advocacy.

When you control a propaganda vehicle, it is tempting to use it to promote your own program.

The Reece Committee said of the Endowment's work:

> An extremely powerful propaganda machine was created. It spent many millions of dollars in:
>
> The production of masses of material for distribution;
>
> The creation and support of large numbers of international policy clubs, and other local organizations at colleges and elsewhere;
>
> The underwriting and dissemination of many books on various subjects, through the "International Mind Alcoves" and the "International Relations Clubs and Centers" which it organized all over the country;
>
> The collaboration with agents of publicity, such as newspaper editors;
>
> The preparation of material to be used in school text books, and cooperation with publishers of text books to incorporate this material;
>
> The establishing of professorships at the colleges and the training and indoctrination of teachers;
>
> The financing of lecturers and the importation of foreign lecturers and exchange professors;
>
> The support of outside agencies touching the international field, such as the *Institute of International Education, the Foreign Policy Association, the American Association for the Advancement of Science, the American Council on Education, the American Council of Learned Societies, the American Historical Association, the American Association of International Conciliation, the Institute of Pacific Relations, the International Parliamentary Union* and others, and acting as mid-wife at the birth of some of them.* .

The Carnegie Endowment was utterly frank in disclosing its propaganda function. It used terms frequently such as the "ed-

* Reece Committee *Report*, p. 171.

ucation of public opinion." This is not "public education," but *molding public opinion.* The Committee report indicated that one thing seemed "utterly clear: no private group should have the power or the right to decide what should be read and taught in our schools and colleges," yet this is what the Endowment sought to do in "educating public opinion."

The influence of this foundation may be illustrated by the functions held by its former president, Alger Hiss. He was a trustee of The Woodrow Wilson Foundation, a director of the executive committee of the American Association for the United Nations, a director of the American Peace Society, a trustee of the World Peace Federation, and a director of the American Institute of Pacific Relations.

The Carnegie Endowment for International Peace made its position clear. Its 1934 *Yearbook* complained about the

> economic nationalism which is still running riot and which is the greatest obstacle to the reestablishment of prosperity and genuine peace. * * *.*

and referred to nationalism as "this violently reactionary movement." Nationalism is held to be "violently reactionary" in the United States, but the organizations supported by the Endowment apparently feel that nationalism abroad is a fine thing. Under the slogan of anticolonialism, they have supported rabid nationalistic movements, often Communist stimulated, in undeveloped areas, and have underwritten measures abroad highly detrimental to American prestige and American private investments.

The 1946 report of The Rockefeller Foundation also minced no words in advocating globalism. It read:

> The challenge of the future is to make this world one world—a world truly free to engage in common and constructive intellectual efforts that will serve the welfare of mankind everywhere.

* *Ibid.,* p. 169.

The ideal of a united world as a basis for permanent peace is a splendid one. But the executives of the international-minded foundations have committed two serious errors in promoting it. One is that they have been in too great haste to translate into immediate action an ideal which might take another century of extremely careful planning and adjustment to accomplish. The other has been that the "common world" which they have envisioned and to which they have sought to rush us is unquestionably an extended, international collectivism.

The Reece Committee came to this conclusion:

> The weight of evidence before this Committee, which the foundations have made no serious effort to rebut, indicates that the form of globalism which the foundations have so actively promoted and from which our foreign policy has suffered seriously, relates definitely to a collectivist point of view. Despite vehement disclaimers of bias, despite platitudinous affirmations of loyalty to American traditions, the statements filed by those foundations whose operations touch on foreign policy have produced no rebuttal to the evidence of support of collectivism.*

In an affidavit filed with the Reece Committee, Dr. Felix Wittmer, former Associate Professor of the Social Studies at the New Jersey State Teachers College, described his experiences as the adviser to one of the International Relations Clubs founded by The Carnegie Endowment.

Dr. Wittmer said that there were about a thousand of these clubs and that, as a result of association with them, a great proportion of the student members had acquired strongly leftist tendencies.† At regional conferences, said Dr. Wittmer, "a large majority of those students who attended favored views which came close to that of the Kremlin."

Speakers were provided by The Carnegie Endowment. Among

* *Ibid.*, p. 169.
† *Ibid.*, p. 174.

the speakers supplied to the club at New Jersey Teachers College was Alger Hiss. When Dr. Wittmer protested against receiving Hiss as a speaker, the Secretary of the Endowment, said Dr. Wittmer, reminded him "in no uncertain terms that our club, like all the hundreds of other clubs, was under the direction of The Carnegie Endowment for International Peace, which had for years liberally supplied it with reading material, and which contributed funds to cover the honoraria of conference speakers."

Radical infiltration in the club of which Dr. Wittmer was adviser became so pronounced that he resigned his position.

THE FOREIGN POLICY ASSOCIATION

Among the literature distributed by The Carnegie Endowment was some produced by The Foreign Policy Association, which it heavily supported. The research director of this organization for years was Vera Micheles Dean. A staff report to the Reece Committee made this comment upon Mrs. Dean:

> Reference has already been made to Mrs. Dean who, according to *The New York Times* a few years ago, made a "plea for socialism" to 600 alumnae at Vassar College, saying our quarrel with communism must not be over its ends but over its methods, and urging a foreign policy backing Socialist programs.
>
> Speaking of her book *Europe and the U.S.* in the book review section of *The New York Herald Tribune* on May 7, 1950, Harry Baehr, an editorial writer for that paper, wrote: "In other words, she considers it possible that the world may not be divided on sharp ideological lines but that there may yet be at least economic exchanges which will temper the world struggle and by reducing the disparity in standards of living between Eastern and Western Europe gradually abolish the conditions which foster communism and maintain it as a dangerous inhumane tyranny in those nations which now profess the Stalinist creed." *

* Reece Committee *Hearings* I, p. 901. See also *Report,* p. 264.

Among the Foreign Policy Association's products were the *Headline Books.* One of these, *World of the Great Powers,* was written by Max Lerner, a leftist who, conceding that "there are undoubtedly valuable elements in the capitalist economic organizations," proceeded to tell the readers to whom The Carnegie Endowment circulated his work that:

> If democracy is to survive, it too must move toward socialism. * * * It is the only principle that can organize the restless energies of the world's peoples.*

THE COUNCIL ON FOREIGN RELATIONS

The Council on Foreign Relations, another member of the international complex, financed both by the Rockefeller and Carnegie foundations, overwhelmingly propagandizes the globalist concept. This organization became virtually an agency of the government when World War II broke out. The Rockefeller Foundation had started and financed certain studies known as The War and Peace Studies, manned largely by associates of the Council; the State Department, in due course, took these Studies over, retaining the major personnel which The Council on Foreign Relations had supplied.

THE "HISTORICAL BLACKOUT"

One of the propaganda objectives of The Council on Foreign Relations was promotion of the "historical blackout." The 1946 Report of The Rockefeller Foundation, one of the supporters of The Council, contained this:

> The Committee on Studies of the Council on Foreign Relations is concerned that the debunking journalistic campaign following World War I should not be repeated and believes that the American public deserves a clear and competent statement of our basic aims and activities during the second World War.†

* Reece Committee *Report,* p. 176.
† *Ibid.,* p. 178.

This statement deserves pause. It has obvious political intention. It cannot be considered objective. Several eminent historians have written books critical of much of the government position in World War I. *It is nothing short of reprehensible for a tax-exempt organization to smear such critical historians with the term "debunking journalism."*

The plan called for a three-volume history of World War II, in which there was to be no "debunking." Note that this clearly was to be no objective study. The official propaganda of World War II was to be perpetuated. As Professor Charles Austin Beard put it: "In short, they hope that, among other things, the policies and measures of Franklin D. Roosevelt will escape in the coming years the critical analysis, evaluation and exposition that befell the policies and measures of Woodrow Wilson and the Entente Allies after World War I.*

Professor Harry Elmer Barnes, in *The Historical Blackout* and *Perpetual War for Perpetual Peace,* described what amounted to a conspiracy to prevent the American people from learning the truth. This conspiracy was foundation-supported. The Rockefeller Foundation allotted $139,000 to the production of the three-volume history which was to debar "debunking." This is the same Rockefeller Foundation whose current president has, in two recent addresses, proclaimed its insistence on continuing to support "controversy."

THE INSTITUTE OF PACIFIC RELATIONS

I have discussed this catastrophic organization in some detail in an earlier chapter. It need only be added that it was one of the most important elements in the complex of international-minded organizations financed principally by the Rockefeller and Carnegie foundations. To the trustees of The Rockefeller Foundation, The Carnegie Corporation, and The Carnegie Endowment for International Peace, I recommend that they place a large sign in each of their board rooms reading "REMEMBER IPR," as a constant reminder of what disastrous results can flow from

* *Ibid.,* p. 178.

abandoning supervision of activities financed by them and delegating their authority and judgment to intermediary organizations.

INTERLOCKS WITH GOVERNMENT
There have been interlocks between the international-minded foundations and the Federal government even as early as World War I. The Endowment went so far as to state in its 1934 *Yearbook* that it

> is becoming an unofficial instrument of international policy, taking up here and there the ends and threads of international problems and questions which the governments (*sic*) find it difficult to handle, and through private initiative reaching conclusions which are not of a formal nature but which unofficially find their way into the policies of governments (*sic*).*

If we turn back to an earlier Endowment report (1925), we may recognize that this proud statement in the 1934 report represents a paean of victory. The 1925 report said:

> Underneath and behind all these undertakings there remains the task to instruct and to enlighten public opinion so that it may not only guide but compel the action of governments and public officers in the direction of constructive progress.†

That a foundation could openly propose a plan to influence public opinion to the point where it, in turn, would coerce government, is really quite astounding. With the great power of its money and its patronage, such a major foundation carries the capacity to do just that.

FOUNDATION-PROMOTED "GLOBALISM"
Considerable evidence exists that some of the major foundations and a group of satellite organizations operating in the field

* *Ibid.*, p. 177.
† *Ibid.*, p. 178.

of international relations had ignored American interests in promoting "internationalism" of an unrealistic and dangerous nature. Professor Kenneth Colegrove testified:

> In my opinion, a great many of the staffs of the foundations have gone way beyond Wendell Willkie with reference to internationalism and globalism. * * * There is undoubtedly too much money put into studies which support globalism and internationalism. You might say that the other side has not been as fully developed as it should be.*

This opinion was emphatically shared by an American diplomat who should know his facts, Mr. Spruille Braden, former Assistant Secretary of State. He wrote to me:

> I have the very definite feeling that these various foundations you mention very definitely do exercise both overt and covert influences on our foreign relations and that their influences are counter to the fundamental principles on which this nation was founded and which have made it great.†

The foundations to which I had referred were: "Carnegie Endowment, Rockefeller Foundation, Ford Foundation, Rhodes Scholarship Trust." To those mentioned might be added the Foreign Policy Association, the Council on Foreign Relations, the Institute of Pacific Relations, and the United Nations Association, all part of what the Committee majority called a "concentration of power."

Professor Colegrove examined a list of books distributed by the Carnegie Endowment through its "International Mind Alcoves" and through the International Relations Clubs and Centers which it created and supported in hundreds of universities and colleges. His comments on some of these‡ run from "globalist," through

* *Ibid.,* p. 168.
† *Ibid.,* p. 169.
‡ Report, p. 173.

"ultra-globalist," "Marxian slant" and "subtle propaganda along Communist lines," to "pro-Communist" and "well-known Communist."

One wonders what kind of an "international mind" The Carnegie Endowment for International Peace intended to promote. The incomplete list of books which Professor Colegrove examined included works by such writers as Anna Louise Strong (a Communist); Owen Lattimore (pro-Communist); T. A. Bisson (pro-Communist); Professor Nathaniel Peffer (who advocated our giving up in Korea, "eating crow," recognizing Red China, assisting her in her financing, and admitting her to the United Nations); and Harold J. Laski (the philosopher of British socialism).

Dr. Wittmer mentioned in his sworn statement that the Endowment had distributed books also by Corliss Lamont (a noted pro-Communist); Ruth Benedict (co-author with Gene Weltfish of a pamphlet finally barred by the War Department; her co-author, be it remembered, refused to state under oath whether or not she was a Communist); Evans Clark (a former executive of the 20th Century Fund of wide Communist-front associations); and Alexander Werth (a European apologist for many Communist causes).

THE INTERNATIONAL "EXPERTS"

The foundations participating in the combination of tax-exempt institutions in international affairs may say that they have used experts where they have found them and that, indeed, if these have been globalist, it is because most experts have the globalist point of view. The Reece Committee report had this to say:

> It may well be said that a majority of the "experts" in the international field are on the side of globalism. It would be amazing if this were otherwise, after so many years of gigantic expenditure by foundations in virtually sole support of the globalist point of view. Professors and researchers have to eat and raise families. They cannot themselves spend the money to finance research and publications. The road to eminence in international areas, therefore,

just as in the case of the social sciences generally, is by way of foundation grants or support.*

Foreign policy is largely made by "experts"—technicians—inside the State Department and other "experts" who influence policy from the outside. Through the operation of the foundation complex in the international field, therefore, the overwhelming majority of these experts, both inside and outside the Department, have been indoctrinated with the globalist point of view which the combine has fostered.

PROPAGANDA FOR UN

The "international-mind" obsession of The Carnegie Endowment and its associated organizations has avidly taken up the United Nations. No intelligent person could doubt the desirability of an effective and sensibly designed international organization. But the group of foundations and organizations of which The Carnegie Endowment is a leading member apparently believes that any organization should be supported if it is international. Nothing else could explain the truly intemperate propaganda which has been launched to indoctrinate our people into *blind* support of the United Nations. There has been no disposition whatever to be objective, to criticize what is fallacious and what is dangerous. There has been no debate on merits. There has been only propaganda in support.

This group of foundations, led by The Carnegie Endowment, pours millions of dollars into propaganda to convince us that the United Nations organization, as now constituted, is our light and our savior. The contrary point of view expressed by many Americans of eminence receives no circulation by this cabal for unconditional acceptance of the United Nations and the multitude of its affiliates and programs.

The detailed operation of the UN remains a mystery to most Americans. Supported to the extent of great sums by our government, the UN has numerous departments, commissions, and

Ibid., p. 182.

agencies busily at work. Some may result in great benefit. Others are unquestionably meddlesome, useless, or dangerous. This is especially so because the proportion of Communist and Socialist representatives on these agencies is usually high. The interests of other nations come frequently into conflict with the national interests of the United States. Under the pressure of foreign governments, exerted often by a combination of collectivists, the United Nations many times has produced resolutions and taken steps in ways inimical to America. The Reece Committee report urgently suggested that the extent to which foundations have promoted "the theory that we must subordinate our own economic welfare to that of the world in order to have peace is worth an investigation of its own."

A recent publication by UNESCO acutely illustrates the need for such an investigation. Several years ago, UNESCO authorized the preparation of a series of books on the social sciences. The first of these has now appeared. It is called *Economics and Action* and was written by the former French premier, Mendès-France, with a collaborator. There will apparently be no other book on economics, so that this volume will stand, and be widely circulated, as the approved, official United Nations bible on economics. It is a strongly anti-capitalist and frankly, ardently collectivist piece of work. Others than Socialists, Communists, and extreme Keynesians will be horrified to read this UNESCO book, largely financed with American dollars.

It will be interesting to see whether The Carnegie Endowment or any of its associated organizations which so urgently propagandize for the United Nations and UNESCO will offer even a modest criticism of this publication.

Who knows what economic worldwide planning is being concocted by UN agencies, much of which will later be promoted domestically by these foundations, following their thesis that UN is the only road to peace? Nor should we forget the attempts to impose on us changes in our own basic declarations of human rights. That proposed by UN ignored the right to hold private property. Indeed in the Economic and Social Council of the

United Nations a resolution, adopted against the opposition of the United States, established the principle that no government may interfere with the right of other nations to expropriate or impair the property of its nationals. This is a discriminatory measure against private American investment abroad.

THE NEA JOINS THE PARADE

The National Education Association has worked overtime to inculcate into our children the idea that UN is a magnificent enterprise, upon which rests the world's hope. Imagine this being included in its *Education for International Understanding in American Schools—Suggestions and Recommendations*, partly financed by The Carnegie Corporation:

> Through its Security Council, every dispute that affects the peace of the world can be brought before an international body endowed with authority to take all necessary steps for the restraint of aggression.*

As the Committee report said:

> To impose this concept upon our children in the schools is to teach them nonsense. The futility of the United Nations in settling international disputes has been tragically evident. And this futility, moreover, is not the result of a failure on our part to be "international minded."

This book was prepared by the NEA's Committee on International Relations, The Association for Supervision and Curriculum Development, and The National Council for the Social Studies. *The use of the term "social studies" or "core studies" should always give pause. It is likely to indicate that children are to be fed "educational" material in accordance with the recommendations of the Commission on Social Studies of the American Historical Association to which I have earlier referred—propaganda toward a collectivism which now has broadened to international collectivism—globalism.*

The same volume asserts that we must conform our national

* *Ibid.,* p. 192.

economic policies to an international world economy; that the "nation-state system" is obsolete; that part of our political independence must be surrendered; that we must engage on a "planned economic cooperation on a worldwide scale"; and that our children must be taught to become propagandists for these ideas.* The school is to be a militant agent in the campaign for the globalist idea.

THE INTERNATIONAL SOCIAL SCIENCE RESEARCH COUNCIL

Significant, too, was the creation of an International Social Science Research Council. This was called into being through UNESCO action and at the instance of Alva Myrdal. Mrs. Myrdal, a militant Socialist who was once denied a visa by our State Department, is the wife of Gunnar Myrdal, the author of *An American Dilemma*. Mrs. Myrdal was director of the Department of Social Sciences of UNESCO when she proposed the formation of an international SSRC in 1951. The first Council meeting took place in Paris in December of that year. Donald Young took part in this meeting and played an important role in the organization of the Council. He was at the time president of The Russell Sage Foundation and had previously been president of The Social Science Research Council; he is one of the central characters of the *dramatis personae* of the foundation complex. Another of the chief American participants was Professor Otto Klineberg of Columbia University, well known as a social scientist far to the left and, incidentally, a contributor to *An American Dilemma*.

This new organization is worth watching. Apparently it is to act internationally in the clearing house and directive fashion in which the SSRC functions domestically. It seems to have intended to ape the undemocratic set-up of its American counterpart. The charter proposed at the organization meeting provided not for a democratic representation of social scientists from the participating nations but, instead, for a method of self-perpetuating domination similar to that which I have earlier described as in use in the domestic SSRC. This form of organization would have

* *Ibid.,* p. 193.

permitted the domination and utilization of this prestige organization by a closed clique, to the exclusion of all dissidents and nonconformists.

FOUNDATION INTERNATIONAL MEDDLING

If only the boards of trustees of great foundations, overwhelmingly composed of responsible and well-meaning men of distinction, would come to realize that the great funds they administer can be used to as devastating an effect in the world of men's minds as can the nuclear bombs in man's physical world! To rely upon professional employees to do their thinking for them can be hazardous to an extreme. If that seems a strong statement, consider the case of Mr. Hiss.

In 1947 Mr. Hiss was president of The Carnegie Endowment for International Peace. Its *Yearbook* then contained Recommendations of the President to the Trustees. Now that the United Nations had been established in New York, said Mr. Hiss, "the opportunity for an endowed American institution having the objectives, tradition and prestige of the Endowment, to support and serve the United Nations is very great." He then recommended that the Endowment create a program centering its activities on popularizing the United Nations and "assisting" it. This program, he said, should be "widely educational" and should not only create public opinion but "aid in the adoption of wise policies, both by our own government in its capacity as a member of the United Nations, and by the United Nations Organization as a whole."

The following section of Mr. Hiss's recommendations is worth reproducing in its entirety:

> The number and importance of decisions in the field of foreign relations with which the United States will be faced during the next few years are of such magnitude that the widest possible stimulation of public education in this field is of major and pressing importance. In furthering its educational objectives the *Endowment* should utilize its existing resources, such as *The International Relations Clubs* in

the colleges, and *International Conciliation,* and should strengthen its relationships with existing agencies interested in the field of foreign affairs. These relationships should include close collaboration with other organizations principally engaged in the study of foreign affairs, such as *The Council on Foreign Relations, The Foreign Policy Association, The Institute of Pacific Relations,* the developing university centers of international studies, and local community groups interested in foreign affairs of which the Cleveland *Council on World Affairs* and the projected *World Affairs Council* in San Francisco are examples.

Of particular importance is the unusual opportunity of reaching large segments of the population by establishing relations of a rather novel sort with the large national organizations which today are desirous of supplying their members with objective information on public affairs, including international issues. These organizations—designed to serve, respectively, the broad interests of business, church, women's, farm, labor, veterans', educational, and other large groups of our citizens—are not equipped to set up foreign policy research staffs of their own. *The Endowment* should supply these organizations with basic information about the *United Nations* and should assist them both in selecting topics of interest to their members and in presenting those topics so as to be most readily understood by their members. We should urge *The Foreign Policy Association* and *The Institute of Pacific Relations* to supply similar service on other topics of international significance.

Exploration should also be made by the Endowment as to the possibilities of increasing the effectiveness of the radio and motion pictures in public education on world affairs.*

To what extent Mr. Hiss managed to get his program rolling before his departure for prison, I do not know. He was not long enough in office to perpetrate on the American public as much damage as he was capable of. But one can well see today the

* *Ibid.,* p. 184.

execution, by his successors, of the policies formulated in the 1947 *Yearbook*. And it is worthy of note that his recommendations speak in terms of using a complex or close interlocking association with other foundations and kindred groups, including the nefarious Institute of Pacific Relations.

A propaganda agency such as The Carnegie Endowment can so easily become a vehicle for intended subversion. What is equally dangerous is that it can fall into the administrative hands of incompetent, negligent, or misguided persons, against whom the trustees, ultimately responsible for its action, can protect themselves only through either the most attentive alertness or through an abandonment of the basically hazardous occupation of propaganda.

As Dr. Frederick P. Keppel, himself president of The Carnegie Corporation, a sister organization to the Endowment, put it*:

> Danger arises whenever any group with power in its hands, whether it be a state legislature, or the board of a university or of a foundation, believes it to be its business to use its power to direct opinion. Any such group is a dangerous group, regardless of the manner of its make-up, and regardless of whether its action is conscious or unconscious, and, if conscious, whether benign or sinister in purpose.

Mr. Joseph E. Johnson, president of The Carnegie Endowment, played down the role of his foundation in world affairs in his statement to the Reece Committee. He attributed changes in American attitudes toward foreign relations to the problems created by modern social and political upheavals, by new inventions, and by two world wars. This argument is not convincing. Even if the Endowment merely reinforced what was a basic trend, its activities could not help but have a strong, accelerating impact on public opinion. The Endowment, in any event, has not confined itself to studies and discussions of public issues but has engaged in political propaganda for particular points of view, much of this propaganda directed to influencing legislation.

* Quoted with approval in Andrews, *Philanthropic Foundations*, p. 203.

8 THE FORD FOUNDATION — GARGANTUA OF PHILANTHROPY

A NEW POLICY?

AMONG THE GIANT FOUNDATIONS, The Ford Foundation is by far the largest. It was established in 1936. In 1949, the trustees finally arrived at a definitive program to "carry out the broader purposes envisaged for the Foundation by its founders and benefactors" and to reorganize within the framework of policies supposedly established by Henry Ford and his son Edsel. This program was the result of a mountain of labor by a committee of advisers under the leadership of H. Rowan Gaither, who later became president of the Foundation. The result did not differ greatly from the pattern of operations of earlier foundations such as those of Carnegie, Rockefeller, Sage, and others created for social and scholarly purposes.

The one real novelty in the Ford operation was its size. It administered billions in capital, and an annual income of some $100,000,000. The challenge and the responsibility of this wealth are beyond comparison with any historic precedent. The power to spend these trust funds for good or for bad, or simply to piddle them away in squandering ventures called for precautions in decision making far more serious than those required in a business enterprise.

In 1956 Dr. Henry T. Heald, formerly president of New York University, became president of The Ford Foundation, succeeding Mr. Gaither, who was moved up from president to chairman

221

of the board. The appointment of Dr. Heald was encouraging, not only because of his ability, character and experience but also because it may indicate a growing awareness on the part of the trustees of the many grave mistakes which had been made by the Foundation during the years which followed the adoption of the 1949 platform.

There are some signs that Dr. Heald realizes that household alterations are in order. He has stated in public utterances that the Foundation's program is subject to continuous review and evaluation; that existing programs are sometimes dropped and that changes and the creation of new programs follow only upon careful study. He must certainly understand the importance of the Foundation's directive personnel and, while only limited alterations have been made to date in the personnel setup, a new broom cannot, after all, always sweep clean overnight.

Dr. Heald stated in one address that four fifths of the money spent by the Foundation to the end of 1956 (about a billion) was devoted to education. His emphasis on education is in itself very encouraging. However, he used the term "education" in its broadest sense. For a foundation "that attempts to work for the public welfare, the principal instrument through which it can work," he said, "is education in general and higher education in particular." In supporting this statement, he uses an argument typical of foundation executives, the alleged need for social change and the benefits of such change. He suggests that it is "virtually impossible to make real and lasting progress for mankind without education and its constant extension in scope and improvement in quality." This statement is beyond questioning. But he explains further: "By definition, improvement implies and involves change. Change is not something to fear or avoid. Change is not only inevitable but desirable. Problems are solved, ills corrected, progress made by change."

He does add: "But first there must be an admission, a recognition that a problem exists. Then men of good will must go about changing things." However, this qualification seems to miss the possibility that, as to many "problems," change is not desirable.

To illustrate, a democracy is certainly inefficient. Thus, a problem exists. That does not mean that change from a democracy is desirable. To illustrate again, a problem is created by the fact that a centralized government could accomplish many functions far more effectively than a federal system. Does that mean that a change is needed or desirable?

Dr. Heald adds: "If nothing needs changing, then we are all wasting our time and our resources, for there is nothing really to be done except to feed and clothe people." This emphasis on change is classic among the executives of the "concentration of power." There is, after all, much that a foundation can do, which does not involve promoting "change," in addition to feeding and clothing people. No one in his right mind would assert that no improvements in our society are possible or desirable, but the emphasis on change by the newly elected president of the largest foundation in the world* implies an eagerness to pursue what Professor Colegrove has called the "pathological" approach to research. Dr. Heald believes in the power of man "to leave the world a better place than it was when he entered it." This is a proposition which, again, one can readily accept. But is it true, as he says, that the challenge can only be met "by changing the environment in which [man] finds himself—always, we hope, for the better; always working for social and economic improvements in the lot of all people * * *"? Does this concern for betterment in the material world of "social and economic improvement" not indicate a neglect of the nonmaterial, the spiritual values which have at least as much importance as the physical?

What could be more obvious than that change is desirable when it is desirable? But the emphasis so frequently put by foundation leaders on "change" often results in advocating change because it is change—as though there were a certainty of improvement if there were a change.

Dr. Heald has adopted the "risk-capital" and "experimentation" concepts. It is not yet clear whether his interpretation of these two

---

* At the October 11, 1956, meeting of the American Council on Education.

terms follows the general line of the complex. It is encouraging to have him say that a foundation sometimes should even support the exploration of unpopular ideas. A dedication to the support of the nonconformist is most laudable, and we can only hope that it is followed. The Ford Foundation has not demonstrated this dedication in the past. Quite to the contrary, it has, in most instances, supported the ruling clique of materialistic social scientists who once were a minority but long since have become, with foundation assistance, a clear majority. I regret that I have not seen, in any of Dr. Heald's public utterances, any consciousness of the danger of supporting this type of conformity.

In many areas this ruling clique in the social sciences, so well supported by The Ford Foundation and others, advocates change of institutions, principles, and methods, and of social, economic, and political mechanisms which a great many people (in some instances a vast majority of the people) wish to have retained as they are. Where is the support for those who wish to protect something we have, against well-financed movements to change it? Is only the man who wants to change something to be given foundation support?

In Dr. Heald's public statements I have found much to be admired and applauded. If I am critical or questioning of some of his remarks it is to bring into focus problems of foundation theory and management which, I believe, sorely need attention and discussion. In an address of April 4, 1957, for example, he touches on the problem of foundation responsibility by saying that "education extends beyond the academic world and into the atmosphere of society, which is made up of beliefs and ambitions of the aggregate of its members." He follows with this statement: "This is where foundations, among others, have an appropriate role to play, not in the shaping of those beliefs and ambitions but in helping to provide people concerned with them and competent to understand, maintain and realize them." Just what does this mean? Is it possible to "provide" people competent to "realize" "ambitions" without, in turn, being responsible for the contents of what these people "maintain"? Can one intentionally deal with change without being responsible for the change which one finances?

If a foundation makes grants "to improve governmental processes," how can it avoid entering the field of politics and partisan action? What constitutes "improvement"? Such a term involves value-concepts and, therefore, offers a problem not subject to solution through a scientific method of approach free of preconceived political concepts of value. So many foundation executives seem to fail to see the determining influence of *a priori* assumptions of the "desirable," of the socially "commendable," and of similar yardsticks for judgment. For this reason they do not seem to realize how much of what they do is political.

Here is an example. The spending of 63 million dollars to advance international understanding, desirable as this goal may appear, is the result of *a priori* assumptions regarding ethical and practical values, ultimate purposes and potentials. There can be no possible objection to the relief of the poor and sick, wherever they may suffer. But the expenditure of 58 million dollars in overseas development programs "to help the emerging new democratic nations of the world to help themselves" cannot be separated from an inherent political intention—or from such *a priori* assumptions as: that these nations are democratic; that their democracy, if they have it, is good for them; that the adoption of some democratic processes necessarily results in the adoption of democratic ideas of peace and justice; that immediate institution of democracy in these undeveloped nations is good for mankind; and that democracy is better nurtured if supported from the outside than if it stands upon its own feet. I do not mean to conjecture which, if any, of these assumptions are wrong, but to emphasize that they are *a priori* assumptions.

In an address on April 8, 1957, Dr. Heald, discussing the Responsibilities of Private Philanthropy, indicates an awareness that the responsibility of foundations to the public goes beyond the mere publication of reports. Foundation activities, he says, involve "risk, and they require intelligence, judgment and wisdom. Their ultimate success or failure forms the basis on which the foundations will be judged by the public they serve and which gives them the freedom and the opportunity they enjoy." But then Dr. Heald seems to fall into an error conventional to the manager of the "concentration." He identifies the responsibilities of a foundation in terms of the promotion of concepts of value. He speaks of a foundation's "freedom to discriminate, to take chances, to try to identify the good and make it better." This amounts not to a mere support of controversy but to an actual taking of sides on controversial issues.

There is no general agreement on what is good for society. In a democratic society the decision of what is good for it (what is right and what is wrong in effect) is decided by a majority. The injection of foundation power into the democratic process by which the majority makes these value decisions creates an imbalance interfering with the concept that public affairs should be controlled by the free will of the people. The freedom referred to by Dr. Heald implies belief in an intellectually aristocratic élite of foundation managers with the right to influence our fate. Consistently with this élite concept, he speaks of the opportunity and responsibility "to pioneer ahead of public opinion, to do * * * things that might not at the time they are done be approved by popular vote, to be ahead but not too far ahead." Such a right to be "ahead" of the people can be exercised by an individual if he cares to exercise it. Whether such a right is attributable to a juridical person operating with public trust funds, is highly questionable. To pioneer ahead of public opinion means indulging directly or indirectly in propaganda of a kind that is the sole privilege of the citizen and not the right of a tax-exempt organization.

I agree with Dr. Heald that "stimulating the development of ideas" is a legitimate concern of foundations. But the development function should be left to others. The foundation should confine itself to giving competing forces a fair and equal chance. Only if equal chance is given can free competition in the market place of ideas take place.

Dr. Heald describes the Ford Foundation's hope of serving our society and thus advancing human welfare in general in this manner: "First, to identify existing centers of excellence and contribute to their continued improvement, and second, to help the number of these centers increase." In selecting these centers, the Foundation expects to find "individuals, departments, organizations, or entire institutions whose curiosity in the realm of ideas holds most promise—as far as this can be determined—for tomorrow's world." This statement again suggests value judgments of a political nature. It is a program which could only be accepted as just and sound if equal chance were given to competing ideas and to the respective representatives or defenders of these ideas. I do not see how those in positions like Dr. Heald's can forget that the tax-exemption privilege is granted by *all* the people, irrespective of their creeds, ideas, and political goals. How can a foundation rightly exhibit partisan preferences at the expense of that part of the public which does not support these preferences! Tax exemption does not make foundations the guardians of the nation in the world of ideas and in planning for the future.

"The Ford Foundation is interested in improving American society," says its president. He says that experiments and research underwritten by the Foundation "may not be uniformly popular, and probably should not be. Problems in the social sciences are not problems of which everyone is aware or on whose easy solution everyone agrees. Yet it is part of the foundation function to cruise ahead of popular notions, to risk being sniped at, when there is a valid gain to be made." This, it seems to me, is the "social-engineering" concept gone wild. Is it not presumptuous of foundation administrators to assume that their choice of values is superior to that of others?

"Ye shall be as gods," said the serpent in Paradise, in offering the forbidden fruit, "knowing good and evil."

It is my own hope that Dr. Heald will take the time to challenge conventional concepts of foundation management, such as I have criticized above, and to think through on his own the difficult problems involved. As the chief administrator of the largest tax-exempt fund in our history, he owes this duty to the people.

THE RECENT PAST

The Annual Report of The Ford Foundation for 1956, signed by Mr. Gaither, contains the latest statements of the Foundation's policies. As I shall explain later, the Foundation started with five major areas of proposed activity. It has now extended into twenty-three major project areas. It continues its plan to set up successive, new, self-contained funds under separate boards of management, thus delegating its jurisdiction and trust functions to others. The report makes much of the relinquishment of control of the Foundation by the Ford family. This step might have been desirable from several points of view, including the desirability of shifting any onus of responsibility from the controlling proprietors of the Ford Motor Company. But the shift from family control to a self-perpetuating, bureaucratic control may not have been so commendable. It took the risk of a characteristic breeding of power cliques of administrators and the use of resources for political ends instead of for charitable donations.

Having been given control of the Foundation, the trustees, says Mr. Gaither, "accepted the challenge of the maturing concept of American foundation philanthropy in which emphasis had shifted over a period of some forty years from the effects of social problems to their *causes*. They agreed that the resources of the Foundation should be committed to the solution of *problems* constituting grave threats or obstacles to human progress—such as the growing demands on the educational structure and the need for improved understanding of and between men and nations." No one could disagree with the desirability of solving the problems which Mr. Gaither mentions. But solutions for such problems are chiefly political. Foundations which take the initiative, the propagandistic leadership, for social change cease to be philanthropic in the legal meaning of the term and enter into the political arena where they do not belong.

The choice of measures to remove unfavorable causes in our body social is clearly a political-partisan matter. So, in effect, is

THE RECENT PAST 229

the defining of what constitutes "progress." Contrary to the belief prevalent among some foundations, the currently foundation-orthodox ideas about progress and the need for change are not universally accepted. There is a noticeable and vehement revolt among American thinkers who oppose materialistic concepts of progress and pragmatic solutions of problems, basing their distaste for them on religious or philosophical convictions.

A good illustration of this revolt is to be found in an address delivered by Dr. Ralph Cooper Hutchinson, President of Lafayette College, on March 21, 1957, under the auspices of the Committee of Sponsors of the Greater Philadelphia Council of Churches. In this address he inveighed against the assault of scientific humanism on ideals. He named four teachings of scientific humanism which constitute "particular dangers." One is that "all is natural and all truth is subject to discovery and determination through science." "As a consequence," he said, "there is no higher law, no law written in the heart, no law on the tables of stones, no law revealed in the sublimities of nature, no law in the inner conscience, no law of God." He described the second danger: "as the belief, following the lead of Bacon, Lenin, Hogben and Bernal," that "there are no values save material and scientific realities." The third danger he says is that "the objective of all life" is deemed to be "social progress." "Here," he continues, "is one of the greatest values and greatest vices of scientific humanism, because of course social progress is good. The scientific humanist has arbitrarily inherited and adopted the concept from the Christian ethic. But he makes it the supreme good and only goal. * * * Social progress is the only norm, the only ideal, the only objective. All other values are dismissed."

Since "social progress is the only value" to scientific humanism, said Dr. Hutchinson in describing its fourth danger, "the end justifies the means," means which may be coercive and ignore the rights of the individual. "All the developing power of science is to be used to bring about the social progress desired. Hence the use of laws to achieve social progress * * *." We are going along with these evils," continued Dr. Hutchinson. "Inflamed by the fad for social progress and reform, we have given up the teaching of social idealism and have embarked on what we call 'liberal movements.' We are achieving social progress by legislation. Instead of persuading men we command them. * * * In our moral judgments we have gone over into the enemies' territory because while not denying God it is becoming very common to deny any higher law. * * * We have substituted an opportunistic and relative ethic for the absolute. We are becoming a compromising relativistic uncertain people recognizing no absolute right or wrong, no higher law."

Have any foundation administrators the moral and ethical right to ignore the position of the great number of intelligent Americans who think as does Dr. Hutchinson and to direct the trust funds which these administrators disburse solely or predominantly to those of the opposing point of view?

There is one hopeful sign in the broadening which the extension of The Ford Foundation's original platform indicates; this broadening at least exhibits some flexibility. We can only hope that the Foundation will move further and further away from the temptation to adjust our body politic to blueprints designed by ideological and political factions. This is so important in the case of The Ford Foundation because of its immense size. Its errors can be huge errors, gigantic in impact. It has no peer in size or potential. When The Ford Foundation takes sides, who can be its match! How can there be a fair test of ideas!

The managers of the Foundation seem to have an exaggerated sense of mission and importance. Without apparently realizing how much it applies to his own foundation, Mr. Gaither quotes Dr. Raymond B. Fosdick, former president of The Rockefeller Foundation, as follows:

> Every social agency, including a foundation, has within it not only the seeds of possible decay but a tendency to exalt the machinery of organization above the purposes for which the organization is created.

Mr. Gaither's belief that the Foundation should decide what social problems exist, endeavor to determine their causes, and find
measures to remedy them, expresses an *excessus mandati*.

Mr. Gaither deems the philanthropic process as "at best a
reasonable system of providing resources and opportunities for
men capable of creative thinking in what has been described as
a gigantic bet on the improvability of man" (emphasis supplied).
This is again tampering with law and with the body social. There
are responsible schools of thought which do not believe in the
"improvability" of man—and this includes the Christian religions.
What Mr. Gaither propounds as a brand of foundation philosophy
is the old Pelagian heresy of the fifth century, opposed by Augus-
tine and later by the Reformation. I do not profess the competence
to discuss whether man is "improvable" or not, but the massive
body of opinion against it would indicate that a foundation should
steer carefully clear of basing a disposition of its vast funds on
the support of the "improvability" theory. Of course, Mr. Gaither
may not have meant what he said. He may have meant merely
"the improvability of man's conditions" or the "improvability of
man's education" or something like that. If that be so, a lesson is
apparent. Foundation managers should not try to be philosophers
or, at least, not attempt to select brands of philosophy upon which
to base the support of research. Such decisions are far too dangerous for foundation managers to handle.

There are some encouraging features in Mr. Gaither's report.
He recognizes the responsibility of a foundation for the results of
its grants, at least to the extent of seeing the need of examination
and review. He says: "The Foundation retains a continuing responsibility to review and evaluate the grantees' accomplishments
under the grant. If the Foundation should conclude that it has
fallen short of the objective, or that a grantee has exhibited poor
judgment in a series of events over a substantial period of time,
the Foundation has the inherent right—and indeed the obligation
—to withhold further support for such a grantee. * * * Thus the
responsibility for making judgments cannot be evaded by those
whose responsibility it is to administer the resources of philan-

thropy." I would hope that Mr. Gaither and others like him would also come to the point of recognizing the social duty to take such corrective or remedial action as may be possible when a project has turned out badly or unfairly.

Encouraging, too, was the 1956 grant to Harvard, even though in the small sum of $25,000, for "improving the understanding of American capitalism." How rarely, indeed, is such a grant to be found among lists of major foundation benefactions. Grants for change, yes. Grants to defend that capitalism upon which our nation has grown strong, that capitalism which gave birth to The Ford Foundation, that capitalism which has been under trip-hammer attack by a multitude of foundation-supported intellectuals, have been almost as rare as hens' teeth.

One reported grant of $195,000 to Columbia University is more difficult to understand, though it may indicate a friendlier attitude toward business. It is for a study of the legal, business, and political problems of Joint International Business Ventures (such as the oil consortium of Iran). Such studies could be well left to the managements of the wealthy corporations involved in such international deals.

Eminently discouraging in Mr. Gaither's report is evidence of the continued extensive use of intermediary organizations to disburse the Foundation's money. Among these, prominently, are The Social Science Research Council and the allegedly non-partisan Foreign Policy Association now under the partisan presidency of Vera Micheles Dean. Most astounding are the grants to other foundations: for example, to The Russell Sage Foundation, The Carnegie Endowment for International Peace, and The Whitney Foundation. The connections with other foundations are so numerous there seems almost to be a mixture of management.

In the most important field of the behavioral sciences, for instance, an Advisory Committee assists the Foundation in the selection of recipient universities. Among the members of this Committee, in addition to the directors of the Foundation-financed Center for Advanced Study in the Behavioral Sciences, are Charles Dollard of the Carnegie Endowment; Hans Speier of The

THE RECENT PAST 233

Rand Corporation; Donald Young of The Russell Sage Foundation; and Fillmore Sandford of the American Psychological Association. Messrs. Dollard and Young are very familiar names. They selected Stuart Chase to do *The Proper Study of Mankind*, the exposition of the current social-science orthodoxy. Their names appear, again and again, in foundation operations. Hans Speier, before coming to this country and serving as a professor at the New School for Social Research and later as director of the social-studies section of the supersecret Rand Corporation, had contributed extensively to radical Socialist publications, especially to Rudolf Hilferding's *Die Gesellschaft*, in Germany.

Here is another example. The Report describes a committee of five which assists the Foundation in awarding grants-in-aid to individual scholars. Of this committee of five, one is the same Hans Speier; a second is the same Charles Dollard; a third is the same Donald Young. On the very next page of the Report appears the name of Professor Paul Lazarsfeld of Columbia, who is reported to be engaged in directing the "improvement" of "advanced training in social research." He, too, is a standard character, appearing again and again on the rolls of the foundation-favored. Are our academies so bereft of scholarship that foundations must use the same few technicians over and over again!

The sorry story of The Fund for the Republic, that strange child of The Ford Foundation, has embarrassed its parent, which has sought to shift responsibility by repeatedly affirming the complete independence of The Fund. But there seem to be left vestiges of the spirit which caused The Fund for the Republic to be created. On page 42 of the Report is a picture of Joseph Welch, who was selected to appear on a television program to expound on the "Constitution's protection of individual civil liberties." Mr. Welch is a lawyer who came into national prominence as the opponent of the late Senator McCarthy. There is a definite controversy associated with the term "civil liberties," a controversy in which Mr. Welch took a fervent side. However excellent a lawyer he may be, to have selected him to discuss "civil liberties" was an exercise of political partisanship.

Similarly, on page 36 of the 1956 Ford Foundation Report, appears a picture of Professor Zechariah Chafee of Harvard, conducting a "regular TV course on human rights." Professor Chafee was an eminent and very articulate partisan in the controversy over "civil liberties," "human rights," and the Fifth Amendment. He was also an endorser of many pro-Communist causes. In his speeches and writings he supported and expounded the same position taken by Dr. Hutchins and by the propaganda of The Fund for the Republic. Grave issues are involved, including the extent to which the doctrine of States' Rights applies to restrict Federal action; the relative importance and leverage of the various individual liberties granted by the Constitution and the Amendments; the significance of the Constitutional reservation of unenumerated basic rights to the people; the proper powers of Congressional committees; the significance and proper use of the Fifth Amendment; the propriety and legality of methods used to fight communism; and others. On these issues, The Ford Foundation has enlisted its enormous power on one side. How was the other side represented? It was not represented. One can only conclude that it was the *intention and purpose* of The Ford Foundation to propagandize for one side of these grave issues. Such a taking of sides by a foundation must surely be condemned bitterly. In the case of The Ford Foundation, its Gargantuan size makes its violation of propriety (and perhaps of law) all the more serious.

It would be interesting to make a thorough study of the recipients of funds for research and the specific projects for which Ford Foundation funds were expended. There seems not the slightest doubt that it would disclose a relatively limited circle of institutions, their academicians, and their graduate students. Familiar names appear and reappear. Samuel Stouffer of Harvard receives a grant with no strings attached. So does Marie Jahoda of New York University (former wife of Professor Paul Lazarsfeld). With Mr. Speier on the awarding committee, we find two of his Rand Corporation staff members, Messrs. Goldhamer and Leites, similarly benefited. And so it goes.

In the field of research and education a foundation does not seem to me to have any right to discriminate and to favor certain groups and individuals. Its funds are in use through the grace of all the people. To exclude individuals or institutions because of their philosophies or religious persuasions seems indefensible. One form of discrimination is most difficult to understand. There are 30 million Catholics in this country, who maintain scores of universities and colleges. Their institutions do not figure among the favored of the foundation complex, nor are academicians connected with them likely to receive research grants from the complex. Perhaps there is a good reason for this discrimination. If so, I cannot guess what it might be. True, Catholic institutions were included among the institutional donees to which The Ford Foundation recently donated a huge aggregate of money, a step which deserved the most enthusiastic approval of the general public. But when it comes to special, individual grants, to find a Catholic institution as a donee is a rarity indeed.

The massive Ford grants to institutions, hospitals, colleges, and medical schools was a very hopeful sign that there might at least be dissension within The Ford Foundation, a conflict between the old school of thought and the new which favors a nonpolitical and constructive use of its funds. The earlier history of the Foundation, especially in the era of Messrs. Paul Hoffman and Robert M. Hutchins, was, to say the least, controversial. The first appointments to the Foundation staff after the 1949 platform was adopted were influenced by these two proponents of radicalism in public affairs. It may take years before this influence, inherited by the new management, can be overcome. It can hardly be overcome unless The Ford Foundation decides to avoid joint ventures with other foundations, to eliminate trustees, executives, and advisers now or recently connected with other foundations or distributing organizations—all this in the interests of trying to effect an unhampered and free contest of ideas.

THE EARLIER HISTORY OF THE FORD FOUNDATION

After an initial period, during which the foundation had no definite policies to govern its grants, a designed program was adopted, upon recommendation of a special committee. This committee was headed by W. Rowan Gaither, Jr., who later became president of the foundation. Mr. Gaither has said that Mr. Ford wanted to know what the people of the United States thought the foundation should use its money for and, accordingly, went out to see "the people." But "the people" turned out to be a large number of "experts" of various kinds—who thought they ought to be able to say what was good for "the people."

The result was a 139-page book, which can be obtained from The Ford Foundation. Its major thesis was that the Ford Foundation should try to help solve the problems of mankind and to do so in five areas:

The Establishment of Peace.
The Strengthening of Democracy.
The Strengthening of the Economy.
Education in a Democratic Society.
Individual Behavior and Human Relations.

Raymond Moley pointed out that the committee which had designed this program was

> composed of a lawyer, W. Rowan Gaither, Jr., now president of the foundation; a doctor; a school administrator; and five professors. None of these were experienced in foundation work. It could hardly be a coincidence that the five "areas" which they recommended for the foundation correspond, to a degree, to the academic departments in which the professors had been teaching.
>
> The plan substantially ruled out medical research, public health, and natural science on the vague ground that "progress toward democratic goals are today social rather than physical." "Democratic goals" are nowhere defined.*

* *Newsweek,* January 9, 1956.

Nevertheless, no one could quarrel with the selection of the five fields of activity, vague as they might be, if the plan were to make only direct and simple grants to desirable institutions and individuals. A grant to Harvard University for so vague a purpose as to "help strengthen democracy" or one to Columbia for "studies in group psychology" could result in nothing but applause, so long as these institutions were to be permitted to determine for themselves how the grants were to be applied. But this was not the Ford Foundation plan. The foundation was to spend most of its efforts in the detailed designing of how its selected purposes were to be achieved.

Whether it was because an overwhelming number of the consulted "experts" were "liberals," or because the initial directive management of the foundation was "liberal" and sought "liberal" justification for a "liberal" program, at any rate The Ford Foundation became a conscious "liberal" vehicle.

(I must here remind the reader of my definition of the term "liberal" as I use it throughout this book. I do not mean a liberal in the traditional sense; the "liberal" to whom I refer is almost the diametric opposite of the classic liberal, who is devoted to personal freedom. The "liberal" to whom I refer is, at the very least, tinged with Marxism, Fabianism, or some other variety of economic collectivism and political centralization. He is a "statist," an advocate of highly centralized government, of "state planning," of paternalism. His direction is away from personal and group management of affairs and toward government management.)

An eminent "liberal," Mr. Paul Hoffman, was selected as chief administrator of The Ford Foundation. His political predilections were well known when he was appointed chairman and have become more evident since. For one of his chief assistants, he selected Dr. Robert Maynard Hutchins, a "liberal" educator and publicist whose ideas are even more extreme than Mr. Hoffman's. The Wall Street Journal said in an editorial: "Money spent in the clouds is money frittered away." And further: "The task of disbursing millions of dollars for so nebulous a goal as 'the welfare of the people' is a formidable one; the very magnitude and vagueness of the goal make it difficult to grapple with on a practical level."* The difficult task was handed over to Mr. Hoffman, who relied heavily on Dr. Hutchins.

Not only these two were "liberals." The major staff members, the men who were to do the principal thinking for the trustees, were almost all "liberals." One cannot believe that this selection was coincidental. These men do not represent a cross-section of American belief. Their selection was not even a case of choosing a "liberal" majority. There were virtually no conservatives on the staff. Dwight Macdonald described the typical Ford Foundation staff member as "youngish" and "of a liberal turn politically, habituated to collective, nonprofit enterprise. . . ."†

As might be expected, the academic advisers who were called in, from time to time, both to advise on, and in many instances to direct, studies or projects, were again overwhelmingly "liberals." There are, in the United States, many academicians of eminence who are either wholly objective politically or who have a conservative cast of mind. You might be able to find one of these associated with Ford Foundation projects if you look long and carefully; but you will find him, if at all, hidden behind a mass of dedicated "liberals."

Thus, the largest foundation ever created became a vehicle for the type of planning which is dear to the hearts of the "liberal." Its chief executives were "liberals," its staff was overwhelmingly, if not wholly, "liberal," and its advisers were selected almost entirely from the "liberal" group.

It would have been possible, to be sure, even with such heavily slanted foundation personnel, to keep on an objective course; strength of purpose, application, and alertness on the part of its trustees could have done so. In the case of The Ford Foundation, however, this did not happen. Mr. Hoffman and Dr. Hutchins were eventually released, after Mr. Henry Ford II and some of the other trustees could stand their activities no longer. In the meantime, great damage had been done with the vast financial power

---

* December 14, 1955.
† *The Ford Foundation*, p. 98.

which the foundation administered. Nor can we be certain that the trustees, having rid themselves of Mr. Hoffman and Dr. Hutchins, are ready to purge the foundation of its strongly "liberal" elements or are even acutely conscious of the social necessity of operating this great public trust with an objective staff.

I wish to make clear, at this point, that I do not take the position that a foundation must be "conservative" or have a predominance of "conservative" employees or even of any particular percentage of "conservatives." But I do criticize The Ford Foundation for having allowed itself to acquire a distinctly, consciously "liberal" character. I maintain that a tax-exempt trust, such as a foundation, should be wholly objective politically and economically—better still, should avoid, as much as possible, injecting itself into areas or projects which are susceptible of being directed by political-minded foundation executions toward propagandistic ends, or in which political opinion may play a directive part.

It has not been uncommon in the United States for a foundation theoretically managed by predominantly conservative trustees to be taken over in operation by a "liberal" group and directed largely by it to political ends. In the case of The Ford Foundation, this process was made very easy through the plan of detailed operation which the trustees permitted themselves to be persuaded to adopt. Under this plan, and it was made utterly clear, the trustees were not to interfere with the staff.

The Report of the Study for the Ford Foundation on Policy and Program, dated November 19, 1949, reads in part as follows:

> Individual members of the Board of Trustees should not seek to decide the technical questions involved in particular applications and projects. Nothing would more certainly destroy the effectiveness of the foundation. On the contrary, the Trustees will be most surely able to control the main lines of policy of the Foundation, and the contribution it will make to human welfare, if they give the President and the officers considerable freedom in developing the program, while they avoid influencing (even by in-

direction) the conduct of projects to which the Foundation has granted funds. (Pages 127 and 128.)

As individuals, the Trustees should learn as much as they can by all means possible, formal and informal, about the program of the Foundation in relation to the affairs of the world. But the Board of Trustees, as a responsible body, should act only according to its regular formal procedures, and usually on the agenda, the dockets, and the recommendations presented by the President. (Page 128.)

The meetings of the Board should be arranged so that the discussion will not be directed mainly at the individual grants recommended by the officers, and institutions to receive them. Nothing could destroy the effectiveness of the Board more certainly than to have the agenda for its meetings consist exclusively of small appropriation items, each of which has to be judged on the basis of scientific considerations, the academic reputation of research workers, or the standing of institutions. If the agenda calls solely for such discussions the Board will necessarily fail to discuss the main issues of policy and will inevitably interfere in matters in which it has no special competence. (Page 130.)

A foundation may wish from time to time to make small grants, either to explore the possibilities of larger programs, or to take advantage of an isolated and unusual opportunity. For such purposes it will be useful for the Trustees to set up (and replenish from time to time) a discretionary fund out of which the President may make grants on his own authority. The Trustees should set a limit on the aggregate amount which the President may award in discretionary grants during a given period, rather than set a fixed limit on the size of a single grant. * * *

The President of the Ford Foundation, as its principal officer, should not only serve as a member of the Board of Trustees, but should be given full authority to administer its organization.

He should have full responsibility for presenting recommendations on program to the Board, and full authority to appoint and remove all other officers and employees of the Foundation. * * * (Page 132.)

The founders of at least two of the larger American foundations intended their trustees to devote a major amount of their time to the active conduct of foundation affairs. Usually this arrangement has not proved practicable. * * * (Page 133.)

* * * for the program of a foundation may be determined more certainly by the selection of its top officers than by any statement of policy or any set of directions. * * *

The Reece Committee report commented on this platform as follows:

> *We cannot escape the conclusion that the trustees of the Ford Foundation abdicated their trust responsibility in assenting to this plan of operation, under which everything except possibly the establishment of glittering generalities could be left to employees.**

In his book *The Ford Foundation*, Dwight Macdonald points out how vexatious a job it is to run a large foundation.† Massive, boring detail is required of those who would expend vast sums on directed research.

> Like an army, the United Nations, and other large, bureaucratic organizations, a foundation excretes an extraordinary quantity of words, most of them of stupefying dullness.‡

Is it the trustees who plough through this material? No, replies Mr. Macdonald. In the case of the Ford Foundation:

* P. 26.
† Mr. Macdonald, incidentally, is no friend of the Reece Committee. His book completely ignores the mass of critical material produced by it and writes off its work with some highly uncomplimentary characterizations. However, he implicitly supports many of the most important criticisms of foundation operation made by the Reece Committee and actually adds valuable illustrative material to the data critical of foundations and of The Ford Foundation in particular.
‡ *The Ford Foundation*, p. 109.

The Foundation's fourteen trustees, prominent and busy men of affairs, are shielded by the staff from the main spate of bureaucratic rhetoric.*

That is, while the trustees are, no doubt, confronted periodically with a certain number of reports presented by their professional employees—and these reports, in themselves, are difficult enough fully to understand—they do not even see the mass of material which the staff uses in deciding upon programs, plans, projects, and grantees. The trustees know only in a general way what is going on. They act only upon what has been filtered up to them from the echelons below. They exercise little more than superficial direction of the foundation's affairs, in relation to directed or designed projects.

After all, what can be expected of a trustee unfamiliar with the gobbledygook which is the *lingua franca* of the professional foundation administrator? The tendency of many foundation executives to avoid writing simply, can be attributed, I am sure, to a certain aping of the social scientists with whom they come into contact and whose obscure writings they so frequently see. Many of these "scientists" have what Professor Sorokin in his recent book, *Fads and Foibles in Modern Sociology and Related Sciences,* calls "speech disorders." One of these speech disorders, he says, is "a ponderously obscure description of platitudes." In an effort to make their "sciences" sound more "scientific," they take over terms which have precise meaning in a natural science and implant them in their own work. Professor Sorokin mentions some of these terms (and others constructed out of whole cloth): *syntality, synergy, ergic, metanergic, valence, cathexis, inductibility, topological medium, hodological space, edience, abience, enthropy, org, animorg.* He illustrates the resulting nonsense by describing certain historical incidents as a social scientist with this speech disorder might do it:

* * * in March 1917 the location of Russia locomoted on a two-dimensional plane (surface) from monarchy to re-

* *Ibid.,* p. 110.

public, with positive cathexis and promotive inductibility of the Provisional government vectorized toward the goal of a democratic regime. In October 1917 this locomotion was followed by a new locomotion in hodological space, fluid and permeable, along the dimensions of Communism, marked by negative cathexis, and contrient inductibility toward a democratic structure of "groupness," "we-ness," "valence," and "syntality." *

Mr. Macdonald gives some actual examples of this foundation language, which no trustee could be expected to understand without an interpreter at his elbow. Take this one relating to a proposed study of the experience of foreign students in the United States:

> The general purpose is to develop techniques for evaluating the impact of exchange-of-persons experiences on foreign students in order to produce, through intensive, controlled investigation, a body of information on the effect of exchange that can serve as a basis for a wider analysis of the many variable factors in particular exchanges.

Mr. Macdonald explains this as meaning that The Social Science Research Council (in this instance) is to spend $225,000 (provided by the Ford, Carnegie, and Rockefeller foundations) on a study which will make it possible to do more studies.

Mr. Macdonald quotes further from an SSRC report on this Ford-supported proposed study:

> The first phase had consisted of intensive exploratory studies of the adjustment of foreign students to life on American campuses * * *. As was hoped these studies focussed the attention of the committee on a number of problems of salient theoretical and practical interests, and resulted in the formulation of many hypotheses about the determinants of various outcomes of the students' sojourn. As is generally the case with intensive studies, however, the data

* See pp. 21-30.

served to document varieties of cross-cultural experience rather than to support firm conclusions about causes and effects. The committee early decided, therefore, that the next phase of its work would be devoted to well-focussed, systematic studies designed to test hypotheses and attack major problems discerned in the initial phase of its research.*

Mr. Macdonald translates these sonorous phrases to mean: they were disappointed in the work which had been done; they did not find out anything; they were starting all over again. Mr. Macdonald comments: "The American academic world, thanks partly to the foundations, is becoming a place where committees accumulate and thought decays."

Into this complex and difficult world the trustees of The Ford Foundation have thrust themselves. Able as they are, they could quite possibly acquire enough information and data to steer themselves through it with sufficient understanding. But to accomplish this would be a full-time job and a very arduous one.

It has been reported that the Ford Foundation trustees meet for two days, four times a year; that they do some homework; that they have informal talks with Mr. Gaither occasionally; and that they act on committees from time to time. This would be enough if the foundation merely made grants of the type which recently won such great acclaim—direct grants to operating institutions for simple and valuable uses. However, because The Ford Foundation operates in obscure and difficult areas of activity and devotes itself largely, if not principally, to designing and directing projects, the trustees could not possibly do their work adequately by devoting, as they do, only one twelfth of every year to the job.

Mr. Henry Ford II is the most important member of the Ford Foundation board. How much time does he spend on its work? He has been quoted as saying: "I rarely take a position on any program until the staff has acted on it." His main job is that of chief executive of the Ford Motor Company, a rather large enterprise to

* *The Ford Foundation*, pp. 105-106.

conduct. He has rightly said: "If I got mixed up in all that" (meaning the detailed work of The Ford Foundation) "I'd never get anything done around here" (meaning the Ford Motor Company).*

Mr. Ford and the other trustees of The Ford Foundation "run" it in the sense that they are the legal repositories of the management power. They "run" it also in the sense that they exercise the right to approve or reject major proposals. They do not "run" it, however, in the practical sense; they delegate their power to others. Even if they were to apply their full time to the work, it would be difficult for them to acquire a sufficient understanding of the vast areas in which the foundation operates to enable them to check the work of their employees. Spending the equivalent of one month per year in the foundation's service, they are dependent on what these employees plan, approve, and execute.

Foundation apologists have tried to draw an analogy with an industrial corporation, holding that the foundation trustee is in the same position as the director of a commercial enterprise. The analogy is not apt. The foundation trustee cannot discharge his duty through the limited type of service which his directorship in a commercial company involves. The ultimate, basic purpose of the trust enterprise which he is to help direct is the selection of grants and grantees. He is, in the true sense, a trustee. His fundamental, essential trust function is to select grants and grantees with understanding, intelligence, and objectivity.

Trustee alertness is sorely necessary, because political slants are so easily introduced into social material. The Reece Committee report extracted an excellent example out of the 1952 report of The Ford Foundation. The trustees who passed that report must have done so in ignorance, for it contained this false statement:

> The high cost of a college and of a higher education in general makes real equality of opportunity impossible. More

---

* Mr. Ford made these statements while chairman of the Ford Foundation board of trustees. Since then, he has retired as chairman, while remaining a trustee. It is to be presumed that he will be able to give no more time to his position as a trustee than he was able to give to that of chairman.

and more the financial burden is being thrust upon the student in the form of higher tuition fees. *In consequence, higher education threatens to become increasingly the prerogative of the well-to-do.**

The fact is exactly the opposite. "More and more," the less well-to-do are getting college educations. Here are the statistics on college attendance:

Year	Students enrolled (by thousands)
1900	238
1910	355
1920	598
1930	1,101
1940	1,494
1950	2,659

And the increase since 1950 has been so great that the colleges are swamped; their facilities are far below the demand. As the Reece Committee report asked:

> Why did representatives of The Ford Foundation, who were well aware of the true facts, make such false statements: Did they intend political propaganda? Did they wish to manufacture a class argument, an attack on the well-to-do who alone are able (which is false) to attend colleges! †

The predominance of "liberal" direction of The Ford Foundation's affairs—the overwhelming predominance of the leftward-tending point of view among its professional staff—makes it all the more dangerous for the trustees to delegate their basic duties. That this leftish predominance has been translated into foundation action appeared clearly from the limited studies which the Reece Committee was able to undertake and from further data which have appeared since its work closed. A complete Congressional study of the operations of The Ford Foundation, to audit

---

* Reece Committee *Report,* p. 123. Emphasis supplied.
† *Loc. cit.*

the discharge of the trustees of their duties to the people of the United States, should be made.

Let us see some of the record to date.

THE (FORD) BEHAVIORAL SCIENCES FUND

The Reece Committee's report included a diagram of the structure of The Ford Foundation and its subsidiaries. This gigantic operation has grown so complex that it is no wonder the central trustees cannot possibly follow all its operations. The diagram shows, as major divisions:

Adult Education
Advancement of Education
East European Fund
Intercultural Publications
Resources for the Future
Fund for the Republic
Center for Advanced Study
TV Workshop
Foundation External Grant
Behavioral Sciences Division
    Research & Training Abroad
    Institutional Exchange Program
    Grants in Aid

The 1956 Report (p. 17) diagrams a still longer list of divisional activities:

International affairs
International training and research
Overseas development
International legal studies
Public affairs
Fund for the Republic
Economic affairs
Resources for the Future
Business administration

Behavioral sciences
Center for Advanced Studies
Mental health research
Fund for Adult Education
Medical education
Hospital aid
Council on Library Resources
National Merit Scholarships
Faculty salaries
Humanities
Education
Educational television
Fund for Advancement of Education
TV-Radio Workshop

And more may be breeding.

Particularly important is the Behavioral Sciences Fund, engaged in a field of operations in which, if it fails to act with the utmost objectivity, it can cause irremediable damage. The Reece Committee report commented upon it as follows:

> This Behavioral Sciences Fund has vast resources at its command. Its list of objectives indicates an underlying assumption that human behavior can be understood as an object of the natural sciences would be, within the framework of limited numbers of cause-effect relationships. This doctrine is not by any means universally accepted, and there is the danger that the huge sum available to the Fund to promote its underlying thesis can make this the ruling doctrine in the social sciences. A full examination of the current and intended operation of this great fund is indicated, as well as a study of why certain institutions have been so greatly favored by it.*

---

* Reece Committee *Report*, p. 82. The behavioral-"science" theories which this Ford unit promotes with tens of millions of dollars largely concern "scientism" or "fraudulent science." The basic fallacy consists of an over-emphasis on fact finding, with an accompanying insufficient regard for the intangible factors which affect human behavior or must be taken into account

The reference in the quotation above to "greatly favored" institutions is based partly upon the following statistical analysis:

A glance at the list of recent recipients of favor from, and consultants to, the *Behavioral Sciences Division* of *The Ford Foundation* indicates a definite concentration among favored institutions or their faculties. Of the committees which formulated policies for this Fund, including a total of 88 persons with university connections, 10 seem to have been from Harvard; 8 from Chicago; 7 from Yale; 5 from California; 5 from Stanford; and 5 from Columbia. A total of 59 of these men (out of 88) represented 12 institutions. There is additional significance in the fact that some of these recipients and consultants were on a multiplicity of committees. For example, Professor Lazarsfeld of Columbia, was on six; Professors Carroll of North Carolina, Merton of Columbia, and Tyler of Chicago, on five; Professors Lasswell of Yale, Simon of Carnegie Tech., and Stouffer of Harvard, on four, etc. Counting the number of times each person with a university connection appears on committees of the Fund, we reach this representation:

University of Chicago	23
Harvard	18
Columbia	16
Yale	13
North Carolina	8
California	7
Stanford	7
Cornell	7, etc.

Note also that associates of *The Rand Corporation* are represented 11 times. This interlock with *The Rand Corporation* is highly interesting.

---

in determining what human beings should do, should be permitted to do, or should be restrained from doing. I shall give an example of this, presently, in discussing the notorious Behavioral Sciences Division-financed jury-tapping incident.

We must add the intriguing fact that the *Behavioral Sciences Fund* provided a grant-in-aid program under which each of fifty persons was to receive $5,000 to be spent at their own discretion for the purpose of enriching their own work. The associates and consultants distributed this largess, and included a goodly number of themselves in their lists.

Note also that *The Social Science Research Council** took part in the policy making of the Fund and that considerable funds were made available to it and through it.

In the Summer of 1950, $300,000 was given to each of seven universities and to *The Social Science Research Council* (beyond other large grants to the *SSRC*). Why this money was concentrated on this limited group of institutions, we do not know.†

The explanation, namely, that what seems to be favoritism is really the selection of the best men in the respective fields of research, is not persuasive. An analysis would show that the men chosen, directly or through the use of selected universities, are overwhelmingly, if not wholly, of one school—that which the Behavioral Sciences Division of The Ford Foundation seeks to promote. There is no objectivity in these selections. Men and institutions are carefully chosen to follow the theories of social-science research to which those who operate the Division adhere.

FORD EAVESDROPS ON JURIES

Were the trustees of The Ford Foundation to confine themselves to direct, undesigned grants to operating institutions, they would be held exonerated if anything unfortunate were done with a grant. Where, however, the foundation has planned or designed the grant, or played any part in determining or approving its detailed subject matter, its objectives, or its method of operation, it is

* See Chapter 3 to orient The Social Science Research Council.
† Reece Committee *Report*, p. 81.

difficult for the trustees to escape responsibility for what happens. The incident of jury eavesdropping is illustrative.

It is also an example, an excellent one, of the fraudulent nature of much of the "science" to which the Behavioral Sciences Division had been addicted.

The Eastland Committee of the Senate recently investigated the installation of microphones in jury rooms to record the conversations of juries in session. These installations were made under a Ford Foundation grant through its Behavioral Sciences Division to the University of Chicago Law School. The project was supervised by Dean Edward H. Levi of the Chicago University Law School and was under the direction of Professor Harry Kalven, Jr.

These were scarcely objective selections to control an investigation with political overtones or connotations. Dean Levi signed a letter to the Chicago *Daily News* in 1948 denouncing the House Committee on Un-American Activities as a "spy-hunting" group. Professor Kalven's similar political disposition is indicated by his letter to President Truman in 1952 asking clemency for the convicted Rosenberg spies and by his work at "Rosenberg rallies." Both these men belong to the group which J. Edgar Hoover has characterized as "fictitious liberals." They are entitled to their opinions. But their opinions would seem to show such a lack of objectivity that one would hardly choose them to study a political institution such as the jury system.

Dean Levi testified that The Ford Foundation originally did not know that juries were to be "tapped" in the investigation which he supervised. On the other hand, it appeared that the original Ford grant had been for $400,000, but, so the dean testified, it had been increased by an additional $1,000,000 after The Ford Foundation had been informed of the eavesdropping procedure.

This was "behavioral *science*."

This was paid for by The Ford Foundation with money dedicated to the public.

Millions of Americans were shocked at the disclosure of this project. As the Boston *Post* put it: "The jury system is far from perfect, but it is not going to be improved by secret eavesdropping in jury rooms. That kind of police-state research can only tear down the confidence of the people in the jury system, and, by the same method, destroy the courts."

The project was designed to be "scientific" and to be undertaken under the auspices of "élite" personnel who presume to know far better than the citizen what is good for him. The people saw the incident clearly, however, as a shocking violation of the right of privacy without which the jury system would be useless as one of the fundamental, Constitution-guaranteed protections of the citizen.*

In a commercial corporation, a fiasco such as the jury-tapping incident would mean that executive heads would fall. In The Ford Foundation this does not seem to be the case. Bernard Berelson, an old friend of Dr. Hutchins, was the operating head of the Behavioral Sciences Division and seems to have been the contact man for the project which eavesdropped on juries. As I write, Mr. Berelson is still head of this great Behavioral Sciences fund.

College presidents and academicians who so urgently (but mostly in private) plead for direct and unrestricted grants to academic institutions freely admit that these institutions themselves can err. It is quite possible that the Chicago Law School, under Dean Levi's deanship, would have itself selected the American jury as a subject of inquiry and conducted it with as little regard to propriety. But there is normally far greater safety to the public in transferring research decisions to recognized educational institutions than in bestowing them on professional foundation managers.

There is the point, moreover, that such a grant could have been made to some other law school presided over by a dean more likely to direct a proper inquiry.

Among the countless condemnatory comments in the press

---

* I do not happen to know what other procedures of investigation the jury project has adopted. But researchers who would stoop to the outrageous and fruitless procedure of "bugging" juries in session may well have used other and worse methods in their "scientific" research.

which greeted the disclosure of the study of the "behaviorism" of juries by "bugging" their deliberations, was an editorial in *The Wall Street Journal* of October 17, 1955, reading in part as follows:

> When the experimenters use the wrong methods to ascertain truth, are the researchers alone responsible? Or are the foundations, which are tax-free, accountable to the public for the transgressions?
>
> *   *   *
>
> Certainly the general public will hold foundations responsible for grants used in irresponsible ways. And unless the foundations themselves assume a responsibility for seeing that their grants are not misused, the unfortunate result doubtless will be that the government will assume it for them.
>
> For a foundation can no more disclaim responsibility where legal research funds are used for tampering with the jury system than it could if some irresponsible people used its funds for research into structural engineering by blowing up some public bridges.

THE (FORD) FUND FOR THE ADVANCEMENT OF EDUCATION

It took courage for academicians to testify before the Reece Committee. To offer any criticism of the major foundations and those organizations with which they interlock is equivalent to writing yourself off their books. They know how to deal with those who dare to disagree. As Professor Charles W. Briggs, professor emeritus of Columbia University, testified, they have terrified many who would be critical. He said:

> It is tragic in a high degree that men who have won confidence and position in the education world should be intimidated from expressing criticism of a foundation whose administrators and policies they do not respect.*

* Reece Committee *Report*, p. 38.

He added these remarks concerning the power of the founda-tions to punish criticism or to suppress it by the inducements of their patronage:

> It has been stated that, unlike colleges and universities, foundations have no alumni to defend them. But they do have influential people as members of their boards, and these members have powerful friends, some of whom are more inclined to be partisanly defensive than objectively critical. Moreover, there are also thousands who, hopeful of becoming beneficiaries of future grants, either conceal their criticisms or else give expression to a defense that may not be wholly sincere.*

Dr. Briggs was one of the courageous few who were willing to criticize when he thought criticism was due. His standing as one of our leading educators was recognized by the Ford Foundation-created Fund for the Advancement of Education, which had ap-pointed him to its advisory committee.

It was with reference to The Fund for the Advancement of Education, that heavily endowed child of The Ford Foundation, that Professor Briggs principally testified. He had resigned from its advisory committee in disgust. Reading from his own carefully prepared statement, he said that all the officers of The (Ford) Fund for the Advancement of Education had been appointed di-rectly or indirectly by one influential executive of the parent (Ford) foundation and (it is worth repeating) that these officers presented to the board of their organization and to the public "a program so general as to get approval and yet so indefinite as to permit activities which in the judgment of competent critics are either wasteful or harmful to the education program which has been approved by the public."

The Fund program was described in the statement of The Ford Foundation, filed with the committee, as follows:

> The Fund for the Advancement of Education concentrates upon five major educational objectives. These are—

* *Loc. cit.*

Clarifying the function of the various parts of the educational system so that they can work together more effectively;

Improving the preparation of teachers at all levels of the education system;

Improving curricula;

Developing increased financial support for educational institutions; and

Equalizing educational opportunity.*

The same statement records that, up to the end of 1953, the Fund had received from The Ford Foundation a total of $30,-850,580, of which it had disbursed $22,242,568. By the end of 1954, it had received $57,000,000 from its parent. Who allocated these vast funds? Professor Briggs tells us:

Not a single member of the staff, from the president down to the lowliest employee, has had any experience, certainly none in recent years, that would give understanding of the problems that are met daily by the teachers and administrators of our schools.

Nor did they listen to competent advice:

As a former member of a so-called Advisory Committee I testify that at no time did the administration of the fund seek from it any advice on principles of operation nor did it hospitably receive or act in accordance with such advice as was volunteered.†

Professor Briggs attacked the theory that foundation leaders were entitled to force upon the public things which it does not want. He said:

The principle that the public should decide what it wants in order to promote its own welfare and happiness is unquestionably sound. An assumption that the public does not

* Reece Committee *Hearings,* p. 1028.
† Reece Committee *Report,* p. 23.

know what is for its own good is simply contrary to the fundamental principles of democracy.*

Among his charges, supported in detail in his carefully prepared statement,† Professor Briggs said that The (Ford) Fund for the Advancement of Education "is improperly manned" with an inexperienced staff "out of sympathy with the democratic ideal of giving an appropriate education to all the children of all the people"; that it has propagandized against programs approved by the public; that it has ignored professional teachers' organizations; that it has been extremely wasteful of public trust funds; that it has "given no evidence of its realization of its obligations as a public trust to promote the general good of the entire nation; and that it either "has no balanced program of correlated constructive policies, or else it has failed to make them public."

Having severely criticized the propaganda of The Ford Foundation against current theories of education, he accused the Fund's officers of an "arrogation" of "an assumption of omniscience" and said:

> All this being understood, we can assert without fear of successful contradiction that any attempt by outside agencies, however heavily they may be financed and however supported by eminent individuals, to influence school administrators and teachers to seek other objectives than those which have public approval or to use methods and materials not directed by responsible management is an impudence not to be tolerated. Though cloaked with declared benevolence, it cannot hide the arrogance underneath.‡

There is no doubt that Professor Briggs was referring to Dr. Robert M. Hutchins when he said that one man was responsible for the staffing of The Fund for the Advancement of Education. The Fund was his creature and his design. It is well known that Dr. Hutchins's ideas on education and the responsibility of teach-

---

* *Ibid.*, p. 21.
† Reece Committee *Hearings*, p. 94 *et seq.*
‡ Reece Committee *Report*, p. 167.

ers runs severely counter to accepted theory; and I believe it safe to say that The Fund for the Advancement of Education has used its millions in great measure to propagate Dr. Hutchins's ideas.

I have no doubt that some of Dr. Hutchins's theories are meritorious and even, in some respects, far superior to prevailing theories of education. Indeed, he has lined himself up with those who have revolted against the scientific humanist theory of progress. In his *Freedom, Education and The Fund** he says (p. 97):

> According to the dogmas of scientism, skepticism, and secularism there is no * * * truth. If there is truth at all, it is truth discoverable in the laboratory, by what is called the scientific method.

Further (p. 126):

> Underneath the writings of almost all writers on education lies the doctrine of social reform. They cannot look at the society around them and like it. How is the society to be changed? There are only two ways: revolution and education.

And (p. 128):

> But I believe it is dangerous as well as futile to regard the educational system as a means of getting a program of social reform adopted. If one admits the possibility of obtaining through the schools social reforms that one likes, one must also admit the possibility of obtaining social reforms that one dislikes. What happens will depend on the popularity of various reformers, the plausibility of their causes, and the pressure they are able to exert on the educational system.

It is "unwise and dangerous," he continues, to look at the educational system "as an engine of social reform."

However commendable some of Dr. Hutchins's ideas on education may be, the fact remains that a system which enables any

* A Meridian paperback book, 1956.

one employee to use the terrific power of a vast public trust fund to propagandize his own educational ideas is not to be tolerated, as Professor Briggs rightly maintained.

Other data assembled by the Reece Committee bear out Professor Briggs's disgust with The Fund for the Advancement of Education. An illustration is the $565,000, three-year grant by the Fund to The Institute of Philosophical Research in San Francisco which, according to the Ford 1952 annual report, is to concentrate on a "clarification of educational philosophy." An objective study of "educational philosophy" could be highly desirable. The committee wondered, however, whether The Ford Foundation had selected Dr. Mortimer Adler to head this study in order to make sure that it would be objective.

Dr. Adler, another old friend of Dr. Hutchins, has made his sympathy with collectivism entirely clear. In an article in 1949 in *Common Cause,* he said that we are in "a quiet but none the less effective revolution." He did not disapprove of this revolution. Its direction was leftist, and he liked it.

He wrote:

> By choice the American people are never going to fall back to the right again. * * * That deserves to be called a revolution accomplished. Either the Democratic Party will move further to the left or a new political party will form to the left of the Democrats.*

Dr. Adler has also expressed himself forcefully to the effect that world peace "requires the total relinquishment and abolishment of the external sovereignty of the United States. . . ." †

This is the man chosen by The Ford Foundation to direct "a dialectical examination of western thought" and "to clarify educational philosophy." Starting in 1952 with his budget of $565,000, Dr. Adler has produced nothing very substantial to date except a report called *Research on Freedom: Report of Dialectical Discoveries and Constructions.*

* *Ibid.,* p. 162.
† *Ibid.,* p. 227.

There are indications that the Ford trustees are not wholly satisfied with the results of their gigantic expenditures through their Fund for the Advancement of Education. Dwight Macdonald, in discussing the jargon used by foundation executivies, said this:

> Thus, President Gaither, a master of foundationese, writes in his 1954 Annual Report, apropos of the trustees' decision to cut the annual rate of support for the Fund for the Advancement of Education from $10,000,000 to $3,000,000, "In adopting this course, the Trustees acknowledged the encouraging results of the Fund's efforts in a relatively short period and reaffirmed their belief that the Fund's assistance to education showed exceptional promise for the future. [Translation: The trustees are cooling off toward the Fund and have decided to spend most of their educational money themselves in the future.]"*

THE (FORD) FUND FOR ADULT EDUCATION

When The Ford Foundation decides to enter some field of operation, it does not do so in modest fashion. Through 1956, its grants to its own Fund for Adult Education totaled $47,400,000. This illustrates clearly enough the dangers inherent in foundation size. Adult education is a worthy area of foundation activity when such education is objectively directed. But $47,400,000 is a tidy sum to hand over to those who may be inclined to use it for social and political propaganda.

One of the projects richly supported by the Fund for Adult Education was the Great Books Discussion Groups, operated by The American Library Association through its American Heritage Project. "Adult education" was to be based on group discussions of the "Great Books" and educational films. Adults were to be brought together in public libraries to discuss the great American documents and "American political freedoms."

The use of the term "American political freedoms" might have given the Ford trustees pause. The word "freedoms" used in this

* *The Ford Foundation*, p. 102.

connection has a special semantic significance. Radicals, domestic and foreign, have been trying for years to reconstruct our basic charter of liberties, our "inalienable rights" by superimposing or substituting for some of them new concepts of "freedom from" various social ills. Much of the thinking behind these new "freedoms" has come out of the United Nations, where Marxists have had their say in limiting the rights to which we adhere and in adding concepts which are foreign to us.

The Reece Committee, unable to do complete research on the work of these Discussion Groups, did find some highly interesting items among the prescribed materials employed. The Committee found that the Great Books project was closely allied, through its directorate, to *The Encyclopedia Britannica,* which issued 16mm. documentary films sometimes used by the discussion groups. The materials which the Committee collected "leaned heavily to civil liberties, political and social action, and international world politics." Many of the authors whose works were studied were extreme leftists. But it was selection of films used by the discussion groups which most induced the Committee to doubt "the objectivity and good faith of those responsible for the selection of individuals and discussion materials." The following is the Committee's description of some of the films:

Due Process of Law Denied

This film, somewhat uniquely paired with "The Adventures of Huckleberry Finn" deals with excerpts from "The Ox Bow Incident," a brutal story of mob "justice." Described in the material furnished to the discussion groups as "forceful re-enacting of a lynching," a more accurate statement is that it is inflammatory and designed to convey the impression that throughout the United States there **is** widespread disregard for law and order.

The Cummington Story

By Waldo Salt, who on April 15, 1951, refused to answer, claiming the privilege of the Fifth Amendment when questioned by the House Un-American Activities Committee regarding his Communist affiliations.

The House I Live In

By Albert Maltz referred to earlier, who refused to answer questions regarding his Communist Party record, and was cited for contempt.

Of Human Rights

Prepared by the United Nations Film Department, it is used with the United Nations Declaration on Human Rights, and is described as follows:

"An incident involving economic and racial prejudice among children is used to dramatize the importance of bringing to the attention of the peoples of the world *their rights as human beings* as set forth in the Universal Declaration of Human Rights proclaimed by the UNP General Assembly in December 1948." [Emphasis supplied.]

The United States government by rejecting this Universal Declaration has gone on record as stating this country does not consider that document—prepared in collaboration with the Communists—as a statement of our "rights as human beings." The rights of citizens of the United States are set forth in the Declaration of Independence, in the Constitution and its Amendments.

Brotherhood of Man

Also suggested for use on the program "Human Rights," this film produced by United Productions of America for the United Automobile Workers of the CIO is distributed by Brandon Films. The Washington representative of Brandon Films testified before the Jenner Committee in May 1951 that Brandon Films advertised in the *Daily Worker* but took refuge behind the Fifth Amendment against self-incrimination when questioned as to his own Communist Party membership.

The film itself is based on the pamphlet "Races of Mankind" written by Ruth Benedict and Gene Weltfish, whose records are included in the Appendix. Following complaints as to its nature and accuracy the pamphlet was withdrawn from the Armed Forces Education Program—*but as recently as September of this year the film was in use at the Film Center at Fort Monmouth.* To this Committee the use of such a film cannot be justified, and it condemns the subterfuge by which a document branded as inaccurate is withdrawn as it were by one hand and surreptitiously reinstated with the other.

With These Hands

Produced by the International Ladies Garment Workers' Union, this film is a highly colored portrayal of violence on the picket lines, featuring the horrors of the Triangle Fire in New York City almost fifty years ago, giving a completely unrealistic picture of present day working conditions.

The Challenge

This is another film on the theme that the guarantee of "life, liberty and the pursuit of happiness" is denied to Negroes and other minority group members in the United States; it is unrealistic, distorted and deceptive.

Such presentations as these cannot be called educational in the opinion of this Committee; they deliberately seek to stress "what's wrong" in present and past group relations rather than provide facts for objective discussion of such relations, and ignore the fact that here in the United States can be found the outstanding example of liberty in action in the world today.

The Fund For Adult Education along with the 20th Century Fund, and the Carnegie Endowment for International Peace, is closely associated with the Film Council of America. Evans Clark is listed as a member and William F. Kruse (at one time connected with Bell and Howell) is in a policy-making position on the Film Council. Mr. Kruse's background is particularly interesting to this Committee since he carries great weight with the Council—and the Council's films find their way into the discussion groups sponsored by the American Library Association with Ford money.

Mr Kruse is reliably reported to have been a Communist as recently as 1943, and there are witnesses who state he still was after that date. As late as 1943 he was listed as sponsoring the Chicago Council of American-Soviet Friendship.

Another individual indirectly associated with the Film Council is John Grierson, who produced "Round Trip," spearhead for a world trade campaign in this country starring Paul Hoffman. Grierson resigned as head of the National Film Board of Canada at the time of the Canadian atomic spy ring revelations. Denied a visa to this country he came in through Unesco and thereafter headed the film section of that organization. Unesco and UNO films are likewise used in the [Great] Books discussion groups.

The 16mm. film is being increasingly recommended for use in all levels of education—including so-called adult education. This Committee would strongly urge that the whole matter of the type of films as well as the subject matter and the individuals and organizations who produce these films, be carefully studied. There is no greater media today through which to propagandize and it is no exaggeration to say that such things as ostensibly "educational" films can well prove to be the Trojan horse of those ideologies which seek to scuttle American principles and ideals.*

The Fund for Adult Education seems also to have been a Hoffman-Hutchins product. The President of the Fund is C. Scott Fletcher, who has been closely associated with both. He was

* Reece Committee *Report*, pp. 164-166.

president of the Encyclopedia Britannica Films, which was once owned by the University of Chicago when Dr. Hutchins was president of that institution. In some way not disclosed to the public, Britannica passed into private hands, among them those of Mr. Benton, with whom Dr. Hutchins has also been closely associated. And Mr. Fletcher had been sales manager of the Studebaker Corporation while Mr. Hoffman was its President.

FORD "EDUCATES" LABOR

The Fund for Adult Education does not confine itself to the education of the general adult public. It also devotes huge sums of money to the "education" of labor as a special class in our society.

This "education" is of a special kind. Its nature may be gathered from the heavy support given by The Fund for Adult Education to The American Labor Education Service, which is devoted to educating labor in how to "Advance Labor's Economic and Political Objectives."*

The American Labor Education Service distributes political pamphlets. Many of these are produced by that other radical organization, *The League for Industrial Democracy.* As an indication of how uninformed the trustees of The Ford Foundation must be regarding the detail of their foundation's operations, one of the pamphlets widely distributed by the Ford-supported American Labor Education Service is entitled "Fordism." It is hardly complimentary to the Ford Motor Company or to the memory of the man who made the Ford Foundation billions available.

That The Ford Foundation might consider establishing general and special courses of instruction for "labor" can be understood; such educational efforts directed especially at factory workers could be highly desirable. There cannot be any possible justification, however, for the use of public trust funds to support organizations devoted to "educating" labor to the leftist ends of such as The American Labor Education Service and The League for Industrial Democracy. It is difficult to believe that the Ford trustees would countenance such appropriations were they aware of their

* *Ibid.,* p. 106.

nature. The answer is that these trustees are quite out of touch with much of the work of the great foundation which they, in theory, administer.

It is difficult to believe that the Ford trustees have any understanding of the nature of the Inter-University Labor Education Committee to which The Fund for Adult Education granted $384,000 from January 1, 1952, to June 30, 1953. The Reece Committee found an undated publication of this Education Committee entitled Labor's Stake in World Affairs. It was marked "Preliminary Draft for Limited Distribution and Comment."

This publication characterized the conflict between Russia and the United States as a "struggle for world power." Labor must fight communism, it indicated, but the impression was given to the "labor" which The Ford Foundation was thus helping to "educate" that the Soviet Union wants peace, is against imperialism and intervention, and wishes to cooperate with the United States. This publication equates the Berlin airlift with the Russian blockade—one was no worse than the other—indeed, what could the Russians do, it said, when the Western Powers restored industrialization to Western Germany instead of persisting in agrarianization?—the Russian blockade was a just retaliation.

The question is asked, should we (labor) fight if Russia attacks? The answer given is "yes." Then the question is asked, But what if *we* start the war? No answer is suggested.

These are illustrations of the tenor of this Ford-financed work of "education" of "labor."*

FORD AND INTERNATIONALISM

On October 5, 1955, a luncheon took place on the premises of The Carnegie Endowment for International Peace, at which Mr. Chester Bowles delivered an address in which he explained the usefulness of private agencies working abroad. He said:

> The voluntary agencies have more force than representatives of the government. They do not suffer from the re-

---

* *Ibid.,* pp. 162-163.

straints imposed on official emissaries. They are free people.*

The same issue of the *Times* which reported this speech also reported one by Mr. Paul Hoffman, former chairman of The Ford Foundation and later chairman of its Fund for the Republic. Mr. Hoffman, like Mr. Bowles, praised "voluntary welfare agencies." Mr. Hoffman was speaking at a dinner of the newly created Fund for Asia.

It is obvious enough that "voluntary agencies" are, in general, most highly desirable when engaged in philanthropic work. When such agencies, however, operate in the international area, considerable risk may be involved. Dealing with the treacherous international situation might better be left to government agencies, whatever their limitations.

The Fund for Asia may be a wholly commendable enterprise. But it would be well to understand whose agency it is to be; what Asians it is to be "for"; who is to distribute its largess; and for what purposes. "Agencies" often have an angelic appearance but turn out to be unfortunate media as distributors of public trust funds.

The Reece Committee found an example of this in the case of The American Friends Service Committee, to which The Ford Foundation made very heavy grants. The Service Committee is an active lobbying organization whose policies have included an acquiescence, at least, in the Communist penetration of China. A report of The American Friends Service Committee contained this astounding statement:

> Our own independence was achieved through a revolution, and we have traditionally sympathized with the determined attempts of other peoples to win national independence and higher standards of living. The current revolution in Asia is a similar movement, whatever its present association with Soviet Communism.†

* *The New York Times,* Oct. 6, 1955.
† Reece Committee *Report,* p. 186.

One cannot get enthusiastic over the use by The Ford Foundation of this agency for distributing its funds—an organization which does not seem to see any material difference between the American Revolution and the Communist movement in China. Yet Ford granted the Service Committee $1,134,000. Its expressed justification for the size of this grant was that the officers of The American Friends Service Committee had demonstrated their capacity "to deal effectively with" conditions which "lead to international tensions."

But was everyone in The Ford Foundation, for example, ignorant of the fact that, in 1950, The American Friends Service Committee had written to President Truman:

> Further intervention will result in the hardening of Chinese resentment against America and the strengthening of Sino-Russian ties. By treating Communist China as an enemy and by refusing to recognize her, we are not isolating China, we are isolating ourselves.*

The American Friends Service Committee was itself a tax-exempt organization. The propriety of such an organization attempting to influence the foreign policy of the United States cannot be defended. Moreover, its public pronouncements had shown that funds distributed by it might well be used for objectives suiting its own theories of foreign relations, regardless of the extent to which these might conflict with those of our government.

One of the grandiose schemes of The Ford Foundation (in its selected area of "The Establishment of Peace") was the creation of Intercultural Publications, Inc., to "increase understanding among peoples." What kind of an "understanding" of the people of the United States has this creature of The Ford Foundation given to other nations? The Reece Committee found among the members of the advisory board of Intercultural Publications, Inc. (and among those who contributed articles to its periodical or whose books were reviewed in it) a large number of persons with

* *Ibid.,* p. 187.

extensive Communist-front associations or of extreme leftist tendencies.

Whatever mistakes our own government may have made, and may be making, in portraying the American people and their political and social ideas to others, it would seem far safer for us to rely upon government than upon a creature of The Ford Foundation to do our international "public relations" job for us.

The Ford Foundation has apparently spent some $90,000,000 in aid of foreign countries. There is considerable doubt whether the American people have received their money's worth for the many billions spent by our government on foreign aid. But at least this has been official spending, authorized by our elected representatives. The millions spent abroad by The Ford Foundation constitute public trust funds, spent by private individuals without the people's consent, knowledge, or understanding.

Time was when foundations confined themselves, in foreign grants, to religious objectives (such as the establishing of missions); educational purposes (such as the creation and support of schools); and public health. Not so today. Some of them, Ford and Rockefeller particularly, have launched themselves widely into foreign projects which might be classed as international "do-gooding," along program lines of their own design. In the case of The Ford Foundation, responsibility can probably be attributed to Mr. Paul Hoffman, who became so accustomed to paying out gigantic sums for foreign aid when he was an administrator of our government's aid program that he could not curtail the habit.

To what extent have these foreign grants of The Ford Foundation interfered or worked at cross-purposes with our State Department? To what extent have they supported ideologies to which Mr. Hoffman and his associates have been attached, though they contravened what is acceptable to the American people? To what extent have these private administrators of public trust funds wasted millions and millions of dollars? I cite one example of waste mentioned by Mr. Macdonald—the grant by Ford to The Carnegie Endowment for International Peace of $100,000 to assist in undertaking "a two year program of studies of national policies and attitudes toward the United Nations." Mr. Macdonald characterized this project as "like making a map of a cloud hovering over a fog."*

Apparently The Ford Foundation, under Mr. Hoffman's guidance, concluded that our relations with some "undeveloped" nations could be improved by the expenditure of great sums in those countries. Our own government had had a similar theory. However, as I have said, it would seem safer to let our government take whatever risks are involved than to permit private agencies to allocate public trust monies for such ends. The millions, for example, which Ford has poured into India—have they been well spent? This enormous nation now shows an increasing distaste for the United States and a rapidly increasing affection for the Soviet government. Should it not occur to the trustees of The Ford Foundation that they have no business using public trust funds to further a Ford Foundation Foreign Policy?

A startling example of Ford Foundation Foreign Policy is its recent grant of $500,000 to allow Polish social scientists, architects, engineers and writers to study in the United States and Western Europe, and for a few American and European scholars to study in Poland. The Rockefeller Foundation has joined this new procession and has announced a $475,000 grant to Poland "for scientific research in agriculture and medicine." † It does not appeal to my sense of logic that we should be assisting the Communist Empire. But, if contrary opinion is valid and the Communists of the Iron Curtain countries should be assisted, should not that decision be made by our President and Congress rather than by the Ford or Rockefeller foundations? After all, The Ford Foundation and The Rockefeller Foundation are dispensing public trust funds. I cannot imagine any stretch of logic or interpretation of propriety which would entitle foundation trustees to apply American, public trust funds to the use of Communists.

One of the most fantastically futile and wasteful projects designed by Mr. Hoffman for The Ford Foundation was a study of

* *The Ford Foundation*, p. 104.
† *New York Herald Tribune*, May 27, 1957.

how we could achieve peace. It was Mr. Hoffman's naïve belief that the expenditure of enough money on "studies" could find the answers which The Carnegie Endowment for International Peace had not been able to discover in all its long history. Apparently, it was Mr. Hoffman's theory, which he convinced the trustees to adopt, that there was no basic problem of Soviet intransigence or of Russian determination to destroy the capitalist world. All that was needed was for a group of scholars to sit down and figure out what we had to do, and what the Russians had to do, so that peace could reign. Something like $100,000 of the Foundation's public trust funds went down this drain.

Nor has the Foundation given up hope that better international relations can be developed if only the American people become more "international-minded." This thesis has governed a large part of the work of The Carnegie Endowment. But the Endowment cannot plunge the way The Ford Foundation can. The latter allotted $6,500, 000 to six law schools "to develop a program of international studies." And the program for "intercultural relations," started by Mr. Hoffman, is being continued with a probable aggregate expenditure of $375,000. Mr. Macdonald has said, "The budget reads like an academic W.P.A."*

Indeed, with so much money to spend, The Ford Foundation obviously must scramble around actively to find ways in which to use its vast funds. Quite a large percentage of its grants might be classed with the "boondoggling" of the 30's. Far more serious than such waste of public trust money, however, are the instances of affirmatively harmful projects. Of these, one of the worst is The Fund for the Republic.

THE (FORD) FUND FOR THE REPUBLIC

The Fund for the Republic is the finest flower of what might be called the "philandering school of philanthropy." It was the brain child of Mr. Paul Hoffman, probably midwifed by Dr. Hutchins. It was born simultaneously with Mr. Hoffman's release as chairman of The Ford Foundation, and it is not unreasonable to suppose

* *Ibid.,* pp. 164-165.

that there was a connection between the two events. It is suspected that Mr. Hoffman was given charge of the $15,000,000 capital of The Fund for the Republic, to use for the promotion of some of his favorite ideas, as a sop to his feelings.*

It was not long before The Ford Foundation trustees decided that they could not stand Dr. Hutchins either, and relieved him of his duties as a principal director, whereupon Mr. Hoffman installed him as president of The Fund for the Republic, to the chairmanship of which Mr. Hoffman had been demoted. Messrs. Hoffman and Hutchins were thus together again. Inasmuch as The Fund for the Republic was given independence by The Ford Foundation, these two were to have their heyday.

The Fund for the Republic holds itself out to be educational in purpose. Its handsome and expensively printed report of May 31, 1955,† includes this statement, written by Dr. Hutchins:

> The object of the Fund is to advance an understanding of civil liberties. The Board of Directors believes that the rights of Americans should not be compromised or lost through neglect or confusion. It believes that the citizen should know what his rights are and what is happening to them.

These noble purposes were put to the test when a proposal was made to The Fund for the Republic that it cause a study to be made of the rights reserved to the people by the Ninth and Tenth Amendments to the Constitution. No grant was requested—the suggestion was merely that the Fund, itself or through others, undertake such a study. It seemed logical enough. The Fund claimed to be interested in "civil liberties" and the proposal was to let the people know what their "liberties" are.

---

* There is even another Hoffman in the picture. Mr. Hallock Hoffman, son of Mr. Paul Hoffman, is listed as "Assistant to the President." Nepotism?

† The Fund has never denied itself. In the first two years of operation, it consumed $410,000 to make grants of $843,000. Its offices, both in Pasadena and New York, have been luxurious. Expense has seemed no serious concern. Salaries have been by no means niggardly. Mr. Hutchins gets along on a $50,000 salary; his assistant on one, I believe, of $35,000; and counsel is similarly compensated.

Certain rights and "liberties" were expressly reserved to the people in the Constitution and its Amendments. The Ninth and Tenth Amendments provided, further, that any rights which the people might have which were not expressly enumerated were also reserved to them. The point is, nobody seems to have any very clear idea what these unenumerated, reserved rights may be. Surely, if The Fund for the Republic is dedicated to the purpose (to use Dr. Hutchins's actual words) that "the rights of Americans should not be compromised or lost through neglect or confusion," one might think it a necessary and basic use of some of its money to have a study made to determine what our rights are. Surely, if Dr. Hutchins meant what he said, that he wanted the citizen to "know what his rights are and what is happening to them," the proposed study was a "must."

The proposal was rejected in writing by The Fund for the Republic on the ground that it did not fit into its program.

This reaction might have been expected. The documents attending the creation of The Fund for the Republic convinced the Reece Committee that one of the Fund's purposes had been to investigate Congressional investigations. It has turned out, in operation, even more dangerous than the Committee anticipated. While the Reece Committee investigation was under way, The Fund kept its skirts moderately clean. Since the filing of the Committee report, however, it has shown its true colors as a propaganda agency for the leftist political ideas of its directing officers, Messrs. Hoffman and Hutchins, and similarly disposed, carefully collected associates.

The Fund for the Republic now has to its credit many monumental achievements in propaganda:

1. A $100,000 study of the Federal loyalty-security program, intended to bring out criticism of the methods used to clear Communists and Communist sympathizers out of government employ. Mr. Walter Millis, a consultant to the Fund, is associated with this project. Mr. Millis, in a recent radio debate with Judge Robert Morris, said: "What I object to is not the procedure in the [loyalty-security] program, but the very fact that the system is there."

2. The subsidization of the Edward R. Murrow project to circulate among schools and elsewhere his extended T.V. interview with Robert Oppenheimer. This project was intended to glamorize Dr. Oppenheimer after he had been stripped of his security clearance—an obvious attempt to discredit the security system.

3. The $150,000 survey of high-school and college teachers to ascertain the degree to which they have "feared" to teach controversial subjects in the classrooms. The intention of this project was to propagandize the false claim that the loyalty-security program and "hysteria" on the part of the anti-Communists has terrorized innocent teachers.

4. $300,000 study of the influence of communism in contemporary American life. This project has distinguished itself by hiring Earl Browder, former head of the Communist Party in the United States and still an ardent Communist. It has also assigned a subproject to one Theodore Draper, who was once a reporter for *The Daily Worker* and graduated from that to *The New Masses*.

5. The $185,500 study of "American attitudes, toward communism and civil liberties." The purpose of this, obviously enough, is to promote the Hoffman-Hutchins theory that our security measures violate "civil rights" and that the protection of these rights may be more important than protecting ourselves against communism.

6. The $64,500 study of the "Communist record," including bibliographies. This project has produced *A Bibliography on the Communist Problem in the United States*. It has been blasted by a great number of informed critics. Professor Philip Taft of Brown University, a leading authority on communism in trade unions, has said that The Fund for the Republic deserves a "vote of thanks from the Communist Party." James T. Farrell, chairman of the American Committee for Cultural Freedom, called it "inexcusable sloppiness." Dr. John A. Sessions, assistant director of the International Ladies Garment Workers Training Institute, has been scorching in his criticism. He said the *Bibliography* "consistently omitted the more important works of many of the very

writers who have done most to illuminate the Communist problem." "If," wrote Dr. Sessions in *The New Leader*, "the Fund seriously wishes to defend itself against such attacks as have been leveled against it by Fulton Lewis and the American Legion, it must do something to make amends for this bibliography."*

7. The $40,000 production of *Freedom to Read,* a film calculated to attack the banning of pro-Communist books from U. S. Information Service propaganda libraries.

8. The purchase and circulation of a propaganda booklet written by Dean Griswold of the Harvard Law School, entitled *The Fifth Amendment Today,* a brief for the Fifth Amendment pleaders. Against the mass of material issued to the public of an anti-anti-Communist nature, the Fund, as far as I have been able to learn, has distributed only one piece of contrary literature. This is an article written by C. Dickerman Williams, which devastates the booklet, *The Fifth Amendment Today,* written by Dean Griswold. But 35,000 copies of the Griswold book were distributed. And only 1,000 of the Williams reply! Regarding Dean Griswold's position, Mr. Williams had this to say in the *National Review,* December 21, 1955:

> * * * it is unfortunate, if not tragic, that the Harvard Law School—with its energy, intelligence and prestige, and its militant stand on the side of disclosure during the investigations of monopoly in the 1890's and 1900's, of corruption in the 1920's and of questionable business practices in the 1930's—should be identified with the cause of concealment today, when the country is confronted with the far more serious danger of Soviet penetration. The "methods" and personalities of congressional investigators, whatever they may be, hardly warrant such a reversal of position.

As far as I know, the Fund For The Republic has not distributed any copies of *Common Sense And The Fifth Amendment,*

* See *Experts Hit Ford Fund Red Guide, New York World-Telegram,* October 28, 1955. A revised Bibliography was subsequently produced but is by no means adequate.

by Professor Sidney Hook of New York University (Criterion Books, 1957), which leaves Dean Griswold's book in shreds.

9. The circulation of a large number of other leftish books, among them

Banned Books, by Anne Lyon Haight;
Faceless Informers and our Schools, by Lawrence Martin;
Freedom Award Speeches, by Freedom House;
The Pseudo-Conservative Revolt, by Richard Hofstadter;
Grand Inquest, by Telford Taylor;
Government by Investigation, by Alan Barth;
Conformity and Civil Liberties, by Samuel A. Stouffer;
The Kept Witness, by Richard H. Rovere;
To Insure the End of Our Hysteria, by Paul Hoffman;
Who "Collaborated" with Russia, by Paul Willen

delivered to legislators, lawyers, judges, college presidents and others who might create opinion or influence legislation.

10. The purchase and wide distribution of a propaganda issue of The Journal of the Atomic Scientists, intended as an attack on our security system.

11. The $100,000 "blacklisting" study: the circulation of a questionnaire to firms using radio and television to discover what anti-Communists are doing.

12. An appropriation of $200,000 (later revoked under sufficient ridicule and, perhaps, fear of losing tax exemption) to put Herb Block on television. Herb Block is a cartoonist for the Washington Post-Times. The 1954 report of The Fund for the Republic lists this project under "Popular Education." David Lawrence described Mr. Block as "a cartoonist who regularly ridicules the security program and is noted for his 'Left Wing' cartoons."*

13. The gift of $5,000 to a Quaker school board for its "courageous and effective defense of democratic principles" in having voted to retain a Mrs. Knowles as a librarian. Mr. Herbert Philbrick, an F.B.I. undercover agent, had testified under oath that Mrs. Knowles had been a member of the very Communist cell

* N.Y. Herald Tribune, Sept. 16, 1955.

which he had joined in his F.B.I. work—and Mrs. Knowles had interposed the Fifth Amendment when asked under oath whether she had ever been a Communist.

14. The employment on its staff of one Amos Landman, three weeks after he had been named under oath as having been a Communist and had himself pleaded the Fifth Amendment when asked whether he had ever been one. His employment by The Fund for the Republic was as a *"publicity man!"* Dr. Hutchins had recently gone so far (it took him quite a while to get there) as to admit that communism was a danger to the United States. Nevertheless, he has stated that he would hire a Communist if he were "qualified" for the job at hand, regardless of the man's previous record.

15. The $25,000 "study" at Stanford University of the testimony of witnesses in proceedings relating to communism. This study was accepted by the dean of the Stanford Law School without the approval of the trustees. The dean is the director of Far Eastern Affairs for The Ford Foundation. The study is to be conducted under one Herbert Packer, a former employee of The Fund for the Republic. The result will no doubt be a deprecation of the testimony of reformed Communists, such as Elizabeth Bentley and Louis Budenz, whose disclosures of Communists have been so important to the security of the United States.

16. The grant of $395,000 to The Southern Regional Council. *The New York Journal-American* reported on November 7, 1955, that the board of directors of this organization "includes 21 members with past pro-Communist affiliations."

David Lawrence, in his column of August 18, 1955, referring to The Fund for the Republic, called attention to the "current wave of appeasement" which is destroying our national ideals, and continued:

> There is, for example, a deliberate attempt to pooh-pooh Communist infiltration in the United States. Scarcely a day passes that some blow isn't struck at those who are fighting Communist subversion. Thus, in the last few days a docu-

ment has been published of a study financed by the Ford Foundation. It selects pieces of testimony and tries to make the security proceedings of the United States look capricious and ludicrous. Nowhere is the full transcript of any hearings given so that both sides of the cross-examination and the reasons for it can be understood.

When Sen. McCarthy stood up in the Senate and gave selected items about individuals suspected of Communist associations, he was pilloried for giving only one side. But when the Ford Foundation study gives only piecemeal items without all the background, no criticism is voiced from "Left Wing" quarters. Recently there has been a hue and cry about anonymous informants but the Ford Foundation study now being publicized is anonymous so far as giving the facts or the story of both sides or the sources of the study.

Nor is any information being given to the public as to why some of the questions asked in hearings could be pertinent to a security investigation. * * * It is only common sense not to let anybody occupy a government position or be given a post in the armed services if he could later be the victim of attempted blackmail.

The American Legion has several times, at its national convention, adopted resolutions urging Congress to make a further and complete study of tax-exempt foundations. National Commander Seaborn P. Collins of the American Legion, according to a *New York Herald Tribune* report of September 11, 1955, called on Legion members to "have no truck" with The Fund for the Republic. He said:

I am issuing this alert to our membership because it appears that the Fund for the Republic, headed by Dr. Robert Maynard Hutchins, is threatening and may succeed in crippling the national security.

He accused the Fund of "constant, loaded criticism of Congressional and Administration efforts to resist Communist infiltration." He said:

> One apparent line of attack is the attempt to persuade Americans that communism is not, and never has been, a serious threat to the United States.
>
> This propaganda is considered by the American Legion to be as dangerous as it is untrue, but we recognize that even such propaganda as that being disseminated by the Fund for the Republic can be sold to many Americans when millions of dollars are behind the sales effort.

After the American Legion had become critical of his work, Dr. Hutchins took a paid full-page ad in the *American Legion Magazine* to defend The Fund for the Republic. The *Legion Magazine*, in commenting on this advertisement, said:

> Incidentally, we are holding in escrow the money paid for the advertisement on the preceding page. There is a difference of opinion as to whether an eleemosynary organization may properly spend money in this way, and we are holding it till such time as this point is adjudicated.

It should concern the Internal Revenue Service whether a foundation is expending its funds for purposes entitling it to tax exemption when it buys advertising space in magazines and when it engages "public relations counselors."

The Fund for the Republic is not without defenders. *The New York Times* of September 25, 1955, reported that Dr. Nathan M. Pusey, president of Harvard University, had said, in an address of the day before, that the attack on The Fund by Mr. Collins of the Legion was "an incredibly misguided action." The *Times* reported further:

> *Noting that several trustees of the Fund for the Republic were present,* Dr. Pusey said that the record would show "to any fair-minded observer" that the Fund had hewed

to its basic aims in two years of operation. (Emphasis supplied.)

Dr. Pusey was entirely correct—that is, if the aims of The Fund for the Republic were, as the Reece Committee suspected, to propagandize for certain extreme "liberal" political views.

In December 1955 Mr. George Meany, president of the merged A.F.L. and C.I.O., delivered a fiery address inveighing against the quiescent attitude of "liberals" toward communism. He said:

> Communism is the very opposite of liberalism. Communism is the deadliest enemy of liberalism. Liberals should be the most consistent and energetic fighters against communism. Liberals must also be on guard against developing a certain type of McCarthyism of their own. They must shun like a plague the role of being anti-anti-Communist.

The Fund for the Republic has not shunned this role. It has become the leader of the anti-anti-Communist movement in the United States.

Not only have Mr. Hoffman and Dr. Hutchins given an anti-anti-Communist leadership to The Fund for the Republic, but it has been a very fuzzy one, indeed. This was brought out in an editorial in the Los Angeles *Times* of August 28, 1955, which discussed the current Fund report. The editorial said that there was a question whether The Ford Foundation had "got its money's worth out of the Fund's $2,514,738 expenditures to date." The editorial reviewed the basic laws which protect our "civil rights" and then said:

> One is tempted to believe that these basic laws have not been carefully read by Dr. Hutchins. For in his report he says:
>
> "The treatment accorded suspected persons in Congressional hearings has not always been that contemplated by the Sixth Amendment:
>
> Here is the Sixth Amendment:
>
> *"In all criminal prosecutions, the accused shall enjoy the*

*right to a speedy and public trial, by an impartial jury of
the State and district wherein the crime shall have been
committed, which district shall have been previously ascertained by law, and to be informed of the nature and cause of
the accusation; to be confronted with the witnesses against
him; to have compulsory process for obtaining witnesses in
his favor, and to have the assistance of counsel for his defense."*

Neither Congressional investigations or administrative
hearings are mentioned in the amendment. For neither of
these is a "criminal prosecution." If there is reasonable evidence of criminality, the normal processes of trial then take
place wherein the individuals concerned have the complete
protection of the Constitution.

These are samples of the hazy thinking about civil rights
in the Hutchins report and a continuation of the bizarre
points of view he has had in these matters. * * *

I must record one more example of Fund For The Republic
absurdity. While the manuscript of this book was in final process
of preparation, the New York Herald Tribune (July 2, 1957) reported an announcement by the Fund For The Republic of the
appointment of a committee of "consultants" who are to undertake an inquiry into "the impact on individual freedom and civil
liberty of two large modern institutions—the industrial corporation and the labor union." The "consultants" are: Adolph A.
Berle, Henry R. Luce, Scott Buchanan, Eugene Burdick, Eric
Goldman, Clark Kerr, the Rev. John Courtney Murray, Isador I.
Rabi, Robert Redfield and Reinhold Niebuhr. While this committee is obviously well-stacked with "liberals"—some extremely
to the left—it has one further interesting characteristic. In his syndicated column of August 1, 1957, Raymond Moley pointed out
that the list reveals "an astonishing absence of people who have
ever had any experience with either corporations or unions. All
except one are professors or college administrators." The one exception (Mr. Luce), said Moley, has had no experience "in the

industrial climate which conditions the problems with which this study purports to deal."

Moley concludes: "The exclusion of people experienced in running corporations and labor unions makes certain that the personal views of Hutchins will have no opposition." The panel of "consultants" is a carefully hand-picked one. An objective report from this group is too much to hope for. I wonder whether the new management of The Ford Foundation is pleased with this project generated by its offspring, The Fund.

THE RESPONSIBILITY OF THE FORD TRUSTEES

The Fund for the Republic raises, in a harrowing way, the problem of trustees' responsibility. Some of the statements filed with the Reece Committee by foundations proclaimed the utterly sound principle that a foundation should not exercise censorship in the execution of a grant. But they used this sound principle to excuse themselves from responsibility for damage which could have been anticipated. There is a great deal of difference between insisting on *controlling* the research engaged in by Professor Jones to whom a grant has been made, and making sure that the professor to be selected for the grant is not one given to radicalism and strong bias in his work. There is a world of difference between requiring conformity of a researcher and insisting on objectivity in selecting him; the former is reprehensible; the latter is a public duty.

Yes, there might be one exception to this conclusion. A grant might properly be made to a person of known bias, if this were part of a program or plan in which the contrary point of view would also be adequately and fairly presented to the public.

According to newspaper reports, Mr. Henry Ford II finally got around to disavowing The Fund for the Republic. He did this in a series of letters to correspondents who asked him why he remained silent in view of the apparent record of the Ford Foundation-created Fund. Mr. Ford said that some of the actions of The Fund for the Republic "have been dubious in character and inevitably have led to charges of poor judgment." This was rather a weak disavowal. Mr. Ford must know that some of the activities of the Fund have been more than "dubious" and that far more than mere poverty of "judgment" was involved. Mr. Ford maintained, in any event, that The Ford Foundation was not responsible in any way, because it had created the Fund as an independent unit, to be managed by its own board.* This position cannot be accepted by the public.

As *The Wall Street Journal* of December 9, 1955, put it in an editorial commenting on Mr. Ford's position:

> So here are a group of men who have been handed $15 million to spend in the Ford name for political and educational purposes without being accountable to anyone. They are not subject to recall or referendum. They appoint their own successors. They could if they chose, adopt projects to "educate" for communism, fascism or whatever fancy struck their heads. And no one could say them nay.

Can Mr. Ford and the other Ford Foundation trustees dodge responsibility by saying that they created an independent and self-governing unit? Can one, fairly and ethically, just pour fifteen million dollars into anyone's lap and say: "Do with this what you will; I wash my hands of what you do"? Yes, perhaps that might be done in making a grant to a university, a church, a hospital, or some other responsible, existing institution with recognizable and acceptable traditions and standards. Otherwise, the maxim *delegatus non potest delegare* applies—that no trustee can delegate his trust function.†

No, the money being so wrongfully used by The Fund for the Republic is Ford Foundation money, and the public, which was required to be made the beneficiary of The Ford Foundation in

* Actually, the umbilical cord between The Ford Foundation and The Fund for the Republic was not wholly severed. It was provided that, if the Fund lost its tax exemption, its remaining money would revert to the parent.

† This maxim was quoted at the Cox Committee hearings by Dr. Henry Allen Moe of *The John Simon Guggenheim Memorial Foundation*. This foundation, itself, made many regrettable grants, some of them to Communists; but at least Dr. Moe did not try to dodge the responsibility of trustees for the application of the funds they administer.

order for the Ford family to reap the tax advantages which went with its creation, is entitled to trace that money and to judge its application.

The grant to The Fund for the Republic was not made unwittingly. The trustees selected Mr. Paul Hoffman to run it. They must have known Mr. Hoffman's opinions and proclivities and understood that its offshoot, placed in his control, would likely follow his bent—just, indeed, as they must have known, when placing Dr. Hutchins in charge of The Fund for the Advancement of Education, that the result would be a Hutchins product.

The Ford trustees might have acquired some insight into the way The Fund for the Republic would be managed when its chairman, Mr. Hoffman, initially announced that it proposed "to help restore respectability to individual freedom"—a statement which the Reece Committee report characterized as "obviously a product of the 'red herring' and 'witch hunt' school of political philosophy" and as "arrogant, presumptuous and insulting."*

The Ford trustees should also have known that there were inherent dangers in the detailed program which Mr. Hoffman presented to them for The Fund for the Republic. This touched delicate political areas. A foundation should not necessarily shy from delicate areas. If it wishes to enter them, however, it is ethically obliged to exercise the greatest circumspection. Every reasonable effort should be made to assure that subjects which contain political dynamite will be handled with the care they require—with full objectivity and fairness. In permitting their creature, The Fund for the Republic, to become a propaganda machine for the advancement of leftist political ideas, the Ford trustees abandoned their duty to the public to whose service they were dedicated by accepting appointment. By suffering The Fund for the Republic to fall into the hands of persons who might have been expected to use it for propaganda, these Ford trustees, by negligence at least, became party to actions against the public welfare.

The statement filed by The Ford Foundation with the Reece Committee said:

* Reece Committee *Report*, p. 114.

The trustees of the Ford Foundation are proud of their act in creating the Fund for the Republic.*

Since then we have had Mr. Henry Ford II's qualified and gentle disapproval of some of the actions of The Fund for the Republic. But his was an expression of personal opinion. There has been no official Ford Foundation repudiation of The Fund for the Republic. As far as the public knows, except for Mr. Ford's moderate criticism of The Fund for the Republic, the trustees are wholly satisfied with all the Ford Foundation's works.

HAS THE FORD FOUNDATION CHANGED ITS SPOTS?

Nothing would be more conducive to better foundation public relations than for these trustees to come forward with frank self-criticism, disclosing to the public (whose interests they represent) exactly how dissatisfied they have been with their performance to date. I am sure they cannot be entirely happy, and an honest self-critical report could constitute a most valuable catharsis.

When the major grants of the Ford Foundation in 1955 were announced, many saw hope that its trustees had come to understand the error of their ways and were ready to abandon the dissipation of their funds in scientism and worse. Such hopes may have been illusions, as the facts narrated in the following syndicated article by Raymond Moley of February 29, 1956, may indicate:

BEHAVIORISM AT HARVARD

The Influence of The Ford Foundation in The
Harvard Graduate School of Business
Administration.

The final report of Donald K. David, signalizing his retirement as dean of the Graduate School of Business Administration at Harvard, provides a vivid example of the immense power that the Ford Foundation is exercising over academic institutions of even the highest rank. And

* Reece Committee *Hearings*, p. 1053.

that influence, it seems, will be directed toward the adoption by such institutions of a very special type of research which seems to have possessed the Foundation since the beginning of its career under Paul Hoffman and Robert Hutchins.

It seems that during the past year the Ford Foundation bestowed upon the school a grant of $2,000,000 for research, with a strong hint that it be used in large part to "further the increased use of the behavioral sciences, especially sociology, psychology and anthropology, in research in and teaching of business administration." When three billion dollars gives a hint, of course, it is a command.

It is interesting that Dean David is also a director of the Ford Foundation, which raises the point of not a conflict, but what might be called a community of interests. It is more blessed to give than to receive. But when you can give and receive at the same time, you may consider yourself twice blessed.

It is also interesting to note that the dean's report was sent to graduates of the school with a covering letter from Thomas H. Carroll, who is not only president of the alumni association but Vice President of the Ford Foundation.

The directive that the funds be used on the "behavioral" sciences follows almost the exact language of the original purposes of the Ford Foundation.

The dean's report points out that research undertaken in the school "must represent the specific interests of the individual members of the Faculty." Apparently the "specific interests" of the present members of the faculty do not provide the preoccupation with "behaviorism" so dear to the Ford people. Accordingly, new talent is to be summoned in the person of Professor Samuel A. Stouffer of the Department of Social Relations across the Charles River.

Dr. Stouffer is well fitted to lead the business school into the mysterious "scientism" desired by the Ford Foundation. He has been a member of no less than four Ford advisory committees. During the war he served in the so-called Information and Education Division of the War Department. Mainly, according to ex-service men, that operation was intent upon performing as many curious behavioristic experiments as possible while the human guinea pigs were under what social scientists call "control." He is co-author of "The American Soldier," a work which will be bitterly remembered by many responsible army officers. At the University of Chicago and later at Harvard he was able to conduct his "controlled" probings on sophomores. At the business school, Dr. Stouffer will work with a team of the faculty leading toward a "new long-range program of research in the area of consumer behavior." One graduate of the school said, after reading of the expected visitation of Dr. Stouffer, that apparently "controlled experiments" which have hitherto been possible only on (a) soldiers, (b) sophomores, (c) guests in state institutions, will now be performed upon (d) customers for the benefit of prospective marketing experts.

So the old rule that the customer is a supreme being who is always right will no longer have that distinction. He is to become a guinea pig along with many other formerly free citizens.

Lawyers well remember the invasion by the behaviorists of the law schools and the strange sociological judicial opinions we have seen in recent years. Now business management is to have its turn.

In any event, this whole matter illustrates the creeping control by the bureaucracy of the Ford Foundation over higher education. It can happen even in a school like this which has won a fine distinction by keeping fairly close to its major interest which, according to its catalogue, is "to provide opportunity for men to develop themselves for positions of responsibility in private business or in the business of government." In short, business was its business.

There is other evidence that the Ford trustees either have not yet assumed full control of the foundation enterprise or else have not yet decided to change the foundation's coloration. In an article in the *National Review* of April 11, 1956, Mr. William Henry Chamberlin deplores the support by The Ford Foundation of The Foreign Policy Association, which apparently expects to receive a further twelve and a half million dollars from the foundation. Mr. Chamberlin points out that the "general influence" of The Foreign Policy Association "on American public opinion has been in the direction of anti-anti-Communism." This he lays chiefly at the door of the guiding genius of the Association, Vera Micheles Dean, now its president. This publication, he says, has borne "over a period of a decade and more, the unmistakable stamp of anti-anti-Communism." The support of this leftward-tending organization has not come from the severed Fund for the Republic but from The Ford Foundation itself. And it is apparently continuing.

There are, as I have pointed out earlier, indications that The Ford Foundation has not changed its spots. But there are signs, on the other hand, which give hope that it may eventually come to measure up to its grave responsibility. One can only hope for the best. As an instrument for good, this fantastically large foundation could be of vast benefit to our people. As one managed without absolute regard to objectivity, it can represent a horrible danger to our society.*

---

* Since the preparation of the manuscript of this book, and even after it was set in type, various announcements have been made by The Ford Foundation of new grants and new programs. Some of these announcements are very encouraging. While many of the Foundation's wheels seem to be running in the same old grooves, there are some sharp innovations. Particularly encouraging are the indications that the original emphasis on the "cultural lag" theory, which largely underlay the Foundation's statement of purposes adopted in 1949, is being toned down considerably. Many recent grants seem to show that the Foundation no longer intends to be confined by the 1949 corset and that it is becoming willing to branch out into deviations from its former orthodoxy. I hope I am right in attributing this change to a realization by the Trustees that the past performance of the Foundation left much to be desired. I hope also that this has been due, partly at least, to the influence of Dr. Heald.

9　FROM HERE ON?

AS IT IS

SINCE THE PUBLICATION of the report of the Reece Committee, there has been more public criticism of foundations than in all the previous history of foundations. Many writers, commentators, and other publicists were shocked at what the Reece Committee found. A hard core remains, consisting of those "liberals" who cannot see anything wrong in the use of public trust funds to accomplish "liberal" political ends. There is a third group, inclined at first to take the revelations of the Reece Committee with a grain of salt, which has had its eyes opened by the blunders of the Ford Foundation's fatuous child, The Fund for the Republic. This should gratify Congressman Reece, the David who had the courage to face the foundation Goliaths and their serried ranks of defenders.

Large foundations such as Rockefeller and Carnegie have contributed greatly (and often spectacularly) to the public welfare through their work in medicine, public health, and other useful fields; a list of their magnificent accomplishments, such as the establishment of the Carnegie libraries and the virtual wiping out of several virulent diseases through Rockefeller-supported research, would be very long indeed. But the wide and rightful publicity given to these great public benefits have tended to dull public sensitiveness to other developments in the foundation world which have not been benign. These unpleasant developments could not easily have been exposed without such an inquiry as the Reece Committee conducted.

Only a small part of the foundation story has been told. The Reece Committee strongly urged a continuance, or a resumption, of its inquiry. It advocated "the most complete possible airing of criticism and the most thorough possible assembling of facts." It concluded that in no other way could "foundation trustees come to realize the full degree of their responsibility, nor the extent of the dangers which they must avoid to prevent foundation destruction."*

A continued Congressional investigation has been urged by resolutions of the D.A.R., the American Legion, and other patriotic organizations. Such a continued investigation is bitterly opposed by most foundation professionals. They consider such organizations as the American Legion "anti-intellectual." Its resolutions only prove to the "liberal élite" of the foundation world that they must increase their efforts to lead the American people into a better way of life.

The Rockefeller Foundation, for one, apparently intends to do just that, if statements by its president, Mr. Dean Rusk, are any indication. In an address at New York University, the president of The Rockefeller Foundation appears to have made his position clear. *The New York Times* of May 22, 1955, commented editorially on this address as follows:

> It is refreshing to be told that, in spite of Representative B. Carroll Reece's jitters about such matters, American foundations are going to deal increasingly with "controversial" issues—especially when this opinion is expressed by those who know most about foundation activities. Both Dean Rusk, President of the Rockefeller Foundation, and F. Emerson Andrews, author of authoritative studies in this field,† said as much at the conference on the problems of the charitable foundations held at New York University last week.

You have to understand the jargon of major foundation professionals like Mr. Rusk to know what they are talking about. The

---

* See the Committee's recommendations, Appendix A of this book.
† Mr. Andrews is an executive of the Russell Sage Foundation.

term "controversial," as I have earlier indicated, does not imply the fair presentation of two sides of an issue. What is meant is the presentation of one side of a controversy, and one side only—the "liberal" side. As *The New York Herald Tribune* reported another speech by Mr. Rusk (this time in Pasadena, in June 1955), he said that The Rockefeller Foundation would *continue* "to support vigorously a program of free and responsible scholarships." This promise would have been encouraging if the word "continue" had not appeared in this news report. The Rockefeller Foundation, when operating in the social sciences, in education, and in foreign affairs, has not always shown a disposition to promote either "free" or "responsible" scholarship. Its support of The Institute of Pacific Relations and some of the worst characters in its *dramatis personae* is but one case in point; as is its support of the "historical blackout."

The same editorial in *The New York Times* which lauded Mr. Rusk and Mr. Andrews for stating that foundations would increase their support of "controversial issues" gave a clue to what foundation executives meant by this term. It praised The Fund for the Republic, which it selected for mention as an example of how right Messrs. Rusk and Andrews were in predicting a general increase in foundation support of "controversial issues." If the Fund for the Republic typifies what we are to be in for, then action by the Congress to protect the people against the misuse of foundation funds is sorely needed.

Happily, the work of the Congressional investigations has not failed to influence foundations. There are indications that some of them have begun to practice greater caution in their operations. The gigantic gifts of The Ford Foundation to colleges and other institutions in 1955, 1956, and 1957 evidenced a new policy of direct support of education with no strings attached. The support of the Kinsey studies by The Rockefeller Foundation ended after the Reece Committee had illuminated the public regarding the origin of the funds used for this project. The Social Science Research Council has come out, in a recent report, for greater support of the unattached, lone researcher. The Rockefeller Foundation has somewhat reorganized its administrative structure; and substantial changes of personnel have taken place in The Ford Foundation. Signs such as these are encouraging.

A PLEA TO THE TRUSTEES

In my initial report on proposed procedure to the Reece Committee* I expressed the opinion that no Congressional action should be taken of a legislative nature unless it were unavoidable. The Committee report concurred. I have not changed my position. Much is tragically wrong with the way some of the foundations have operated, much that has heavily damaged our society and can continue to injure us. But there is hope that reform can come about from within the erring foundations. I shall not, therefore, conclude with any discussion of what legislative measures might be considered in order to prevent further injury to our society, but rather with what measures might be taken by trustees of foundations in order to correct the unhappy situation from within and thus forestall the otherwise inevitable, restrictive legislation.

1. It seems to me clear that no one should permit himself to be a mere figurehead trustee of a great foundation. How much time or application may be necessary for the proper discharge of a trustee's duty to the public depends on the size of the organization and the complexity of its structure and of its program. Whatever the answer is, it should be faced squarely.

2. The alternative to resignation, if the trustees find themselves unable to contribute the time and attention which duty to the public requires, is to simplify the program of the foundation to the point that trustees can adequately discharge their duty directly and without delegating their most essential functions to subordinates or to other distributing organizations.

3. Unless the trustee is certain that he reasonably understands the ramifications, intricacies, and implications of a proposed, designed grant, it would seem improper for him to acquiesce in it. The preferable alternative would be to make a grant direct to an existing operating institution of recognized character, of the type

* See Appendix C.

of a college, university, hospital, or church, leaving the focusing and designing of the project to it.

4. Trustees of foundations should avoid any situations involving a conflict of interest. They should not serve on granting and receiving boards of tax-exempt organizations simultaneously. They should also insist on their employed executives exercising similar cautions.

5. The avoidance of multiple trusteeships seems highly desirable, to eliminate a concentration of power through interlocks.

6. The practice of so unreasonably favoring a few of the large universities with research grants should be abandoned. The justification given for this favoritism, that the best men and the best equipment are to be found at these institutions, is not wholly true. Much research requires no equipment whatsoever; and all the best brains in academic life are not to be found in the great universities. Moreover, more widespread research grants, in themselves, would tend to widen the intellectual field, enable smaller institutions (and men in them) to attain greater stature and reputation and contribute more heavily to the development of our intellectual and practical life.

7. Trustees of those foundations like The Ford Foundation which have excluded themselves substantially from the natural sciences might reconsider whether this decision has been wise. At the 1956 annual dinner of The Research Corporation, a foundation devoted to the development of natural science, an address was made by Professor Robert Burns Woodward, an eminent scientist of Harvard to whom the foundation's annual award had been presented. Dr. Joseph W. Barker, the president of the foundation, had previously made a plea for greater support of scientific studies and for the crying need to develop science teachers in order to produce more scientists, so badly needed. This plea was echoed and amplified by Professor Woodward.

Whenever foundation apologists seek to defend the foundations against criticism, they point invariably to the great things which foundations have done for our country. These great things have indeed been done, and the foundations responsible for them (some large, like the Rockefeller and Carnegie foundations, and some smaller, like The Research Corporation and many others) are almost invariably in the fields of natural science, medicine, and public health, and some in the humanities. When major foundation accomplishments are listed, how many fall within the so-called *"social* sciences"? Very few, indeed! Is the theory sound, then, that because enough is being done in true science fields, foundations should "risk" their capital and income predominantly in "social" directions? Ask Professor Woodward, who has synthesized cortisone, quinine, and cholesterol. Ask him what he could do with the millions wasted by The Ford Foundation and others on useless compilations of statistical material and on the drafting and publication of masses of reports on "social" subjects which will lie buried forever, useful to no one.

In exposing the crying need for further support of pure science, Professor Woodward attacked the "culture-lag" theory, which is at the bottom of the policy of some of the major foundations of spending so much on organized social-science research. The Ford Foundation has been the greatest sinner in this direction. Its initial trustees succumbed to pressure by social-science advocates of the cultural-lag theory—that we have developed science so rapidly that we have not caught up socially. Out of this theory comes the idea that organized projects should be financed to make pathological studies of our society and of our behavior in order to find ways of enabling society to catch up with science.

This, in a way, is fiddling while Rome burns. I quote from the concluding paragraphs of an address made by Admiral Strauss at the Sixth Thomas Alva Edison Foundation Institute on "The Growing Shortage of Scientists and Engineers" on November 21 and 22, 1955:

> The extent to which science has become a major factor in our living, our environment and our fate, is something now apparent to all who will examine the facts. Our position of

eminence and influence in the world has been due to the prudent and vigorous applications of technology to the development of our resources and our potential.

*   *   *

If we value these possessions which have made for our eminence and influence, we must be prepared to defend them. Our greatest possession—freedom—is itself partly the product of science, since it was technology which made slavery unprofitable, and under freedom and only under freedom all our other treasures flourish.

It is a paradox that we should find ourselves at this point in history suddenly poorer in the very means by which our greatness was achieved.

This is the cold war of the classrooms.

In five years our lead in the training of scientists and engineers may be wiped out, and in ten years we could be hopelessly outstripped. Unless immediate steps are taken to correct it, a situation, already dangerous, within less than a decade could become disastrous.

It may well turn out that The Ford Foundation and the other foundation followers of the cultural-lag theory have made an irretrievable error in not recognizing that what we face is not a cultural but a scientific lag.

FURTHER RECOMMENDATIONS

I do not propose that foundations should not support any social-science research. I do propose that they should abandon almost all of the vastly expensive, directed group-research procedures which have been so characteristic of recent foundation operations and have been so ridiculed by even warm friends of the foundations. The individual social-science researcher should receive support for his own selected project. No group-research project would have produced an Einstein. No group social-science research has yet produced anything of monumental significance; but individual social scientists have produced, and ever will produce, much of great value to our society if permitted to go their own selected way.

The saving in abandoning those group-research projects which have been so dear to the hearts of the executives of the foundation combine would make available tens or hundreds of millions which could be used to advance us in pure and applied science, in medicine, and in public health, with ever greater speed. Nor do I mean that the humanities should be neglected. Attention to the humanities offers far more hope of preventing or curing any "cultural lag" than any combination of group-research projects in the social sciences.

Some of the largest foundations have virtually abandoned the support of existing educational and other types of operating institutions on the theory that the government is now spending so much money on direct support that private funds can be better used elsewhere. This is a most regrettable position for foundation trustees to take. It may well have behind it the conviction of some of the most leftward-thinking foundation professionals that such institutions should be supported, and therefore controlled, by the state—an aspect of the paternal theory of government. It seems essential to our social system, however, that there be private institutions which can remain wholly outside any government control.

The fact is that private educational institutions have been desperately in need of funds. Hospitals and other social institutions so necessary to human comfort need money badly. The partial change of plan in The Ford Foundation which resulted in heavy grants to such institutions in 1955, 1956, and 1957 deserves the highest praise, and offers an example which other foundations might well emulate.

One of the admirable characteristics of The Rosenwald Fund was that it was to be expended and not carried on in perpetuity. Perhaps perpetuity should be proscribed by law except in certain specific instances. At any rate, where trustees have the power to expend their capital, should they not consider carefully whether it might not be better to allocate it gradually to institutions such as universities, which can so well employ it, rather than to carry on forever and spend only the income?

What is most important for the trustees of most of the major foundations to understand is that they have lent themselves to the virtual suppression of freedom of inquiry and freedom of expression in the social-science areas. There is no blinking the facts. The "liberal" academician has a relatively easy time, and the conservative a very difficult one, getting a grant from one of these organizations. True, a conservative academician may still write as he pleases and speak as he pleases, but research costs money; the preparation and publication of written works costs money; and professors usually are poor men. If "liberals" are heavily subsidized, and subsidization is denied their opposite numbers, a form of suppression occurs which no one can justify in a public trust.

Were this situation reversed, were the foundations in question to favor conservatives and to exclude "liberals," the Americans for Democratic Action, the American Civil Liberties Union, the propaganda agencies of organized labor, the "liberal" press, the "liberal" publishing industry in general would speak up in no uncertain terms. These are silent now.

As I have said earlier, this book is no plea to convert the "liberal" preponderance within major foundations and their associated organizations into a "conservative" preponderance. It is a plea to foundation trustees to make certain that the organizations they manage operate with complete political disinterest. The privilege of tax exemption is justified whenever a foundation confines itself to truly educational, scientific, or other nonpolitical activities. When it reaches clearly into politics, the tax exemption is not justified. There is a borderline, very difficult to delineate, of course, in which there is uncertainty. This uncertainty does not necessarily mean that inquiries and action even in these border fields are inadvisable. But it suggests greater caution. It calls for wisdom. It calls for the perspicacity and willingness to avoid a hortatory and partisan advocacy of political goals and to stick to an objective presentation of facts, figures and ideas.

If the foundation is merely a granting foundation, confining itself to institutional grantees and making no attempt to say what the donee institutions are to use the grants for, it would make little difference what the political complexion of its executives might be. Or if the foundation confines itself to areas of activity in which political connotations are absent, it would be of little consequence whether its executives were predominantly conservatives or radicals. Where, however, the foundation determines the lines of inquiry to which its funds are to be applied and these touch social areas in which political predilection could play a part, then it becomes of the greatest importance for the trustees to assure themselves that the executives they employ act without political bias.

This requires extraordinary alertness. It also requires a careful scrutiny of the foundation's employees to make sure that there is at least a balance of political predilection, set up in such a way as to create an effective objectivity of result. This is not merely a matter of balance in numbers. One or two Communists in strategic posts in a cabinet have been able to pave the way for the absorption of a nation into communism. One or two political-minded foundation executives, placed in strategic posts within the organization, can turn it to active and effective political use.

In his *Philanthropic Foundations,** Mr. E. Emerson Andrews suggests that foundations should

(1) before voting a grant, make certain of the integrity and competence of the persons involved, the responsibility of the organization, and the worth of the project; (2) after voting the grant, make no attempt to influence appointments or internal policy of the organization, avoid membership on its board, and give counsel only if asked; (3) when requesting financial and progress report, avoid any suspicion of control over the nature of findings or their distribution.

* P. 223.

He adds:

> In the unlikely case of complete misapplication of funds or other malfeasance, discontinuance of further payments or action for recovery is warranted.

With all this I agree, but it does not finish the story of the duty of trustees in connection with grants. I believe it to be the duty of trustees to examine the product to determine whether it has (a) been produced with bias, and (b) has materially affected our society, or could so affect it. The purpose would be to decide whether corrective *action* is indicated. Such action might take the form of a public repudiation of the product in some instances—a broadcast notice to the public that the foundation which made it possible does not support what its money misproduced. In most instances corrective relief would call for the financing of a counterproject to create at least a balance.

Had The Carnegie Corporation, for instance, adopted such a procedure in the case of the report of the Commission on Social Studies of The American Historical Association, much damage to our educational system could have been avoided. These comments apply, clearly enough, wherever the subject matter touches "controversy."

Mr. Andrews repeats his position regarding responsibility in an introduction to *The Public Accountability of Foundations and Charitable Trusts** by Eleanor Taylor. He speaks of the inadequacies of much foundation reporting, expresses concern over the possibility of restrictive legislation which might harm all foundations, and affirms that it is "wholly proper that the foundation or trust should be held accountable for its stewardship." However, along with the author of the book, he used the term "accountability" strictly in a financial sense. He says: "Society should have the means of protecting itself against the theft, squandering, or unreasonable withholding of the promised" benefits intended for the general welfare. He says: "The operations of the exempt organizations should be fully and regularly reported with adequate provi-

* Russell Sage Foundation, 1953.

sion for review by a public authority possessing power to correct abuses. This constitutes accountability."

But Mr. Andrews does not support any form of "control" other than financial auditing. He demands "real freedom" for the givers of funds and the administrators who manage them. He deems this especially important in the field of the social sciences. He is all for the "venture-capital" theory, and he wants no "control" over the freedom of ventures. What Mr. Andrews, and those who think like him, do not see is the logical weakness of their proposed distinction between "accountability" (as they define it, limiting it virtually to a statement of what they have paid to whom and for what projects) and "control."

The true measure of "accountability" is not merely proof of what they have done with the money entrusted to them. Those to whom they have the duty to account surely must have the right to know not only how the money was spent, and whether or not some of it was dissipated, but also what the theory, objectives, and results of the expenditures have been. "Control" could take the form of the right of censorship or penalty or remedial relief after the act, exercised by governmental authority, of course. But that is not part of the concept of "accountability" which I maintain should be applied. "Accountability" in its true sense should be to the public, the beneficiary of the trust which a foundation admittedly represents; and the public has the right to know how the managers and operators of a foundation have interpreted their trust duty.

Accountability for financial propriety alone is not enough to protect the public against abuses of substantive power. There is need for a form of accountability which will protect the people in the areas of intellectual concern; to insure that nothing has been done to curb true academic freedom; to make certain that the free competition of ideas has not been impaired; to see that the rights of the nonconformist have been protected.

The foundation needs to look closely at what its financing has produced. It needs to explain or expose publicly what motivated its selections and to explain also how, in so selecting, it was alert to the necessity of preventing bias and of promoting objectivity. It needs, further, to renounce publicly that which has turned out misbegotten and to announce and take such steps as might reasonably be necessary, and are feasible, to correct any damage which has been done. If this process, which begins to effect true public "accountability," is generally adopted by foundations, no movement for government intervention would collect any substantial support. The very process of self-audit, combined with the resultant public accounting, should quickly enough correct errors of management.

The foundations which are bent on a public mission should be grateful for any public scrutiny of their deeds and of the significance of their actions. In the absence of controlling authority, public scrutiny alone can supply them with sound yardsticks of performance. It is my hope that, in the constant adjustment of social institutions, to which foundations are as subject as other bodies of men, the stimulus of outside criticism will, in the end, prove to be a most constructive contribution to their work.

FINDINGS AND CONCLUDING OBSERVATIONS OF THE REECE COMMITTEE

THE FINDINGS

THE COMMITTEE FINDS AS FOLLOWS:

1. The country is faced with a rapidly increasing birth-rate of foundations. The compelling motivation behind this rapid increase in numbers is tax planning rather than "charity." The possibility exists that a large part of American industry may eventually come into the hands of foundations. This may perpetuate control of individual enterprises in a way not contemplated by existing legislation, in the hands of closed groups, perhaps controlled in turn by families. Because of the tax exemption granted them, and because they must be dedicated to public purposes, the foundations are public trusts, administering funds of which the public is the equitable owner. However, under the present law there is little implementation of this responsibility to the general welfare; the foundations administer their capital and income with the widest freedom, bordering at times on irresponsibility. Wide freedom is highly desirable, as long as the public dedication is faithfully followed. But, as will be observed later, the present laws do not compel such performance.

The increasing number of foundations presents another problem. The Internal Revenue Service is not staffed to adequately scrutinize the propriety and legality of the work of this ever-enlarging multitude of foundations.

2. Foundations are clearly desirable when operating in the natural sciences and when making direct donations to religious, educational,

scientific, and other institutional donees. However, when their activities spread into the field of the so-called "social sciences" or into other areas in which our basic moral, social, economic, and governmental principles can be vitally affected, the public should be alerted to these activities and be made aware of the impact of foundation influence on our accepted way of life.

3. The power of the individual large foundation is enormous. It can exercise various forms of patronage which carry with them elements of thought control. It can exert immense influence on educational institutions, upon the educational processes, and upon educators. It is capable of invisible coercion through the power of its purse. It can materially predetermine the development of social and political concepts and courses of action through the process of granting and withholding foundation awards upon a selective basis, and by designing and promulgating projects which propel researchers in selected directions. It can play a powerful part in the determination of academic opinion, and, through this thought leadership, materially influence public opinion.

4. This power to influence national policy is amplified tremendously when foundations act in concert. There is such a concentration of foundation power in the United States, operating in the social sciences and education. It consists basically of a group of major foundations, representing a gigantic aggregate of capital and income. There is no conclusive evidence that this interlock, this concentration of power, having some of the characteristics of an intellectual cartel, came into being as the result of an over-all, conscious plan. Nevertheless, it exists. It operates in part through certain intermediary organizations supported by the foundations. It has ramifications in almost every phase of research and education, in communications and even in government. Such a concentration of power is highly undesirable, whether the net result of its operations is benign or not.

5. Because foundation funds are public funds, the trustees of these organizations must conscientiously exercise the highest degree of fiduciary responsibility. Under the system of operation common to most large foundations this fiduciary responsibility has been largely abdicated, and in two ways. First, in fact if not in theory, the trustees have all too frequently passed solely upon general plans and left the detailed administration of donations (and the consequent selection of projects and grantees) to professional employees. Second, these trus-

tees have all too often delegated much of their authority and function to intermediary organizations.

6. A professional class of administrators of foundation funds has emerged, intent upon creating and maintaining personal prestige and independence of action, and upon preserving its position and emoluments. This informal "guild" has already fallen into many of the vices of a bureaucratic system, involving vast opportunities for selective patronage, preference and privilege. It has already come to exercise a very extensive, practical control over most research in the social sciences, much of our educational process, and a good part of government administration in these and related fields. The aggregate thought-control power of this foundation and foundation-supported bureaucracy can hardly be exaggerated. A system has thus arisen (without its significance being realized by foundation trustees) which gives enormous power to a relatively small group of individuals, having at their virtual command, huge sums in public trust funds. It is a system which is antithetical to American principles.

7. The far-reaching power of the large foundations and of the interlock, has so influenced the press, the radio, and even the government that it has become extremely difficult for objective criticism of foundation practices to get into news channels without having first been distorted, slanted, discredited, and at times ridiculed. Nothing short of an unhampered Congressional investigation could hope to bring out the vital facts; and the pressure against Congressional investigation has been almost incredible. As indicated by their arrogance in dealing with this Committee, the major foundations and their associated intermediary organizations have intrenched themselves behind a totality of power which presumes to place them beyond serious criticism and attack.

8. Research in the social sciences plays a key part in the evolution of our society. Such research is now almost wholly in the control of the professional employees of the large foundations and their obedient satellites. Even the great sums allotted by the Federal government for social science research have come into the virtual control of this professional group.

9. This power team has promoted a great excess of empirical research, as contrasted with theoretical research. It has promoted what has been called an irresponsible "fact finding mania." It is true that a balanced empirical approach is essential to sound investigation. But

it is equally true that if it is not sufficiently balanced and guided by the theoretical approach, it leads all too frequently to what has been termed "scientism" or fake science, seriously endangering our society upon subsequent general acceptance as "scientific" fact. It is not the part of Congress to dictate methods of research, but an alertness by foundation trustees to the dangers of supporting unbalanced and unscientific research is clearly indicated.

10. Associated with the excessive support of the empirical method, the concentration of power has tended to support the dangerous "cultural lag" theory and to promote "moral relativity," to the detriment of our basic moral, religious, and governmental principles. It has tended to support the concept of "social engineering"—that "social scientists" and they alone are capable of guiding us into better ways of living and improved or substituted fundamental principles of action.

11. Accompanying these directions in research grants, the concentration has shown a distinct tendency to favor political opinions to the left. These foundations and their intermediaries engage extensively in political activity, not in the form of direct support of political candidates or political parties, but in the conscious promotion of carefully calculated political concepts. The qualitative and quantitative restrictions of the Federal law are wholly inadequate to prevent this mis-use of public trust funds.

12. The impact of foundation money upon education has been very heavy, largely tending to promote uniformity in approach and method, tending to induce the educator to become an agent for social change and a propagandist for the development of our society in the direction of some form of collectivism. Foundations have supported text books (and books intended for inclusion in collateral reading lists) which are destructive of our basic governmental and social principles and highly critical of some of our cherished institutions.

13. In the international field, foundations, and an interlock among some of them and certain intermediary organizations, have exercised a strong effect upon our foreign policy and upon public education in things international. This has been accomplished by vast propaganda, by supplying executives and advisers to government and by controlling much research in this area through the power of the purse. The net result of these combined efforts has been to promote "internationalism" in a particular sense—a form directed toward "world govern-

ment" and a derogation of American "nationalism." Foundations have supported a conscious distortion of history, propagandized blindly for the United Nations as the hope of the world, supported that organization's agencies to an extent beyond general public acceptance, and leaned toward a generally "leftist" approach to international problems.

14. With several tragically outstanding exceptions, such as *The Institute of Pacific Relations*, foundations have not directly supported organizations which, in turn, operated to support Communism. However, some of the larger foundations have directly supported "subversion" in the true meaning of that term, namely, the process of undermining some of our vitally protective concepts and principles. They have actively supported attacks upon our social and governmental system and financed the promotion of socialism and collectivist ideas.

CONCLUDING OBSERVATIONS—SOME SUPPLEMENTAL COMMENTS

THE PROBLEM OF FOUNDATION SURVIVAL

A number of foundations have complained bitterly about a "second" investigation, bemoaning the inconvenience of repeated inquiries. Whatever the inconvenience, this Committee urgently recommends a continued inquiry. The fullest possible study is necessary adequately to expose certain weaknesses and errors of operation, the failure to recognize which might, some day, result in a growing movement to destroy the foundation as an institution by wholly denying it tax exemption.

There are many today who believe that foundations should not be permitted. Among them are one group of advocates of "state planning," who take the position that all the functions now performed by foundations should be in government control; that foundations prevent the over-all coordinated planning in Washington which, they say, should be our goal. Others feel that the privilege of giving away the public's money (tax-exempt money) should not be subject to the idiosyncrasy of the donor or the disposition of a self-perpetuating group of foundation managers. There are others who resent, on a simple motivation of human envy, the presence of great sums of money segregated to the directed desires of some person of great wealth.

None of these points of view are received sympathetically by this Committee.

There is another group, however, which says that nothing would be lost by abolishing foundations, except factors which are undesirable or unpleasant. That is, they say, a donor could still make all the charitable donations he wished, by conferring his benefactions on existing institutions such as colleges and universities, hospitals, churches, etc. He could still get the same tax benefit for himself and for his estate, and save the equity control of a business for his family through such transfers. He could give himself the same egotistical satisfaction, if that is important to him, by attaching his name to a fund. He could even designate a purpose for which a recipient college, for example, must use his grant. He could even attach reasonable conditions and restrictions to his gifts.

All that would thus be lost by abolishing foundations, say these critics, would be (1) the inability to use a foundation itself as a vehicle for maintaining control or partial control of a business and (2) the inability to insist upon the management of the fund through family members or other self-perpetuating, designated persons. We would thus still have the equivalent of foundations, but they would be administered by universities and other responsible institutions instead of by those appointed by a miscellaneously selected board of private trustees and by "clearing houses."

This argument cannot be lightly dismissed. Nor can it be defeated by the insistence that foundation funds are most valuable as "risk capital." If the risk capital theory is sound, would it not be a safer "risk" to society to have such funds administered by responsible university trustees? The delineation of scope of purpose in a deed of gift could very easily warrant the taking of reasonable "risks."

While we recognize the weight of these arguments, we do not support the proposal that foundations be abolished or refused Federal tax exemption. One reason is that foundations are generally creatures of state law and it does not seem to us that the Federal government should, through the power of its taxing arm, virtually prevent the states from retaining the foundation as a permissible institution if they wish to.

Another reason is that some foundations have accomplished so much that is good. Institutions which are capable of doing for the American people the magnificent things which foundations have been responsible for, in medicine, public health and elsewhere, indicate that they should be saved if they can be. But the foundations cannot rest on their beneficial accomplishments alone. Not only must their balance sheets show a preponderance of good—that preponderance must be truly overwhelming. That they have improved the public health, for example, cannot offset that they have permitted themselves to be used to undermine our society and some of our most precious basic concepts and principles.

If they are to be permitted to continue and to wield the tremendous power which they now exercise, it must be upon the basis of complete public acceptance—because they will have committed mere venial sins and not mortal ones. For this reason we so strongly advocate the most complete possible airing of criticism and the most thorough possible assembling of facts. In no other way can foundation trustees come to realize the full degree of their responsibility, nor the extent of the dangers which they must avoid to prevent foundation destruction.

THE PROPOSED CONTINUED INQUIRY

Various suggestions have been made as to the proper or most advisable vehicle for a continued inquiry. One is that a permanent subcommittee of Ways and Means be created to complete the investigation and to act as a permanent "watch-dog." Another is that the whole problem be turned over to the Joint Committee on Internal Revenue Taxation. A third is that something in the nature of a British "royal commission" be created. Whatever the means used, we urge that the investigation be retained under the control of the legislative branch of the government, where it belongs.

How should that continued inquiry be conducted? We have pointed out that such an inquiry is primarily a matter of laborious research. Facts are best secured by this method, rather than through the examination and cross-examination of a parade of witnesses.

Some foundation spokesmen have alluded to "Committee witnesses" and "foundation witnesses" in connection with the current investigation. There has been no such division of witnesses. All who came, or were to come, before us were, or were to be, "Committee witnesses." What these foundation spokesmen have attempted to do is give this proceeding the character of a trial, rather than an investigation. It has been no trial, and could not be.

There has been a growing insistence on the part of some groups of extreme "liberals" that Congressional investigations be changed in character to approach very closely to trial practice. Such suggestions fly in the very face of the nature of Congressional investigations and seek to undermine the independence of the legislative arm of the government by depriving it of the right to unhampered inquiry.

The use of a trial method, with complaint, answer, reply, rebuttal, surrebuttal, etc., as to each issue, would mean utter confusion and make of each investigation an endless "circus."

This Committee has been much maligned, in part by the press and by foundation spokesmen, because it first placed critical witnesses on the stand. This was done, with the unanimous approval of the full Committee, in order to be utterly fair to the foundations by letting them know, in advance of their own expected appearances, the main lines of inquiry which were to be followed. This was explained repeatedly by the Chairman and by Counsel, and appears in the record again and again. In the face of these statements foundation spokesmen, echoed by parts of the press inimical to this investigation for whatever reasons of their own, have cried "unfair!"

The insistence on something close to trial practice is illustrated by a telegram from *The Rockefeller Foundation* to the Committee which says:

"We must assume that the Committee's decision [to discontinue the hearings] means that it will not submit a report to the Congress containing any material adverse to our foundation on which we are not fully heard." (*Hearings*, p. 1062.)

This statement is made as though this condition were advanced as a matter of right. We reject it emphatically. We are not "trying" the foundations; we are investigating them. To require us, in advance of a report, to submit to a foundation every piece of evidence or comment which our staff may have collected would be an absurdity, hampering a committee such as this to the point of destroying its effectiveness.

The Rockefeller Foundation statement goes even further than demanding to see every piece of material which might be used in criticism of it. It says: "We suggest that the Committee insure this [refraining from unfairly injuring the foundations] by affording the foundations an opportunity to be heard on the draft of any report which the

Committee proposes to submit." That is both intolerable arrogance and an absurdity. Perhaps this will be added to the list of things which the advanced "liberals" are asking of Congressional procedure —that no Congressional committee be permitted to file any report until all persons interested have had an opportunity to see it in draft and comment upon it to the committee!

Such procedure, aside from its interference with the independence of Congress, would involve the endless protraction of investigations. In our case, for example, there are some seven thousand foundations. Does Mr. Rusk, who signed the Rockefeller statement, believe that only *The Rockefeller Foundation* should have the right of examination? Or does he believe all foundations should have that right? Does he suggest they be called in one by one, or all in a group? The impossibility of his suggestion is obvious enough. And how about the cost? We have heard no foundation voice raised to assist this Committee in securing adequate financing.

THE ATTITUDE OF THE FOUNDATIONS

United States News and World Report of October 22, 1954, page 104, contains excerpts from an article in *Harper's* Magazine for February, 1936, concerning Congressional investigations, written by Supreme Court Justice Hugo L. Black. Justice Black describes how pressure against an investigation commences before the investigation even begins.

> At the first suggestion of an investigation the ever-busy, ceaselessly vigilant Washington lobby sounds the alarm."

The instant a "resolution is offered, or even rumored, the call to arms is sounded by the interest to be investigated."

> "High-priced political lawyers swarm into the Capitol. Lobbyists descend upon members. Telegrams of protest come from citizens back home protesting against the suggested infamy."

Certain newspapers can generally be depended upon to raise a cry against the proposed investigation. The opposition does not end when a resolution passes; the next step is to try to influence appointments to the Committee. Finally, pressure is put upon the controlling legislative Committee to restrict the activities of the investigating committee by limiting its funds.

Justice Black's article is worth reading. It goes on to describe the difficulties which confront Congressional investigations when they do get under way.

Unfortunately this Committee concludes that some of the foundations have followed the traditional course which Justice Black described as taken by "the interest to be investigated." Nor have we been impressed with the general willingness of foundations to submit their performance to public scrutiny.

This Committee can judge the attitude only of those foundations with which it has had intimate contact. These, as well as the "clearing house" organizations, have been fully cooperative in supplying information. Both groups, however, have demonstrated an intolerance toward criticism. This unwillingness even to consider that they might, in any respect, be guilty of serious error, we find distressing and discouraging. We can only conclude that it emanates from a sense of power and security, even *vis-à-vis* the Congress. Some of the foundations have gone so far as to imply that it is an injustice for Congress to investigate any complaint against them.

They have filled their statements with cliché material regarding the desirability of "free speech," and "freedom of thought," and "academic freedom" as though they had a monopoly on the defense of freedom and there were serious danger that Congress might unfairly curtail it. A form of arrogance and a pretension to superiority leads them to believe that critics must, *per se,* be wrong. Foundations are sacred cows. The men who run them are above being questioned. This Committee, continues their general attitude, is bent upon the destruction of the sacred right of foundations to do as they please; it is full of malice; its staff is manned with incompetents who have called in incompetents as witnesses; no one who criticizes a foundation could be competent.

One gathers the impression from some of the filed statements that the foundation officers who have signed them believe that they have a vested and inalienable right to do as they please, and that it is an outrage that a Congressional Committee should dare to question any of their actions. The fact is that they have a limited privilege—limited by what the public may determine is for its own good; and the public, in this sense, is represented by the Congress.

This Committee has even been attacked by foundations which it has not investigated in any detail. Several such attacks, for example, have been launched by the Anti-Defamation League of B'nai B'rith, one appearing in its October, 1954, *Bulletin,* which begins by announcing—before the completion of our investigation, that it has failed. The lengthy article refers to the Committee members and staff as "actors" in a "charade," and refers to the witnesses called by the Committee as "a strange group." It is replete with vituperation and prejudges in vicious manner before the publishing of a report upon which alone any final judgment of this Committee's work could be made. The concluding sentence of the article is:

> "Its failure as a Congressional investigation is a great victory for the American people."

There can be no possible justification for such an attack by a tax exempt organization in the course of a Congressional investigation.

This Committee is quite conscious of the possibility that it may itself have erred in some facts or in some judgments. Unlike some of the foundation-supported social scientists and some of the foundation executives (to judge them from their own statements) we do not consider ourselves Olympian. It is partly for this reason that we strongly recommend a completion of the project of an investigation of foundations—so that all possible facts in the criticized areas may be adduced which might be favorable to them. Based on an incomplete inquiry, all final conclusions are subject to possible revision.

On the other hand, we are quite shocked that some of the foundations have presumed to imply malice and an intention by this Committee to do a biased and prejudiced job. We should like to print in full the initial report prepared by Counsel to the Committee under date of October 23, 1953, outlining his proposals for the conduct of the work. It is a measured, objective and thoroughly unprejudiced document running to 22 pages, the result of extremely careful thought; it formed the basis upon which the Committee built its operations. We shall quote merely part of it to indicate the attitude which this Committee has had in its work.*

> *"Control as a Basic Problem.* This brings us to the basic control problem. We would assume that the Committee would be disposed to a minimum of Federal control. The rights, duties and responsibilities of foundations are, in our opinion, primarily

* See Appendix C.

matters of state law with which the Federal government should not interfere unless grounds of national welfare, strong enough to induce an application of a broad Federal constitutional theory, should appear. For the moment, then, the only available mechanism of control available to the Congress is the tax law. Congress has the clear right to place reasonable conditions upon the privilege of tax exemption. It has done so, as to income tax, gift tax and estate tax. If amendments to these tax laws come to appear desirable it is the province of the Committee on Ways and Means, as we understand it, to consider such amendments. We conceive our function in part to be to produce the facts upon which that Committee may, if it chooses, act further. We deem it within our province to state the facts which have appeared, collate them, and suggest areas of consideration for Ways and Means if the Committee finds this desirable.

"If acute or chronic foundation ailments should appear, the remedies may not, in every case, be through legislation. A disclosure of the ailments may, to some extent, induce reform within the ailing foundation itself. And the very statement of the facts may induce the public to take an interest of a nature to bring about reform through the force of public opinion."

This measured language does not indicate an intention to "railroad" the foundations or to impose restrictions on them which might, as some of the foundations purport to fear, destroy their usefulness. To quote once more from this initial and guiding report of Counsel:

"Starting with the premise that foundations are basically desirable, excessive regulation, which would deprive them virtually of all freedom, might well destroy their character, their usefulness and their desirability. Therefore, regulatory measures should be approached with great caution. We are not prepared at this time even to suggest that further regulation is needed. It seems essential to us that as scientific a collection and integration of facts as possible be accomplished before anyone, whether in this Committee or outside, arrives at any precise conclusions."

This is the spirit in which this Committee started its work and in which it has continued through the preparation of this report.

SPECIAL RECOMMENDATIONS NOT FULLY COVERED IN THE PREVIOUS TEXT

We shall not burden this already lengthy report with a repetition of all the various observations, conclusions and recommendations stated in its course. Because of the incompleteness of the inquiry, we have been disinclined to arrive at many final and fixed recommendations. We shall, however, discuss briefly some features of foundation operation which seem to require additional or fresh comment.

THE JURISDICTION OF WAYS AND MEANS

Wherever suggestions are made herein for possible changes in the tax laws, we are mindful of the superior jurisdiction of the Committee on Ways and Means and respectfully offer such suggestions to that Committee for its consideration.

REFORM FROM WITHIN THE FOUNDATIONS

This Committee has never swerved from the concept laid out in the initial report of Counsel to it that whatever reform of foundation procedure is necessary should, if possible, come from within the foundations themselves. We are not overly encouraged, from the content and import of the statements filed by some of the foundations, and their general attitude, that much willingness exists among executives of the foundations and of the associated organizations to institute any reform whatsoever. A prerequisite to such reform from the inside would lie in a recognition that it is needed. If these foundations and organizations persist in their attitude that they are sacrosanct, that they have not committed and cannot commit any serious errors, and that they, therefore, need no reform whatsoever, then Congressional action in various directions seems inevitably necessary, even to the possible extent of a complete denial of tax exemption.

LIMITATIONS ON OPERATING COSTS

Suggestions have been made that the operating cost of foundations is sometimes excessive, resulting in a waste of public funds. There is much to this allegation, particularly in the case of heavily staffed foundations with complex machinery of operation, and those which double overhead by using intermediary organizations to distribute some of their funds. There seems to be no reasonable way, however, to control such waste through any form of regulation. It is our opinion that this is one of the areas in which reform from the inside is the only kind possible. We urge foundation trustees to consider it carefully.

"COLLECTING" FOUNDATIONS

Special attention might be given to abuses by foundations used for the purpose of collecting money from the public. These have been extensively investigated in the State of New York and elsewhere, and organizations like the National Better Business Bureau can supply much data concerning them. The chief complaint against many of these organizations is that their costs of operation often far exceed the net amount available for distribution to "charities." Legislation to protect the public against abuses of foundations of this type is possible, perhaps in the form of a limitation on a percentage of permitted overhead. This Committee has not had time, however, to study this specific problem nor did it feel it advisable to duplicate any of the work done, for example, by the investigation in the State of New York.

WASTE IN GENERAL

The evidence indicates that there is a good deal of waste in the selection of projects, particularly mass research projects in which large sums are expended, and the services of a substantial number of researchers employed, when the end to be achieved does not measure favorably against the aggregate expenditure of valuable manpower and of money. This error seems to us often to relate to an excessive interest in empirical research. The services of ten or more researchers might be used to assemble "facts" on some narrow subject when the same money spent on this piece of mass-fact-production could support those ten or more men, each in valuable, independent research. It would not be difficult, for example, to find a better use for $250,000 than the mass research on the Taiping Rebellion concerning which Professor Rowe testified. We urge foundation trustees, who alone can prevent such waste, to scrutinize carefully the proposed end-objective of any suggested research project involving possible waste of manpower and public funds. We suggest to them, further, that foundation money is precious; that the capacity to distribute it is not a right but a privilege, a privilege granted by the people—that, therefore, waste should be avoided even more strictly than in the use of one's personal funds.

DEFINING FOUNDATIONS

In order that statistical material of great value may be produced by the Bureau of Internal Revenue, and so that special rules might be applied to foundations (and "clearing house" organizations) as distinguished from the miscellany of organizations included within the scope of Section 101 (6) (now 501 [c] [3]) of the Code, we suggest that the Committee on Ways and Means consider a division of that section into two parts.

INTERNAL REVENUE SERVICE MANPOWER

It is the opinion of this Committee that, although complete observation of foundation activity by the Internal Revenue Service is impossible, the subject is of sufficient social importance to warrant an increase in the manpower of the pertinent department of the Bureau to enable it more closely to watch foundation activity.

FULL PUBLIC ACCESS TO FORM 990A

We consider it an absurdity that the public does not have open access to the full reports filed by the foundations and known as Form 990A. Why any part of the activity or operation of a foundation, a public body, should not be open to the public eye, we cannot understand.

A "RULE AGAINST PERPETUITIES"

Many have urged that a "rule against perpetuities" be applied to foundations in the form of an aggregate limit on life of, say, from ten to twenty-five years. We strongly support this proposal. It should be applied primarily to foundations and other non-institutional organizations whose sole or chief function is distributing grants. Some operating research organizations might, possibly, be exempted from the rule and classed with institutional organizations such as colleges, universities, hospitals, churches, etc. And careful study may disclose other types of foundations which might be excluded from the proposed limitation on length of existence. It would not be easy to define these classes or to draw the lines of demarcation; but the difficulty of delineation should not prevent the undertaking.

Measures to forestall evasion would have to be considered. For example, a foundation, shortly before its duration-expiration, might pass its assets to another foundation created for the purpose or having similar objectives and management. There are other problems requiring difficult study. But it seems wise to proscribe perpetual foundations of the general class. This would minimize the use of the mechanism to enable a family to continue control of enterprises *ad infinitum;* avoid the calcification which sometimes sets in on foundations; and, among other desirable objectives, minimize the seriousness of the danger that a foundation might, in some future period, pass into the control of persons whose objectives differed materially from those which the creator of the foundation intended.

ACCUMULATIONS

Foundations may not accumulate income "unreasonably." The pertinent provision of the tax law is analogous to Section 102 applying to ordinary corporations, and has a sound principle behind it. Yet it seems to us to sometimes work out unhappily. Foundations should not be overly-pressed to distribute their income, lest they do so casually or recklessly. We suggest, therefore, that this rule be changed so that:

> 1. a foundation be given a period of two or three years within which to distribute each year's income, but that
> 2. within that period, *all* of that year's income be paid out.

If a "rule against perpetuities" were applied, our suggestion might be that a foundation be given an even longer period of income accumulation.

CAPITAL GAINS

With the objective of preventing any accumulations (beyond the limits discussed above), we suggest that capital gains be treated as income. That is, all capital gains realized should be subjected to the same rule as to accumulations, as though they were ordinary income. Whether or not capital losses should be allowed as an offset for the purpose of treating accumulations is debatable.

RESTRICTIONS ON CORPORATION-CREATED FOUNDA-TIONS

We have suggested that such foundations require the thorough study which we have not been able to give them. We are not in a position to make final recommendations. We do suggest that, while such foundations seem entirely desirable, they should be subjected to some restrictions which would prevent them from aggregating enormous capital funds with which they could (1) exercise powerful control of enterprises through investment and (2) come to have a very strong impact upon our society. One method might be to treat all donations to such foundations as income for the purpose of compelling distributions and proscribing accumulations. That is, whatever rule is applied, directed at the improper accumulation of income, should be applied to a corporation's annual donations as though these were income to the foundation.

NATIONAL INCORPORATION

It has been suggested that foundations be either compelled or permitted to incorporate under Federal law. We adopt neither suggestion. This Committee does not advocate any unnecessary extension of Federal jurisdiction. Federal incorporation would have the advantage of permitting regulations to be enacted on a broader base than the tax law. But we feel that the further centralization of government function would be an unhappy invasion of states' rights.

RETROACTIVE LOSS OF EXEMPTIONS

This Committee has pointed out that, upon violation by a tax-exempt organization of the rules of the tax law relating to subversion and political activity, the only penalty is the future loss of income tax exemption (and the corresponding right of future donors to take tax deductions for gifts or bequests). We urgently recommend that means be studied by which the initial gift tax and/or estate tax exemption, granted upon the creation of the organization, may be withdrawn and the tax due collected to the extent of the remaining assets of the organization. It impresses us as absurd that, having been guilty, for example, of subversive activity, a foundation whose funds were permitted to be set aside because of tax exemption, can go right on expending its capital for further subversion.

REMOVAL OF TRUSTEES

A sensible alternative to the imposition of the retroactive penalty described above, would be the immediate removal of the trustees or directors. This is primarily a matter of state law, and the Federal government could not force such removal. It could, however, we believe, provide that the retroactive penalty be assessed unless all the trustees or directors forthwith resign and arrangements are made for the election of directors appointed by a court or an agency of the state of incorporation or of the situs of the trust.

PUBLIC DIRECTORS

The suggestion has been made that each foundation should be required to have, upon its board, or as one of its trustees, a member selected by a government agency, perhaps the state government. The purpose of the suggestion is that the public would thus have a direct representative who could watch the operations of the foundation and take whatever action he might deem necessary if he found a violation of good practice or of law. The suggestion may have merit; it may be well worth the consideration of the Committee on Ways and Means.

REVOLVING DIRECTORATES

Directed against the calcification which may set in upon a foundation, the suggestion has been made that a director or trustee be permitted to sit upon a board for only a reasonably limited number of years, after which he would be ineligible for reelection. This suggestion also seems to have considerable merit, and may be worth the attention of Ways and Means.

SELECTION OF WORKING TRUSTEES

We urge most strongly upon those who control the great foundations, in particular, that they fill their boards with men who are willing to take the time to do a full job of trust administration. This is meant as no personal criticism of those many estimable men who sit upon foundations boards. We have gone into this matter elsewhere in this report. The president of a great corporation cannot possibly give to the management of a foundation the time which should be required. Many of the weaknesses of foundation management might be avoided if the trustees were selected from among men able and willing to give a large amount of time to their work.

RELIEF FOR THE ALERT CITIZEN

As it is obvious that the Internal Revenue Service cannot, except at prohibitive cost, follow the activities of the individual foundations to ascertain whether violations of law exist, this Committee believes that some additional method should be established to protect the people against a misuse of the public funds which foundation money represents. An interesting suggestion has been made, which deserves careful study, that legal procedure should be available in the Federal courts under which a citizen could bring a proceeding to compel the Attorney General to take action against a foundation upon a showing, to the satisfaction of a Federal judge, that a *prima facie* or probable cause exists.

PROHIBITED ABUSES

The Internal Revenue Code specially taxes "unrelated income" and proscribes certain transactions and uses of foundations. Among them are the unreasonable accumulation of income and certain prohibited transactions between the foundation and its creator or other closely associated persons and corporations. Within the limitations of time and funds faced by this Committee it did not feel warranted to enter this area of research which is, in any event, peculiarly the province of the Committee on Ways and Means. Doubtless certain defects in the existing law covering these areas need attention, but these must be left to consideration by the controlling Committee.

FOUNDATIONS USED TO CONTROL ENTERPRISES

One subject which does need careful consideration by the Congress is the use now so frequently made of foundations to control businesses. In an early section of this report we alluded to the extent to which foundations are being currently created in order to solve estate and business planning problems. We mentioned also the possibility that so great a percentage of enterprises may, someday, come into the hands of foundations that this very factor in itself may oblige legislative relief. We believe the Congress and the public should be sharply aware of this factor of enterprise control through foundations; it has already had some effect on our economy.

There is nothing now in the law prohibiting such control. A donor or testator can transfer the controlling stock of an enterprise to a foundation and it may hold it in perpetuity, its self-perpetuating directors or trustees voting the stock as they please. It is conceivable that certain situations of a special character might be attacked by the Internal Revenue Service. For example, if the continued holding of one stock by a foundation seemed to prevent it from using its funds to the best advantage in relation to its dedicated purposes, it is possible that a court might cut off its tax exemption. But such instances would have to be extreme and irrefutably clear to promise relief. In the ordinary case, nothing will interfere with the continued holding. By the same token, foundations holding only a minority percentage of the voting stock of a corporation can act in consort with other stockholders, perhaps of one family, to become part of a controlling group; there is nothing in the law to prevent this either.

To prevent a foundation from receiving any substantial part of the securities of an industrial enterprise would extremely limit the use of the foundation mechanism for the solution of the problem of how to meet the heavy death charges in estates whose assets consist chiefly of securities in a closely held enterprise. On the other hand, the retention of a substantial holding in any enterprise may, in the long run, operate against the general public interest. We are not absolute in our conclusion, but suggest to the Committee on Ways and Means that it consider the advisability of denying the tax exemption to any foundation which holds more than five or ten per cent of its capital in the securities of one enterprise—and, in the case of an initial receipt of such securities, it might be well to give the foundation a period of two to five years within which to bring its holdings down to the prescribed maximum level.

AREA EXCLUSIONS AND RESTRICTIONS

We qualifiedly support the theory of the foundations that their capital and income is often wisely used in "experimenting" in areas which the government or other private philanthropic organizations do not enter—we support this theory, however, only as to such areas where there is no grave risk to our body politic and to our form of society. With this limitation, the theory of "risk capital" seems sound and its observation accounts for many of the great boons to society for which foundations have been responsible, particularly in medicine and public health.

The question comes—should foundations be excluded from any special fields, such as the social sciences? Some ask that they be restricted to certain limited fields, such as religion, medicine, public health and the physical sciences. We do not support this theory. We believe they should be prohibited from using their funds for "subversive" purposes and from all political use, and we shall discuss this further. Beyond that, we believe that foundations should have full freedom of selection of areas of operation.

In giving them this freedom, there is a great risk of waste. This risk must be taken at the alternative cost of such hampering of operations through controls as to make foundation independence a virtual fiction. But we urge again that foundation trustees exercise great care in avoiding waste.

TYPE EXCLUSIONS

Suggestions have also been made that foundations be restricted in various ways as to type of operation. These suggestions are of all sorts, some of them conflicting:

>That they should not be permitted to act as operating units;
>That they should only be permitted to operate, and should not be permitted merely to make grants;
>That they should not be permitted to create subsidiaries, affiliates or progeny foundations or operating units;
>That they be permitted to make grants only to existing operating units of certain types, such as colleges, universities, hospitals, churches, etc.;
>That they be denied the right, in the social sciences, to attach any condition to a grant, as to detail of operation, personnel, etc.;
>That they be excluded from grants to other foundations, including "intermediary" organizations;

and many others.

If any of these and similar suggestions are to be considered, we recommend that this be done only after a truly complete investigation has been had; and then only after the most careful study. It is the general position of this Committee that no restraints should be put upon the operation of foundations which do not seem inevitably necessary for the protection of our society.

PROTECTION AGAINST INTERLOCK

Many detailed suggestions have been made to prevent the growth and even the continuance of the concentration of power to which we have given considerable attention. These suggestions, for the most part, should also await the completed study and should be approached with great care. Some of the intermediary organizations should perhaps be continued, to go on with whatever valuable and safe activities they now pursue; but efforts should be made to induce or prevent them from acting in any coercive role, whether by intention or by the very nature of the structure of the foundation world.

Some few suggestions are, however, worthy of immediate consideration. One is that no trustee, director or officer of any foundation or intermediary organization be permitted to act as a trustee, director or officer of another, except where members of constituent societies may be associated with a parent body.

Another is that the fullest democracy be imposed on the election of members of such associations of societies and similar organizations to prevent the self-perpetuance which exists, for example, in the *Social Science Research Council.*

For the moment, we believe that the problem of "power" urgently demands the attention of foundation trustees. In order to escape an eventual substantial curtailment of foundation independence, trustees will have to understand how powerful their organizations are and how much care must be exercised so that no abuse of this power occurs. They must also understand the terrific social impact which a concentration of foundation power entails and avoid, like the plague, operations or associations which tend to coerce, or even carry the propensity for coercing or in any way effecting, social controls, compulsions toward uniformity or any form of pressure on society or on those who are or are to become its intellectual leaders.

GREATER USE OF COLLEGES AND UNIVERSITIES

Among other approaches to the solution of the problems raised by a concentration of power, this Committee urges trustees of foundations more frequently to use colleges and universities as media for research operations, suggesting further that grants to such institutions be made as free as possible of conditions and limitations.

THE EXCESS OF EMPIRICISM

This Committee is entirely convinced by the evidence that the foundations have been "sold" by some social scientists and employee-executives on the proposition that empirical and mass research in the social sciences is far more important than theoretical and individual research, and should be supported with overwhelming preponderance. We are conscious of the fact that Congress should not attempt to exert any control over the selection of methods of research or the relative distribution of foundation funds over various types. Nevertheless, this Committee suggests that foundation trustees consider carefully and objectively our conclusion, from the evidence, that an overindulgence in empiricism has had results deleterious to our society, particularly in subordinating basic and fundamental principles, religious, ethical, moral and legal. In such consideration, we also suggest, as we have previously in this report, that they consult not alone with their professional employees who are the advocates of overwhelming empiricism but also with those scholars and students who are critical of the preponderance.

POLITICAL USE AND PROPAGANDA

It is the opinion of this Committee that the wording of the tax law regarding the prohibition of political activity of foundations should be carefully re-examined. We recognize that it is extremely difficult to draw the line between what should be permissible and what should not. Nevertheless, the present rule, as interpreted by the courts, permits far too much license. While further study may be indicated, we are inclined to support the suggestion that the limiting conditions of the present statute be dropped—those which restrict to the prohibition of political activity *"to influence legislation"* and those which condemn only if a *"substantial"* part of the foundation's funds are so used. These restrictions make the entire prohibition meaningless. We advocate the complete exclusion of political activity, leaving it to the courts to apply the maxim of *de minimis non curat lex.* Carefully devised exceptions to this general prohibition against political activity might be made in the case of certain special types of organizations, such as bar associations.

Whatever the difficulties which foundations may face in determining when a proposed activity may have political implications, we cannot see any reason why public funds should be used when any political impact may result.

LOBBYING

An astonishing number of tax-exempt foundations are registered as lobbyists in Washington. Under the present law, it seems clear that lobbying in itself is not held to be political activity of a type which might deprive a foundation of its tax exemption. Moreover, registration may, in many instances, take place to protect the foundation against a technical violation of the law requiring registration, when the only activity approaching true lobbying may consist of merely keeping an eye on developing legislation in some special field of interest. Nevertheless, there is evidence to indicate that much true lobbying goes on. The whole area needs investigation. Whether tax-exempt organizations should have the privilege of lobbying is at least extremely doubtful.

SUBVERSION

The prohibition against the use of foundation funds to support subversion also needs wholesale revision. As the law stands it is only the support of Communism and Fascism which is prohibited. It may be that the adequate revision of the law regarding political use would suffice, but it is clear to us that all support of socialism, collectivism or any other form of society or government which is at variance with the basic principles of ours should be proscribed. This subject, too, requires considerable study. We well understand that some research clearly not intended to have any political implication may, nevertheless, incidentally impinge on the political. We also understand that the effect may relate to what is merely one facet of an aggregate of collectivist thought. Yet we feel that the whole field of the social sciences is of such a nature that "risk" is not desirable. As much as we support taking "risks" in the physical sciences, in medicine and public health and other areas, it is clear to us that risks taken with our governmental, juridical or social system are undesirable. If there is a burden placed on the foundations through the difficulty of drawing a line between what is in the broad sense "subversive" or "political" and what is not, it is better that the foundations suffer this burden than that they take risks with our happiness and safety.

FOREIGN USE OF FOUNDATION FUNDS

In this area this Committee has not been able to do sufficient study to come to a final evaluation. However, we offer this suggestion tentatively and subject to further investigation of the extent and significance of foreign grants and grants for foreign use—that such grants be limited to ten per cent of the annual income of the foundation or, if it is disbursing principal, ten per cent, in the aggregate, of its principal fund. An exception should be made in the case of religious organizations, such as foreign missions, and perhaps in some other instances of peculiar and historic nature.

FURTHER AREAS OF INVESTIGATION

We have limited ourselves in the scope of our inquiry, in order not to scatter over the entire, gigantic field. We urge, however, that the proposed continued inquiry cover those sections which we have perforce omitted. Among them is that of organizations which have religious names, or some connection with religion or a religious group, which have engaged in political activity. There is evidence that such groups exist in all three major sects. The right of a minister, priest or rabbi to engage in political activity is clear enough. When such activity takes place, however, under the shelter of a tax-exempt organization which is not in itself a church, we question its permissibility.

There are some special types of tax-exempt organizations which seem to us seriously to need investigation. Among them are the co-operative organizations, some of which seem to engage in political activity and even to promote a form of collectivism. Some labor and union organizations also might be studied to see if they have not crossed the border from privilege to license in matters political. Among unions, for example, there is the basic question whether dues payable by the members should be used for political purposes which the members have not authorized.

There are some special foundations or similar organizations to which we have been able to give insufficient attention in some cases and none in others. These should all be studied. Among those which we have not heretofore mentioned (or mentioned only briefly) are these:

The Public Administration Clearing House;
The National Citizens Commission for Public Schools;
The Advertising Council;
The Great Books Foundation;
The American Heritage Council;
The American Heritage Program of the American Library Association;
The American Foundation for Political Education;
The American Friends Service Committee;
The Institute of International Education.

Another special group requiring study is the so-called "accrediting" organizations. These (apparently tax-exempt) organizations are extra-governmental, yet they act, in effect, as comptrollers of education to a considerable degree. For various reasons colleges, universities and specialized schools and departments today require "accreditation," that is, approval of one or more of these organizations which presume to set standards. Some of these accrediting organizations are supported by foundations; through such support, they may well control them. An incidental factor involved in this accrediting system imposed on American education is its often substantial expense to the institutions themselves. The Committee is informed that some colleges are obliged, through this system, to pay as much as $20,000 per year to enable them to stay in business. The standards set may perhaps in every instance be beyond criticism, yet the system in itself is subject to question in so far as it imposes on institutions standards set by private organizations not responsible to the people or to government.

As we have been able to devote intensive study only to some of the major foundations, we suggest that a selected number of the more important foundations of what might be called the second rank in size should be examined carefully. A study of these may produce type or sampling material of great value in considering the over-all foundation problems.

We have been unable to do much concerning small foundations and their problems and difficulties. Some of these involve matters which should be primarily the concern of the Internal Revenue Service, but we have pointed out that its capacity for watching over the foundation field to discover breaches of law and offensive practices is very limited. A thorough study should, therefore, perhaps solicit from the public complaints against smaller foundations, as well as large, in order that studies may disclose what weaknesses exist in the operation of these smaller organizations.

* * *

While this Committee has spent little time in investigating the activities of foundations in the natural sciences on the ground that their performance in this area has been subjected to very little criticism, a continued inquiry might well give attention to this field in relation to the problem of subversion. There is evidence that some foundations and foundation-supported scientific enterprises have been used by Communists, through a special form of infiltration which has escaped the notice of those in control. Several important scientific projects seem to have been so employed for Communist purposes. They have become clearing centers for building up the reputation of persons of hidden Communist persuasion and subsequently placing these pseudo-scientists in situations where they are able to engage in espionage. The process includes using the assistance of scientists who are fellow-travellers or outright Communists to provide the material which is then used by the infiltrate to establish his scientific reputation. This is all done so adroitly that the foundations which support such projects know nothing of it.

THE STORY OF THE REECE COMMITTEE

PRELUDE: THE CREATION OF THE COX COMMITTEE

On August 1, 1951, in the 82nd Congress, Congressman E. E. Cox of Georgia, a Democrat, introduced a resolution in the House of Representatives to direct a thorough investigation of foundations. In an accompanying "extension of remarks"* he applauded foundations for the work they had done in various areas of activity but asserted that, of those which

> had operated in the field of social reform and international relations, many have brought down on themselves harsh and just condemnation.

He cited foundation support of such men as Langston Hughes, Hans Eisler, Louis Adamic, and Owen Lattimore. He named The Rockefeller Foundation,

> whose funds have been used to finance individuals and organizations whose business it has been to get communism into the private and public schools of the country, to talk down America and to play up Russia * * * .

He cited the Guggenheim foundation, whose money

> was used to spread radicalism throughout the country to an extent not excelled by any other foundation.

He listed The Carnegie Corporation, The Rosenwald Fund, and other foundations among those badly needing scrutiny. And he said:

* *Congressional Record,* April 1, 1951, p. A-5046.

There are disquieting evidences that at least a few of the foundations have permitted themselves to be infiltrated by men and women who are disloyal to our American way of life. They should be investigated and exposed to the pitiless light of publicity, and appropriate legislation should be framed to correct the present situation.*

There had been much bitter criticism of foundation activity for many years, and a Democratic Congressman had finally shown the courage to bring the subject to Congressional attention.

His resolution was referred to the Rules Committee, on which he was the ranking Democratic member, and was reported out by it† on August 15, 1951, and referred to the House Calendar, but Mr. Cox must have run into difficulties, for he never called it up for action by the House.

The following year, Congressman Cox tried again. On March 10, 1952, he introduced an identical resolution‡ which was reported out by the Rules Committee on March 18th.§ On April 4, it was called up by Congressman Smith (Democrat) of Virginia, and a highly interesting debate ensued on the floor.†† Mr. Cox had criticized foundation support of Langston Hughes, a Communist who achieved notoriety, among other things, for his poem *Good-bye Christ*. Because Hughes is a Negro, Mr. Cox was accused of racial prejudice. Because he had criticized The Rosenwald Fund for having made grants to Communists, he was accused of anti-Semitism.

At the conclusion of the debate, however, the resolution passed. The vote was:

Yeas 194	Democrats 100
	Republicans 94
Nays 158	Democrats 88
	Republicans 69
	Independent 1
Not voting 78	

* *Congressional Record*, August 1, 1951, p. A 5046.
† H. Res. 881.
‡ H. Res. 561.
§ H. Res. 1553.
†† *Congressional Record*, April 4, 1952, pp. 3537, 3539 *et seq.*

Thus the resolution passed with a majority of both Democrats and Republicans.

In this Democrat-controlled Congress, 100 Democrats had voted for a resolution presented by a Democrat, and 88 Democrats had voted against it. When it came to appointing the four Democratic members of the Committee, however, two were selected who had voted against the resolution:

Yea	E. E. Cox of Georgia
Yea	Brooks Hays of Arkansas
Nay	Donald L. O'Toole of New York
Nay	Aime J. Forand of Rhode Island

The three Republican appointees had all voted for the resolution or been "paired" for it!

B. Carroll Reece of Tennessee
Richard M. Simpson of Pennsylvania
Angier L. Goodwin of Massachusetts

Congressman Wayne Hays of Ohio, who was later to become the major obstacle preventing orderly completion of the assignment of the Reece Committee, voted against the Cox resolution.

On May 8 an allowance of $100,000 was requested, but the House Committee on Administration cut this request to $75,000 and this sum was appropriated on July 2. The vote on the appropriation was:

Yeas 247	Democrats 111
	Republicans 135
	Independent 1
Nays 99	Democrats 62
	Republicans 37

Among those who voted against this appropriation was Mr. Wayne Hays of Ohio.

THE WORK OF THE COX COMMITTEE

Though the Cox Committee came in like a lion, it went out like a lamb.

Most of the testimony taken by this Committee was by officers and trustees of large foundations and by persons associated with them. It consisted largely of adulatory statements praising the work of the major foundations. Fourteen representatives of foundations were heard, of whom The Rockefeller Foundation provided three; The Ford Foundation, five; and the Carnegie foundations, six. A number of academicians appeared, all of whom praised the foundations and had no serious criticism to offer.

No critics of foundation activity were heard except Alfred Kohlberg, who had been responsible for unearthing the malfeasances of The Institute of Pacific Relations, and four witnesses called to prove that there had been conscious Communist penetration of foundations. None of the foundation representatives was put under oath. In contrast, witnesses who testified to Communist penetration were sworn in.

The final report of some fifteen pages was unanimous, except for the appended statement by Mr. Reece, to which I shall later refer. The report held to be unwarranted almost all the criticisms which had been made of foundation activity.

The Cox Committee did find that there had been a Communist, Moscow-directed plot to infiltrate American foundations and to use their funds for Communist purposes. The final report* of January 1, 1953, said:

> There can be no reasonable doubt concerning the efforts of the Communist Party both to infiltrate the foundations and to make use, so far as it was possible, of foundation grants to finance Communist causes and Communist sympathizers. The committee is satisfied that as long as 20 years ago Moscow decided upon a program of infiltrating cultural and educational groups and organizations in this country, including the foundations. The American Communist Party, following the program laid down in Moscow, went so far as to create a subcommission of the Agit-Prop (Agitation-Propaganda) or Cultural Commission which gave specific attention to foundations. The aims were to capture the foundations where possible, and where this proved impossible, to infiltrate them for the purposes (1) of diverting their funds directly into Communist hands, and (2) procuring financial assistance for projects and individuals favorable to commu-

* No. 2514, 82nd Cong. 2nd session.

nism while diverting assistance from projects and individuals unfavorable to communism. A few small foundations became the captives of the Communist Party. Here and there a foundation board included a Communist or a Communist sympathizer. Occasionally a Communist managed to secure a position on the staff of a foundation or a staff member was drawn into the Communist orbit.

The Cox Committee referred to the "unhappy instances where the committee is convinced infiltration occurred. There remains," it said, "the ugly unalterable fact that Alger Hiss became the president of The Carnegie Endowment for International Peace. And this despite the fact that his nomination and election came about through the efforts of men of proven loyalty and broad experience in public affairs."

The report said that the Committee was "hurried by lack of time" (which was certainly true) and could not do much research in this area. It went so far as to say, however, regarding foundation grants to Communists and for Communist use:

> In the aggregate, the number of such grants and the amounts involved are alarming.

The report hastened to add:

> Proportionately, when viewed in the light of the total grants made, they are surprisingly small.

The use of the word "surprising" *is* surprising. It would indeed have been "surprising" if a large percentage of foundation grants had gone to Communist use.

The Cox Committee report did mention the support given by The Rockefeller Foundation, The Carnegie Corporation and The Carnegie Endowment for International Peace to The Institute of Pacific Relations, to the extent of millions of dollars. But the report discharged the tragic IPR incident with this statement:

> The whole unhappy story of the IPR, which was largely supported by foundation funds, has been so fully revealed by the investigation of the McCarran committee that there is no need to make further reference to it here.

There was, indeed, good reason for discussing the IPR story in detail. The McCarran Committee had investigated subversion. The Cox Committee investigated foundations. The grave misuse of foundation funds, involved in the IPR incident, with catastrophic effect upon our foreign policy, deserved more analysis by the Cox Committee than the brief, quoted reference. There were lessons to be learned from the support by the Rockefeller and Carnegie foundations of The Institute of Pacific Relations. The Internal Security Committee had determined

> * * * that the IPR has been in general, neither objective nor non-partisan; * * * that the net effect of IPR activities on United States public opinion has been pro-Communist and pro-Soviet, and has frequently and repeatedly been such as to serve the international Communist, and Soviet interests, and *to subvert the interests of the United States.**

While the Cox Committee report recognized Communist penetration of the foundation world, it said

> that very few actual Communists or Communist sympathizers obtained positions of influence in the foundations.

Having softly disposed of the issue of Communist infiltration in foundations, the report treated even more gently the frequent criticism that some foundations had "supported persons, organizations, and projects which, if not subversive in the extreme sense of the word, tend to weaken or discredit the capitalist system as it exists in the United States and to favor Marxist socialism." (It took the position that the support foundations had given to socialism was "educational" only.)

This quotation from the Cox report recognizes the use of the term "subversion" in its true, primary meaning of an undermining. Yet when the Reece Committee later termed broad foundation support of socialism to be "subversive," it was bitterly criticized for using the dictionary meaning of "subversion" instead of limiting its use strictly to Communist-socialist penetration.

Many of leftward persuasion protested against the investigation by the Reece Committee on the ground that it was unnecessary because the work had already been done by the Cox Committee. But the Cox

* Internal Security Committee *Report*, p. 84. Emphasis supplied.

report itself stated in no uncertain terms that the Committee had had insufficient time to do its job.

Here is but one of such admissions, relating to an area of investigation the omission of which, alone, was sufficient ground for a renewed investigation. The Cox Committee report propounded this (7th) critical question:

> *Through their power to grant and withhold funds have foundations tended to shift the center of gravity of colleges and other institutions to a point outside the institutions themselves?*

It commented upon this criticism as follows:

> This question arises from a criticism *which has come to the committee from persons well informed generally and situated in positions from which a strategic view of the situation can be had.* THE COMMITTEE DOES NOT CONSIDER ITSELF SUFFICIENTLY WELL ADVISED ON THIS POINT TO HAZARD A VIEW. [Emphasis and capitalization in this paragraph supplied.]

This line of criticism, that foundations had exerted great and excessive influence over educational institutions, was levied, as the report says, by persons of authority. It is one of the gravest charges entered against foundation activity in the United States. If the foundations have exercised a powerful influence on our schools and colleges, tending to control them from outside their academic walls, the Congress and the people of the United States were entitled to know about it. That the Cox Committee had been unable to expend the time to study it, called for a renewed Congressional investigation; it would be only through a committee of Congress that all the relative facts could be brought to light.

The Cox Committee had also received much criticism concerning the alleged favoritism of some foundations for "internationalism." This criticism, the report held to be unsound. The Cox Committee had no adequate basis for coming to this conclusion. It had not collected or studied the facts. It would have been better to say, as it did in the case of foundation influence on educational institutions, that it did not have adequate time to investigate—instead of arriving at a categorical conclusion based on obviously insufficient data.

The Cox Committee report erroneously concluded that, although there might have been some derelictions on the part of foundations, it was the *little* ones which had been guilty and not the *great* and *powerful* foundations; these were beyond criticism.

Its conclusions were considerably weakened by its admission that it had inadequate time to do the job assigned to it. Moreover, the succeeding Reece Committee found in the Cox Committee files a considerable amount of material critical of foundation operations which had not been used by the latter.

Upon examining the Cox Committee files, which it received soon after going into action, the staff of the Reece Committee immediately reported to the Clerk of the House that many important documents and memoranda were missing.* As an example, a file marked "Robert Hutchins" was found to be completely empty. Whether such data were destroyed by the Cox Committee staff or were purloined by others, was never ascertained.

Congressmen are extremely busy men. The members of the Cox Committee were confronted with a gigantic research job, the satisfactory conclusion of which would have required far, far more time than they were allotted. Moreover, as is inevitably the case, they must have left the burden of organization and direction almost entirely to their chairman, Congressman Cox. It may well be that, even with the handicap of lack of time, the Cox Committee would have been more productive had Mr. Cox not been stricken down. He fell gravely ill while the investigation was under way and died before the report was filed.

BIRTH OF THE REECE COMMITTEE

At the end of the Cox Committee report appeared this endorsement by Congressman Reece:

> As pointed out and stressed in this report, the select committee has had insufficient time for the magnitude of its task. Although I was unable to attend the full hearing, I feel compelled to observe that, if a more comprehensive study is desired, the inquiry might be continued by the Eighty-third Congress with profit in view of the importance of the subject, the fact that tax-exempt funds in very large amounts are spent without public accountability or official supervision of any sort, and that, ad-

* Reece Committee *Hearings,* pp. 6-7.

mittedly, considerable questionable expenditures have been made.

In the Eighty-third Congress, Mr. Reece introduced a resolution for a new investigation, accompanying it with a speech.* He referred to the work of the Cox Committee as "unfinished business." He stated that, while this Committee had disclosed serious malfeasance by some foundations, its work had been far too limited to warrant legislative proposals being based upon it. He cited, in particular:

> That the Cox Committee had been given inadequate time;
> That foundation officers and trustees had not been sworn as witnesses;
> That these persons had been permitted to excuse the improper grants made by their foundations as "unwitting" or as made through "ignorance";
> That these witnesses were not asked why they were continuing to make grants "to organizations, projects and persons which are promoting special interests or ideologies," and even "outright political objectives"; and
> That the Cox Committee had failed to use much of the critical documentary evidence in its possession, relating to "subversive and un-American propaganda activities which attempted to influence legislation."

Such a resolution passes into the hands of the Rules Committee, and here this one stayed a long while. But the Rules Committee finally voted the resolution to the floor of the House, where it was presented, toward the end of the session, on July 27, 1953.

Mr. Reece accompanied the calling up of the resolution with a speech which pleaded for further investigation of tax-exempt foundations by referring at great length to suspicions of substantial foundation delinquencies.† This speech was no "prejudging" of the foundations, as some of the opponents of the investigation have claimed, but was intended to bring forcefully to the attention of the House of Representatives the seriousness of the complaints which had been made of certain acts of certain foundations.

The resolution passed, by a substantial majority:

* *Congressional Record*, April 23, 1953, p. 3776.
† *Congressional Record*, July 27, 1953, p. 10188 *et. seq.*, included in the Reece Committee *Hearings*, p. 25 *et seq.*

Yeas 209   Republicans 140
           Democrats 69

Nays 163   Republicans 49
           Democrats 113
           Independent 1

The Committee authorized by the Reece resolution was directed to report before January 3, 1955, which gave it approximately a year and a half of life. This was almost a year longer than the life of the Cox Committee, and it seemed as though a reasonably thorough inquiry might be had.

The first step was to appoint a Committee. Three Republicans were appointed and two Democrats. *Of the appointed Committee of five, three had voted against the resolution*—Republican Congressman Goodwin (who had been a member of the Cox Committee), Democratic Congressman Wayne Hays of Ohio, and Democratic Congresswoman Gracie Pfost of Idaho. The other two Republicans (and the only members who had voted for the resolution) were Congressmen Carroll Reece of Tennessee and Jesse Wolcott of Michigan. The majority (Republican) members were appointed by Representative Martin, Speaker of the House; the minority (Democrat) members by Rayburn, the minority leader.

MANDATE TO THE COMMITTEE

The enabling resolution read in part as follows (I have italicized several parts to emphasize its essential character):

> The committee is authorized and *directed* to conduct a full and complete investigation and study of educational and philanthropic foundations and other comparable organizations which are exempt from Federal income taxation *to determine if any foundations and organizations are using their resources for purposes other than the purposes for which they were established,* and especially to determine which such foundations and organizations are using their resources *for un-American and subversive activities; for political purposes; propaganda, or attempts to influence legislation.*

Thus the Committee was not directed to judge how beneficent foundations had been, but to determine whether any had been guilty of undesirable conduct. Yet abuse has been heaped upon the Committee majority because its investigation was critical. The term "unfair" has been hurled at it because it dared to research the serious criticisms which had been leveled at some of the foundations, not by "crack-pots" but, as even the report of the Cox Committee admitted, by well-informed citizens.

These attacks came, in part, from the very same professional managers of some of the foundations whose acts were subjected to criticism. They came also in large part from persons whose political and social ideologies made them sympathetic to the questioned acts which had been brought to light. After all, it is a matter of whose foot the shoe pinches. An investigation of "the stock market" or of the "munitions interests" or the "power monopoly" or some other critical investigation of an activity associated with free enterprise capitalism would be supported enthusiastically by those same persons to whom an exposure of the collectivist activities of foundations would seem an outrage.

PREPARATION FOR THE HEARINGS

Just how should a committee of this kind go about its work? Should it start hearings immediately, put foundation representatives on the stand, and ask them to state whether they thought any criticisms of foundation activities were justified? That was largely the procedure of the Cox Committee, and it partly explains the failure of that Committee adequately to discharge its mandate. Obviously, it would be futile to rely upon witnesses for the foundations to disclose their own delinquencies. They could hardly be expected to beat their breasts and cry *mea culpa*.

Some committees, operating in dissimilar areas, could rely wholly on the power of subpoena, and bring in witnesses from whose lips the full facts could be forced. Such procedure would have brought the Reece Committee nowhere. The activities of the foundations are reflected in a mass of printed matter. As the majority report stated:

> The materials of most value are to be found in voluminous literature, reports and records. Deciding among points of view becomes chiefly a matter of processing the mass of research material which is available, and determining, not on the basis of

witnesses' opinions but on a judicial weighing of the factual evidence, which are correct.*

The Committee drew an analogy with the work of the Temporary National Economic Committee (TNEC), which "conducted hearings but leaned heavily on staff reports published in over fifty volumes."

THE COMMITTEE MEMBERS

Mr. Reece automatically became Chairman because he had presented the resolution.

I had not met him before I took the assignment as General Counsel. I had had some correspondence with him, some years before, upon the occasion of an admirable speech which he had made on foreign policy, from which I later quoted in a book.† In my first meeting with him, I quickly concluded that we could have a happy relationship. He is charming, courteous and understanding. My long association with him has resulted in mounting respect for his intelligence, sincerity, and integrity.

The violence of some of the attacks on Carroll Reece as a result of this investigation were amazing. He has been accused of plotting against the foundations, of conspiring to defame and damage them for some mysterious reason of his own relating to personal political ambition. I have never found the slightest evidence of personal, political ambition in Mr. Reece.

At no time did Mr. Reece ever dictate procedure to me; at no time did he ever seek to influence my mind; at no time did he ever give me a thesis to prove. Mr. Reece had no motive whatsoever other than to ascertain whether the severe criticisms of foundations which had come to his attention were correct. What he was after, and he so instructed me, was to find out what the facts truly were.

Mr. Reece has been called an "anti-intellectual" by his detractors. This is an absurdity. After graduating from a southern college, Mr. Reece took graduate work at New York University and at the University of London. He became an instructor in economics at New York University, and assistant secretary of that University. He later became director of its School of Commerce, Accounts and Finance. He has two honorary doctorates.

* Reece Committee *Report*, p. 15.
† *The Myth of the Good and Bad Nations*, Regnery, p. 40.

He is a member of the Tennessee and D.C. bars; president of several banks, and the publisher of a newspaper. His has been one of the longest records of service as a Congressman. He was formerly Chairman of the National Republican Committee.

Mr. Wolcott, the only other member of the Committee who had voted for the resolution, was one of the busiest, ablest, and most respected men in the House. He was Chairman of the Banking and Currency Committee. This Committee, engaged in constant and important work, took so much of his time that he was able to attend hearings of the Committee on Foundations only at rare intervals. It was easier to get his attendance at meetings of the Committee itself, which could be arranged to the convenience of all members. Here his wisdom, equability, and strength of character were of great service.

The Reece Committee sorely missed Mr. Wolcott when he could not attend. His contribution was, nevertheless, very substantial, and I am deeply grateful to him for his constant courtesy, his willingness to be consulted even in a press of work, and his warm and earnest support.

The third Republican member was Mr. Goodwin of Massachusetts. He remains an enigma. I have rarely met a man more kindly, gentle, and thoughtful. But he did vote against the resolution and, unless the ranking minority member of the Committee, Mr. Hays, lied from the rostrum, Mr. Goodwin had stated privately to Mr. Hays that he was "on his side." It is difficult to believe that Mr. Goodwin had made up his mind in advance to oppose findings of the Committee which might be critical of foundations, but that is what Mr. Hays implied in this vicious thrust at Mr. Goodwin:

> I heard you say you are getting tired. Do you know what I am getting tired of? I am tired of you taking one position in public with pious speeches and then running to me in secret and saying, "You know whose side my sympathies are on." Why don't you act like a man?*

The strange separate opinion which Mr. Goodwin filed, after voting for the report with the right to file a reserving statement, expresses some conflict within himself.

* Reece Committee *Hearings,* vol. 1, p. 863.

Mrs. Pfost, one of the Democratic members, was uniformly pleasant. She was somewhat overshadowed by her vociferous fellow Democrat and inclined to follow where he led. I say this not unkindly, however, for I found Mrs. Pfost willing to observe congressional protocol, and a woman of poise and charm.

The belligerent member of the Committee was Mr. Wayne Hays, the ranking Democrat. He was frank enough to tell us that he had been put on the Committee by Mr. Rayburn, the Democratic Leader in the House, as the equivalent of a watchdog. Just what he was to "watch" was not made clear until it became apparent that Mr. Hays was making it his business to frustrate the investigation to the greatest extent possible.

My professional relations with him were complicated by a succession of his intemperate outbursts. From the start, I was anxious to work with all the Committee members as closely as circumstances would permit. Mr. Norman Dodd, the Director of Research, and I made every effort to convince Mr. Hays that we wished to work closely with him. Mr. Dodd, in particular, had many conversations with Mr. Hays; he outlined to him the nature and theory of the most grave criticisms which had been made of foundations and which we intended to investigate. Nothing was withheld from him. We were utterly sincere in our offers to work intimately with him and to keep him as much abreast of our research as he might wish. But we were met with suspicion and distrust and a succession of scenes which were quite unpleasant to live through.

It was difficult enough to work with Mr. Hays in the initial stages of the investigation. When it came to the hearings, he conducted himself with quite fantastic belligerence.

APPOINTMENT OF COUNSEL AND STAFF

I was officially designated as general counsel at a meeting of the Committee attended on September 15, 1953, by Messrs. Reece, Goodwin, and Hays. My law partner, Arnold T. Koch, was appointed associate counsel. I had suggested him because he is a trial lawyer of the first rank, a man of great wisdom and balanced judgment. His contributions to the success of the Committee's work were most important.

The major problem in collecting a staff was to find a research director qualified by experience and interest. After many interviews,

Mr. Norman Dodd was selected. He had spent many years, and much of his own money, on research of a nature which intimately touched the foundation world.

Mr. Thomas McNiece was selected as assistant research director. He had wide experience and was a researcher of exceptional ability and statistical experience.

Two of the staff were personal selections of my own. One was Dr. Karl Ettinger, the story of whose release before he had completed his work, I shall tell later. Dr. Ettinger's contributions, while he was with us, were vitally important. A deep student, incisive in his thinking, encyclopedic in his learning, both a theorist of the first quality and a researcher of unusual rapidity and thoroughness, he pursued many avenues of inquiry which would have been closed to a less qualified and searching mind. He advocated the use of scientific research methods in the Committee inquiry. Much of the rich material collected by the investigation was assembled by him for the purpose of objective, quantitative and qualitative analysis.

My other selection was Miss Kathryn Casey, a member of the Washington bar. She became a "legal analyst," and was an indefatigable and sound investigator. In later stages of the investigation, when our financial situation reduced the staff to a skeleton, she filled many separate functions with terrific energy and was priceless.

Mr. Hays had asked to have the right to designate one staff member, and the Committee had readily assented. His first selection was unacceptable, as he himself later agreed. His second, Miss Lucy Lonergan, daughter of the late Senator Lonergan, was wholly acceptable and she was appointed a research assistant.

RESEARCH STARTS

It was well into the fall of 1953 before intensive research could begin. Meanwhile, I had spent considerable time analyzing the general problem of how the investigation might be conducted. The Reece Committee has been accused by the "liberal" press of having prejudged the foundations. The fact is that I accepted my assignment only on the condition that I could direct an objective inquiry. My own ideas of how the work should be conducted are to be found in an initial report of Counsel on procedure made to the Committee under date of October 23, 1953. It follows as Appendix C. This report was acquiesced in and became the basis for the staff's work.

LIMITATIONS ON THE STUDY

The work of the staff was concentrated on a comparatively small number of foundations, and necessarily so. To review even a substantial number of the existing organizations in sufficient detail to make any sense would have been impossible. Moreover, the complaints registered with the Committee and the critical material which it encountered centered principally in some of the largest of the foundations and certain intermediary and satellite organizations which they chiefly supported. It was felt better to do as thorough a job on this limited few as we could, than to scatter our work among many. It is also obvious enough that, if unhappy practices exist in the foundation world, it would be of more service to the country to disclose those which were backed by great wealth than to spend precious time on the questionable practices of comparatively inconsequential foundations.

The Reece Committee interested itself almost solely in the so-called "social sciences," education, and international affairs. Little criticism has ever been made of the work of foundations in other areas, such as pure science, medicine, public health, and the direct support of existing institutions of the character of hospitals, schools, and churches.

MONEY TROUBLES

Mr. Reece had initially applied for an appropriation of $125,000. Appropriations are referred to the Committee on Administration, which is the financial watchdog of the House of Representatives. This Committee was, at the time, Republican controlled. Its Chairman was Congressman Le Compte of Iowa. A member of the Reece Committee was also on the Administration Committee—unfortunately, this was Mr. Hays, who had consistently voted against investigating foundations.

The Administration Committee met and recommended a reduced appropriation of $50,000 instead of the $125,000 which Mr. Reece had requested. No one in his right mind expected that this would carry the Committee through its year and a half of life, for the Cox Committee had spent $50,000 in about six months. So the Reece Committee was given $50,000 with the expectation that it would apply at the end of the calendar year (1953) for an additional appropriation to carry it through a full remaining year of work.

Shortly after the beginning of the following year (1954) Mr. Reece made his expected application for additional funds. The staff had estimated that $120,000 would be our minimum requirement. After studying a tentative budget carefully, Mr. Reece agreed that this figure was reasonable, and applied for it.

It was expected that our application would be acted on promptly. But nothing happened for a long while, and we began to worry. We had expected to schedule hearings in February, or in March at the latest, but it was impossible to do any precise planning until we were sure of the appropriation, which now seemed doubtful indeed. During this period of uncertainty, when we did not know whether we were to be permitted to carry on or not, Mr. Reece did everything he could to hasten the consideration of our appropriation, but Mr. Le Compte would not budge.

Finally a break came. Mr. Hays, who had been "bumped off" the Administration Committee on some seniority basis, now was suddenly restored to that Committee, and immediately threw himself into the appropriation issue.

This is how he operated. He came to Mr. Reece and made certain demands. If these were accepted, he would vote for our appropriation. If they were not accepted, he would vote against it. Control of the Administration Committee was Republican and Mr. Reece was a Republican, but the ways of politics are often mysterious. Mr. Hays had told us that his Party had given him complete discretion regarding the Committee on Foundations—that it had been left to him to decide whether to try to kill it or let it continue. What power did he really have? Who knows! Issues frequently cross party lines, and those faced by the Reece Committee certainly did. All Democrats were not against us. All Republicans were not for us. If Mr. Hays, therefore, had delegated power to turn the entire Democratic membership of the Administration Committee against us, and if one or two Republicans were against us also, we were out of business. So Mr. Reece deemed it best to listen to Mr. Hays.

These, then, were Mr. Hays's proposals. The Committee was to drop two members of its staff, Dr. Ettinger and Mr. George DeHuszar; and Mr. Hays was to be given a member of the staff to help him write a minority report if he decided to. This last condition was easy enough to comply with. He had already appointed a member of the staff, Miss Lonergan, and it was no burden to agree to let her stay on until the reports were in. But to be obliged to give up the expert services of two productive staff members was a different matter.

Nevertheless, Mr. Reece felt compelled to accede in order not to take any chance that the investigation might be starved out of existence. Shortly after that, the application for an appropriation was acted upon. A sub-committee of the Administration Committee met and recommended $100,000. Although this was less than we believed we needed, we breathed a sigh of relief to have been awarded even that. But our pleasure was short-lived. The whole Administration Committee later met and cut us down to $65,000, a sum palpably inadequate.

LOSS OF ETTINGER AND DeHUSZAR

Mr. Hays knew what he was doing when he coerced the release of Dr. Ettinger and Mr. DeHuszar from our staff. He was in frequent consultation with representatives of some of the more important foundations and their allies.

Mr. DeHuszar had already shown his capacity on the staff of the Cox Committee, to which he had contributed a mass of critical material which was not used. In his work for the Reece Committee he had begun to assemble significant data on particularly unpleasant examples of the practices of major foundations. When he was released, this research came to an end.

In the case of Dr. Ettinger the loss to the inquiry was tragic. Many of our most valuable lines of inquiry were devised or initiated by him. He had insisted on the tabulation of questionnaire returns and a systematic collection of complete sets of data. He had, in the short period of his services to the Committee, assembled substantial data on foundation activities in education and research. Some of these he was able to bring to sufficient completion to enable us to use much of his material. Many of his projects, including some of primary significance, came to an end when he was released. It was impossible for the busy, curtailed staff to take up where he had left off. In this way, some of our potentially most important material was lost to the Committee.*

---

* Among these uncompleted studies of Dr. Ettinger were a survey of foundation support to colleges, to discover patterns of giving, and preferences for certain types of institutions in social-science support; a survey and study of the learned journals, so often an instrument of power in the hands of small professional cliques, with a resultant effect upon the volume and quality of professional papers; a study of the relationship of foundations and inter-

To make certain that Mr. Hays's appointee, Miss Lonergan, would be in the heart of things, we had assigned her to assist Dr. Ettinger. She was thus familiar with all his important work. While Mr. Hays did not succeed, by any of his tactics, in destroying the investigation, he did deal it an extremely serious wound in forcing the release of this brilliant investigator. Had he remained on the staff, a much greater volume of material would have been available to judge objectively the social implications inherent in the operations of some of the major foundations and their satellites.

Mr. Hays's expressed reason for demanding Dr. Ettinger's release was that he was a Socialist. This is rather amusing, since Dr. Ettinger's work consisted in substantial part of unearthing examples of foundation support of socialism. At least since 1925 Ettinger had been active in publicly opposing Socialist programs, and in consequence for more than thirty years he had been identified by his writings and activities as an advocate of the free-enterprise system.

TROUBLE FOR COUNSEL

On February 15, 1954, but as of January 1, 1954, Congressman Le Compte, the chairman of the Administration Committee, which is the housekeeping committee of the House of Representatives, removed both Mr. Koch and me from the payroll through an order sent to the Clerk of the House. This was done without previous discussion with Mr. Reece—in fact, while Mr. Reece was out of Washington; Mr. Le Compte merely directed the Clerk of the House to wipe our names from the payroll of the Committee, and notified Mr. Reece by letter that he had done so. Mr. Le Compte's action was taken on a wholly fictitious set of facts indicating that Mr. Koch and I had violated the Federal statute proscribing a conflict of interest.

Mr. Koch and I had retained our professional relationship with our law firm in New York. Mr. Le Compte assumed that our firm was engaged in "tax practice," with the implication that we were currently trying tax cases against the government. An obvious conflict

---

mediary organizations to these journals; special studies on the interlocks existing between foundations, professional groups, certain government advisory and research institutions, and a few leading universities; an inquiry into college-accrediting organizations; and several more studies of importance relating to the activities of foundations and their associated organizations in education and the social sciences. His interest was in a wholly objective analysis and weighing of the activities of foundations in the social-science world.

of interest would have been present if Mr. Le Compte's assumed facts were correct. Mr. Koch and I would have had no right to remain in the employ of the government if, at the same time, we were litigating against it.

The facts were that our firm was not in "tax practice" in the sense of specialists engaged in litigation against the government. I had never tried a tax case in my life. Mr. Koch, while an eminent trial lawyer, had never tried a tax case while associated with our firm. Moreover, Mr. Koch and I had directed our firm to withdraw from even such routine tax matters as the settlement of an estate-tax return or an income-tax return at any point where direct controversy with the Government resulted.

Mr. Le Compte made no attempt to get the true facts before taking action. The facts were communicated to Mr. Le Compte promptly but without result. All our efforts to see and talk to Mr. Le Compte were met with rebuff. *Mr. Le Compte would not see us and examine us as to the facts.* Nothing was accomplished until I wrote to Speaker Martin on March 17 explaining our situation, which Mr. Koch and I found intolerable, and urgently requesting his immediate intercession.

This letter was handed to Mr. Martin by Mr. Reece. Not long thereafter, Mr. Koch and I were restored to the payroll, with retroactive pay.

MR. HAYS AND "THE WHITE HOUSE"

President Eisenhower is very conscious of the separate prerogatives of the Congress and would not knowingly countenance any interference by the executive with the functions of the legislature. But it is utterly clear, unless Mr. Hays has sorely prevaricated, that someone in "the White House" was actively opposed to the investigation of foundations.

Mr. Hays reported to us on two separate occasions that "the White House" had been in touch with him regarding our investigation.

One of these occasions had to do with our request for an executive order to examine a form known as 990A. This is an information form required to be filed with the Internal Revenue Service by foundations. Most of it is open to public inspection; one part is not and can be seen only through an executive order. Why any part should be secret I do not know. Foundations are, necessarily and admittedly, public trusts, and information concerning them should be open to the public, which is their beneficiary.

As the 990A forms contained information of great value to the investigation, Mr. Reece applied for the necessary executive order as early as November 16, 1953. Nothing happened for months.

Our first news regarding the application came when Mr. Hays informed us that he had been telephoned by "the White House" and asked whether he objected to our having access to the 990A forms. He had replied, he said, that he did object, and on the ground that they were "confidential tax returns." I explained to him that they were not "tax" returns but "information" returns and that, as far as we were concerned, they were not confidential as we had the right to extract the full information from the individual foundations by subpoena. Some time later, on February 1, 1954, an executive order was issued giving us access to the forms. (Note that we applied on November 16, 1953.)

Did we get the forms immediately? We had indicated which foundation forms we were most interested in, but apparently no efforts had been made to call these in from the regional offices. Finally, on April 8, 1954 (I emphasize that we applied on November 16, 1953), we were informed that we could now examine the 990As. Even then, however, all the forms we had requested had not been called in; we were forbidden to take any forms from the office of the Internal Revenue Service; we were not permitted to photostat any; and we were permitted to examine such forms as were ready for us only in a designated room in the presence of a representative of the Service.

After the order had been granted, I visited an assistant commissioner, accompanied by Miss Casey, to arrange for an examination of the 990As. The assistant commissioner told us that certain documents had to be prepared, and gave Miss Casey the necessary instructional forms. These were complied with, and the forms were typed and signed at once; but the Service required four successive revisions before we were told that the documentation was satisfactory.

When we finally got access to the forms, the hearings were so imminent that no effective use of the materials to be extracted from the 990As could be made.

COINCIDENCES?

The reader may have noted certain coincidences.

After fantastically long delays in each instance, the final granting of our (tragically reduced) appropriation, the final restoration of Mr. Koch and myself to the payroll, and the final granting of access to the 990A forms, were just about simultaneous.

Coincidence?

MR. HAYS AND "THE WHITE HOUSE" AGAIN

The second incident involving "the White House" and Mr. Hays was even more remarkable. Mr. Hays is no Senator George. He is not one likely to be called into conference on policy as a representative of the Democratic Party. He is a relatively unimportant member of the House, who has attained no eminence and acquired only notoriety by his conduct on the Reece Committee.

Yet *Mr. Hays told us one day that "the White House" had been in touch with him and asked him if he would cooperate to kill the Committee.* His reply, he said, was that he would let the Republicans fight their own battles.

We could not believe, of course, that the incident had any official significance. We concluded that the call from "the White House" must have been the act of an individual, without sanction of the President, and without his knowledge. But it was uncomfortable to be led to believe that someone close to the President, perhaps one of his advisers or someone charged with delegated executive power, could have been guilty of such conduct. It was additional indication that the long arms of the foundations extended even into high places.

MR. HAYS AND THE STAFF

Congressman Reece has been criticized for not having taken a more aggressive attitude as Committee chairman, opposing Mr. Hays's constant harassment. Mr. Reece is a brave man who has given evidence, both in his astounding and much-decorated military career and in his political life, that he can fight. But Mr. Reece understood, soon after our investigation started, if not before, that we would be met with every obstacle which could be put in our way. He was determined to finish the job which he had undertaken and not to be diverted into personal controversy. His attitude reminded me of the Chinese proverb: "The wise man is like water, the softest thing which yet breaks the hardest thing."

Sometimes a Congressional committee starts with a honeymoon, later to be disrupted by quarrels. There was no honeymoon for the Reece Committee. From the very start Mr. Hays began to harass the staff and to complain and obstruct.

He complained frequently that he did not know what the staff was doing. The fact is, he knew more about what was going on than any other member of the Committee, not excepting the chairman. Once my original report to the Committee had been approved, Mr. Reece permitted us to go ahead without restraint, understanding that our job was fact finding and that time would be wasted by detailed reports until we had virtually completed the study period of the investigation. As suggestions, inquiries, and data came to Mr. Reece, he would transmit them to us for attention. Beyond this, he left us free to test whether complaints regarding foundation activities were justified.

Mr. Hays, on the other hand, had a personal reporter on the staff. Nothing was withheld from Miss Lonergan, Mr. Hays's personal appointee. All records were open to her inspection. Our instructions to her were clear—she was to report to him whatever she chose to report and whatever he might be interested in. This she did, and with frequency.

Mr. Hays accused us of engaging in research not authorized by the Committee. This accusation was an absurdity. The general line of our research carefully followed the authority given to the Committee by the resolution which created it. This in turn was not materially different from that which created the previous Cox Committee. Mr. Hays's position seemed to be that every detail of proposed research had to have express approval of the Committee before we could spend any time on it. This Mr. Reece told us was not so—that, as long as we stayed within the four corners of the authorizing resolution, we were free to research what we thought advisable, except insofar as the Committee instructed us to abstain.

Despite all his earlier complaints, Mr. Hays well knew that he had received every possible cooperation from the staff, as he acknowledged during the hearings as follows:

> Mr. Chairman, let me say that I may be seeming to ask some critical questions, but I do not want to imply that there has been

any trouble between myself and the staff. It may be that I do not see eye to eye on a good many things, but the staff has been very responsive any time I have asked them a question to come up and explain it, or to make the files available, or anything like that. There has been no difficulty whatsoever on that score.*

MR. HAYS AND DR. KINSEY

Several lines of inquiry enraged Mr. Hays particularly. One, which disclosed his reluctance to permit freedom of inquiry, was a proposed study of the Kinsey reports. It was undoubtedly reported to him by Miss Lonergan that Dr. Ettinger had dug up some significant material about foundation support of the Kinsey projects. This brought Mr. Hays to a steaming rage, and he asked to see our entire Kinsey file. It was produced for him, and he angrily declared to Mr. Dodd that we were to go no further with this particular investigation, contending that every member of Congress would be against our doing so. Neither Mr. Dodd nor I could see any reason why Dr. Kinsey's foundation-supported projects should not bear as much scrutiny as any other foundation operation. But Mr. Hays then introduced another element into the situation. Our appropriation for 1954 had, at the time, not yet been approved, and Mr. Hays stated emphatically to Mr. Dodd that *he would oppose any further appropriation to our Committee unless the Kinsey investigation were dropped.* His unreasoning opposition to any study of these projects was so great that he threatened to fight against the appropriation on the floor of the House.

As we were already fearful that an appropriation might not come through, and our work would be frustrated, Mr. Dodd concluded that Mr. Hays must be appeased. He suggested, therefore, that Mr. Hays take the entire Kinsey file and lock it in his personal safe so that he would know the material could not be used without the express consent of the Committee. This Mr. Hays did: the file remained in his safe throughout the hearings. For all I know, he may still have it.

The Kinsey reports did, in the course of the open hearings, become part of the Committee evidence through the testimony of Professor Hobbs, who used them as apt examples of "scientism," but the valuable material in our Kinsey file never saw the light of day.

* Reece Committee *Hearings*, p. 54.

MR. HAYS AND FACTS FORUM

On a number of occasions, I urged Mr. Hays to give us any complaints against foundations of which he became aware, so that we could run these down. I told him particularly that almost all the complaints with political connotations which we had received concerned left-wing activity, and that I had made every effort to dig out complaints against foundations which might be engaged in activity at the other end of the political spectrum. None of sufficient importance to warrant further inquiry had come to my attention. I made clear that I was interested in investigating extremism at either end.

His only major contribution in response was repeatedly to insist that we investigate *Facts Forum*. We complied with all his specific requests. We collected for him voluminous detailed data on *Facts Forum*. *He wanted control of these data himself.* They were all handed to him—whatever he asked for was procured and delivered.

This material was never used by Mr. Hays, except to prepare a personal, private brief of his own against *Facts Forum,* which he caused to be published in the *Congressional Record.* None of his material was offered to the Committee of which he was a member. None of it became part of the Committee's record, from which he withheld it.

Mr. Hays thus failed to use the forum presented by the Committee of which he was a member but chose, instead, to attack this particular foundation in a forum where it could not possibly defend itself or even file a protest—the floor of the House of Representatives.

MR. HAYS AND THE COMMITTEE PROCEDURE

In his minority report, Mr. Hays indulged in gross misstatements concerning my recommendations regarding procedure. He said:

> In the early meetings of the committee the general counsel, Mr. Wormser, advanced the proposal that the inquiry be made without public hearings and without seeking the testimony of interested persons, suggesting instead that the staff be directed to devote its time to independent study and inquiry, the results of which would be brought to the committee when concluded. It apparently never occurred to Mr. Wormser, a member of the bar, that such a proceeding, in a matter so sensitive, inevitably con-

flicted with constitutional guarantees of free speech and violated every American principle that individuals and groups, subjected to accusations in the course of an inquiry, be permitted to defend themselves.*

On reading the minority report, I wrote at once to Mr. Hays calling his attention to a misstatement regarding the identity of Mr. Koch and myself and also to this absolutely false description of my proposals for procedure. Regarding the latter, I wrote as follows:

> You state that I suggested closed hearings without the presence of witnesses. This is not the fact. I did suggest that we might consider having closed hearings, but only in order to avoid the publicity which you yourself had objected to and for the purpose of preventing any injury to the reputations of individuals who would be called as witnesses. You, later on, yourself urged the Committee to hear some of the testimony in private, a procedure which I had thought from the start might be advisable for the same reasons you came to understand were persuasive. I never suggested to you or anyone else that we dispense with calling witnesses.

Mr. Hays replied immediately and apologized for his misstatements, but they remain in the printed minority report.

Fortunately, Mr. Reece thoroughly understood that detailed research was essential to satisfy our mandate. There was never any question of avoiding hearings, but hearings without research would have been futile.

As the time for hearings approached, lawyers for a number of foundations asked me how we expected to proceed. I informed them that it was planned first to put a series of critical witnesses on the stand, to introduce enough substantive evidence to support whatever criticisms the staff had found *prima facie* to be justified. In this way, the foundations themselves would know to what to reply. Foundation representatives had then asked whether they could not be presented with a "bill of particulars." I was very sympathetic to this suggestion and assured them that we had no intention of surprising them with critical material, that every effort would be made to let them have it in advance of foundation appearances on the stand.

* Reece Committee *Report,* p. 426.

The canard has been spread widely that the Reece Committee "prejudged" the foundations. It was the Committee's own fairness of approach which was used as a basis for this slander. At a meeting of the Committee, about a week before the day set for the opening hearing, I proposed that we give the foundations the "bill of particulars" which they had requested. This recommendation was approved unanimously and, in the case of Mr. Hays, with enthusiasm. Yet he himself later accused us of having "prejudged" by presenting this very "bill of particulars."

THE "DODD REPORT"

In the presence of the Committee, and with its approval, I requested Mr. Dodd, the director of research, to prepare this "bill of particulars." He did this in the form of a report which he read at the first hearing, disclosing to the foundations the main lines of criticism of foundation practices which he had found sufficiently supported by evidence to warrant the attention of the Committee.

For the "Dodd report" to have been distorted into a report of the Committee itself, constituting a final verdict against the foundations, was a palpable absurdity; yet this became the cry of the pack which yelped at our heels during the entire investigation. That report was in no sense a report of the Reece Committee. *No member of the Committee, not even the chairman, knew what was in it before it was read. It was a personal report of the director of research to the Committee.* It reviewed the methods he and his assistants had used. It stated the lines of inquiry which he suggested. It listed the criticisms of foundation activity which he, personally, had concluded were justified, based on the research which had been conducted. It was intended to be, and was, the very "bill of particulars" which the foundations themselves had requested.

Mr. Dodd was careful to state that the conclusions contained in his report were meant to be only tentative—he was, after all, merely presenting material for inquiry. Both the chairman and I made it explicitly clear, at the first and second hearings, May 10 and 11, that the purpose of the Dodd report was "to give the foundations an opportunity to know what most important matters we want to go into in relation to them."

During the investigation I was to learn that faith in the reasonable accuracy of news reporting was naïve. Many of the reporters who attended the hearings dozed or chatted while vitally important testimony was being taken; but awoke to scribble notes whenever Mr. Hays staged one of his antics. Few newspapers gave the public even a reasonable summary of what was taking place. A wisecrack by Mr. Hays would make headlines while the story of a tragically serious foundation error would go unreported. On some papers, notably *The New York Times*, *The New York Herald Tribune* and *The Washington Post-Times*, the editors were apparently determined, whatever might transpire at the hearings, to persuade the public that the Committee majority members were persecutors and that Mr. Hays was a knight in shining armor, protecting the virtue of the immaculate foundations. I do not remember one instance in which any of the three newspapers I have named commented critically on Mr. Hays's amazing behavior.

These papers knew that the duty of the Committee was to investigate criticism, yet they castigated it for presenting critical material. They knew that the Dodd report was merely a personal report by the research director, yet they deliberately misconstrued it into an official and final report of the Committee itself. They knew that its purpose (repeated again and again throughout the hearings) was to inform the foundations and to forestall surprise; yet they beat Mr. Reece about the ears incessantly for having dared to permit the issues to be named which the staff thought worth investigating.

Mr. Koch and I had not had an opportunity to see the last draft of Mr. Dodd's report until the evening before the first hearing, at which it was to be presented. While it was to be his personal report, it was appropriate for counsel to examine it to see whether any constructive suggestions could be made. Accordingly, although it had already been mimeographed because time was so short, we did make suggestions for change, chiefly of a literary and emphasis character. With all possible speed, a final draft was prepared and mimeographed and presented to the Committee the following day, but after the first hearing (a morning hearing only) had closed. This gave rise to an involvement with Mr. Hays which exposed his plan to throw all possible confusion into the hearings.

In some not too mysterious fashion, he had gotten possession of the earlier draft of the Dodd Report, though this had been distributed to no one. Immediately, he invented a plot. He accused Mr. Dodd of having produced two reports, one "doctored" to fool the Committee, or the foundations, or the public, or perhaps just Mr. Hays. This required Miss Casey to take the stand to explain that the draft was only a working draft, not issued to anyone, and that there had been no "doctoring."

In questioning Mr. Dodd concerning this incident, Mr. Hays reminded him that he was under oath. It was a rather sorry procedure on Mr. Hays's part—an attempt to make it look reprehensible that a draft of a report had been revised before it was submitted.

I asked Mr. Hays to delete his use of the word "doctored" from the record, and he refused to. To the end, he tried to leave the impression that there had been two reports and that, for some felonious purpose, the staff had "doctored" one of them. It was typical of the Hays campaign to discredit the staff; and this obvious red herring was exploited gleefully by some newspapers, happy to try to disparage the investigation.

THE WITNESSES

Pursuant to the agreed procedure, the report of Mr. Dodd was followed by a succession of witnesses, intended to present material substantiating the criticisms which had been leveled at foundations. With our budget for the year cut almost in half by the Committee on Administration, we had to plan for enough sessions to bring in representatives of those foundations against whom the principal criticisms had been made. Our decision was to call a minimum of carefully selected critical witnesses of demonstrable credibility and to supplement their testimony with detailed staff reports, preliminary to hearing the foundation representatives themselves.

The witnesses not representing foundations called by the Committee can be put into three groups. The first consisted of staff members (Mr. Dodd, the research director; the assistant research director, Mr. McNiece; and the legal analyst, Miss Casey) who presented prepared reports. The second group consisted of four academicians: Dr. Thomas H. Briggs, professor emeritus in education at Columbia; Dr. A. H. Hobbs, an assistant professor in sociology at the University of Pennsylvania; Dr. David N. Rowe, a professor of international affairs at Yale; and Dr. Kenneth Colegrove, a former professor of politics at Northwestern. The third group consisted of
, persons who produced special testimony. This included Mr. T. Coleman Andrews, the Collector of Internal Revenue, and Mr. Sugar-

man, then one of his assistants; Mr. Ken Earl, an attorney from the State of Washington who had been on the staffs of the Internal Security Subcommittee and of the Immigration Subcommittee of the Senate; and Mr. Aaron Sargent, an attorney of San Francisco.

Mr. Hays and his friends have referred to these witnesses by a variety of deprecatory and insulting terms. Mr. Hays himself several times called them "crackpots" and added that the chairman had "dredged them up" and "dredged deep." Dr. Hutchins has called them "witnesses of dubious standing." Mr. Henry Edward Schultz, national chairman of The Anti-Defamation League, has referred to the investigation as a "charade" in which part of the cast was "a strange group of witnesses."

Typical is the case of the late Mr. Bernard DeVoto who, in an article in *Harper's,* almost exhausted the thesaurus in selecting words of insult. He said of the report: "This mass of innuendo, insinuation, allegation, and misstatement is too insubstantial to be dealt with critically." Unable to deny the facts, Mr. DeVoto sought to blast the individuals who were connected with the report. He called the staff "paranoiacs" and by other choice epithets. He suggested that some of the witnesses before the Committee were psychiatric cases. He opined that the staff must have been either insane or dishonest—adding that insanity was not likely to be the answer.

Of similar nature was a recent attack on the Reece Committee by Mr. Dwight Macdonald, in his series of "Profiles" on The Ford Foundation in *The New Yorker.** Although Mr. Macdonald himself provided column after column of severe criticism of foundation operation, much of it echoing specific criticisms levied by the Reece Committee report, he had this to say about the Committee:

> The hearings * * * were largely devoted to the animadversions of obscure crackpots and the scarcely more lucid testimony of the Reece Committee's staff.

Among these witnesses labeled as obscure "crackpots" were Professor Emeritus Briggs of Columbia, Assistant Professor Hobbs of Pennsylvania, Professor Rowe of Yale, and Professor Colegrove of Northwestern.

The Committee report, said Mr. Macdonald, was "a patchwork of data botched together." He called the report "a lengthy exercise—four

* Since published in book form.

hundred and sixteen pages—in irrelevance, insinuation, and long-range deduction." He did not deal with the facts which the Committee disclosed—Mr. Macdonald did not deign to discuss them. The way to get at the Reece Committee was to call its personnel names! This was the "smearing" procedure of critics of the type of Messrs. DeVoto and Macdonald.

A large part of the daily press was equally prejudiced against the Committee and avoided an objective presentation or appraisal of its findings and activities.

I can well realize how difficult it was for the man in the street to understand that organizations which had done so much good in some areas could also have behaved so badly in others.

MR. HAYS BROWBEATING A WITNESS

It was during the testimony of Mr. Aaron Sargent that Mr. Hays conducted himself in a manner without any precedent. In order to prevent testimony unfavorable to certain foundations and tax-exempt organizations, he treated this witness, and the Committee itself, contemptuously and offensively. His intention to prevent an orderly hearing became soon apparent.

Mr. Sargent was so well informed regarding foundation operations in education that he had been approached by Congressman Cox, chairman of the Cox Committee, to act as counsel to that Committee. As the Cox Committee had been created by a Democratic-controlled Congress, this made it difficult for Mr. Hays to attack the witness' credibility directly, but he found a way to do it by accusing him of perjury.

Mr. Hays asked Mr. Sargent on the stand whether he had been offered the position of counsel to the Cox Committee. The latter replied that he had, but had declined for personal reasons. Actually, no official offer had been made. Congressman Cox had asked him if he would consider taking the position, and the Committee itself had authorized Chairman Cox to do this. But Mr. Hays made a great to-do about the fact that Mr. Sargent had answered "yes" when he was asked if he had been "offered" the job. This, said Mr. Hays, was "perjury!"

Mr. Sargent began to testify at 10 o'clock A.M. on May 24 but was unable to give uninterrupted testimony for more than a few moments at a time; Mr. Hays heckled him all day. He was not satisfied to wait for any substantial testimony to be given and then to cross-examine; he cluttered the record with irrelevancies and tried his best to upset the witness. Here is an example of Mr. Hays's questioning:

> MR. HAYS. Do you believe in astrology?
>
> MR. SARGENT. No, sir; not I.
>
> MR. HAYS. Could you give me any reason why there are so many peculiar people drawn to southern California?
>
> MR. SARGENT. I don't live in southern California, and I wouldn't know.
>
> MR. HAYS. You know, it is a funny thing, but every time we get an extremist letter in my office—and it is either on the left or the right—you don't have to look at the postmark. It either comes from southern California or Houston, Texas. I just wonder if there is some reason for it.

There were endless interruptions of this illuminating kind; Mr. Hays's histrionics for the benefit of the gallery of newsmen were at the same time calculated to confuse the witness, an objective in which he failed utterly. But he resorted to far nastier tactics also, hoping to irritate the witness into an indiscretion; in this he failed as miserably. But he did succeed, through theatrical touches and "colorful" antics, to intrigue a newspaper claque.

It would take too much space to quote all his breaches of decency during Mr. Sargent's testimony. But one remark was typical. He said, "I will tell you if we bring any more down here like some we have now I am in favor of the committee hiring a staff psychiatrist." * This could only have referred to the witnesses who had testified up to that time. These were three members of the staff and Professor Briggs, Professor Hobbs, and the witness before him, Mr. Sargent. But later, Mr. Hays explained, "I did not mean to cast any reflection on the other 2 witnesses as much as I did on the one here, to be frank about it." †

Mr. Hays sought to induce the Committee to stop Mr. Sargent's testimony in open hearings and to resume it in secret session. When the chairman refused to accede, Mr. Hays "took a walk" accompanied by his cohort, Mrs. Pfost, leaving the hearing room. As only three members of the Committee were present at the time, this left the chair-

* Reece Committee *Hearings,* p. 222.
† *Ibid.,* p. 230.

man alone and he was forced to close the hearings for want of a quorum. That was at 3:20 P.M., very little having been accomplished in the taking of testimony, for the whole day virtually was consumed by Mr. Hays's antics.

The Committee met again at about 10:30 the next morning, at which time the full membership was present. Proceedings were opened with a statement from the Chairman, in part as follows:

> * * * As a convenience to the foundations, an initial report was submitted outlining the main lines of major criticisms of foundations which a preliminary study by the staff had shown were sufficiently supported by evidence to warrant considering carefully.
>
> We are now in the first stage of assessing these criticisms by hearing some of the supporting evidence. We shall later hear evidence supplied by the foundations themselves, defending against these criticisms. We shall not prejudge. We shall not try to prove a case. We are here to learn what the truth may be.
>
> Needless to say, criticism cannot be expected to come from the foundations themselves. It must come, if at all, chiefly from persons not directly connected with foundation matters. We shall give foundation representatives respectful attention. We do not see why persons who have criticism to offer are not entitled to the same courteous treatment. Failure to give them such courtesy and inclination to condemn them for daring to criticize frankly and even severely would seem to me to deny such witnesses the privileges of citizens and to fail to give them the consideration to which we believe they are entitled from members of the committee.

Mr. Hays then raised the point of order that the witness Sargent had not prepared a written statement for submission to the committee under the House rules which provided that such statements should be required "so far as practicable." The point of order was overruled on the ground that it was impracticable in Mr. Sargent's case. The following colloquy then took place:

> MR. HAYS. The Chair would not uphold any point of order that he did not agree with, no matter what the rule said. That has become pretty obvious in these hearings.

THE CHAIRMAN. Now—

MR. HAYS. Don't start interrupting me, or you better bring in the sergeant at arms, because I am going to be heard just the same as you are. You may be afraid of Fabian socialism, but I am afraid of Republican dictatorship. Let us get it out in the open. You brought in the shock troops here, so let us fight it out.

MR. GOODWIN. I understood we were going to hear the witness.

MR. HAYS. We are going to have more points of order.

The second point of order is that the committee is in violation of the rules of the House and the Reorganization Act, inasmuch as the minority of the committee has been deprived of one single staff member.

THE CHAIRMAN. The Chair overrules the point of order.

MR. HAYS. I will say the Chair did not keep his word. When I helped the Chair get his $65,000, so you would not look stupid when they were going to shut you off, you promised me a staff member. Did you or did you not?

THE CHAIRMAN. No one has individually a member of the staff.

MR. HAYS. You have the whole staff.

THE CHAIRMAN. There is a member of the staff that was employed on the recommendation of the gentleman from Ohio.

MR. HAYS. As a stenographer.

THE CHAIRMAN. No; not as a stenographer.

MR. HAYS. That is what she does.

THE CHAIRMAN. As an analyst or researcher, I am not sure what her title is. That is what our understanding is.

MR. HAYS. I have a motion to make. I move that we hear this witness in executive session in order to prevent further name dropping and any further hurting of people who have no place in this hearing.

MRS. PFOST. I second it.

MR. WOLCOTT. As a substitute for that, Mr. Chairman, I move that the witness be allowed to proceed with his statement without interruption.

MR. HAYS. You can pass all those motions you want, but I will interrupt whenever I feel like it. How do you like that? So you might as well save your breath, Jesse.

Mr. WOLCOTT.   I should like to.

Mr. HAYS.   You run the Banking and Currency Committee without proxies, but in this committee you run it with proxies. You make the rules as you go along for the majority, and I will make the rules for myself as I go along, and if this fellow does not want to bring in a statement, I will interrupt him whenever I feel like it. He better get a bigger mouth than that.

Mr. WOLCOTT.   As I understand it, this committee made the rules, and we are proceeding under the rules adopted by this committee.

Mr. HAYS.   You know there is no such rule on this committee. When did we make this rule?

Mr. WOLCOTT.   I understand we can vote by proxy. If we do not, I shall make a motion that we do vote by proxy. I understood that I have given the chairman a proxy and there had been no objection to it.

Mr. HAYS.   I just want the record to show that you rule one way in the committee of which you are chairman and another way here.

Mr. WOLCOTT.   You can make that record if you want to. The Banking and Currency Committee of 29 members have asserted themselves on a good many occasions, and we get along very nicely in that committee and with the rules of the House. Until the Banking and Currency Committee changes the rules, we will abide by the rules which have been adopted, if any have been adopted. I do not remember that any have been adopted. We operate under the rules of the House.

Does anybody want to support a substitute motion? I move a substitute motion to the motion made by the gentleman from Ohio that the witness be allowed to proceed with his statement without interruption, and at the conclusion of his statement that he subject himself to questioning.

Mr. GOODWIN.   Second.

Mr. HAYS.   I have something to say on that motion. It might take quite a little while. In the first place, what this motion entails is that this fellow can come in here and do what he did yesterday.

Mr. GOODWIN.   Who is "the fellow," may I inquire?

Mr. HAYS.   Right down here.

MR. GOODWIN. You mean the witness?

MR. HAYS. I will call him anything I like. We understand each other.

MR. GOODWIN. Mr. Chairman, I have something else to do besides—

MR. HAYS. Go ahead. Whenever you go, the minority will go, and that will be the end of the hearing.* If you can just stay here and be patient, I have a right to be heard on the substitute and I am going to be heard on the substitute.

THE CHAIRMAN. Reasonably.

MR. HAYS. I will decide what is reasonable. In other words, you know the trouble around here—and this is pertinent, too—that there have been too many committees in which the minority has allowed itself to be gaffled into submission and silence. I am going to be the kind of minority that does not go so easy for that gaffle stuff.

MR. WOLCOTT. You have been in the minority for 20 years.

MR. HAYS. You know the funny part of it is that most of you fellows are still in the minority, because you don't seem to have the responsibility to run this Congress. That is why the great crusade is in reverse.

MR. WOLCOTT. If the minority will allow us to assume our responsibility, we will get along.

MR. HAYS. The minority on this committee is not going to sit here silent and have peoples' characters assassinated at will by dropping their names in as Senator Douglas' name was dropped in yesterday, deliberately, because it was one of only two names the witness mentioned out of a whole series of names. He had his name underscored in the pamphlet that he was reading from. He had the name "Paul Douglas" underscored.

THE CHAIRMAN. But the others were being put in the record.

MR. HAYS. At my insistence, let the record show.

THE CHAIRMAN. No, they were being put in the record.

MR. HAYS. No, they were not being put in the record. The only thing that was going into the record was what this gentleman was going to say. I said if you are going to read—the record is here, and if you want to start reading from the record, I will read from the record.

* A threat to do another "walkout."

MR. WOLCOTT.   I ask for the question.

MR. HAYS.   I am still talking.

MR. WOLCOTT.   I ask for the question.

MR. HAYS.   Go ahead and ask. I say the gentleman is coming in with a shotgun and shooting in all directions, and the committee does not want to give protection to the people whose characters he is going to assassinate. That is what the substitute motion does. I think it is bad and in violation of the rules of the House. It is in violation of the rules of orderly committee procedure which you seem to be so concerned with. I just want the record to show that if the majority wants to let people like this come in and do that, that is up to them.

THE CHAIRMAN.   All in favor say "Aye."

MR. WOLCOTT.   Aye.

MR. GOODWIN.   Aye.

THE CHAIRMAN.   Opposed, "no."

MR. HAYS.   No.

MRS. PFOST.   No.*

After this and another exchange among the Committee members, Mr. Sargent's testimony was resumed, only to be broken into constantly by Mr. Hays. When Mr. Wolcott reminded Mr. Hays that a motion had been passed that the witness be permitted to conclude a statement before being questioned, Mr. Hays threatened to leave the hearing again and stop it for lack of a quorum. He also accused Mr. Wolcott of trying to "gag the minority," and continued his constant interruption.

These persistent interruptions, violating the perfectly proper rule made by the Committee (after unconscionably numerous interruptions by Mr. Hays made it necessary) that the witness was to be questioned only after he had completed his testimony, ultimately resulted in a conference among the Committee members, in which Mr. Hays finally agreed that the witness be permitted to complete his testimony without interruption and be available for full questioning thereafter at any length. After the announcement of this agreement had been made, Mr. Sargent proceeded with his testimony but was immediately interrupted by Mr. Hays, in violation of his agreement, and the interruptions continued at Mr. Hays's normal pace, which meant that

* *Ibid.*, pp. 237-240.

the witness could hardly finish a sentence before Mr. Hays tried to divert him.

MR. HAYS DISTINGUISHES HIMSELF

At one point, Mr. Sargent had cited *Fabianism in Great Britain,* an authoritative work on English socialism written by Sister Mary Margaret McCarran, a daughter of the late Senator McCarran.

After Mr. Sargent's testimony was later resumed, the following discussion took place:

> MR. HAYS. ******* Another thing you did, you brought in the name of Sister Mary Margaret, and then you pause for emphasis and put in the name of McCarran.
>
> I submit to you that ordinarily people in the orders do not use the last name and I wonder if it is in the flyleaf of the book.
>
> MR. SARGENT. It is. I gave you the information about the author and the book.
>
> Previously you had been questioning authority for the statements I was making. I want to make clear that I was relying on a high-type of research book in the statement that I made.
>
> MR. HAYS. Maybe we ought to subpoena the officials of the Catholic University and find out how high type this is.
>
> I happen to know something about the background of the author of that book, and how long it took her to get a degree, and so forth, and even that there was a little pressure used or she would not have it yet.*

The rector of Catholic University wrote to Mr. Reece† stating that Mr. Hays's allegations were "completely false." The publisher of Sister Mary Margaret's book had this to say‡:

> The attack upon the character of Sister Mary Margaret Patricia as a nun, devoted to a life of teaching, with a vow of poverty and complete worldly abandonment, is one of the most irresponsible, thoughtless, and uncharitable acts that has ever come to my attention.
>
> I do not believe that in the records of the House of Representa-

---

* *Ibid.,* p. 231.
† *Ibid.,* p. 945.
‡ *Ibid.,* p. 946.

tives there could be found a more striking example of an irresponsible statement by a Member of that body.

Mr. Hays may well have created a record for intemperate and unparliamentary behavior while a member of the Reece Committee.

His interruptions of the testimony must have established a *world's* record—the count was 246 interruptions during 185 minutes of Mr. Sargent's testimony.

It seemed most incredible that none of the newspapers which attacked the proceedings with such vigor ever thought anything Mr. Hays did was subject to any criticism. *The New York Times, The New York Herald Tribune, The Washington Post-Times*—none of these ever saw anything reprehensible in Mr. Hays's conduct.

MR. HERRING TAKES THE STAND

I had prepared a tentative schedule of intended foundation witnesses who were to follow the initial, critical witnesses. This schedule included representatives of the following foundations and tax-exempt organizations:

> Rockefeller Foundation
> Carnegie Corporation
> Carnegie Endowment for International Peace
> Ford Foundation
> Fund for the Republic
> Social Science Research Council
> American Council of Learned Societies
> American Council on Education
> National Education Association
> American Historical Association
> League for Industrial Democracy
> American Labor Education Service

No foundation witness was to be compelled to appear, but such as felt themselves aggrieved or as wished to be heard were to be given the opportunity. Those listed above had indicated that they wished to appear. I kept in touch with most of these organizations and tried to inform them, as closely as I could, when they might be called upon to appear if they wished to. And I made clear that they could appear by representatives of their own choosing, as we did not want any criticism based on a contention that they had been unable to present their own "case" in their own way.

We also anticipated calling Facts Forum, which had been subjected to reiterated attack by Mr. Hays during the hearings and had asked to appear. In addition, it was expected that we would give an opportunity to some individuals who had been mentioned in the testimony adversely, to present their "defenses."

The first foundation witness called was Mr. Pendleton Herring, president of The Social Science Research Council—on June 16, 1954. He was selected because his organization was one of those most directly concerned in the inquiry and because he, himself, was one of the ablest publicists for the foundations. During his testimony other foundation representatives were present, ready to testify. One, in fact, Dr. Arthur S. Adams, president of The American Council on Education, the expected second foundation witness, even handed in his prepared statement, anticipating that he would be called immediately on the conclusion of Dr. Herring's testimony. But Dr. Adams was never called to the stand. The hearings ended during Mr. Herring's testimony.

Mr. Herring was treated with every possible courtesy. He was permitted to testify at great length, reading in detail from prepared statements without any interruptions except those of which he himself approved, introducing whatever material he cared to. He testified, in his own way, for one entire afternoon. His testimony continued through part of the next morning.

After the witness had exhausted his own material, Arnold Koch, the associate counsel, began to question him on behalf of the Committee. Mr. Koch's questions were gently put. No pressure was exerted. It was not cross-examination, in the true sense. There was no insistence on a direct answer. If Mr. Herring, as he sometimes did, chose not to respond directly to a question, as he would have been required to in a court of law, the question was dropped and Mr. Koch passed on to another.

But all this did not last long. Mr. Hays did not intend to permit any foundation witness to be subjected to orderly questioning. At the beginning of Mr. Herring's testimony, the chairman had suggested again that the witness be permitted to make his statement and then be questioned. In contrast to his earlier conduct, Mr. Hays observed this admonition and, while Dr. Herring was making his own statement, questioned him rarely and only with the greatest politeness. His manner changed, however, when Mr. Koch began his examination on behalf of the Committee; then Mr. Hays proceeded to inject frequently, this time intent not on interrupting the witness but on interrupting the questioning by counsel.

This unpleasant situation came to a head when someone from the audience passed a paper to Mr. Hays, after which he quoted a verse from the Bible: "Should a wise man utter vain knowledge, and fill his belly with the east wind?" This was a direct insult launched at Mr. Koch.

There resulted a colloquy among Mr. Hays, the chairman, and Mr. Goodwin, in which Mr. Hays, in violent temper, his voice loud and strained, committed insolence after insolence. He accused the chairman of not being interested in getting at the facts. He referred to the previous witnesses as "crackpots." He asserted that Mr. Herring was the first witness "who has dealt with factual matters." He referred to other witnesses as "people that you have gone out and dragged up and dredged up." He continued:

> And, Mr. Reece, you must have had to dredge to find Mr. Sargent, and I could mention one or two more. You really had to dredge. You went way down with your dredge to get them. They are not reliable, responsive. [The chairman used the gavel.] Go ahead and hammer. I will keep right on talking when you get through.

This followed:

> MR. GOODWIN. Now, Mr. Chairman, if the gentleman from Ohio indicates that he is not going to respect the gavel, as he just indicated, I am going to bring up here the question of whether or not these hearings are being conducted according to the rules of the House of Representatives, which are the rules of this committee.
>
> MR. HAYS. Well, I have brought that question up before and been overruled.
>
> MR. GOODWIN. I am rather tired of this. We have an eminent witness, who must, I suspect, or he may in his innermost con-

sciousness, be coming to the realization that he spoke a little too early in his praise of Congress, if this is an example of the way congressional hearings are conducted.

MR. HAYS.   I heard you say you are getting tired. Do you know what I am getting tired of? I am tired of you taking one position in public with pious speeches and then running to me in secret and saying, "You know whose side my sympathies are on." Why don't you act like a man?

MR. GOODWIN.   Mr. Chairman, I am going to ask for the rules of the House, and I am going to say that the gentleman from Ohio is out of order. He is impugning the motives of the chairman and the members of this committee.

MR. HAYS.   You wouldn't say I am not telling the truth, would you?

THE CHAIRMAN.   The gentleman is out of order. He has impugned the integrity of every man about whom he has talked.*

After a few more exchanges of this nature, and one or two questions put to the witness, the hearing was adjourned to the afternoon.

The chairman had employed unlimited patience throughout the hearings, in the face of constant insolence and personal attack by Mr. Hays. Mr. Reece had been determined not to let anything break up the investigation. But there was a limit to what anyone could stand. The explosion which I have just reported reached that limit in the case of Mr. Reece and the other two majority members of the Committee. The cold record of the hearings cannot bring the incident, or Mr. Hays's many previous disturbances, into proper light. It would take a tape recording to add Mr. Hays's arrogant voice, and a film to record his aggressive and offensive manner.

I think Mr. Reece would have swallowed his pride and gone on with the hearings, regardless of how much insolence he would have had to continue to face, had it not been that Mr. Hays had now made clear that he was not satisfied merely to have harassed the first group of witnesses. He had shown his intention to block an orderly examination of foundation spokesmen.

In a conversation with me immediately following the Committee adjournment, Mr. Reece expressed concern about how to find the best way to discharge our duty to the Congress and the people. He

* *Ibid.*, pp. 861-864.

wanted time to think. Accordingly, when the afternoon session was called to order, Mr. Reece made this statement:

> The chairman feels very deeply the responsibility which he has to protect the witnesses who appear before the committee, the employees of the committee, and the members of the committee, and to maintain the dignity of the committee, the dignity of the House, and to uphold the rules of procedure of the House and of the committees which operate under the procedures of the House. In view of the very unfortunate incident that happened this morning, following similar incidents, coupled with the fact that Mr. Goodwin cannot be here at this time due to another very important engagement which has developed, and also to give time to reflect upon this very serious situation that confronts the committee, the committee will stand in recess until 10 o'clock Tuesday morning.

After this statement, Mr. Hays contributed a lame and only partial apology for his distressing conduct of the morning, which was not entered in the record and was hardly adequate to obliterate the unhappy incident which he had precipitated.

The hearing was then recessed until Tuesday, June 22. This hearing was postponed until June 24, because of the chairman's absence from Washington, and that, in turn, was postponed subject to later call when Mr. Hays left Washington on June 24 to attend a funeral in Hawaii.

In the meantime, on June 21, Mr. Goodwin had written to the chairman as follows:

> I cannot be at the meeting on foundations tomorrow and in the meantime want you to know I think there should be an immediate cancellation of all public hearings.

THE DECISION IS MADE

On July 2, after Mr. Hays had returned from Hawaii, the Committee met in executive session and the following resolution was passed:

> *Now be it resolved that in lieu of further public hearings and in order to expedite the investigation and to develop the facts in an orderly and impartial manner, those foundations and others*

whose testimony the committee had expected to hear orally be requested to submit to the committee through its counsel within 15 days sworn written statements of pertinence and reasonable length for introduction into the record—such statements to be made available to the press—and that the committee proceed with the collection of further evidence and information through means other than public hearings.

The basis of this decision, concurred in by the chairman, by Mr. Goodwin and by Mr. Wolcott, was that, in view of Mr. Hays's conduct, it was impossible to continue hearings with propriety. The following separate statement by Mr. Reece, attached to the majority report of the Committee, reviews the facts leading to this decision:

STATEMENT OF B. CARROLL REECE SUPPLEMENTAL TO THE MAJORITY REPORT

In view of the decision of the ranking minority member of the Committee to file a minority report, copies of which will not be made available to the other members of the Committee until released to the press, I feel it is desirable to include a brief summation of the attempts to frustrate the work of the Committee for which the ranking minority member has been responsible.

It was made clear at the outset that the inquiry was to be an objective study. In line with this purpose and after consultation by Counsel with attorneys for some of the foundations, the Committee decided to inform the foundations in advance of the main lines of criticism into which inquiry would be made, giving sufficient supporting evidence so that they would know what to reply to in their own testimony. This decision was unanimous. It seemed the most fair approach for the foundations.

In accordance with the unanimously agreed procedure, and also by unanimous assent, Mr. Dodd, the Director of Research, prepared an initial report to the Committee which was read into the record at the first two hearings. This report, representing his tentative personal observations after initial studies had been made, was intended to indicate the main lines of inquiry. His report stated:

"As this report will hereafter contain many statements which appear to be conclusive, I emphasize here that each one of them must be understood to have resulted from studies which were essentially exploratory. In no sense should they be considered proved. I mention this in order to avoid the necessity of qualifying each as made."

This statement could not be clearer. On the first day both the Chairman and Counsel made the purpose of the report utterly clear—it was "to give the foundations an opportunity to know what most important matters we want to go into in relation to them." During the hearings this identification of Mr. Dodd's report was repeated both by the Chairman and Counsel. Yet the ranking minority member repeatedly asserted that the majority had arrived at pre-judged decisions. Newspapers reported him as having said that this was an "Alice-in-Wonderland" investigation in which a decision had been made in advance of the trial of a case. The majority submits that in taking this attitude the ranking minority member intended to discredit and harass the investigation, and to impugn the good faith of the majority and of the staff.

From the start, Mr. Hays has assumed an attitude of aggressive suspicion and insulting distrust of the majority members and the staff. He has said frequently that he has known in advance what the majority was going to decide. The shoe is, in fact, on the other foot. Mr. Hays could not have made clearer, from the beginning of our work, that he intended to frustrate the investigation to the limit of his abilities, and to attempt wholly to "whitewash" the foundations.

The lines have not been drawn in this Committee on a political party basis. The opinions of the majority are not party-line opinions. They are not "Republican" opinions, any more than the opinions of the minority are "Democratic" opinions. Many Democrats voted for the establishment of this Committee, and many Republicans voted against it. There is no party significance whatsoever in this Committee's work, which crosses party lines, and I am confident that our findings will find both supporters and opponents in both parties.

Sixteen public hearings were held, in the course of which the patient attempt was made by the Chairman to follow the procedure unanimously agreed upon in advance: that the main lines of criticism to be investigated were first to be aired, with sufficient evidence to show the reasonableness of investigating them, after which the foundations were to be brought into the hearings to state their positions.

The last public hearing was held on June 17th. Further public hearings were discontinued by a resolution passed by the majority at an executive meeting on July 2, 1954.

The reason for the cessation of hearings was that the attitude and conduct of the ranking minority member had made it impossible to conduct orderly hearings. Among the obstructive and harassing acts of Mr. Hays—all of them during the public sessions—were these:

He interrupted witnesses beyond all reason, attempting to frighten witnesses and to disorganize both the initial presentations and orderly interrogation by others. In one session of 185 minutes he interrupted 246 times.

When, after harrowingly frequent interruptions by Mr. Hays, great numbers of which were on extraneous matters, a rule was passed by a majority that a witness was to be permitted to finish his presentation before being questioned, Mr. Hays angrily remarked that he would pay no attention to any such rule and would interrupt whenever he pleased; and this he continued to do.

His interruptions were very frequently intemperate, both in tone and substance, and in purposeful disregard of parliamentary procedure and the rules of the House.

He repeatedly, and from the rostrum, vilified the staff and accused it of having prejudged the complaints against the foundations.

He repeatedly, from the rostrum, vilified other members of the Committee and questioned their good faith. He publicly accused the Chairman of lying and being a coward; and accused Mr. Goodwin of duplicity and of cowardice. The following excerpt from the record of the hearings which I, as Chairman, had deleted from the printed record in an effort to achieve harmony and to maintain the dignity of the Committee and the House, is illustrative of the violent and abusive remarks of Mr. Hays:

THE CHAIRMAN. Now, the gentleman from Ohio, I am sure, is not going to get anybody worked up or irritated here. If he has that in mind he might just as well subside, because the Chairman for one has made up his mind that he is not going to let any byplay get him out of temper. That would impair the usefulness of this committee.

MR. HAYS. Let me say to the Chairman that I took his word and he assured me his word was good, and if the time arose when I felt that we needed somebody on the minority side that the Chairman would put somebody on.

THE CHAIRMAN. The conversation was that if the gentleman from Ohio and his colleague should finally decide to write a minority report, that a member of the staff would be made available to cooperate with them on that.

MR. HAYS. No, that was not the agreement, because I don't want any member of this staff writing a minority report for me.

THE CHAIRMAN. I said cooperate.

MR. HAYS. Or to cooperate either.

THE CHAIRMAN. And assist. That was the conversation. I do not know what the gentleman had in mind.

MR. HAYS. I will say this to the gentleman, that out where I come from we have a saying that if a man doublecrosses you once, that is his fault; if he doublecrosses you twice, that is your fault. I just want you to know you won't get the second opportunity.

THE CHAIRMAN. Even that statement is not going to provoke the Chairman, but there is no living man can justifiably say that this Chariman—that this man who happens to be Chairman at this time—has ever doublecrossed anybody or he had failed to keep his word.

MR. HAYS. I am saying both.

THE CHAIRMAN. That is all right.

MR. HAYS. Is that clear enough? There is no inference there, is there?

THE CHAIRMAN. That does not disturb me a particle.

MR. HAYS. I know. You are pretty hard to disturb. I thought they had more guts in Tennessee.*

---

* *Author's footnote:* In World War I, Congressman Reece was decorated with the D.S.C., the D.S.M., the Purple Heart, and the Croix de Guerre with palm. He was cited for bravery by Generals Edwards, Hale, and Lewis and by Marshal Pétain.

THE CHAIRMAN. You are not going to provoke me. You need not worry, I have already made up my mind on that.

In an effort to discredit a staff witness, he employed quotations from papal encyclicals, bringing in by inference a religious issue where it had no bearing.

He cast aspersions on the character and record of a Catholic nun, the daughter of Senator McCarran.

He repeated vilified and openly insulted witnesses appearing before the Committee. In a letter dated May 30, 1954, Professor Kenneth Colegrove noted that Mr. Hays had insulted, vilified and browbeaten a witness "in the most brutal fashion." "*On thirty or more occasions,*" wrote Prof. Colegrove, "*Congressman Hays deliberately insulted the witness, and on numerous occasions, he inferred that he was a liar. Throughout three days, Congressman Hays was allowed to interrupt the testimony with irrelevant questions and to make distracting and insolent remarks. On the second day, even after Congressman Hays promised to refrain from interruptions [see page 638], he continued to interrupt and insult the witness without rebuke from the Chairman.* [Note that the record will show that the Chairman used unlimited patience to try to induce a reasonable attitude on the part of Mr. Hays without converting the hearings into an open brawl.] *I doubt whether the entire history of Congressional investigations will show more unfair or cowardly attack upon a witness than the treatment accorded to Mr. Sargent. Obviously no self-respecting scholar will care to testify before such a Committee under such conditions.*"

Mr. Hays referred in scurrilous terms to witnesses who had been heard, using such expressions as suggesting that the Committee should have a psychiatrist present; referring to witnesses as "crackpots"; asserting that they had been "dredged up" by the majority or the staff; asserting that not one single fact had been adduced by the testimony; etc. Among these witnesses were professors of repute and eminence. In a letter to the Chairman dated June 21, 1954, Professor Hobbs referred to the conduct of Mr. Hays and said that an atmosphere was created "*of fear among competent persons who might otherwise question the omniscience of the directors of those foundations. Witnesses are thereby warned that no matter how objective their testimony, no matter how legitimate their questions, their character will be smeared and their testimony ridiculed. Such threats add substance to an existing awareness that any pointed questioning of anti-intellectual or unscientific activities of these foundations will seriously handicap or permanently destroy an academic career."*

The first witness who might be called a spokesman for the foundations was Mr. Pendleton Herring, President of the Social Science Research Council. After Mr. Herring had stated what he wished, and at great length, the Committee's Associate Counsel began cross-examination, whereupon the ranking minority member of the Committee immediately made plain that he would not permit sequential, orderly examinations. Starting with an insult to the Associate Counsel, he indicated by his conduct that he intended to frustrate the cross-examination of foundation representatives by counsel and to prevent the eliciting of any material unfavorable to the foundations. The record of that last hearing on June 17th will show that a final incident of interference by Mr. Hays with orderly procedure justified the majority in concluding that no further hope existed of conducting public hearings properly in view of Mr. Hays' intransigence and refusal to obey rules of decency and propriety.

Among the other difficulties for which the ranking minority member was responsible was the loss, in the middle of its work, of two of its ablest investigators, released at the insistence of the ranking minority member who indicated that he would otherwise oppose any additional appropriation for the Committee. It was felt advisable to comply with this demand rather than to risk the abandonment of the investigation for lack of funds. The loss of the two investigators was a severe one. Several extremely valuable projects which had been started by the released investigators were left unfinished, and the remainder of the staff could not add the completion of these studies to their own heavy schedules. It is the belief of the undersigned that the demand for the release of the two investigators was prompted by their very evident ability and information.

One more comment upon the termination of the hearings. Some of the foundation statements filed with the Committee have been more than intemperate in castigating this Committee for ending the hearings. The Ford Foundation, for example, said: "We therefore regard the decision of the Committee to discontinue public hearings and to limit the foundations' defense to written statements or closed sessions as a puzzling and unexpected act of injustice."

The Carnegie Endowment for International Peace was even more belligerent. It commenced its statement with an introductory paragraph which is an affront to a committee of the Congress of the United States. Other foundations approached this insolence in their statements.

What impresses this Committee, in relation to these unwarranted and intemperate remarks, is the fact that none of these foundations interposed any objections to the harassments to which this Committee was subjected in the course of its work. Indeed, some foundations very obviously worked closely with the ranking minority member of the Committee in his attempts to frustrate the investigation.

B. CARROLL REECE

So the end came. It had been bad enough to have to sit through Mr. Hays's indecent treatment of the previous witnesses. When he made clear that he would not permit the orderly examination of witnesses for the foundations by Committee counsel, the majority of the Committee, after thinking the problem through very carefully, decided that hearings must close. The time which would have been consumed in listening to Mr. Hays and getting nothing out of the foundation witnesses except what their written statements contained, could be better used in sober analysis of the testimony to date, the collateral written materials, and statements which the foundations might wish to submit.

Some critics of the investigation have implied that the hearings were closed as part of a preconceived plan to prevent the foundations from defending themselves. This is a preposterous falsehood.

THE FOUNDATION STATEMENTS

The problem remained of giving the criticized foundations a fair opportunity to put into the record, for the Committee's consideration, whatever material they deemed of consequence.

The canard has been spread that the foundations were not given a chance to present their "case." An example of the spread of this falsehood is to be found in a booklet of which 35,000 copies have been purchased and circulated free by that creature of The Ford Foundation, The Fund for the Republic. This propaganda booklet is entitled The Fifth Amendment To-Day, and was written by Dean Griswold of the Harvard Law School, who is himself a trustee of The Fund for the Republic.

In his booklet, Dean Griswold, referring to the Reece Committee, had this to say:

> After developing the case against the foundations, this committee closed its hearing without giving the foundations a chance to present their defense. Such conduct is hardly calculated to foster confidence in the fairness of committee investigations.

Such writing as this is "hardly calculated to foster confidence in the fairness of" an educator. Dean Griswold knew that many foundations filed full statements with the Committee, including The Fund for the Republic, of which he is a trustee, and its parent, The Ford Foundation, which in its statement exhibited pride in the work of its progeny. He must have known also that these statements were immediately released to the press upon receipt by the Committee and were printed in full in the record of its proceedings.

Foes of the Committee have quite consciously misrepresented the facts to the public in failing to state fairly the reasons for the majority decision to terminate the public hearings—and in falsely implying, instead, that the purpose was to forestall the foundations' defending themselves. The fact is that the foundations were given the fullest opportunity to present their positions, of which they took fullest advantage.

They followed the hearings closely. Most had representatives present, eminent counsel as well, and even "public relations counselors"! They received daily transcripts of the testimony. They knew exactly what criticisms had been made of them. They had plenty of time, personnel, and money to answer in full, and they were given the opportunity to do so. They did, in fact, present long statements. The printed record contains about 70 pages devoted to the full testimony of Mr. Herring, president of The Social Science Research Council and a major spokesman of the foundation complex. In addition, the printed record contains statements of other foundations as follows:

Carnegie Corporation	over	25	pages
League for Industrial Democracy	over	22	"
American Council of Learned Societies		11	"
American Council on Education		7	"
Ford Foundation	over	36	"
Fund for the Republic	over	2	"
Carnegie Endowment for International Peace		10	"
Rockefeller Foundation and General Education Board		85	"
National Education Association		8	"
Foreign Policy Association		6	"
TOTAL over		212	"

In addition, the following statements were included which had been submitted by individuals associated with foundations:

Bernard L. Gladieux, of The Ford Foundation		13	pages
Joseph H. Willits, of The Rockefeller Foundation		5	"
Walter Gellhorn, of Columbia University	over	4	"
Mortimer Graves, of The American Council of Learned Societies, in the form of an answer to questions of Committee Counsel		9	"
TOTAL		31	"

Thus, the total extent of the printed record devoted to material supplied by foundation representatives and associates, including the testimony of Mr. Herring, aggregated 313 pages.*

The statements filed by foundations were printed in full, without deletion or alteration in any respect, just as they had been filed. They were, in their mass, extremely disappointing. They were characterized by an evasion of the specific issues raised in the testimony and a failure to face the detailed evidence. They were glib, self-adulatory, given to glittering generality, frequently abusive; in general, they main-

---

* Pages of about 650 words each, in the case of the statements.

tained that the respective foundations were beyond and above any serious criticism.

By filing statements without being subjected to questioning on the stand, the foundations could, and certainly did, make many statements which would not have stood up under questioning. They avoided the danger of being confronted, in open hearing, with the necessity of attempting to explain acts and procedures which were extremely difficult to justify.

Nor did they lose the opportunity to have their case get to public notice. Their statements received the widest newspaper treatment, in many instances being printed in full in some of the press, particularly in *The New York Times,* which gave publicity to these statements far wider than would normally have been the case in the event of a mere reporting of testimony. The filing of the uncensored prepared statements, promptly delivered under authority of the Committee to individual newspapers and to the press services, gave the complaining foundations the widest possible publicity for their "case."

THE PREPARATION OF THE REPORT

When the hearings closed, early in July, at least four or five more months of intensive research should have been possible, and an adequate staff to assist in assembling, digesting and organizing the materials. But its financial condition forced the Committee to release the entire staff by August 1, except for a skeleton crew necessary to do what was referred to as "house-cleaning." The associate counsel (Mr. Koch), the director of research (Mr. Dodd), his assistant (Mr. McNiece), and almost all the rest of the group left on August 1. The only major staff member remaining was Miss Casey. Miss Lonergan was still on the payroll but, once the hearings had started, she had ceased to be of any service in research or in other ways to the Committee in general—she spent all her time assisting Mr. Hays.

Miss Casey took the burden of the extensive executive work which remained, while I worked on the draft of the report, clearing frequently with Mr. Reece. In some miraculous way, perhaps by working twenty-six hours a day, Miss Casey managed to complete some additional and very valuable research.

After the Committee members had had time to study the draft of the report, a meeting was called at which all were present except

Mrs. Pfost, who was represented by Mr. Hays as proxy. Miss Casey and I were also present. In the discussions which ensued, it was understood that certain material was to be added to the draft which had not been included but was carefully described, including its Appendix, which I did not prepare.

I had expected "fireworks" at this meeting from Mr. Hays. To my amazement, he was calmness itself. He voted, on behalf of himself and Mrs. Pfost, against the report. But his only concern seemed to be that he be given an opportunity to present a minority report. Messrs. Wolcott and Reece approved of the majority report in its entirety and voted for it. Mr. Goodwin voted for it but stated that he objected to parts of it and asked the right to file a separate statement with the report, dissenting in part.

This was all arranged amicably. A date was set for the public release of the majority report, and it was agreed that a minority report might be filed and released simultaneously, even though the majority would not have had an opportunity to read it before its release. It was also agreed that any Committee member might file a separate, personal statement at the same time.

The minority report was filed in accordance with this agreed procedure, and the majority did not see it until it was released to the press. Mr. Goodwin missed the deadline and did not get his separate statement in until after the full document had gone to press, was finally printed, and was released. His separate statement was, however, separately mimeographed and released promptly to the press after receipt.

The short minority report set the theme for the subsequent criticism of the Committee by its foes. It ignored the mass of convincing evidence upon which the majority's findings were based, and resorted to considerable misstatement and to vituperative attacks on the majority, counsel, and staff.

THE "STRAW MEN"

I have referred to the practice of the critics of the Reece Committee of setting up straw men to have the pleasure of knocking them down. I shall identify some of these creatures which they have tried to foist upon the Committee.

1. *The allegation that the Committee disapproved of foundations.* (The Committee expressly held that foundations are very desirable.)

2. *The allegation that the Committee was critical of all foundations.* (The Committee criticized only a small number of the great multitude of foundations.)

3. *The allegation that the Committee disregarded the wonderful work which some of the criticized foundations have accomplished for society.* (The Committee expressly applauded the many wonderful works of some of the foundations which it criticized most heavily for works which were not so wonderful. Its position, however, was that many good works do not excuse those which are bad. The analogy may not be expressly apt but it is illustrative—that a man cannot be excused for an arson because he has been kind to the poor.)

4. *The allegation that the Committee held that the advocacy of certain social and philosophical concepts, largely identified with socialism, should be repressed.* (The position of the Committee was that an individual was entitled to advocate radicalism of any color as much as he pleased, but that it is a far different matter when we are dealing with foundations. These are public trusts dedicated to the public and operating with tax-exempt funds; it is to be expected of them, therefore, that they refrain from advocacy in the area of politics if they claim continued tax exemption.)

5. *The allegation that the Committee opposed "empirical" research.* (The Committee recognized not only the value but the necessity of empirical research. It commented only on the excessive, unbalanced favor for projects and persons identified with a faction among social scientists dedicated to a pragmatic philosophy, to materialistic concepts of history, and to Socialist goals. It considered the conformism resulting from such favoritism as a danger for research, scholarship, and education and as a political force ultimately controlling our government and affecting public welfare. Empirical research therefore was not criticized in the intention to restrain scholarly pursuits or academic freedom, but reviewed for the purpose of pointing to dangers for our public life from the support by foundations of one ideological and theoretical faction at the expense of all others. The Committee wanted to attract attention to dangers of conformism and the resulting fads and foibles in the social sciences.)

6. *The allegation that the Committee was trying to exercise "thought control" and advocated uniformity and conformity.* (The Committee could not have felt more strongly that it is essential to our society that the freedom of research, freedom of inquiry, freedom

of opinion and freedom in general be maintained and protected. Indeed, what disturbed it most was the mass of evidence leading to the conclusion that some of the foundations and their cooperating, intermediary organizations have tended to exercise or create a form of "thought control" in the social sciences and education through an imposition of conformity and uniformity by various means of intellectual coercion. It was critical of the extent to which social scientists have been tempted to conform to the favorite ideas, attitudes, and research methods of the advisers and managers of grant-dispensing organizations. The observant scholar in search of support for a research project soon learns to design his application for a grant so as to conform with the known preferences of the decision-making executives. Because these executives of the major foundations and intermediary organizations cooperate, the result is uniformity of thought, of goals, and of methods.)

REPORT OF COUNSEL TO THE COMMITTEE ON THE PROPOSED OBJECTIVES AND METHODS OF INVESTIGATION

HOUSE COMMITTEE ON TAX EXEMPT FOUNDATIONS

October 23, 1953.

This memorandum, prepared by Counsel in collaboration with the Director of Research, is the result of intensive application to the very difficult task of planning the work of the staff. It must, necessarily, be incomplete and tentative. The work itself, as it progresses, will determine in great measure more precise directions. This is, moreover, merely our own (tentative) conception of how our service to the Committee should be rendered. We shall proceed upon it as a base, except in so far as the Committee may direct us otherwise. We solicit directions from the Committee and individual suggestion from all its members.

We ask that this memorandum be kept confidential to avoid accidental or premature publicity, or the transmission to others of plans which are only tentative.

The intended lines of inquiry for this Committee are set forth in detail in certain projects later herein described. Those questions which have been most often raised and discussed (and they are specially covered by House Resolution 217) are:

The extent to which foundtion funds have been used for un-American and subversive purposes; and
The extent to which foundation funds have been used for political purposes, propaganda or attempts to influence legislation.

Before setting forth the proposed projects and all of the areas of inquiry, we offer some reflections in the way of background material.

* * *

GENERAL BACKGROUND

Tax exempt foundations have already played an extremely important part in our society, and are likely to become increasingly important. We do not agree with the opinion voiced by several witnesses before the Cox Committee that the birth rate of large foundations will decline in the future because of the impact of the tax laws. The tax laws themselves tend to stimulate the use of foundations to solve the problems (1) of paying the death taxes without sacrificing an enterprise, and (2) of management continuance. It is safe to say that the use of foundations for basically tax purposes is on a rising curve. Great numbers of foundations with but small capital today are essentially vehicles to receive huge grants upon the death of their respective creators. We are personally aware of prospective foundation funds aggregating many hundreds of millions of dollars which will come into use upon the death of various individuals. It is our belief that the next two or three decades should amplify the total capital of the foundations by some billions of dollars.

Accordingly, the eventual, aggregate financial power of the foundations will be immense. This power, intended to be benign, may not always be so. The very financial power, carrying with it the ownership of a considerable section of American industry, could wield a strong influence upon our economic, political, and social life. In an address at the University of Chicago last winter, on the subject of Family Enterprises, General Counsel to this Committee predicted that, after a period of years, a large part of American industry would come into the hands of certain special ownership groups, such as pension trusts, foundations, labor unions, and insurance companies. He pointed out that such a development might, some day, necessitate the enactment of laws similar to the *Statutes of Mortmain* in England which confiscated lands of the Church because it had acquired so great a section of the British landscape. While such extreme relief may never come to be necessary, there is no denying that the aggregate power of foundations may become formidable.

To the extent that this power is granted freedom, it can act for good but also for evil. Further and closer regulation is possible; but it is possible, also, that regulation would not prevent abuses of this aggregate power, or of sections of it, unless it proceeded so far as to wholly deprive foundations of independence. Starting with the premise that foundations are basically desirable, excessive regulation, which would deprive them virtually of all freedom, might well destroy their character, their usefulness and their desirability. Therefore, regulatory measures should be approached with grave caution. We are not prepared at this time even to suggest that further regulation is needed. It seems essential to us that as scientific a collection and integration of facts as possible be accomplished before anyone, whether in this Committee or outside, arrives at any precise conclusions.

We believe, however, that, as the work of the Committee proceeds, it should be aware of the several basic philosophical and legal problems involved and of such new ones as may appear from the work. Though all decisions should be postponed and the investigation approached with as little bias as is humanly possible, an understanding of some of the basic philosophic questions which have been directed against foundations, can act as a stimulus to a more intensive, intelligent and comprehensive investigation, and a more desirable result in the production of data of value.

A. *Is the foundation socially desirable?* A minority of Americans answers this in the negative; some on the "statist" basis that the Government should take over all "charitable" functions and that private giving thus conflicts with this function; others on the ground that foundations have or may acquire too great economic or extra-governmental power; still others on the ground that individuals should not be given the privilege of giving public money (to the extent that foundation funds are, in part, tax-free funds and, therefore, the equivalent of a public grant) as they, idiosyncratically, please; and there are other objections to the foundation as an institution. But the unquestionable majority of Americans believes in private "charitable" giving, in the foundation as a proper medium for such giving, and in the right of the individual, within wide limits, to be idiosyncratic if he chooses.

B. *If foundations are desirable, should limitations be put upon their use?* In this area there are all sorts of proposals. The tax law has already created some limitations of which you are, no doubt, aware.

Under Section 3813 of the Internal Revenue Code, certain transactions are prohibited—in general, transactions tending to benefit the donor of the foundation, or his family, or controlled trusts or corporations. "Unrelated income" is made taxable, as well as "Supplement U Income"—the objective being to prevent the use of foundations for indirect business or personal purposes. Unreasonable accumulations of income are prohibited. And foundations may not engage in certain activities, of which subversion and political activity are the most important.

It is possible that extensions of these restrictions may become advisable. It is also possible that no further restrictions are needed. The disclosed facts should determine. Proposals range all the way from (a) restricting foundation purposes and donations to certain direct fields, such as religion, medicine, health and education, to (b) restricting them to either direct donations without constricted or directed purpose or to what might be called operating, as against donating, foundations. "Proposal (b)" is sometimes based on a dislike of the theory that because Government is more and more taking over the functions of security for the individual, foundation funds should be applied as "risk capital" to social experimentation.

Another type of restriction which is sometimes suggested is that the individual (or the individual foundation) should have considerable freedom, considerable discretion, but that there should be limitations or supervision to prevent the waste of money which is admittedly (all the major foundations seem to admit it) a public trust, through application to objectives which are deemed unsocial, undesirable or capricious.

Many more suggestions for restriction have been made. Another is that the rule against perpetuities, or some other limitation on the life of a purely donative foundation, should be applied to prevent a perpetuation of the fund. Still another is that a violation of any of the restrictions of the tax law should not result merely in a loss of the income tax exemption (the present limit of punishment) but, retroactively, a loss of the initial gift tax or estate tax exemption. We cannot list all of the suggestions which have been made, but merely wish here to indicate how varied the critical suggestions for reform have been.

We repeat our opinion that a full discussion of any proposals for reform should await the facts we disclose; any predisposition to a remedy may risk serious error. We wish to emphasize our staff theory that *if* any remedies are to suggest themselves, it should be because intelligently and fairly assembled facts prompt them.

C. *Control as a basic problem.* This brings us to the basic control problem. We would assume that the Committee would be disposed to a minimum of Federal control. The rights, duties and responsibilities of foundations are, in our opinion, primarily matters of state law with which the Federal government should not interfere unless grounds of national welfare, strong enough to induce an application of a broad Federal constitutional theory, should appear. For the moment, then, the only mechanism of control available to the Congress is the tax law. Congress has the clear right to place reasonable conditions upon the privilege of tax exemption. It has done so, as to income tax, gift tax and estate tax. If amendments to these tax laws come to appear desirable, it is the province of the Committee on Ways and Means, as we understand it, to consider such amendments. We conceive our function in part to be to produce the facts upon which that Committee may, if it chooses, act further. We deem it within our province to state the facts which have appeared, collate them, and suggest areas of consideration for Ways and Means if the Committee finds this desirable.

If acute or chronic foundation ailments should appear, the remedies may not, in every case, be through legislation. A disclosure of the ailments may, to some extent, induce reform within the ailing foundation itself. And the very statement of the facts may induce the public to take an interest of a nature to bring about reform through the force of public opinion.

D. *Should further foundations be encouraged?* This question is put in the light of the present tax laws which are an invitation to create foundations. Foundations were formerly almost always created from an entirely charitable impulse. They are now most frequently created for reasons basically involving the tax laws, even though the charitable purposes are sincere. Do we want to continue this encouragement, or go back to permitting foundations as a simple privilege? The answer to this question is again one for Ways and Means, which should perhaps consider, in the light of our disclosed facts, whether reforms in the tax law might not be desirable, directed at reducing the pressure to create foundations. For example, making easier the problem of liquidating frozen estates (closely held stock cases) to pay death taxes, might well reduce the number of foundations created in the future. On the other hand, the answer might be that the tax pressure operates benignly and should not be reduced.

E. *Do foundations influence public opinion and is this influence desirable?* This basic and vital question could be broken down into such categories as these:

> Education.
> Public affairs.
> Politics and the theory of government.
> Economics.
> International affairs.
> Labor relations.
> Etc.

Recognizing the unquestionably magnificent contributions which the foundations have made to society in certain areas, we are inclined to exclude from our studies the application of funds to certain of these specific areas, notably religion, medicine and health, except where exceptional reason for a study may exist. An example of an exception might be a religious organization engaged in anti-Catholic or anti-Semitic activity, or a foundation expending great sums internationally on medicine or health—this last in connection with the general question of the extent to which foundations to use, and may be justified in using, tax free American money abroad.

* * *

The following are specific projects which we have outlined to guide the staff work. Some overlap, of course, on others.

PROJECT I.

THE COLLECTION OF ACCESSORY MATERIAL AND MAKING AVAILABLE COLLATERAL GOVERNMENTAL AND PRIVATE SERVICES.

1. Coordination with Federal committees on subversion for the purpose of checking existing material on foundations.
    a. Secure copies of records and reports of other committees to establish collateral library.

   b. Arrange for access to other materials of such committees.

   c. Request such committees for foundation leads.

 2. Coordination with similar State committees.

   a. California Un-American Activities Committee has a mass of material, including much on foundations and their penetration of educational institutions.

   b. The California Senate Committee on Education (Mr. Dilworth, Chairman) may have still better material.

   c. Contact similar other state committees.

   d. Assemble library of reports, etc.

 3. Coordination with Attorney General.

   a. Get his list of subversive organizations for check purposes and keep up to date.

   b. Get leads.

 4. Coordination with Internal Revenue.

   a. Get its list of foundations.

   b. Arrange to keep it up to date.

   c. Get access to their statistical material.

   d. Get access to their foundation annual reports.

   e. Procure their criteria for judging illegal activities which would deprive a foundation of tax exemption —for example, definition of political use and propaganda. We are not necessarily bound by such definitions but might start with them.

   f. Get leads.

 5. Coordination with FBI.

   a. Probably very doubtful, but we may get substantial assistance in checking subversives.

 6. Miscellaneous library material.

   a. There are organizations which collect data on foundations. We should assemble as much as possible. Example, Russell Sage Foundation material. We might solicit the foundations to give us whatever material they may have in the way of studies of foundation work and their place in society, as well as any plans they may have for future studies.

 7. Assistance from individuals.

    a. Make check list of individuals who may have material resulting from their own studies of foundations.

    b. Make contact with each to secure leads and cooperation.

8. As soon as possible, build up a quick reference file or card file to save time in cross-checking. Designing a filing system which could be used in reference work is an allied project.

PROJECT II.

GENERAL DATA.

It is proposed to assemble, classify and sum up facts concerning the tax-exempt Foundations in the United States since 1918 in such a manner as will enable the Committee most rapidly and conveniently to determine, among other things:

    a. The extent and nature of their resources.

    b. The purposes to which these resources have been devoted.

    c. The qualifications of those charged with the responsibility of directing their resources toward the achievement of these purposes.

    d. The size, composition and organization of the staffs maintained to supervise their operations.

    e. Operating costs and the relation which they bear to their total resources.

    f. The number and nature of grants made.

    g. The number and nature of grants refused.

    h. The degree of control which they exercise over the recipients of such grants.

    i. The directional policies and practices relied upon to insure the effectiveness of these controls.

Broadly speaking, these facts are essential to any effort to pass judgment upon or appraise the value of an enterprise or a segment of American wealth. In addition, it is intended that these facts shall be classified according to Foundations which are distinguishable from each other because of:

    a. Purpose.

    b. Size of either endowment or quantity of annual contributions.

    c. Nature of investments.

    d. Type of organization (i.e., corporate or fiduciary).

    e. Methods of operation.

Finally, it is contemplated that, to facilitate the interpretation of these "findings," the staff will present to the Committee its own objective summation of the trends which have characterized such essential aspects of life in the United States since 1918 as education, politics and finance—drawing for this purpose upon resources which, in its opinion, can be qualified as authoritative, objective and unprejudiced.

PROJECT III.

ANALYSIS OF FORMER HEARINGS.

This should be done by the Research Director himself, or a top assistant, to determine what material should be amplified and what subjects should be carried further or integrated with other projects.

PROJECT IV.

TREATMENT OF QUESTIONNAIRES.

1. Analysis of existing questionnaires.
   a. Selection of cases for study.
   b. Identification of reasons for study.
   c. Determine whether follow-up questionnaire should be sent; should such be uniform or designed to fit each case?
   d. Follow-through, in some cases, on operation of projects started by foundations last year.
2. Additional mass questionnaires?
   a. Should any be sent?
   b. To large, middle or small groups?
   c. Should we, by this method or any other, try to show evidence that a great number of now small foundations are actually vehicles to receive larger funds at death of donor?
3. Questionnaires to selected list of donees to see what other foundation grants they have received. Also, to check what work they have done.

PROJECT V.

DEFINITIONS.

1. In the work of identification of individuals, projects, purposes and operations, we must check against standards. We shall have to take the risk of determining these standards; they should be defined as closely in relation to legal precepts as we can. We can start with Internal Revenue, F.B.I. and other Committee definitions. It might be wise, in connection with hearings, to prepare a list of definitions for submission to prospective witnesses to avoid semantic bogs.
2. Among them are:
   a. propaganda.
   b. political purposes or uses.
   c. socialism.
   d. communism.
   e. fascism.
   f. subversion.
   g. slanting.
   h. anti-social activity.
   i. radicalism.
   j. leftism.
   k. rightism.
   l. lobbying.
   m. un-American activity.
      etc., etc., etc. (There may be many more.)

PROJECT VI.

ADMINISTRATIVE CHECK-UP WHERE THERE
HAVE BEEN DISCLOSED REGRETTABLE AWARDS.

1. To cover cases as to which there has already been testimony, or as to which we may have new material, and where:
   a. There have been subversive grants;
   b. There has been political use; or
   c. There has been gravely slanted use.
2. A factual presentation in this area would be of great value exposing:

    a. The dangers which deserve the administrative attention of good foundations;

    b. Areas in which remedial legislation by the states might be desirable; and

    c. Areas of consideration for Congress.

3. Except where wicked intention is clear, we take goodwill for granted and assume that no impropriety was intended.

4. Then—How did it happen? Who was responsible? Why? What caused such unintended results?

5. This can, in part, be reduced, perhaps, to a somewhat statistical result. That is, we can list instances in which an improper award was made for such reasons as:

    a. Lack of sufficient investigation or check of the project.

    b. Lack of supervision or control in operation.

    c. Calculated design at the source of the appointment (prompting of the appointment, perhaps, by a subversive or extremist on the staff).

    d. Lack of security check.

    e. Inattention by trustees.

    Etc., etc., etc.

6. In cases where an admittedly unfortunate donation was made and the foundation has expressed regret and asserted that it would not willingly or knowingly make such an award, should we not run down the extent to which the foundation has tried to ascertain whether an error in procedure existed and take steps to try to prevent a recurrence?

PROJECT VII.

POLITICAL USE.

1. A list should be prepared of foundations which have registered as lobbyists. In each case, the nature of the lobbying must be investigated carefully. Some of these cases will be innocent. Others will be *per se* violations of the tax exemption rule.

2. Other cases will appear in which the literature produced is of a political character or has been used politically.

3. There will be other cases in which though no political literature is used, the foundation has engaged in politics.

4. There is a very difficult area, where the foundation has not engaged directly in politics but has produced what might be called "politically slanted" material.

PROJECT VIII.

ROUTINE PROCEDURE WITH FOUNDATIONS WHICH ARE SUSPECTED OF IDEOLOGICAL "SLANTING."

1. List of trustees.
2. List of officers.
3. List of administrative officials.
4. Is there an extraordinary preponderance of ideological proponents, or an effective direction by ideological proponents?
5. Then see if there is a reflection of this preponderance in the operation:
   a. By identity of awards.
   b. By dollar value of awards.
   c. By identity of donees.
   d. By identity of administrators of awards.
   e. In each case (a.b.c.d.) collateral material may be needed for the characterization.

By this means we might show that, when extremists predominate in control of a foundation, the result is at least a slant to its operation, with political implications—whether sufficient to result in exemption loss or not.

Note: There are some instances in which, although there will be no numerical predominance, it can be shown that the non-extremists were inactive and that the extremists directed the show.

Note: Where the correlation between control and result can be proved and there was a partial use of funds for subversive purposes, or an administration or use of funds by a subversive, a further tie-in may be possible.

Note: We cannot expect uniformity or stand-patishness. We shall have to define the term "ideological," but we mean it roughly to cover communism, socialism, fascism, and other ideologies which tend to change radically our form of economy or society.

PROJECT IX.

INTERNATIONALISM.

1. The delicate area is religion. To even question the right to use foundation money for foreign religious missions, etc., is dangerous.
2. In many other instances, the wide use of tax free money abroad is subject to question:
    a. On the ground that it is transporting the taxpayer's money without his consent.
    b. On the ground that it has an effect on foreign policy independent of and sometimes contrary to the official policy of government. In some cases, it is "meddling."
3. The problem here is simply to present factual and statistical information and, upon it, to base the question: Are such grants justifiable or desirable?
4. A mass questionnaire on this subject by itself might be advisable.

PROJECT X.

INTERLOCKS AND FAVORITISMS.

1. Extent to which foundations give money to each other.
    a. Extent to which this results in a shifting or ducking of responsibility.
    b. Extent to which this indicates an interlock.
    c. Extent to which this indicates an informal control of foundation operations in general.
    d. Extent to which a trend of political or social character can be traced to this interlock.
2. Extent of interlocking trusteeships.
    a. Interlocks within the boards.
    b. Interlocks with the universities.
    c. Certain favored universities.
    d. Obvious exclusions through such interlocks.
    e. Some statistical study of this result.
3. Extent of interlock in foundation officers and administrative officials.
    a. Same breakdown as above (a.b.c.d.e.)

    b. Probable that most of the mischief takes place at this level.
4. Markedly favored individual donees.
5. Markedly favored projects.
6. Markedly favored institutional donees.
7. Tracing ideological patterns?

PROJECT XI.

CONTROL OF EDUCATION.

1. This subject should be integrated with or partly based on Project X.
2. Favoring of certain universities and institutions.
3. Interlocks and their part in controlling education and the development of educational theories through association with favored colleges and favored professors.
4. Describe the pattern of control. (It has been suggested that there is a sort of inner group and associates who act as a self-perpetuating controlling board—not formally, but by mutual support.)
5. Difficulty of getting allotments for individuals and organizations not within the inner group or on its periphery.
6. Extent to which government funds find their way into the same control (National Science Foundation?).
7. Trace the charge that there was a pattern or plan of Communist and Socialist infiltration into foundations to affect education, etc.

PROJECT XII.

TAX AND BUSINESS ABUSES.

1. A discussion of the tax uses of foundations is important as a background to current and future developments. Abuses come into play through business use when foundations are created for tax purposes primarily. These deserve mention, at least, though they are for the eye of Internal Revenue.
2. Some analysis might be made of foundation portfolios and of the holdings of donors and their families to see whether control of enterprises takes place indirectly.

3. A general study of the financial import of foundation management might also be undertaken.

* * *

FOLLOW-UP ON COX COMMITTEE'S WORK.

In the report of the Cox Committee, a list of criticisms of foundation operation was given in the form of questions, and the report gave answers to some of these questions. We understand it to be the position of this Committee that the Cox Committee had inadequate time to consider these posed questions with thoroughness. We propose, therefore, to reconsider these questions and attempt to produce more elaborate material upon which answers to them can be based, though the Committee may not choose to give precise answers.

The questions asked by the Cox Committee were these:

1. Have foundation funds been diverted from the purposes established by the founders?
2. To what extent have foundations been infiltrated by Communists and Communist sympathizers?
3. Have foundation funds been channeled into the hands of subversive individuals and organizations, and, if so, to what extent?
4. Have foundations supported or assisted persons, organizations, and projects which, if not subversive in the extreme sense of that word, tend to weaken or discredit the capitalistic system as it exists in the United States and to favor Marxist socialism?
5. Are trustees of foundations absentee landlords who have delegated their duties and responsibilities to paid employees of the foundations?
6. Do foundations tend to be controlled by interlocking directorates composed primarily of individuals residing in the North and Middle-Atlantic States?
7. Through their power to grant and withhold funds, have foundations tended to shift the center of gravity of colleges and other institutions to a point outside the institutions themselves?
8. Have foundations favored internationalism?

9. To what extent are foundations spending American money in foreign countries?
10. Do foundations recognize that they are in the nature of public trusts and are, therefore, accountable to the public, or do they clothe their activities in secrecy and resent and repulse efforts to learn about them and their activities?
11. Are foundations being used as a device by which the control of great corporations are kept within the family of the foundation's founder or creator?
12. To what extent are foundations being used as a device for avoidance and tax evasion?

Most of the questions are covered in the projects outlined above.

* * *

METHODS.

We intend to produce a record at hearings. Whether these hearings are to be public or private is the Committee's decision. Some documentary evidence will be accumulated and introduced; other evidence will come out of the mouths of witnesses under oath. We hope that early hearings will not be required. We feel that a great amount of preliminary research should be finished before, and in preparation for, hearings. Some of this involves independent study by the staff; some necessitates conferences with foundation executives; and some will come to us in the form of material solicited by mail from the foundations.

* * *

This report to the Committee is, as we have said, intended to be tentative. We reserve the privilege of amplifying or varying it within its general import. We fully understand, however, that we are the servants of the Committee itself and subject entirely to its direction. Moreover, we welcome whatever cooperation or direction the Committee members can take the time and trouble to give us.

René A. Wormser
General Counsel
Arnold T. Koch
Associate Counsel
Norman Dodd
Director of Research

INDEX

404 INDEX